D0620952

From the
Library of:
Brother Mark McVann
F.S.C.

THE GOOD NEWS ACCORDING TO MARK

THE GOOD NEWS ACCORDING TO MARK

Eduard Schweizer

TRANSLATED BY DONALD H. MADVIG

JOHN KNOX PRESS
ATLANTA

New Testament Scripture quotations are from *Good News for Modern Man, The New Testament in Today's English Version,* copyrighted 1966 by the American Bible Society and used with permission. Old Testament Scripture quotations are from the *Revised Standard Version of the Bible,* copyrighted 1946 and 1952.

Fourth Printing 1977
Standard Book Number: 8042-0250-8
Library of Congress Catalog Card Number: 77-93828

Printed in the United States of America

•

To Elisabeth and our four children,
who, through their very existence,
have contributed to this book
more than they may ever imagine.

•

CONTENTS

INTRODUCTION

1

Long ago it was observed that the first three Gospels (for the word "Gospel" cf. 1:1) show remarkable agreement in their presentation of the ministry of Jesus. For this reason they have been called the "Synoptic Gospels" (i.e., those which have a common perspective).

Correspondence is found in the wording, which frequently is identical even in the most minute details (compare, for example, Matthew 3:7b-10 with Luke 3:7b-9, or Mark 8:34b-37 with Matthew 16:24b-26 and Luke 9:23b-25). Even more striking is the agreement in the order of the material's presentation. Matthew rearranges the material rather freely, whereas Luke follows the sequence of Mark for the most part. A notable exception is found in 9:51—18:14, where Luke inserts a quantity of special material. This phenomenon can be accounted for only if the later Gospel writers were acquainted with the earlier book. The most plausible solution, which has stood the test of more than a century, is the so-called "two-document hypothesis." According to this theory Mark is the earliest Gospel and was known and used by the writers of the other two Gospels. They used in addition the so-called sayings-source (abbreviated "Q" from the German word *Quelle* meaning "source"), which was a collection of the sayings of Jesus, interspersed occasionally with brief historical sections. This source has been utilized in those places where Matthew and Luke are in general agreement in wording as well as in the order in which the individual sections from Q appear. In this process other information —e.g., from Mark—was introduced between these sections. At the same time both writers have appropriated much, individually and jointly, from oral tradition, just as Mark has. It is possible that

Luke, at least, also knew other traditions which had been written previously. Although it is not likely that Mark knew Q, we cannot exclude the possibility that he was acquainted with this collection but deliberately made no use of it, or that the sayings of Jesus which he reports are derived in part from this source.

2

Is it possible to assert that the oldest Gospel, at least, is a true presentation of actual happenings? We shall return to this question in section five and see that it all depends upon how one interprets that statement. Before we do this it will be necessary to review the observations and findings of the research of the last century.

As early as 1913 Albert Schweitzer in his *Quest of the Historical Jesus* affirmed that it was no longer possible to write a "Life of Jesus" on the order of a biography. Before this, William Wrede's book, *Das Messiasgeheimnis in den Evangelien* (1901; 2nd ed. 1913), showed that many details in the order of events in Mark are very improbable and that all the information essential for a real biography must be filled in by the imagination. Mark's objective is to proclaim Jesus as the Son of God. It is not his purpose to produce a description of the life of Jesus which deals with his inner and outward development. This insight was confirmed when K. L. Schmidt analyzed the "framework of the life of Jesus." He examined all the minor transitions, introductions, conclusions, and the occasional short summaries of the deeds of Jesus which frame and unite the individual sections. It became evident that this framework was rather arbitrary and that many of the statements could not be historically correct. For example, although the events recorded in 1:14-34 (or at least 1:21-34) probably occurred at different times, they are presented as if they took place on one single day. This is most apparent in Matthew, whose account of this same day includes the entire Sermon on the Mount and continues as far as 8:16 where the statement about the coming of evening has been appropriated from Mark. This statement has significance in Mark, since this particular day is depicted as a Sabbath when it would not be permissible to bring the sick to Jesus until after sunset. In Matthew, however, the statement is no longer meaningful. The indication of the day and hour in Mark 4:35 is even more difficult to explain. Here Jesus is sitting in a boat, as in 4:1; however, in 4:10 he had withdrawn from the people in order to be alone with his disciples. Moreover, in Mark 4:35 it is evening, which indicates that according to Mark it is the end of the day which began in 4:1. He does not report anything concerning the following night. He has Jesus step directly from the boat to the healing of the Gerasene, travel back to the western shore, heal the woman and raise the daughter of Jairus, in order that Jesus might leave that place and go to Nazareth. Even if one assumes that the first crossing of the lake had taken an entire night and that Jesus spent the next night in some other place, it is still clear that Mark has no interest whatever in precise chronology. The same may be said concerning the geographical locations mentioned, some of which are highly improbable (see 5:1; 7:31; 10:1; 11:1). The brief parenthetical remarks between the sections frequently are stereotyped. The expression "at once," which is typical of Mark, occurs repeatedly. It is often said that Jesus was "in the house," but nothing more specific is ever related concerning that house. This is simply the means by which we are informed that Jesus was, or wanted to be, alone with his disciples (cf. 2:1). In a similar manner, "mountain" indicates that Jesus is seeking the presence of God or that he is speaking in a special way at God's direct command. It is very clear that the order in which Mark presents his material is determined on the basis of subject and not by the desire to write a biography. For example, in 2:1—3:6, he assembles the stories of a number of controversies.

The Gospel writer was a collector of traditions which had come to him, as a general rule, in the form of individual stories or sayings which he put into a framework and thereby added to the whole. The process, which may be compared to the work of a child who is arranging beads on a string, leads to an extremely important conclusion—*the particular message which Mark is endeavoring to express will be found, for the most part, in this very "framework" and in the special arrangement of his Gospel.* These are the things to which we must give careful attention. A simple example will illustrate this. According to Mark 11:1-25, Jesus entered Jerusalem and returned to Bethany in the evening. Then on the next morning he cursed the fig tree, drove the merchants from the temple, and then went away from Jerusalem again. On the third morning his disciples discovered the withered fig tree as they re-entered Jerusalem with him. Thus the cleansing of the temple is put into the framework of the cursing of the fig tree, which for Mark symbolizes the judgment threatening Jerusalem and the temple. At the same time the sayings about the power of prayer in vss. 22-25 are closely joined to the saying "a house of prayer for all peoples" which is so extremely important to Mark (vs. 17; see comment on 11:12-26). Matthew, for literary reasons, records the triumphal entry and the cleansing of the temple as happening on the first day, and thus places both the cursing and the withering of the fig tree on the second day. In this way not only are the events brought closer together, but the miracle of the cursing becomes more obvious. From a purely historical perspective (in the modern sense of the word) it is impossible to harmonize these two presentations. Each of these Gospel writers employs a specific order of events in order to proclaim what he considers to be an important facet of things which happened at that time, even though this may have been something which only a believer could perceive. It is most interesting to observe what Mark has accomplished in his introduction to 3:20-35. (See also the comment on 15:25.)

When one follows carefully the way Mark employs transitional verses, parenthetical remarks, and short summaries, and the way he chooses, arranges, and assembles his material, his theology comes to the fore. This theology is the concern of his proclamation. A few typical words which are repeated frequently in such verses show the editorial work of Mark and characterize his message (see comment on 1:1-8 and 1:21-28). We shall attempt to summarize that message in the Epilogue. This method of research is usually called redaction criticism, because it explores the editorial activity of the Gospel writers.

3

Redaction criticism is a relatively new branch of biblical research. Tradition criticism, which is much older, deals with the history of the individual literary units before Mark received them. Is it possible, however, to ascertain anything about that history? Although many things are uncertain and will continue to be, it is possible to make a few observations. It is quite clear that certain sayings of Jesus and stories about him had been collected and arranged before they came to Mark, as is indicated by the introductions to 2:13-17; 3:7-12; 5:21-43; 9:41-50. The last section reveals how such collections originated. The church wanted to teach certain important sayings of Jesus about true discipleship; for example, in the instruction of candidates for baptism. In order that these sayings might be remembered more easily they were arranged according to certain catchwords (see 9:41-50). The Passion narrative was told as a continuous story at a relatively early date (see comment on 14:1 f.). It may have been recited again and again at worship services during Holy Week, or, perhaps, at each observance of the Lord's Supper (in abbreviated form? See 1 Cor. 11:23 and Mark 14:22-25). Later this story was written down and then read aloud.

Form criticism is a special method of tradition criticism which attempts to trace the history of the individual sayings or stories before they were collected. It proceeds on the assumption that the form in which these sayings now appear in the Gospels reveals their so-called *Sitz im Leben* (life-setting), i.e., the situation in which the sayings or stories were developed and used by the church for specific purposes. This process is easiest to trace where the church has subsequently placed one of the sayings of Jesus into a situation similar to its own. Luke 13:34 f. places the lament over Jerusalem during the Galilean ministry of Jesus at the conclusion of his announcement that he would go to Jerusalem to be killed there. In this way it emphasizes how important it is that Jesus suffer and die in this particular place. Matthew 23:37-39 associates the same lamentation with a discourse against the Pharisees, so that this lamentation became especially relevant for the church in its own conflict with contemporary counterparts of the Pharisees. On the other hand, there are cases where the church simply added the description of a situation to a traditional saying. Thus, for example, the saying of Jesus from Luke 6:46 is found in the writing of Clement (Hom. 8:7) from the third century A.D. It has been enlarged by the description of a new situation added at the beginning and by an explanatory appendix. It reads: "to one who often called him, 'Lord,' but did not do anything that he commanded, our Jesus said, 'Why do you call me, Lord, Lord, but you do not do what I say? It is not saying which profits anyone, but doing.'" This illustrates how sayings of Jesus were explained by additions, and their significance emphasized by placing them in a specific setting. Since the ancient narrator was not able to employ quotation marks or footnotes to keep his own commentary distinct, he simply added it directly to the saying of Jesus. In this manner descriptions of the historical setting in which Jesus uttered this or that saying were added before Mark, to emphasize what these sayings meant to the church (see the introductions to 2:13-17; 7:1-23; 9:33-37; etc.). Consequently, the main point in these stories is the saying of Jesus; the narrative has been added to serve that point. Furthermore, it was possible to choose events which were either the same as or similar to whatever happened in Jesus' time (see 2:13-17). The actual situation or question may not have arisen until later in the experience of the church, but was related as having occurred during the life of Jesus (see 9:38-40). An interesting example of this process is found in Matthew 12:11, which parallels Luke 14:5. In both instances the saying is applied to the question of the lawful observance of the Sabbath, which was an important issue in the church, but the stories that are told in connection with it are different in each instance. Mark 3:1-6 contains the same story as is found in Matthew, but a different saying of Jesus is given as the response (vs. 4). The fact that those who were watching Jesus were Pharisees is not mentioned until vs. 6, which can be traced to Mark. By this means Mark has made Jesus' rejection of legalism apply more forcefully to the specific argument which the church had with the Pharisees. That this man whom Jesus healed was a mason, dependent upon the use of his hands to earn his living, is a detail which is added in a later Gospel known in Jewish-Christian circles. In this way the later writer presents even more clearly how urgent it was that Jesus heal the man, and how unjust was the legalism of the Pharisees which would have prevented the cure.

Where in the experience of the church can this "life-setting" be found? In this connection the controversies with the antagonists, particularly with the teachers or other representatives of the Jewish church, were very important. Several examples of these controversies are given above, and in Mark 2:1—3:6 there is a large collection of such stories, each of which centers around some saying of Jesus and provides instruction applicable to the questions which were debated between the Jews and the followers of Jesus. These questions dealt with the forgiveness of sins and obedience to the law (see the introductions to 2:13-17 and 11:27-33). Moreover, sayings of Jesus and stories about him were collected and revised as they were used in the instruction of heathen who wished to join the church. Thus 9:36 f. probably describes the conduct becoming to one who wished to follow Jesus. Sayings of Jesus which describe the life appropriate for a disciple are collected in 9:37-50 for purposes of instruction (see the introduction to this passage). Other sayings had become important for missionary preaching or for preaching within the congregation. These were sayings which promised salvation to the hearer; threatening words which called him to repentance; words of admonition which governed the life of the church; prophecies which illuminated the future and stimulated hope; and, finally, sayings which described the significance which Jesus has for faith. Many sayings of Jesus are pertinent to later problems of the church without any adaptation. Other sayings could be made to apply to such problems only by means of an explicit reference to some situation corresponding to the issues faced by the church. In addition to this, some sayings have been reformulated. A particularly impressive example of this kind of development is mentioned in the introduction to 4:10-12 and 13-20 (cf. 12:1-12); naturally, parables are especially well suited to reinterpretation in new situations and from new and different points of view; at times they may be interpreted as instruction concerning the significance which Jesus has for the church, and at other times as consolation in temptation or as guidance for the life of the church.

A first stage in this inevitable transformation resulted because Jesus and the early disciples spoke Aramaic, while a part of the Jewish church in Jerusalem was already speaking Greek (Acts 6:1), as were most of the congregations of Gentile Christians. Therefore, it was necessary to translate these sayings, and in the process they frequently were transformed or reformulated into altogether new forms of speech and thought (cf. 4:10-12). Mark, who lived in the Greek-speaking world, received his tradition in the Greek translation, which was the form in which it had already been transmitted for some time.

The very fact that the church did not view Jesus as dead but as a living Lord made it imperative that, as it encountered problems, the church should listen to Jesus' sayings again and again. For the same reason the church had to relate his sayings to changed situations and adapt them as necessary (see comment on 10:12 and 11:26). According to 2 Corinthians 3:17 and Revelation 2:1 and 2:7, the living Christ speaks through the Holy Spirit. Since this is true, it is not only permissible to reformulate the sayings of Jesus, but it is even necessary if they are not to become ancient relics—revered but outmoded—which do not speak in the present time. Yes, it is inevitable that as one listens to this Word and is united with the living Christ he even dares to utter new sayings in Christ's name, in new situations. This is what the seer does in Revelation 2:1 ff. and Matthew does when he makes a command, "Drink it, all of you" (26:27), out of what is a simple report in Mark's description of the Last Supper, "They all drank from it" (14:23). Of course, it is necessary to test these new sayings by the old, and learn from the old where one might go astray. Although the old are normative, this bold updating is still necessary, because many old sayings of Jesus do not become really dynamic until they have been reformulated.

4

Similar observations may be made about the stories. A comparison of the Synoptics has shown that the stories were handed down much more freely than the sayings of Jesus. Except for minor changes, the dialogue in Matthew 8:8-10 agrees with Luke 7:6-9, whereas the story itself is quite different. In the one instance it is the officer himself who speaks with Jesus; in the other, his friends speak to Jesus, while he himself remains at home. Moreover, the fundamental truths stated by Jesus in Matthew 8:11 f. appear in an entirely different context in Luke (13:28 f.). A harmonization of the two versions is out of the question.

The way the stories were developed can be determined by a comparison of the four Gospels. Mark 14:47 reports that in Gethsemane one of the bystanders cut off the ear of the high priest's slave with a sword. Matthew 26:51 says, more explicitly, that it was someone accompanying Jesus who cut off the ear, and adds Jesus' statement of a fundamental truth. Luke 22:50 informs us that it was the right ear. Finally, John 18:10 gives the names of the men concerned—Peter and Malchus. In addition, he introduces a different saying of Jesus. This development of the stories continued after the close of our Gospels. A Jewish-Christian Gospel, for example, reports that at the baptism of Jesus a great light suddenly illuminated the place, and that the Baptist was amazed. The voice of God rang out once more, directed to John, who then fell down before Jesus (The Gospel of the Ebionites 4). Another Gospel relates a conversation between Jesus and his family before his baptism, in which he asserts that he is sinless and for this reason considers baptism unnecessary (The Gospel of the Nazarenes 2). Furthermore, a certain Gospel declares that "the whole fount of the Holy Spirit" descended upon Jesus at his baptism, and that the Spirit had waited long for Jesus but now had found his resting place in him (The Gospel of the Hebrews 2). In the middle of the second century one of the church fathers speaks of a fire which was kindled in the Jordan when Jesus stepped into it (Justin, *Dial.* 88, 3). Countless other examples show that it is only in rare instances that such further expansions of the tradition can be traced to records which are historically reliable. (See comment on 15:27-32.)

Here form criticism has helped to clarify a few things. Many stories of miraculous healings circulated among both Jews and Gentiles. These stories were formulated according to a set pattern which was used over and over. The long duration or severity of the illness was described; occasionally the fact was mentioned that the aid of the physicians was of no avail. The difficulty of the healing and the manipulations of the miracle-worker were related, particularly his touching the sick and his words, which often were strange formulas in a foreign language. Finally, the desired result was reported and confirmed by a demonstration, such as the carrying of his bed by the one who was healed. The story usually ended with the onlookers praising the miracle-worker. Since the use of this narrative pattern was widespread, it was natural for the church to employ it in telling and retelling the stories of Jesus' healings, of which there were undoubtedly a great number. Most of the features mentioned above can be found in the Gospel accounts. It may be supposed that many of these features were added or developed in an effort to conform to the pattern. The church even created new stories in the same style.

It is here that the difference between the Gospel accounts and those of the Jews and Gentiles can easily be seen. Very little, if any, mention is made of manipulations by Jesus or of mysterious magical movements or efficacious magical formulas. Seldom is the process of the miracle itself described. Jesus' conversation with the sick person before or after his healing is almost always the central concern. Frequently, it becomes clear that it is not the healing which is decisive but Jesus' encounter with the person, which leads to faith (see 5:34). There are stories such as the nature miracles, which do not relate Jesus' encounter with any person but portray his power over nature. Nevertheless, the question of faith is still presented even though it is done in a different way. There are Jewish and Gentile parallels to this type of story also, so it is necessary to inquire to what extent these stories have served as models. The miracle, however, had not been performed simply to reveal a divine power which is greater than the storm or some other natural phenomenon; on the contrary, the question of faith is clearly put to the witnesses of the miracle (cf. the excursus to 4:35-41, also 5:43 and 6:5).

None of these stories has been told simply to inform us that miraculous things happened long ago in a distant land. No, all are intended to proclaim the One who encounters the hearer or reader today in the same fullness of power and seeks his faith. This One wants to call him, to justify him, and to restore him to fellowship with God. It is very significant that stories were used for this purpose. Ideas and theological statements alone are not able to change his thinking or to save him. What is effective is the story of an event which took place in Palestine at a very specific time—an event which still applies to him today and is designed to create faith. Consequently, the church must tell these stories in such a way that this claim will be seen clearly.

This is, perhaps, even more emphatic in certain other stories about Jesus, particularly in the Passion narrative. It is clear that this story is very human, very ordinary, and very humble. In itself it presents nothing either miraculous or astonishing. And yet, when Mark tells this story he continually introduces Old Testament language into the narrative. He alludes primarily to the innocent sufferer of the Psalms (cf. 15:23 f.), occasionally adding new details. In this way he declares that this event, so insignificant in itself, is indeed an "eschatological" event, i.e., one in which the Old Testament is fulfilled and which is, therefore, God's ultimate act—the act which applies to all times and to all men. The very fact that these Old Testament passages are not found collected together in the earliest stages of tradition and that they are not cited with specific references shows how very natural and automatic it was for the faith of the narrator to express itself in biblical language. The narrator is able to affirm what really happened only by employing Old Testament terminology, even if this describes details which could not be recorded on a sound-film.

5

The question of truthfulness, then, must be approached in an entirely different manner than would be used by a modern historian. To be sure, the historian knows there can be no purely objective presentation of history, since every narrator chooses the events which for one reason or another he considers important, while others are omitted and allowed to be forgotten. Nevertheless, the problem is more complicated when dealing with Mark's

Gospel. The example mentioned above will help to make this clear. If we had a sound-film of the crucifixion of Jesus, we would have much better knowledge concerning a hundred details, but still we would not know what really happened in this death. That is something which only a witness can tell us—a witness who speaks to us with the authority of the Holy Spirit. The statement of the army officer in Mark 15:39 may not be historical in the sense that we would be able to hear it on such a film. Nevertheless, this statement is more true than a hundred details which the film could show, because it tells what actually happened on that day in history—"This man was really the Son of God!"

The fact of the matter is that we are dependent upon Mark for our information about what happened at that time. This applies not simply to our knowledge of the theological reflections of the church or of the Gospel writer, but also to our knowledge of the events during the few months or years between the baptism in the Jordan and the discovery of the empty tomb. What really took place there can be told to us in no other way than by the witness of faith. The ones who are reporting and testifying in this case are not trained modern historians who can distinguish accurately between reported fact and interpretive witness. It was necessary for the witnesses to resort to a great variety of alterations and additions, although they did not report anything extra or different—just that which really happened. In no other way could the hearer and reader be enabled to comprehend what took place at that time—something which is still relevant for him today.

It is for this reason that the prehistory of the text will be assigned greater importance in this commentary than it was in the commentary of J. Schniewind, whose fine translation I often follow, although at times I have revised it to make it correspond more nearly to the original text. The important thing, of course, is the text which is presented by Mark, and its message. For this reason the reader will want to refer repeatedly to J. Schniewind's exposition. Even though there is always a measure of uncertainty in any effort of this kind, it is still necessary to clarify the earlier stages of Mark's proclamation, because otherwise we would deprive ourselves of something of great value. Our task, then, is not the production of another literal translation. We must encounter the living Christ and then repeat in our own words what the New Testament witnesses are saying to us. The variety of voices is helpful in achieving our goal, as is an examination of the gradual development of their statements. Throughout the centuries the church has taken pains to find the best way to express what it believes has happened in Jesus. It may not be easy for us to follow the progress of this effort on the part of the church, but if we simply want to accept and repeat a ready-made answer without any effort and without any regard for this struggle, then we may never be able to hear their message correctly. When confronted by the Word of the living Christ which permeates the multitude of words, it is this variety of voices which compels us to penetrate the plethora of words and formulate for ourselves what it is that happened in the life, death, and resurrection of Jesus.

He who listens in this way may detect something of the wonder that despite all the doubtful and contradictory voices, and in the midst of the confusion, the original Christ-event still prevails. Thus the declarations about that event remain consistent in the essentials, although they were interpreted differently in different situations and must continue to be so interpreted. And so we learn that it is never possible to express the Word in timeless abstractions, but each witness must use his own contemporary language. Knowledge of this fact will lead us to listen attentively and humbly to the various witnesses. We will not be bewildered by their diverse emphases; on the contrary, we will listen carefully in order that we may repeat the same message in our own idiom and proclaim it in such a way that men in our day also will understand what the Word is saying to them. This entire matter of proclamation is a living process because Jesus himself stands at the beginning with his word and actions, his death and resurrection; and because he himself lives on whenever the message is unfolded. It is this truth which Mark emphasizes.

6

What Mark has done is a tremendous theological achievement; he has created a new literary form—the "Gospel." At the time of his writing, the word still meant "good news" (see 1:1), and good news is the very thing he wants to set forth. Consequently, his book resembles a volume of sermons more than a biography. But he is preaching by telling about the ministry and death of Jesus. The historical books of the Old Testament and perhaps the book of Jonah are the only real parallels. Mark understood that God's Word came to the world in the totality of the ministry, death, and resurrection of Jesus. God's Word did not come in the individual sayings of Jesus in such a way that he might remain simply a teacher whose wisdom we could receive without ever knowing him personally; nor in individual miracles so that we could honor Jesus as a divine magician; nor in an exemplary suffering so that Jesus merely influenced others to imitate him; nor in an abstract proclamation of divine grace which could be received independent of Jesus. This is why Mark wrote a book which lacks all the characteristics essential to a biography; for example, there is no mention whatsoever of Jesus' childhood (see 1:9). The contents of the book are, by and large, only the things which are indispensable for the proclamation of the gospel and which continue to speak to the reader. And yet it is really a history book, since Mark knows that these essentials will not be found anywhere except in the record of the events of these years (perhaps Mark even thinks it all occurred in one single year) which he describes (cf. the Epilogue).

We do not know who the author was. It is conceivable that Mark was his real name. The superscriptions of the biblical books were not added until the second century, but it was necessary, at least orally, to distinguish between the Gospels as soon as there was more than one. If the title had been given at a later time when the real author was not known, certainly a more prominent name would have been chosen than that of some unknown Mark. He is hardly to be identified with the Mark mentioned in Acts 12:12, 25; 13:5, 13; Philemon 24; Colossians 4:10; 2 Timothy 4:11, since he does not seem to know the geography of Palestine (cf. section 2). Furthermore, he writes in a very polemical way against Jewish customs, which he explains to his Gentile-Christian readers (see 7:1-23).

The only mention of the author of this Gospel is found in Papias, a bishop in Asia Minor (*ca.* 130): "Mark, having become the interpreter of Peter, wrote down accurately everything that he remembered, without however recording in order what was either said or done by Christ. For neither did he hear the Lord, nor did he follow Him; but afterwards, as I said, [attended] Peter, who adapted his instructions to the needs [of his hearers] but had no design of giving a connected account of the Lord's oracles. So then Mark made no mistake, while he thus wrote down some things as he remembered them; for he made it his own care not to omit anything that he heard, or to set down any false statement therein." For this information Papias refers to a certain "elder"; perhaps it was John, the elder (see the introduction to 2 John). Papias' testimony is not free from suspicion since he refers to similar sources for other material which is purely legendary (see 16:18). It is very unlikely that Peter carried on missionary work with the help of an interpreter, and the expressions "instruction" and "memories" (i.e., "Memoirs") are fitting neither for Peter's preaching nor for Mark's book. The primary objection is that there is no evidence of any particularly Petrine tradition in Mark. The very most one can say is that there are some traces of it (cf. 1:29-31). First Peter 5:13 might be evidence of some kind of relationship between Mark and Peter (it is not likely that Peter wrote the verse). On the other hand, this reference could be the source of the information which reached Papias. It had been asserted ever since Clement of Alexandria (*ca.* 200) that Mark wrote in Rome. A number of expressions occur in the Gospel which are reminiscent of Latin and could be indications of this, but such expressions were common wherever the Romans had been (cf. 15:21). All we can say with certainty is that the Gospel was written in the Roman Empire for Gentile readers (cf. 7:3 f.). So far as the date is concerned, some year in the 60's is most likely since there is no reference to the destruction of Jerusalem in A.D. 70 (the case is altogether different in Luke 21:20 ff.), although Mark 13:14-20 appears to presuppose a time in Judah when war was anticipated, such as the period shortly before the Judaic-Roman War (A.D. 66-67).

7

The expositions of the individual passages most often consist of three parts which are separated by a larger space: introduction and tradition criticism, detailed exegesis, theological remarks.

The English language edition is based on the text of *Today's English Version (Good News for Modern Man),* copyrighted by the American Bible Society, 1966, and used by permission of the American Bible Society and Wm. Collins Sons, Ltd., London.

Critical Commentaries: A. Schlatter, *Markus, der Evangelist für die Griechen,* 1935; E. Klosterman, *Das Markusevangelium* (*Handbuch zum Neuen Testament,* Vol. 3), 4th ed. 1950; V. Taylor, *The Gospel according to St. Mark,* 1952; W. Grundmann, *Das Evangelium nach Markus* (*Theologischer Handkommentar zum Neuen Testament,* Vol. 2), 2nd ed. 1962; E. Lohmeyer, *Das Evangelium des Markus* (*Kritisch-exegetischer Kommentar über das Neue Testament,* Vol. I/2), enlarged by G. Sasz, 16th ed. 1964. Popular Expositions: J. Weiss, *Das Markus Evangelium,* in *Die Schriften des Neuen Testaments,* Vol. 1, 3rd ed. 1917; G. Dehn, *Der Gottessohn* (*Die Urchristliche Botschaft,* Vol. 2), 1953; J. Schniewind, *Das Evangelium nach Markus* (*Das Neue Testament Deutsch,* Vol. 1, which has been replaced in the series by the present volume), 10th ed. 1963; J. Schmid, *Das Evangelium nach Markus* (*Regensburger Neues Testament,* Vol. 2), 5th ed. 1963 (Catholic); D. E. Nineham, *St. Mark* (*The Pelican Gospel Commentaries*), 1963; R. Grob, *Einführung in das Markus-Evangelium,* 1965; E. Haenchen, *Der Weg Jesu,* 1966. Articles and Monographs: W. Marxsen, *Mark the Evangelist,* 1969; E. Schweizer, "Die Theologische Leistung des Markus," *Evangelische Theologie* 24 (1964), 337-355. With Reference to the Passion Narrative: E. Lohse, *Die Geschichte des Leidens und Sterbens Jesu Christi,* 1964. Apocrypha and Pseudepigrapha: E.

Kautsch, *Die Apokryphen und Pseudopigraphen des Alten Testaments,* 2 vols., 2nd ed. 1921 (the standard work in English is R. H. Charles, *The Apocrypha and Pseudepigrapha of the Old Testament,* 2 vols., 1913); P. Riessler, *Altjüdisches Schrifttum ausserhalb der Bibel,* 1928; E. Hennecke and W. Schneemelcher, *New Testament Apocrypha,* Vol. 1, 1963, Vol. 2, 1965. With Reference to the Qumran Scrolls: J. Maier, *Die Texte vom Toten Meer,* 2 vols., 1960. Contemporary Judaism: H. L. Strack and P. Billerbeck, *Kommentar zum Neuen Testament aus Talmud und Midrasch,* Vol. 1, 3rd ed. 1961 (Matthew), Vol. 2, 2nd ed. 1956 (the other Gospels), Vol. 4, 2nd ed. 1956 (Excursuses). The following works are particularly helpful with reference to the topics discussed in the Introduction: M. Dibelius, *From Tradition to Gospel,* 1935; R. Bultmann, "The Study of the Synoptic Gospels" in *Form Criticism,* F. C. Grant, ed., 1962; R. Bultmann, *History of the Synoptic Tradition,* 1963; W. Marxsen, *Introduction to the New Testament,* 1968. A harmony of the Gospels in English will be of considerable help also; e.g., B. H. Throckmorton, Jr., ed., *Gospel Parallels,* 1949.

I

THE BEGINNING
1:1-13

John the Baptist 1:1-8;
cf. Matt. 3:1-12 and Luke 3:1-18

[1]This is the Good News about Jesus Christ, the Son of God.
[2]It began as the prophet Isaiah had written:

> " 'Here is my messenger,' says God; 'I will send him ahead of you to open the way for you.'
> [3]Someone is shouting in the desert:
> 'Get the Lord's road ready for him,
> Make a straight path for him to travel!' "

[4]So John appeared in the desert, baptizing people and preaching his message. "Turn away from your sins and be baptized," he
told the people, "and God will forgive your sins." [5]Everybody from
the region of Judea and the city of Jerusalem went out to hear
John. They confessed their sins and he baptized them in the Jordan
river.

[6]John wore clothes made of camel's hair, with a leather belt
around his waist; he ate locusts and wild honey. [7]He announced to
the people: "The man who will come after me is much greater than
I am; I am not good enough even to bend down and untie his sandals. [8]I baptize you with water, but he will baptize you with the
Holy Spirit."

(Vs. 2: Mal. 3:1; Exod. 23:20. Vs. 3: Isa. 40:3.)

When Mark wrote this section he had much material at his disposal. The statement from Malachi 3:1 (Mark 1:2) is applied to the Baptist similarly in Matthew 11:10 (Q), where the quotation is augmented, as here, by the words "ahead of you," which correspond to Exodus 23:20. The church, then, had already used this Old Testament saying in reference to the Baptist before Mark.

Perhaps the church had made this application because Malachi speaks of the return of Elijah. Isaiah 40:3 (Mark 1:3) is cited in John 1:23 also. A century earlier than this the Jewish group living near the Dead Sea had justified their flight to the cloister in the wilderness by that passage (1QS 8:14), because they had seen in it a reference to the dawning of the end-time. The first quotation is attributed incorrectly to Isaiah. A plausible explanation is that this passage was found in a collection of Bible quotations treasured by the church, in which it originally followed the one from Isaiah, so that later the second quotation was considered Isaianic also. The name "Baptist" was not unknown, as it appears in the writings of the Jewish author Josephus. That John preached repentance in the wilderness is reported in Matthew 11:7 and 3:8 (Q), and that he was regarded widely as Elijah who had returned to earth is attested by Luke 1:17 and Mark 9:11-13. The description of his belt is taken almost word for word from the story of Elijah in 2 Kings 1:8 (LXX), and the clothing of hair is an allusion to the hairy mantle of the prophets which is mentioned in Zechariah 13:4. Finally, Mark 1:8 is found also in Matthew 3:11 (Q) with slightly different wording.

If we wish to discern what it is that Mark is trying to say, we must observe the way he uses his material. He places these two Old Testament citations at the beginning so that although they refer directly only to 1:4-8, they still function as a preface to the whole book and introduce everything that follows as the fulfillment of all God's dealings with Israel. Thus he declares at the outset that God has acted in a unique way. In the material that follows Mark continues to give preference to that which made a special impression on him. Consequently, he postpones the traditional description of the Baptist and the contents of his preaching until vss. 6-8. Mark's real concern is made clear in vss. 4 f. This can be demonstrated even on the basis of the language used, because the word "preach" occurs only in those sections in which Mark comments on the stories he has received from the tradition. The same is true for the expression "turn away from your sins," and the description of the success of Jesus by the expression "everybody." We must pay careful attention, therefore, to what he wants to tell us by means of this onset of "preaching" and its astonishing results.

[1] Mark begins with the "beginning" just as the first book of the Bible and the Gospel of John do.* God is not the eternally fixed idea; God acts. Accordingly, his history has a very definite beginning. It is this beginning which is reported by the "Good News."

Gospel. The Greek word *euaggelion* denotes "good news," primarily of a victory in battle. This term figures prominently in stories of the lives of the Roman emperors who were honored as gods. We read, for example, of the "good news" of the emperor's birth, of his enthronement, etc. An equivalent concept is not found in the Old Testament although the corresponding verb is used a number of times (Isa. 52:7; 61:1; and 40:9; 41:27; Ps. 40:9, where it has been weakened in the LXX). In the New Testament it is primarily Paul who uses *euaggelion,* and for him it indicates Christian preaching. He employs the word for the event of preaching as well as for the content of that preaching, which is, as a rule, the death and resurrection of Jesus. Therefore, "Good News" already designated the Word, which speeds throughout the world and tells the story of Jesus in such a way that it reveals the significance of that story for faith. In that Word, God himself calls the world to faith in Jesus and to salvation in him. According to Mark, this preaching begins with John (1:4), resounds in the teaching of Jesus (1:14 f.), and continues to spread in the preaching of the world-wide church (13:10 and 14:9). "Good News" or "Gospel" first appears as the title of a book, in the way we are accustomed to use it, with Justin *ca.* A.D. 150.

In several manuscripts, the title "The Son of God" is not found; apparently it was added later in the process of copying. Nevertheless, it is in conformity with Mark's linguistic style (see 15:39). Since Mark never begins a sentence with "as" and since in the New Testament any quotation with such an introduction always comes after, never before, the proposition which it confirms, it is better to recognize vss. 2 f. as confirming the assertion in vs. 1 rather than that which follows in vss. 4 f. This means that the ful-

---

* The TEV transfers the word "beginning" from vs. 1 to vs. 2.

fillment of the Old Testament is not found in some mere detail, but rather in a fresh inbreaking of God. Everything which follows is set in this light, so that even before he appears Jesus is proclaimed as the one in whom the plan of God is fulfilled. Only one who believes can speak in this way—one who already knows about Easter. The fact that God was at work in the preaching of the Good News, which began with the Baptist and continued in the worldwide church, can be heard and understood only as the testimony of faith.

[2, 3] Both quotations were already a part of the church's tradition. Since the writing of Malachi 3:1, the return of Elijah as the forerunner of God was expected to occur shortly before the end. (This is still true in Luke 1:16 f.) It is not certain whether the Judaism of Jesus' time considered Elijah to be, in addition, the forerunner of the Messiah (Mark 9:11). Here the church is underscoring his coming as forerunner of the Messiah when it adds "ahead of you" and speaks in vs. 3 of a path "for him" instead of one "for our God" (Isa. 40:3; 1QS 8:14). The church, therefore, clearly considered John to be the forerunner of Jesus in the program of God. He is presented in this way in all four Gospels and in the summaries of the faith of the church (Acts 10:37; 13:25; cf. 1:22). Jesus, however, understood the time of his own activity as the time of the inbreaking of the Kingdom of God and, consequently, as surpassing and fulfilling the time of John. This is indicated by Matthew 11:12, which is clearly an authentic saying of Jesus. It is for this reason that Jesus no longer practiced John's baptism and custom of fasting (Mark 2:18), although he himself was baptized by John.

[4] Thus the information has come to Mark from the tradition of his church that John as the forerunner of Jesus had fulfilled Old Testament prophecy, and that as a second Elijah he preached repentance and baptized in the wilderness. Now Mark takes the phrase "in the desert" from vs. 3 and applies it to the place where the voice of the herald resounds, whereas in Isaiah 40:3 it indicated the place where the way of the Lord should be prepared. Apparently the fact that Elijah had also spent time in the wilderness (1 Kings 19:4 ff.) is not a factor. It is more likely that the desert is important as the place where God wants to be alone with his people (Hosea 2:14), and primarily as the scene of the salvation-time after the exodus from Egypt. On the basis of Isaiah 40:3 a recurrence of this exodus was expected in the end-time (cf. Deut. 18:15-18 and Acts 3:22 f.; 7:37). Consequently, again and again in that century various prophets led their disciples out into the wilderness.

The fact that the preaching of the Good News has begun and has gone out into all the world is more important to Mark than the traditional picture of a preacher in the wilderness who is a second Elijah, and it is more important than the reference to the coming of Jesus. God's special salvation-time has begun; therefore, this preaching resounds through the world. The preaching has been mentioned already in vs. 3, and baptism has been indicated as the substance of that proclamation (vs. 4). The Baptist (1:4, 7), Jesus (1:14, 38 f.), and the twelve (13:10; 14:9) are all preachers, according to Mark. In this manner he designates the entire period beginning with John and continuing in the world-wide church as a special salvation-time. This applies also to his description of this preaching as "Good News" (see vs. 1) and as a call to turn away from sin. The Greek word for "turning away from sin" (literally meaning "a change of mind," a meaning which had lost its force) translates the Hebrew word "return." The prophets summoned the people to return time and again. Therefore, it is not the changing of the characteristics and actions of a man that is emphasized, but the transformation of the total direction of his life, that is, of his relationship to God. This, of course, includes every aspect of his inner and outward behavior. It has importance, however, only as an expression of such a new direction, and not as an achievement which may be separated from it—just as no amount of extra exertion will help the runner who is running in the wrong direction, so long as no one makes him turn around. It is not clear whether it is baptism or the returning which brings "the forgiveness of sins." The latter is favored by certain Old Testament passages and the explicit statement of 1QS 3:4-12; 5:13 f.—that there is no forgiveness of sins without repentance, and that baptism can be only a subsequent indication of this repentance. In the Old Testament, as in the writings of the Dead Sea community, the acknowledgment is added quickly that such a return can be granted and accomplished only by the Spirit of God who, like water of purification, will free the church from its sins in the end-time (Ezek. 36:25-27; 1QS 4:21; cf. Zech. 13:1).

There are other passages in the Old Testament which speak of the forgiveness of sins (Isa. 33:24; 40:2 [right next to vs. 3!]; 53:5 f.; Jer. 31:34; Micah 7:18). Paul never uses the expression (except in Colossians and Ephesians which, presumably, were written by one of his disciples). John uses it only in 20:23. It is used, of course, by the writers of the first three Gospels, in Acts, and in the later Letters. Luke 1:77 shows that even among the disciples of the Baptist the expression "the forgiveness of sins" was borrowed from the Old Testament.

[5] The procession of the people into the wilderness and the confession of sins appear to be understood by Mark as the expression of the repentance which occurred and to which God gave his sign of favor in the form of baptism. Mark delights in describing the success of this preaching with expressions such as "Everybody from the region of Judea and the city of Jerusalem." The fact that everything was astir indicated that the special salvation-time had begun in which the gospel would reach out to the whole world (13:10).

[6] At this point, the Baptist is described as being like Elijah. This, obviously, had long been the traditional description. In any case, Mark makes no specific reference to the parallel with Elijah. Certain ascetic characteristics are attributed to the Baptist in Luke 1:15 also. Nevertheless, John demands of others neither withdrawal into the wilderness nor renunciation of wine and civilized life (cf. Num. 6:1 ff.; Jer. 35:6 ff.); his diet simply corresponds to the diet of poor nomads. Therefore, he was not one of those hermits among whom Josephus lived between A.D. 53 and 56 and of whom he reports that they had despised everything of human creation and denied themselves meat as well as clothing. Jesus will separate himself even more radically from any asceticism which is understood as a way of salvation (2:18-22). The physical appearance of the Baptist, which would be of the greatest importance in any story, is incidental to Mark. He is not interested in the Baptist as a sensational, rather bizarre figure. What interests him is the beginning of that preaching which is directed to the whole world.

[7, 8] This very preaching points to "one greater." Both of these verses are transmitted in a different form in Matthew 3:11, and its parallel, Luke 3:16 (Q), which may be reminiscent of John 1:26 f. These two statements, therefore, had been repeated frequently. Apparently, Mark preserves the more ancient form where the one statement follows the other, in contrast to Matthew 3:11 (Luke 3:16) where the one encompasses the other. Conversely, in the case of vs. 8 Matthew and Luke have retained the original tradition, in which the coming One baptizes "with the Holy Spirit and fire." In the oldest wording of the Baptist's statement "fire" certainly means the judgment (Matt. 3:10-12). One may even wonder whether originally judgment was the only thing implied, since the word for "spirit" also means "wind" or "storm." Fire and wind (which is needed for winnowing) appear in Matthew 3:12 as well (cf. Isa. 29:6; 30:27 f.; Ezek. 1:4). Both ideas are combined in the Jewish apocalypse 2 Esdras 13:10, 27, which is from the first century A.D. Rabbis join Malachi 4:1 and Isaiah 41:16 in their description of the judgment. Either the word "holy" was added by the Christian church or it may be that John was thinking of the twofold task of the judge—the one to cleanse with the Holy Spirit (see vs. 4), the other to destroy with fire. In Joel 2:28-32 and in 1QS 4:13, 21 these two ideas occur in proximity to one another, and there may be a direct connection between them.

It is no longer possible to determine with any assurance whether it was the Messiah or God himself whom the Baptist expected to come for judgment. Vs. 8 may be understood in this latter sense also. The fact that there were disciples of John who saw in him a kind of messiah and expected no other may be inferred from Luke 1:16 f. and Acts 19:2 f., and from the polemic against such a conception (e.g., John 1:19 ff.) which became sharper and sharper in the Christian tradition, as well as from later reports which clearly state this. On the other hand, the expectation of the coming of a messiah was alive at that time, and it is difficult to understand vs. 7 in any other way. Moreover, the Baptist's doubting of Christ as the Messiah in Matthew 11:3 could hardly be a later invention. Nevertheless, his image of the coming Messiah was that of a judge. The Christian church, on the other hand, knows of the fulfillment of this saying of the Baptist. It has experienced the Holy Spirit as the great gift of Jesus Christ which judges all that is evil and perverse, and creates all things new. Whether Matthew 3:11 means a baptism of fire like that which is recorded in Acts 2:3 remains entirely uncertain. It is not likely that Luke does, since in Acts 1:5 and 11:16 he quotes the saying of the Baptist without the reference to fire. Thus it is more likely the Christian church which saw in it an allusion to the judgment. But the church knows that this judgment, in a certain sense, has already been fulfilled. Since John expected the judgment in the future, he summoned a band of penitents to be sealed through their returning and the baptism of repentance, in order to escape the horror of the coming judgment. The Christian church knows, however, that the baptism with the Spirit has been accomplished already, and that in this very experience God's judgment upon all sin has been fulfilled for those who submit themselves to baptism; and it always continues to be fulfilled.

The historical antecedents of John and his baptism are unclear. Ceremonial washings were practiced by the Dead Sea community, whose members immersed themselves regularly. John's baptism differed from theirs in that it was not repeated, and in that it involved the participation of the one who baptized. The chief difference was that John invited all the people to the baptism, not just a choice group who were members of a particular order. Recently some have held the opinion that at one time John had been a member of the Qumran community; this is misleading, because this Jewish "order" had separated itself from the nation by its fanatical observance of the law. Furthermore, John's baptism, which was God's one-time gift in the final hour, is conspicuous in its contrast to ceremonies which were repeated regularly. If at that time the Gentiles who were converted to Judaism purified themselves by a single immersion (which is very uncertain), John, in a sense, would have classified all Israel with the unclean Gentiles by his practice of baptizing Jews. It is more likely that he revolutionized the purification ceremonies which were practiced by the shore of the Dead Sea, and which were expected to have an ultimate and once-for-all character on the day of judgment (1QS 4:21).

The word of judgment concerning the "baptism" with "fire [and storm]," which forms a contrast to the baptism of John, is surely Mark's original creation, whereby he can establish a connection with the concept of a river of fire (in Persia) or a lake of fire (Rev. 19:20; 20:10, 14 f.; 21:8). If this assumption is correct it brings into even clearer focus the conceptual connections and reformulations of the church.

The church retained the insight that the coming of John signifies the "beginning" of a new age; that with him Elijah reappeared —hence the possibility of repentance and forgiveness of sins before the end. But he is indeed "the beginning" of the new age, and not simply a flaming sign before the end. The baptism which is coming surely is not the all-consuming fire; it is Jesus' baptism with the Spirit—the baptism which became a reality in the Christian church and initiated the age of the world-wide "preaching" of "repentance" and of the "Good News." This alone gives the Baptist and his baptism their meaning. It is not the ethical content of the Baptist's preaching (Matt. 3:7-10; Luke 3:7-14) which is important to Mark and his church, but only the two statements in vss. 7 f. This underscores their orientation toward the one who is coming. It also poses the question which must be answered in the following material, namely, "What constitutes the incomparable greatness of Jesus?"

The Baptism of Jesus 1:9-11;
cf. Matt. 3:13-17 and Luke 3:21 f.

9Not long afterward Jesus came from Nazareth, in the region of
Galilee, and John baptized him in the Jordan. 10As soon as Jesus
came up out of the water he saw heaven opening and the Spirit
coming down on him like a dove. 11And a voice came from
heaven: "You are my own dear Son. I am well pleased with you."
(Vs. 11: Ps. 2:7; Isa. 42:1.)

Although even this has been questioned recently, it is likely that the baptism of Jesus by John is historical, since it caused the church much difficulty. Matthew 3:14 f. declares explicitly why this baptism was necessary. No unbiased person reading Luke 3: 21 f. after Luke 3:20 would guess that it was John who baptized Jesus. There is no statement in John 1:29 concerning the baptism of Jesus. Mark's account is straightforward but extremely concise since his interest is confined to vss. 10 f.

How many of the details are historical is open to question. It is probable that some experience in connection with his baptism induced Jesus to separate himself from the Baptist and he related this experience to his disciples. Even if we could be sure of this, it would make little difference since we would know only that Jesus experienced a call like that received by many true and false prophets before him. That God has actually spoken here can be declared only by the believer, and this is exactly what the church does in telling the story. Every detail makes this assertion, whether it is based upon a report about Jesus or has been included to make the event represent the fulfillment of the Old Testament. In support of the latter supposition one may refer, for example, to the opening of heaven in Isaiah 64:1 and Ezekiel 1:1, or to the descent of the Spirit on the Messiah in Isaiah 11:2. Compare this with Isaiah 63: 14 LXX ("a spirit [or: wind] came down from the Lord"), and 63:11 ("who put his Spirit within him" [that is, in Moses as shepherd of the sheep]), as well as Ezekiel 1:4 ("a stormy wind [or: spirit] came out of the north"). The English translation of "Messiah" (Hebrew) or "Christ" (Greek) is "an anointed one." As early as in 1 Samuel 10:1, 6, 10, and Isaiah 61:1 the Spirit is conferred by anointing. Mark recounts everything from the standpoint of Jesus' subjective experience, whereas Matthew in reporting the opening of heaven treats it as an objective event, just as Luke does in describing the descent of the Spirit. Matthew 3:17 further strengthens this objectivity in that the voice from heaven speaks in the third person; Luke emphasizes the bodily form—like a dove. The message of the voice of God seems to be a combination of Psalm 2:7 and Isaiah 42:1. The wording of this message very likely results from the church's combining of these two Bible passages which were considered important (cf. 1:2 f.). The manner in which Isaiah 42:1 is quoted in Matthew 12:18 probably represents an Aramaic form current at that time, and it is very similar to the message of this voice at Jesus' baptism. In addition, this passage from Isaiah contains a reference to the conferring of the Spirit. The Greek word *pais* which is used here can mean either "son" or "servant." Since the word "servant" is found in the Hebrew text of Isaiah 42:1, it has been supposed that, in the original account, the divine voice at Jesus' baptism addressed him as the servant of God, but that the Greek-speaking church replaced the ambiguous word *pais* with *huios,* which clearly means "son." In this case no other text would be needed to serve as a pattern. The story in its original form would have considered Jesus' baptism as the fulfillment of Isaiah 42:1 and therefore as the beginning of the ministry of God's servant to all peoples. A third possibility is suggested by a Jewish source. The Qumran community expected a priestly messiah in addition to a royal messiah. This priestly messiah is mentioned in the Testament of Levi 18:6, 7: "The heavens shall be opened, / And from the temple of glory shall come upon him sanctification, / With the Father's voice as from Abraham to Isaac. / And the glory of the Most High shall be uttered over him, / And the spirit of understanding and sanctification shall rest upon him . . ." (Cf. Isa. 11:2.) Is it possible that in similar fashion the early church viewed Jesus as the High Priest of the end-time? Could the church have seen him as another Isaac who offers himself, for in the LXX Isaac is designated as an only "beloved son" (Gen. 22:2, 12, 16)? But Jesus is not called a high priest until the Epistle to the Hebrews, which is very late in the New Testament. The parallel in the Testament of Levi is questionable, since the author may have been a Jewish Christian who wrote as late as A.D. 200. On the other hand, even a Jewish author may have had his view of the future influenced by hearing the story of Jesus' baptism from Jewish Christians in the same way that the New Testament writers were influenced greatly by Jewish and Hellenistic views. Consequently, the historicity of the passage remains uncertain.

We may ask whether or not this story is historical; whether it is concerned with just one of many baptisms; or whether it deals with a subjective experience of Jesus which could be explained psychologically. In so doing, however, we would not be asking the decisive question concerning the event. In order to appreciate what this question is we need to realize that the church which first described the baptism of Jesus gave a very definite answer to it. The Old Testament passages cited show that the opening of heaven, the coming of the Spirit, and the resounding of the voice of God are signs of the end-time. In this way the church has stated from the very beginning that here God's actions are conclusive, setting forth clearly the significance Jesus has for every man. In Psalm 2:7 God addresses his king at the time of his enthronement. The allusion to this passage indicates that the baptism of Jesus was considered to be his induction into the eschatological office of the Son of God, corresponding to the enthronement of an Israelite king (see the excursus on 15:39). Mark's interest is no longer centered in this strong apocalyptic orientation toward the end-time—after all, 40 years have passed since that event occurred at the Jordan River. The concept of some kind of adoption as the Son of God satisfies him even less. This event is described in eschatological language; by placing it at the beginning of the story of Jesus, Mark turns this episode into a divine "epiphany." This epiphany reveals the "dimension" in which everything told about Jesus must be viewed. It is the dimension of the conclusive act of God in the "Son," and this act is effectual for all men (cf. vs. 11 and 15:39).

[9] The characteristics which distinguish Jesus from the masses are not biographical data—his family, his particular training, his early abilities and successes. A "Life of Jesus" similar to the biography of some great personality is not found here. All we are told is his name. The reference to his home town serves the same function as our family names, and Nazareth is so insignificant that it is not mentioned in any other source. Nothing else is said about him—nothing concerning his age, appearance, family status; the latter is especially surprising in the light of the fact that bachelors were a rarity in that day.

[10] It is what God does for Jesus that gives him his unique position. Although Mark is narrating everything from the standpoint of the subjective experience of Jesus, he has no interest in the modern question as to whether the event might be explained in terms of a psychological process in the mind of Jesus. The only thing which is important is that God has spoken here. Therefore, the events described here have "actually" occurred; they are not merely subjective experiences stimulated by some predisposition of the mind of Jesus. Whether anyone else saw or heard the same things is not important to Mark. The determining factor is that this transaction between Father and Son is an ultimate secret which no human being can fathom. This is what sets Jesus apart from all others and gives him his unique position.

The opening of heaven signifies God's decisive intervention. After a long period which has been devoid of the Spirit, God begins to speak again—this time conclusively. His silence is over, even though for the time being the Son is the only one who is aware of the fact.

The significance of the appearance of the Spirit as a dove is still obscure. Doves were used as sacrifices. They were also thought to house the human spirit in its transmigrations. A dove plays a role in the story of the flood, and at times rabbis utilized the dove as a symbol of the Spirit of God brooding over the chaos (Gen. 1:2), whereas birds of various species were chosen by other interpreters. Perhaps this imagery may be understood more easily in the light of the fact that in Judaism the voice of God in the temple and, in one late instance, the voice of the Holy Spirit are compared to the cooing of a dove. It is purely coincidental that the Hebrew letters of the word for the "presence of God" also mean "that which is like a dove." Perhaps the dove was chosen as a symbol simply because it was a familiar bird (Matt. 10:16).

[11] The focal point of the whole story is the voice of God which designates Jesus as the "Son." The event recorded in vss. 9 f. resembles the choosing of a prophet, as indicated by the formula "I am well pleased with you." From time to time God had summoned the newly chosen king of Israel to his office with the statement "You are my son" (Ps. 2:7). Consequently, one could say that God is adopting the man Jesus and making him his son. This, however, is not the real issue in this section. Who Jesus might have been before his baptism or even before his birth is a question which might be asked in modern times, but is not being asked here. A Jewish contemporary of Jesus who was influenced by the Old Testament might answer that from God's point of view Jesus had indeed been the Son of God from all eternity, because all things are reality to God including those which will not occur until much later in history. This does not in any way alter the fact that what is important to Mark is the beginning of Jesus' sonship in the world, i.e., the point in time when he began to exercise his sonship. According to this story, then, it is not the eternity of Jesus' sonship which distinguishes him from the other "sons" of God—the kings of Israel (2 Sam. 7:14; Pss. 2:7; 89:27 f.), and indeed all Israelites (at first it was predicated only of the nation as a whole: Exodus 4:22 f.; but later of individuals also: Isaiah 1:2; Wisdom of Solomon 2:16 ff.; Ecclesiasticus 4:10). Perhaps there are others who could be called sons of God in a similar way. Even in the first formulation of our section the statement is made that heaven, which has been closed for a long time, is open once more; that the Holy Spirit is working again; and that God's voice is again sounding forth. Everything was viewed as the ultimate fulfillment of all that was only provisional and symbolic in the Old Testament. This is even more true for Mark (cf. 1:1-3 and the excursus on 15:39). The unique character of Jesus' sonship is indicated by the adjective "dear" which is often translated "only" in the LXX. The uniqueness of his sonship is maintained consistently throughout the New Testament. According to all four Gospels, Jesus speaks only of "my Father" or "your Father." Never does he include the disciples with himself in saying "our Father." Jesus does not pray the words of Matthew 6:9 with his disciples; he is simply instructing them in prayer. It is only through participation in the Spirit of *the* Son that men are made sons of God (Gal. 4:4-7; Rom. 8:3, 14-17). *The* Son, according to John, is the only one who can transform others into "sons of the light" (John 12:36; cf. Rev. 2:18; 21:7; Heb. 1:2-8, etc.; 2:10). With reference to the above compare Christ as the Son of God in Romans 1:1-7.

The Temptation of Jesus 1:12-13;
cf. Matt. 4:1-11 and Luke 4:1-13

[12]At once the Spirit made him go into the desert. [13]He was there forty days, and Satan tempted him. Wild animals were there also, but angels came and helped him.

This story has been preserved in greater detail in Q. Matthew and Luke have appropriated that version and combined it with details from Mark. Mark omits not only the details of the temptation, but the fasting of Jesus as well. In Greek the word meaning "they served" is in a form indicating an action of long duration. This word is used especially for "wait on" or "provide with food," which makes it clear that Mark assumes the angels fed Jesus for forty days. It is likely that the church had related everything in greater detail before Mark (see below); however, Mark tells the story in a very abbreviated form and is interested solely in Jesus' victory over the devil. This indicates once more that what happened in the life of Jesus is no mere human or earthly event. No, it is God's battle against Satan.

[12] As in the stories of the prophets, the Spirit of God appears here as an overpowering force which seizes certain men and drives them to various places (cf. 1 Kings 18:12; 2 Kings 2:16; Ezek. 3:12, 14 f.; 8:3; 11:24; Acts 8:39 f.). This not only confirms the close connection between this passage and 1:11, but also asserts that it is God himself who sends Jesus into this battle. From the very beginning Jesus' path leads not to heavenly glory but into the wilderness where Satan is.

[13] According to Isaiah 11:6 f., peace will reign among the wild animals in the kingdom of the Messiah. God's angels protect the righteous one of Psalm 91:11-13 and the wild animals cannot harm him (similarly Job 5:22). The Jewish Testament of Naphtali 8:4 promises the righteous: "And the devil shall flee from you, and the wild beasts shall fear you . . . and the angels shall cleave to you." According to Jewish tradition the battle with the wild animals began with the Fall; previously Adam had been lord over them and the angels roasted meat and filtered wine for him. Accordingly, when the church told this story it was thinking that Jesus had come as the righteous one of the end-time. He, like Adam, was led by God into temptation immediately after his commissioning; but, unlike Adam, Jesus withstood his temptations and thereby restored paradise. This interpretation is more plausible than the one in which the animals merely represent the horror of the wilderness, and this section is left open and unanswered until 3:22-30. It is difficult to say how much of this was understood by Mark. The only thing of importance to him is that Jesus has come as the one promised by the Old Testament—the one who withstands Satan in the wilderness where God and the angels are the only witnesses.

The way these brief stories are narrated is the consequence of the church's desire to preach and, with some modification, Mark's own desire to proclaim the "Good News." Therefore, it is not of critical importance how many details are historical or what took place only in the mind of Jesus. What is crucial is the question placed before us by the church and by Mark: Is it true that Jesus has come as the new Adam who has counteracted the Fall? Is it true that Jesus has come as the one promised in the Old Testament, the one through whom heaven and earth are reconciled once more? Stated concisely, Is it true that God has acted in Jesus? Faith alone can answer, just as Mark and the church before him attempt to do when they proclaim: In Jesus heaven again has opened, God has intervened, and since that time the Spirit of God is at work once more. Consequently, both the battle with Satan and the peace of God have begun on earth. He who approaches Jesus, therefore, approaches the open heaven as well as the wilderness where the command of the Spirit leads him into battle and temptation; and he meets not only the attack of Satan but also the peace of God in the midst of the wild animals.

II

THE AUTHORITY OF JESUS AND THE BLINDNESS OF THE PHARISEES 1:14—3:6

A. The Authority over Demons and Illness 1:14-45

Jesus Proclaims the Kingdom of God 1:14-15;
cf. Matt. 4:12-17 and Luke 4:14 f.

14After John had been put in prison, Jesus went to Galilee and preached the Good News from God. 15"The right time has come," he said, "and the Kingdom of God is near! Turn away from your sins and believe the Good News!"

Mark gives a brief summary of the preaching of Jesus. "Preaching" and "Good News" are Mark's favorite expressions (cf. 1:1). The call of Jesus is accurately summed up in vs. 15, where the association of repentance and faith reveals the language of the church (Acts 5:31; 11:18; 20:21). Mark's concern is to make clear that in this preaching Jesus continues to go forth into the world and that his call, therefore, is being directed also to the one who reads this Gospel today. Consequently, this section may serve as a caption to the whole Gospel (cf. the Epilogue).

[14, 15] The time of the ministry of Jesus is clearly distinguished from that of John (contrast John 3:24). The word *paradidomi,* which is translated here by "put in prison," means "deliver up," whether into prison or unto death. It is used frequently of martyrs, but also of criminals. The parallel to the fate of the Son of Man is quite clear (9:31; 10:33; 14:21, 41; cf. 14:10 f., 18, 42, 44; 15:1, 10, 15). None of the biographical details of

John's imprisonment are important; accordingly, they are not given until 6:17 ff., and then only to fill a lacuna. The progress of preaching is the one thing which is important. Since the character of the special salvation-time is already present in John's preaching, the two preachers do not appear simultaneously, but one after the other. Jesus, however, does not signify simply the beginning of the Good News (1:1, 2); he marks the fulfillment of the special salvation-time which is distinguished from all other time (this is perhaps what is indicated by the Greek word for "time" in vs. 15). Thus there are different periods of time—some in which God prepares events which will take place in the future, and other times in which those things actually occur.

The Kingdom of God. When Jesus proclaims that the Kingdom of God (literally, the kingly rule of God) is near, he is adopting a concept which was coined in the Old Testament. Although it denotes God's sovereignty over creation (Pss. 103:19; 145:11 ff.), it refers primarily to his unchallenged sovereignty in the end-time (Isa. 52:7). Judaism in the time of Jesus spoke of the sovereignty of God which one accepted if he submitted obediently to every commandment; in addition, it spoke of the reign of God which comes after the annihilation of every foe and the end of all suffering. In the one instance its coming was entirely dependent upon human decision, and in the other case it was seen as something which happens in the normal course of events. In the New Testament the Kingdom of God is conceived, first of all, as something in the future (Mark 9:1, 47; 14:25; Matt. 13:41-43; 20:21; Luke 22:16, 18; 1 Cor. 15:50, et al.) which comes from God (Mark 9:1; Matt. 6:10; Luke 17:20; 19:11). Therefore, it is something man can only wait for (Mark 15:43), seek (Matt. 6:33), receive (Mark 10:15; cf. Luke 12:32), and inherit (1 Cor. 6:9 f.; Gal. 5:21; James 2:5), but he is not able to create it by himself. Jesus' manner of speaking distinguishes him from the Judaism of his day. He rarely spoke of God as king, nor did he ever speak of the establishment of God's sovereignty over Israel or over the world. Instead, he spoke frequently of one's entering the kingdom. Therefore, the kingdom is more like an area or a sphere of authority into which one can enter, so "realm" would be a better translation (Mark 9:47; 10:15, 23-25; Matt. 5:20; 7:21; 18:3; 19:23). To be sure, Jesus refused to calculate the time of the coming of the Kingdom of God, or speculate about it, although he could speak very concretely of sitting down at table and eating and drinking in that kingdom (Mark 14:25; Matt. 8:11; Luke 22:30). Instead of any such speculating he speaks of the nearness of the kingdom (Mark 1:15; Matt. 10:7), about its having come already (Matt. 12:28), and of its presence in the midst of his hearers (Luke 17:21). Men are entering it at the present time (see above), and it is already under attack (Matt. 11:12) because a stronger one is already here (Luke 11:22), one who is more than Solomon or Jonah, the temple or the Baptist (Matt. 12:41 f., 6; 11:11)—one who can say, "But now I tell you" (Matt. 5:21 ff.). For this reason demons are being driven out (Mark 1:26; Luke 11:20) and men are being called to discipleship (Mark 1:16 ff.). Therefore, the kingdom has both present and future aspects. Of course, that aspect of the Kingdom of God is future, where men will have fellowship at table with Jesus in his glory, where death and pain will have been abolished, and where faith will have passed into sight.

But the one who meets Jesus cannot continue to wait for the kingdom to appear sometime in the next ten to one thousand years. In the acts and words of Jesus the future kingdom has come upon him already. It is decided at that very moment whether or not he will ever be in the kingdom. For this reason he actually enters the future kingdom now, and the power of the coming kingdom begins to take effect immediately in the table fellowship of Jesus with his disciples and in the dinner of the congregation as well as in experiencing the power of Jesus and being moved by his words. Thus Jesus unites the present and the future. This is what forms the contrast to the viewpoint of the Judaism of that day: to Judaism the Kingdom of God was far more important than the Messiah, whereas here everything depends upon fellowship with Jesus. In Judaism the world was expected to be either transfigured or destroyed in the fire of Judgment, whereas this saying of Jesus placed his disciples and their duties in the midst of the world; at the same time, however, it makes them inwardly free from the world, and as a consequence, the world is neither condemned nor exalted. Jesus, therefore, has no expectation of a triumph of Israel or of the church, and the condemnation of everyone else. To a disciple of Jesus, what God's judgment says to him is the only essential.

If the coming of the Kingdom of God is not dependent in any way upon the deeds of man, it nevertheless lays claim upon him and all his thoughts and deeds. "Turning about" (this is the meaning of the Old Testament word which in Greek is translated "change of mind," i.e., repentance) results from the coming nigh of God's kingdom and the fulfilling of the time. This sequence is decisive. "Repentance" is nothing less than a wholehearted commitment to the "Good News." This is like the conduct of Jesus himself who, with astonishing patience, left everything to God. He did not prepare for a missionary campaign, first against Jerusalem and then into the rest of the world; no, he remained in insignificant Galilee. For "believe," cf. 5:34-36; with reference to the amazing fact that he did not proclaim himself as the Messiah see the excursus "Son of God" on 15:39.

The Call to Discipleship 1:16-20;
cf. Matt. 4:18-22; Luke 5:1-11

16As Jesus walked by Lake Galilee, he saw two fishermen, Simon and his brother Andrew, catching fish in the lake with a net.
17Jesus said to them, "Come with me and I will teach you to catch
men." 18At once they left their nets and went with him.
19He went a little farther on and saw two other brothers, James
and John, the sons of Zebedee. They were in their boat getting their
nets ready. 20As soon as Jesus saw them he called them; so they
left their father Zebedee in the boat with the hired men and went
with Jesus.

Apparently Mark has added this story in an effort to show in a concrete way what such a new commitment could mean. Nothing is said about time or exact place, or about any other details. It is only in passing that we are told that, since Simon and Andrew are poor, they fish with a net weighted with stones around the outside. When thrown out into the water the net is drawn together at the bottom and encloses the fish as in a pouch. The story is like a woodcut in that only the important features are presented. In the arrangement of his material Mark has created an impression that is far more important than such information as where or when the calls were issued or whether or not they occurred on the same day (cf. 6:7). The fewer the details told and the more closely it resembles an imaginary scene, the easier it is for the reader to find himself in the story. Since there is no real parallel in Jeremiah 16:16 (cf. Amos 4:2; Hab. 1:14 f.; 1 QpHab. 1:14 f.) the Greek-speaking church appears to have formulated the metaphor "to catch men," following the Greek peripatetic philosophers who spoke in a similar manner. This passage is not concerned with the sending out of the disciples, as is 6:7-13. An event in the time of Jesus is being told by the church in such a way that it can recognize itself and its own situation in the event. For the historical questions see comment on 6:7-13; for the theological questions, see the Epilogue.

[16, 19] Discipleship always begins with Jesus' looking at a person (1:16, 19; 2:14; 10:21; Luke 19:5; in the Old Testament, cf. 1 Sam. 16:1; Ezra 5:5; Zech. 12:4) and calling him. Those who are called have had no specific preparation, nor have they even been among those who heard Jesus' preaching (1:14 f.). **[17, 20]** Jesus does not encounter men in some special religious sphere, but in the midst of everyday life where they really live. Men are made disciples by the call of Jesus, which is as powerful as the creative word of God (Ps. 33:9; Isa. 55:10 f.), and whatever those who are called may become will be the work of Jesus. **[18, 20]** It is clearly for this reason that the call of the disciples is related without any indication that the fishermen might have had time for reflection or might have had to overcome certain difficulties before responding. So it is that God's grace operates without the necessity of deliberation. As a result, discipleship is neither an individual ethical decision nor a thoughtful acceptance of propositions; yet in a very substantial way it is a new manner of acting and thinking which is sustained by the event of grace. Vs. 20, which speaks of the rending of family ties and the forsaking of certain wealth, shows a definite advance over vs. 18, as Simon and Andrew had neither boat nor servants.

This concept of discipleship is Jesus' own creation. The Greeks and the later rabbis spoke of "disciples of God"; however, they meant by this "becoming like him" in an ethical sense, or the obedience to his commandments (2 Macc. 8:36; cf. Deut. 13:5; Dan. 4:31 LXX). The relationship of the rabbis to their students seems to be a closer parallel to this discipleship. The primary difference is that the rabbi does not call his disciples—he is sought by them (cf. Matt. 8:19 ff.; the case of Elijah is exceptional, 1 Kings 19:19 ff.). Above all, the rabbis never could have conceived of a call so radical as to make clear that being with Jesus is more important than all of God's commandments (Mark 10:21; although the idea is found already in this passage). A disciple of a rabbi might dream of some day becoming even better, if possible, than his master; but a disciple of Jesus could never expect that some day he himself might be the "Son of Man." Jesus never debates with his disciples as a rabbi would have done. Thus the word "follow" received a new sound when Jesus said it, a sound which it has nowhere else except in those passages of the Old Testament which declare that one must follow either Baal or Yahweh (1 Kings 18:21; cf. the idea in Prov. 7:22).

The Demonstration of the Authority of Jesus 1:21-28;
cf. Luke 4:31-37

21They came to the town of Capernaum, and on the next Sabbath day Jesus went into the synagogue and began to teach.
22The people who heard him were amazed at the way he taught.
He wasn't like the teachers of the Law; instead, he taught with
authority.
23Just then a man with an evil spirit in him came into the synagogue and screamed: 24"What do you want with us, Jesus of Nazareth? Are you here to destroy us? I know who you are: you are

God's holy messenger!" [25]Jesus commanded the spirit: "Be quiet, and come out of the man!" [26]The evil spirit shook the man hard, gave a loud scream and came out of him. [27]The people were all so amazed that they started saying to each other, "What is this? Some kind of new teaching? This man has authority to give orders to the evil spirits, and they obey him!" [28]And so the news about Jesus spread quickly everywhere in the region of Galilee.

It is already clear in vs. 21 that Mark formulated vss. 21 f. as a separate unit. Not only is nothing said of any disciples accompanying Jesus, but most important is the fact that the event in vss. 16-20 could not have happened on the Sabbath, when fishing and the repairing of nets were strictly forbidden. It is clear, then, that Mark has added vss. 21 f. as a transition between two sections which had been transmitted to him. This shows his indifference to matters of time and location, inasmuch as his interest is centered in the significance which the event has for the church.

In vss. 23-26 the story of a healing by Jesus is recounted as it had been told over and over again in the church, and as it had been used in preaching and instruction. It may be that it was set down in writing before Mark. In vss. 22 and 27 f. Mark gives us the message he wants to convey: The miracle is an evidence of the authority of Jesus' teaching. While we are told that the Baptist, Jesus, the twelve, and the church have preached "repentance" and the "Good News" (cf. 1:4), according to Mark, Jesus is the only one who "taught" (15 times, each time indicating a continuous activity; moreover, the word "teaching" occurs 5 times. In 6:30 a different Greek form expresses a single momentary action). Jesus' teaching, therefore, differs radically from the general preaching done both before and after him. As is true here, the content of his preaching either is not indicated at all or is told only in brief summary. Therefore, Jesus was distinguished from others not because he taught something completely different, but because he taught with such authority that things happened. Men were moved to action and sick persons were healed. In brief, God is speaking to men in the teaching of Jesus in such a way that those who have been separated from God are brought back into fellowship with him. Grace is bestowed. This is how Mark uses the story of a miracle (cf. 4:35-41) to show the special "dimension" in which Jesus taught. In his word heaven actually breaks in and hell is abolished. His word is action. This explains why Mark is so impressed with the fact that even the powers of the netherworld proclaimed Jesus as "God's holy messenger" (see vs. 34).

[21] The synagogue is the place where the congregation regularly assembled on the Sabbath for the prayers, Scripture reading and exposition in which everyone was permitted to participate (see Luke 4:16 ff.). Jesus was no revolutionary; he conformed to the normal religious life of his people. **[22]** The astonishment of the people is the visible symbol of the authority of Jesus. It was as true then as now that faith alone can perceive that God confronts us in Jesus. In this section Mark gives us that testimony of faith before he reports anything of what Jesus taught. Matthew, in contrast to Mark, bases the same statement on the content of Jesus' teaching; accordingly, he transfers it to the end of the Sermon on the Mount (Matt. 7:28 f.). The teachers of the law were the professional theologians and, since the Old Testament was the code which regulated every aspect of life, they were the lawyers. Most of them belonged to the religious sect of the Pharisees, who considered the keeping of the law in everyday life to be more important than the temple cult. On the other hand, many Pharisees were laymen in spite of the fact that their legalism, which was becoming more and more strict, required increasingly better knowledge of the law and thus training in the Scriptures. They differed from Jesus in that they claimed to possess merely a derived authority. The law alone possessed authority, and their authority was derived from a proper interpretation of the law. They possessed the Spirit, as it were, only in a prepackaged form.

[23] At that time, illness, and particularly insanity, was generally attributed to unclean spirits. This concept contains the truth that illness, in the final analysis, is something which God has not willed—something which is hostile to God (even if in individual instances it can be a blessing: 2 Cor. 12:9).

[24] Gentile and Jewish stories also relate instances where the demon which is being assaulted calls out the name of the exorcist. The belief was widespread that knowledge of the name of another gives one power over him (cf. the fairy tale about Rumpelstiltskin or the magical papyruses).

"God's holy messenger" is an ancient title which is found nowhere else in the New Testament except in John 6:69 where it is translated "the Holy One from God." In the Old Testament it is found only in Judges 13:7; 16:17 in the LXX (cf. the related title in 1 Kings 17:18 accompanied by the same angry question which is found at the beginning of our verse), whereas other versions read "Nazarite." Perhaps Nazarene (cf. Matt. 2:23 Greek) and Nazarite have been confused because they are similar in sound. Consequently, "God's holy messenger" could be the church's interpretation of the name "Nazarene" (i.e., Man from Nazareth). It may have happened the other way around; that is, first of all Jesus was designated a Nazarite, as Samson was, and afterwards the discovery was made that Nazarite was similar to Nazareth in sound. In any case, this reveals a very early stage of development in which Jesus was seen as a charismatic leader moved by the Spirit of God; one in whom the former salvation-time of God's Spirit, who lived in Israel, had returned after a long period of spiritual drought. The fact that in most instances the possessed one speaks in the plural would be regarded today as a symptom of schizophrenia. The New Testament idea of a whole "mob" (5:9) of spirits indicates that the man has been overwhelmed by his difficulty.

[25] The command to be quiet is Jesus' battle cry here, as it is in 4:39. Mark, of course, interprets it in another way (see vs. 34). To be sure, healings such as this actually occurred, and just as surely they may be explained psychologically. Nevertheless, in all this discussion nothing has been said as yet about the secret of this authority of Jesus which is so great that it prevails in this manner. **[26, 27]** The loud scream of the departing demon demonstrates the intensity of the battle and the magnitude of the victory, whereas the amazement which came over the people shows that they experienced something of the presence of God. This destroys all false peace and security and leads to a healthy doubting and questioning. Moreover, the crowd correctly perceives that the important thing is not this miracle upon a single sick person. What is decisive is the authority of Jesus which has been exhibited through the miracle, which confronts everyone in Jesus' teaching, and with which he wants to reach them all. **[28]** Therefore, the effect of this act of Jesus spread far beyond Capernaum.

The Healing in the House of Simon 1:29-31;
cf. Matt. 8:14-15; Luke 4:38-39

29They left the synagogue and went straight to the home of
Simon and Andrew; and James and John went with them. 30Si-
mon's mother-in-law was sick in bed with a fever, and as soon as
Jesus got there he was told about her. 31He went to her, took her
by the hand and helped her up. The fever left her and she began to
wait on them.

This is another story revealing Jesus' authority, which followed the preceding one in the tradition (see 1:32-39). **[29]** The phrase "with James and John" (Greek) is noteworthy because it may stem from an old Petrine tradition formulated in the first person: "We came with . . . "

[31] The story concludes with an act of service (described as continuous by the Greek form) which is the specific manner of discipleship for a woman (15:41; Luke 8:3; John 12:2; also Mark 9:35; 10:43-45, et al.). Jesus appears to have been more liberal than the rabbis, who disapproved of women serving at the table. In this respect this story goes further than the preceding one. Amazement and questioning do not find God's intended objective in a characterization of Jesus which is more nearly correct than the one given in vs. 24, but in the discipleship of service (see 1:20, 34; 8:34).

The Significance of the Authority of Jesus 1:32-39;
cf. Matt. 8:16-17; Luke 4:40-44

32When evening came, after the sun had set, people brought
to Jesus all the sick and those who had demons. 33All the people
of the town gathered in front of the house. 34Jesus healed many
who were sick with all kinds of diseases and drove out many de-

mons. He would not let the demons say anything, because they knew who he was.

[35]Very early the next morning, long before daylight, Jesus got up and left the house. He went out of town to a lonely place where he prayed. [36]But Simon and his companions went out searching for him; [37]when they found him they said, "Everyone is looking for you." [38]But Jesus answered: "We must go on to the other villages around here. I have to preach in them also, because that is why I came." [39]So he traveled all over Galilee, preaching in the synagogues and driving out demons.

Vs. 32 has little significance unless the setting of the sun marks the end of the Sabbath, so that from that time on it was permissible, once more, to carry the sick. It does not have this meaning for Mark, since whenever he refers to Jewish customs he explains them to his readers (7:3 f.). It is likely, then, that vss. 23-26, 29-32, 34a, 35-38 had been told in a connected form before Mark. Of course, Mark has revised the style extensively. In vs. 32, for example, the first of the two statements which give the time of the day reveals typical Markan style. Mark's editing is seen, perhaps, in the addition of "all" in this verse and the insertion of vss. 33 and 39, since he underscores again and again the far-reaching influence of Jesus. Mark's hand is seen principally in his new interpretation of the command to be silent in 1:34b. An instruction to early Christian missionaries which we know from Didache 11:4 f. forbids their remaining too long in one locality. It is not impossible that the wording of vs. 38 has been conditioned by that directive.

[32] Mark emphasizes that Jesus is present in every difficulty and that his influence extends to everyone. **[33, 34]** That which is most important to him is the "Messianic secret," i.e., the command which prohibits the proclamation of Jesus' special honor and authority.

The Messianic Secret. The command "Be quiet" in the ancient story found in vss. 23-26 was intended to bring an end to the demon's activity, as is true of the other command, "Come out." According to Mark, however, the demons are not permitted to reveal what they alone know (3:11 f.), any more than the disciples are (8:30; 9:9). The persons who are healed are not even allowed to tell about Jesus' miracle (1:44; 5:43; 7:36; 8:26?). The fact that Jesus is the Messiah must be kept secret; but why? Certain contradictions are evident. Why does Jesus perform miracles in public? According to 5:35-38 many people are present. How can the command in 5:43 be obeyed by all of them? How can 2:7-11 be possible if Jesus wished to keep the fact secret that as the Messiah he works on behalf of God? Since the Messianic secret is Mark's own creation, we must listen carefully to what it is that he wants to say by means of it.

Jesus never speaks openly of the mystery of his work (cf. J. Schniewind on 1:44) but always in parables (or in enigmatical expressions such as "Son of Man"); moreover, a certain reserve may be observed on the part of Jesus and in the report of the church before Mark in connection with the healings (1:35-38; 7:33; 8:23). It is significant that in Judaism and in the rest of the New Testament a mysterious character is always attributed to God and his activity. The people from Qumran as well as Paul and his followers know that God's activity can never be comprehended fully in words, but can be understood only as a miracle which, in the final analysis, cannot be grasped by the human mind. In the New Testament, but not in Judaism, this secret has become something unique: It is Jesus Christ himself, or, more exactly, his cross (1 Cor. 2:6 ff.) or his journey through the world on his mission (Col. 1:26 f.; 2:2 f.; Eph. 3:1 ff.; Rom. 16:25 ff.; 1 Tim. 3:16). Mark, to be sure, wants to say more than this. He makes no sharp distinction between those who are in on this secret and those who stand outside, as is done in all these other passages. Even the disciples themselves prove to be blind (cf. 8:17-21). To Mark it is significant that Jesus' command to be silent is broken again and again (1:45; 7:36; cf. 5:20; 7:24), because the authority of Jesus is actually the authority of God and therefore it cannot remain hidden. Ultimately, the declaration of the demons (3:11) or that of Peter (8:29), or even of God himself (9:7), is not wrong or unsatisfactory in any way. Why, then, the secrecy? Mark's answer is that the time for proclamation has not come, since the secret of Jesus will become really apparent only on the cross, and one must follow him in the way of the cross to be able to really understand it (see 8:34). For this reason the proclamation of the demons, the healed, or even the disciples, however exact it may be, can only do harm until Jesus' path to the cross makes it possible for men to follow and even makes that following an irrevocable requirement. Although Mark employs a miracle story about the silencing and driving out of a demon he sees something far more profound in it. Jesus is combatting not only the demons that afflict this one man; he is also combatting those who think that all one must do to be saved and to wriggle out of the demands of discipleship is to know the right name (see 1:24), or to have a proper view about Jesus or a proper "faith" in his divine Sonship. It may be that the less historical the details the more Mark has hit upon the heart of Jesus' actions and proclamation. In this text we are faced with the question of whether we really understand Jesus' healings (which are subject to psychological explanation) as the inbreaking of God who is seeking us. Do we see them as something very ambiguous when taken alone, and which can be comprehended only in the light of the cross of Jesus by one who is following the Crucified?

[35] Vss. 35-38 underscore this truth. We are told again and again that Jesus prayed alone. Prayer was an essential part of his service and continually guarded that service from overactivity as well as from indolence. It was at the same time a refuge from an enthusiastic recognition on the part of individuals who did not desire to become disciples. **[36, 37]** For the first time the disciples' lack of understanding becomes evident. They (on the basis of an old Petrine tradition?) are seen as a group gathered about Simon (it can scarcely be thought of as his family). **[38, 39]** The mission for which Jesus "came" is, however, the call to all people—to all Galilee, as Mark emphasizes. His actions are only symbols of that call.

The Influence of the Authority of Jesus in Spite of the Command to Be Silent 1:40-45;
cf. Matt. 8:2-4 and Luke 5:12-16

[40]A leper came to Jesus, knelt down, and begged him for help.
"If you want to," he said, "you can make me clean." [41]Jesus was
filled with pity and reached out and touched him. "I do want to,"
he answered. "Be clean!" [42]At once the leprosy left the man and
he was clean. [43]Then Jesus spoke harshly with him and sent him
away at once. [44]"Listen," he said, "don't tell this to anyone. But
go straight to the priest and let him examine you; then offer the
sacrifice that Moses ordered, to prove to everyone that you are
now clean." [45]But the man went away and began to spread the
news everywhere. Indeed, he talked so much that Jesus could not
go into a town publicly. Instead he stayed out in lonely places,
and people came to him from everywhere.

(Vs. 44: Lev. 13:49; cf. Lev. 14:2-32.)

The statements about the Messianic secret and its being divulged probably originate with Mark. This would include vss. 44a, 45 (see 1:34). Perhaps the ancient narrative contained a command to be silent, which was limited until such time as the healing was confirmed by the priest, and the subsequent publication of the miracle. The story is placed here to serve as a climax.

[40] Leprosy is a dreaded disease because it excludes one from the general population and thus from the people of God. The afflicted one must cry from a distance, "Unclean, unclean," so that no one will approach him (Lev. 13:45). The rabbis considered him a living corpse and his cure as difficult as a resurrection from the dead. This leper broke through the barrier and committed everything to Jesus' authority. Although there is here by no means any clear knowledge of the real nature of Jesus, true faith is seen in the complete dependence upon him, in the courage to put trust in Jesus' unlimited power, and in the humble consciousness that everything depends upon Jesus' will and nothing can be expected from man.

[41, 42] Jesus' anger (the ancient reading is "was angry" and not "was filled with pity") applies to the horror of the misery which accompanied the disease (cf. John 11:33-38), which is just as contrary to God's plan of creation as is the action of the demons in 1:24 f. If this is true, then Jesus' pity is not the reason for this healing. The reason is to be found in the far more comprehensive campaign which is waged against every ungodly thing and in which the special authority of Jesus is revealed. The healing is accomplished by a word. Nevertheless, not only is the sovereign "I will" (RSV) mentioned explicitly, but also the fact that Jesus touched him (in contrast to 2 Kings 5:10). God's power lives, almost sacramentally, in the bodily nature of Jesus and will lay hold of the bodily nature of man also. **[43]** As is true of the "snorting" of Yahweh in the Old Testament, the "speaking harshly" (literally "snorting") on the part of Jesus is because of the blindness of man who praises the miracle-worker, to be sure, but wants nothing to do with his cross (cf. 3:5 and Matt. 9:30). **[44]** The fact that Jesus abides by the commandment in Leviticus 14:1 ff. should shield him from suspicion of pushing the law of God aside in a revolutionary manner (see comment on 1:21). This may even be the reason why Mark placed this story before 2:1—3:6. Perhaps the original story told how the man who was healed obeyed so that the miracle was confirmed officially, becoming a witness even to the priests. **[45]** With respect to the command to be silent and its being violated because God's inconceivable power does not permit itself to be kept secret, compare 1:34.

In this passage, also, Mark's method of narration becomes obvious. The presence of the power of God in Jesus is presented in a rather strange manner: His simple touch heals, and the power of that touch cannot be kept secret. At the same time, it is clear that nothing is settled simply by faith in the miraculous, so long as one will not accept Jesus' unique gift which breaks through all boundaries between clean and unclean, between the people of God and outsiders, because this is the reason for Jesus' anger and his command to be silent. This is how Mark asks the reader whether he will surrender himself to this confrontation with God in Jesus and allow the traditional boundaries to be destroyed. The ancient church detected something of this intention in Mark; therefore it had the leper say, according to a papyrus, "Lord Jesus, you who walk with the lepers and eat with them in the inn . . ."

B. THE AUTHORITY OVER SIN AND THE LAW 2:1—3:6

The Authority to Forgive Sins 2:1-12;
cf. Matt. 9:1-8; Luke 5:17-26

[1]A few days later Jesus came back to Capernaum, and the
news spread that he was at home. [2]So many people came together
that there wasn't any room left, not even out in front of the door.
Jesus was preaching the message to them [3]when some people
came, bringing him a paralyzed man—four of them were carrying
him. [4]Because of the crowd, however, they could not get him to
Jesus. So they made a hole in the roof right above the place where
Jesus was. When they had made an opening, they let the man
down, lying on his mat. [5]Jesus saw how much faith they had, and
said to the paralyzed man, "My son, your sins are forgiven."
[6]Some teachers of the Law who were sitting there thought to themselves: [7]"How does he dare to talk against God like this? No man
can forgive sins; only God can!" [8]At once Jesus knew their secret
thoughts, so he said to them: "Why do you think such things?
[9]Is it easier to say to this paralyzed man, 'Your sins are forgiven,'
or to say, 'Get up, pick up your mat, and walk'? [10]I will prove to
you, then, that the Son of Man has authority on earth to forgive
sins." So he said to the paralyzed man, [11]"I tell you, get up, pick
up your mat, and go home!" [12]While they all watched, the man
got up, picked up his mat and hurried away. They were all completely amazed and praised God, saying, "We have never seen anything like this!"

After 1:14-45, where the authoritative acts of Jesus are described, a series of disputes follows in 2:1—3:6, some of which, at least (2:18—3:5 or perhaps 2:15—3:5), had been brought together before Mark (cf. Introduction 2).

There is a break in the narration at the end of vs. 10. The expression from vs. 5 is repeated in vs. 9 in order to introduce another statement addressed to the paralyzed man. When vs. 12 declares that "all" were praising God, this would include the teachers of the law from vs. 6, in complete contradiction to the rest of the picture (cf. 2:16). Furthermore, reference is made only to the healing and not to the discussion in vss. 6-10. Jesus probably spoke of himself as the Son of Man (see 8:31), but it is not likely that he regarded the Son of Man as a heavenly figure (in contrast to "one on earth"). It is questionable whether Jesus would have formulated vs. 9 so ambiguously that one might suppose he meant that to forgive sins was easier than to heal. Therefore, it has been conjectured, and justifiably so, that the original account contained no more than vss. 1-5 and 11 f. The promise of forgiveness, which is given before the man is healed, moved the church to point out in vss. 6-10 the conflict existing between Jesus and the teachers of the law which frequently broke out into the open. The church directed attention to this conflict in order to accentuate the emphasis inherent in the ancient story: All of Jesus' healings are symbols of a much more profound authority and of the forgiveness of sins which restores men to fellowship with God. This, of course, is exactly what Jesus meant. These are the decisive verses for Mark, because this story about the beginning of the controversies indicates that the hostility which ultimately leads to the cross (3:6) breaks out at the center of Jesus' ministry.

[1] We are given no indication of when this took place, nor any detailed description of the house. **[2]** The house is mentioned simply to indicate that Jesus desires to withdraw, but the overwhelming impression he makes prevents him from doing so (cf. 3:20) and this desire to be alone makes the gathering of the crowd much more conspicuous (7:17, 24; 9:28, 33; 10:10). The expression "preaching the message" reappears in 4:33 and 8:32 (Greek) with some significant differences. In this place Mark uses it to indicate the beginning of a theologically important section which extends through 3:6 (see below).

[4] A Palestinian house usually consisted of a single room. The roof, which had to be repaired each fall before the rainy season, was constructed of wooden beams overlaid with branches and covered with mud. Very often an outdoor stairway led to the roof. Whether it would be possible to break through the roof while the house was jammed full of people is questionable. **[5]** The boldness and determination with which the four press on to Jesus is called "faith" by Mark, and it is obvious that these characteristics are more important than a complete knowledge of the person and character of Jesus. Therefore, it is a question of the faith of the carriers first of all, and not of the sick man's openness to suggestion or of his inner preparation for God. Consequently, what happens is entirely the work of God. The real need is exposed by Jesus' answers. It is not as if this sick man were unusually sinful, but his case makes the universal separation of man from God more conspicuous and illustrates the truth which is proclaimed over and over in the Old Testament, that all suffering is rooted in man's separation from God. For this reason, Jesus must call attention here to man's deepest need; otherwise the testimony of this healing would remain nothing more than the story of a remarkable miracle. **[11]** On the other hand, the second of Jesus' sayings makes it clear that forgiveness of sins is never merely a subjective experience, but that it restores the sovereignty of God even over a man's physical nature.

[6, 7] The teachers of the law (see 1:22) are absolutely right: God alone can tear down the wall of separation which men have erected against him. Judaism had never expected the Messiah to forgive sins. Jesus acts as if he really were the representative of God. Jesus does not deny in any way that God is the one who forgives sins through him, even though in keeping with the customary practice of all pious Jews he reverently avoids the use of God's Name. In response to this angry question Jesus revealed what really happened when he sat down with tax collectors and when he opened the way for prostitutes to come to God. **[8]** Moreover, the fact that Jesus looks through men so that they are not able to hide anything from him is an indication of the presence of God. **[9]** Jesus replies with a question intended to make them think. Certainly Mark considers the forgiveness of sins to be the more difficult thing to do. The opponents, however, think such a thing is easy to say if it is not necessary to prove that anything really happened. **[10]** So vs. 10 leads back to the story and re-emphasizes the fact that the authority of the Son of Man (see 8:31), in which heaven and earth are reunited, is the center of all that happens. **[11]** What follows must be understood as a demonstration of this fact.

[12] Other healings had occurred before this one, but the people understood this healing as a sign of something which had "never been seen before." This is exactly what the church had in mind when it inserted vss. 6-10. Therefore, it is no longer possible for the reader to escape the question whether he really recognizes in Jesus God's presence and authority. His presence and authority find expression in the assurance of the forgiveness of sins through Jesus (2:5), in his association with tax collectors (2:13-17), and in his freedom from the law (2:18—3:6). In this way, Jesus' victory over illness and demons is understood as a complete victory, i.e., victory over sin and the law, even as Paul declares in his theologically more exact language (1 Cor. 15:55 f.; Gal. 4:3, 8-10; cf. Col. 2:14 f.).

The Meal with Outcasts 2:13-17;
cf. Matt. 9:9-13; Luke 5:27-32

13Jesus went back again to the shore of Lake Galilee. A crowd came to him and he started teaching them. 14As he walked along he saw a tax collector, Levi the son of Alphaeus, sitting in his office. Jesus said to him, "Follow me." Levi got up and followed him.

15Later on Jesus was having a meal in Levi's house. There were many tax collectors and outcasts who were following Jesus, and some of them joined him and his disciples at the table. 16Some teachers of the Law, who were Pharisees, saw that Jesus was eating with these outcasts and tax collectors; so they asked his disciples, "Why does he eat with tax collectors and outcasts?" [17]Jesus heard them and answered: "People who are well do not need a doctor, but only those who are sick. I have not come to call the respectable people, but the outcasts."

Apparently vss. 13 f. and vss. 15-17 were two independent stories at one time. A completely new beginning is made in vs. 15 without any indication that these events took place shortly after the calling of Levi. In fact, there is no further mention of Levi, so it is not clear whether Jesus was staying in his own house (perhaps one placed at his disposal by Peter, 1:29-31) or in Levi's house. It is possible to distinguish older and newer material even within these sections. Vs. 13 is rather general and probably is an introduction formulated by Mark. Jesus' teaching (see 1:21-28) and its results, described by the phrase "a crowd came to him" (see 1:5), are what is important to Mark; the "shore of Lake Galilee" is the usual scene of Jesus' activity (cf. 1:16). Vs. 14 speaks with the conciseness of a woodcut in which everything is reduced to the essentials, and in this respect is very similar to 1:16-20. The question of principle, raised in vss. 15-17, concerning the righteousness of the law, occupied the church for a long time. Has Jesus come only for the Jews who live according to the law, or has he come for the Gentiles also? Later on a very similar question presented itself to the church: Has Jesus come for those who commit obvious sins after their baptism? A metaphor which was a favorite of the peripatetic Greek philosophers is found in vs. 17. When one of them was reproached for his association with lower-class people he said, "Physicians do not usually teach among the healthy, but where the sick are." Apparently this is how the Greek-speaking church summed up the activity of Jesus—with this metaphor which was familiar to them. In the second half of the verse they explained the metaphor because it was an answer to the question which was threatening them. Moreover, reference is made only to "outcasts" here, and not to "tax collectors and outcasts." Presumably, in vs. 15 the church has chosen as an illustration something which occurred commonly in Jesus' life, and in vs. 16 it has the customary opponents of Jesus ask the question which was troubling the church. Nothing is said in regard to where these teachers of the law have come from. Moreover, the formula "tax collectors and outcasts" is very appropriate in vs. 16b which is concerned with the teachers of the law, because they designated everyone who was not living according to the law as an "outcast." It is out of place, however, in vss. 15 and 16a. As a result, "and outcasts" is omitted from Luke 5:29 (cf. 5:30). In Mark's time the church was no longer Jewish; consequently, tax collectors were not excluded as lawless. Therefore, the church had to add the words "and outcasts" three times in order to show that the question was relevant in their time as well. The disciples are the ones who are interrogated in this section, even though it is Jesus who answers. This is the way it was after Easter: The disciples were questioned, but the answers had to come from Jesus. The awkward insertion of "There were many tax collectors and outcasts who were following Jesus" was necessary so that the word "follow" might appear once more in order to indicate that Jesus' association with the outcasts is parallel to his treatment of Levi.

These unhistorical details indicate that in telling this story the church was thinking of its own situation: The Pharisees are merely the personification of the legalism which might become a temptation for the church also. By placing these stories together in this section 2:1—3:6 (see 2:1-12), Mark presents the call of Levi as an act of forgiveness and a crossing of the boundary that separates the sinner from God. This establishes a general principle that has continuing validity. It also shows that the association of sinners with Jesus is a form of discipleship which is possible above and beyond this one instance. This explains why Mark did not place 2:14 after 1:16-20, but in section II B after 2:6 f., 10.

[13] Jesus teaches first in public, as he did in 1:14 ff. **[14]** It is obvious once again that as Jesus walks along he sees (and then chooses) a man who did not belong to the circle of those who heard his preaching. As in the previous passage, Jesus' authoritative word creates that discipleship which results as a matter of course. This passage, in that it is greatly abbreviated, becomes a more simple proclamation of Christ than 1:16-20. It does not concern itself at all with the psychology of the disciple. The event of the grace of God is accentuated most of all by the fact that the one who is called is living outside the walls of the church. Tax collectors were "outcasts" because they continually defiled themselves in dealings with Gentiles and because they were employed by unbelievers—the Romans or Herodians. Furthermore, the collecting of taxes was consigned to that chief tax collector who bid highest. As a result, he was almost forced to subject his employees, the tax collectors, to pressures which led to dishonorable practices. Consequently, the Jews despised these men as much as they despised the Gentiles. In Jesus' call to discipleship, therefore, men are reconciled and brought back to the church of God. **[15]** The story which has been appended shows that this is no exceptional case, but is valid as a general principle.

The fact that Jesus reclines (the literal translation of the Greek) at the table with the tax collectors clearly indicates that this is a banquet. That the outcasts fare very well in the company of Jesus and his disciples (consequently, in the church) shows that complete reconciliation includes the physical as well. In the awkward sentence that follows, Mark calls this table fellowship "following" Jesus. The Greek form in this verse indicates a continuous action, whereas the form in vs. 14 denotes an action which happens only once—an instantaneous visible "conversion." Mark makes no clear distinction between one who experiences a spectacular conversion and one who grows slowly into the fellowship of Jesus and his disciples. **[16]** The antagonism of the Pharisees (cf. 1:22) is incited by what Jesus does; not by any debatable dogmatic propositions. **[17]** The metaphor in Jesus' answer is no longer a mere comparison, because something like the healing of a fatal illness has happened in Jesus' association with the tax collectors. Jesus disregards all religious barriers, and the narrating church comprehends discipleship in such broad terms that it refuses to make a distinction between the converted and the inquirers. Jesus' claim is unprecedented—he calls the outcasts. When Luke adds that he calls them "to repent," he is not wrong, but he does not get to the heart of the matter. Mark intends to say that Jesus calls them to God—to the God who confronts them in Jesus. There is no denial of the fact that there are righteous persons, yet it is here that we see the particular temptation of the righteous. Theirs is the temptation to think they do not need God day by day. As a result, they may not even recognize God when he comes. The danger which threatens the righteous, though it is not the same as that which threatens the outcasts, may cut them off from the living God just as effectively.

Following, in part, the precedent of the church, Mark has combined the various components of 2:13-17. He has placed the passage in this particular context and has used a style of narration which accentuates the universal truth expressed in Jesus' action. By these various means Mark is proclaiming who Jesus is: The one who reconciles outcasts by his actions as well as his words. At the same time Mark is asking his readers whether they need this Jesus or think they are able to get along without him.

The Freedom from Religious Ritual 2:18-22;
cf. Matt. 9:14-17; Luke 5:33-39

18On one occasion the followers of John the Baptist and the
Pharisees were fasting. Some people came to Jesus and asked
him, "Why is it that the disciples of John the Baptist and the disciples of the Pharisees fast, but yours do not?" 19Jesus answered:
"Do you expect the guests at a wedding party to go without food?
Of course not! As long as the bridegroom is with them they will
not do that. 20But the time will come when the bridegroom will
be taken away from them; when that day comes then they will
go without food.

21"No one uses a piece of new cloth to patch up an old coat.
If he does, the new patch will tear off some of the old cloth, making an even bigger hole. 22Nor does anyone pour new wine into
used wineskins. If he does, the wine will burst the skins, and both
the wine and the skins will be ruined. No! Fresh skins for new
wine!"

Vss. 19a and 21 f. may be the words of Jesus. The introduction has been formulated by the church. This explains why the problem concerns the disciples' failure to fast and not Jesus' own failure to do so. This also explains the fact that those particular groups arrived on the scene who continually vexed the church with their practice of fasting; among them the Baptist's movement represented an especially formidable antagonist. The Pharisees had no disciples; this order simply had its adherents. It is likely that the reference to the Pharisees was added when this section was put into the larger collection of disputes with the Pharisees and the teachers of the law. Therefore, we cannot be sure who is really asking the question. Vs. 19a may be a part of the original story, since the difference between Jesus' teaching and the Baptist's movement was most noticeable in the matter of fasting. Vss. 21 f. may consist of proverbs which Jesus appropriated, or of metaphors formulated by him. It is not likely that they were uttered in connection with vs. 19, since the number of varied figures weakens the point of that verse. When rightly understood, vs. 21 contains a warning against the forsaking of the old. The Gospel of Thomas (47) speaks of old patches on a new garment. Of course, this is a later correction, since the opposite formulation is found there also in the case of the wine. Could these words at one time have been a warning in the same sense as Luke 14:31 f. and Mark 10:38? It is more likely that they have always formed a general warning against any compromise which would unite the old and the new, as, for example, the union of rejoicing over God's nearness and persisting in legalism. In any case, this is the way the words are to be understood in the present context. Vs. 20 may represent a misunderstanding by the church which in part reintroduced fasting after Jesus' death (Acts 13:2 f.; 14:23; added later by a copyist in Mark 9:29 and 1 Cor. 7:5). Perhaps the church added vs. 19b in order to emphasize the fact that Jesus' answer applied only during his lifetime on earth. On the other hand, it is possible that Mark added this phrase, since it is not found in several manuscripts nor in Matthew or Luke. For Jesus the picture of the bridegroom was still an appropriate parallel—as no one fasts during a wedding feast, so no one fasts during the special salvation-time—while the church immediately identified the "bridegroom" with Jesus. Vs. 20 can only be understood to be one of Jesus' sayings if it refers to exclusion from the banquet of the end-time, when Jesus would be snatched away from them in the judgment day. But who would get this idea from such a brief statement, especially since it is not Jesus, but the condemned, who will be snatched away? The remarkable phrase "when that day comes," which in the Greek seems to be an afterthought, likely promotes Friday as a fast-day. The same thing is done in Didache 8:1: "Let not your fasts be with the hypocrites, for they fast on Mondays and Thursdays, but do you fast on Wednesdays and Fridays." Surely Mark did not suppose that vss. 21 f. applied only during the time of Jesus' earthly life.

[18] This question is typical of those who wish to perform some meritorious religious acts. Fasting was required only on the Day of Atonement or in times of special need; yet some groups took it upon themselves voluntarily. **[19]** Jesus' justification of the conduct of his disciples is remarkable: Great joy makes any consideration of special religious performances impossible. This metaphor poses the question which is concealed and yet is clear to attentive hearers: Has the coming of Jesus brought such joy that God's giving simply overwhelms the man who wants to rely upon his own achievements? This metaphor is especially meaningful since a wedding was considered so important in Palestine that a rabbi would even interrupt his biblical instruction in order to join in the celebration. Therefore, what is required of Jesus' disciples is the kind of conduct which issues from joy over God's giving, and this may involve the neglect of everything else (2:14). They are not required to perform any special religious acts designed to bring a distant God near.

This truth is made even clearer by the fact that the wedding served the church as an illustration of the glory of the end-time. Without hesitation, they saw the "bridegroom" as an allegorical representation of Jesus, so that the wedding is not mentioned simply to compare his time with a feast. **[20]** The "as long as" in vs. 19b and the clear statement in vs. 20 reintroduce the possibility of fasting after the death of Jesus. This, however, contradicts the surrounding verses which see the presence of the exalted One, as well as the earthly life of Jesus, as marking the beginning of the special salvation-time. In no other way could these verses have any significance for Mark's readers. Nevertheless, the idea of fasting after Jesus' death contains a kernel of truth because neither Jesus nor the church has forgotten that salvation will be complete only when sin and death are abolished. One can view the earthly ministry of Jesus (as Luke is inclined to do) as an especially prominent sign of the future end-time—a sign which terminates with Jesus' death. It is possible to do this even if the church in hope views the presence of the exalted One, and the proclamation of what has happened and what is still future, in the light of the end-time.

If, therefore, the remaining verses accentuate the fullness of God's gift, namely, the end-time which has begun already and in which the church lives, then vs. 20 is reminiscent of the fact that Jesus' death reveals that sin and death, legalism and temptation, are still real powers although in principle they have been conquered. It also reveals that the church would be ill-advised if it became so fanatical as to suppose it were already freed from these powers. In this way even fasting can have a good sense as 1 Corinthians 9:25-27 shows: not as an act of merit, but as a help in the life of Jesus' disciples. However, this aspect is not expressed in this passage where fasting is presented simply as a custom of the church. **[21, 22]** The double metaphor at the end of this section warns against halfheartedness. We cannot use the new for repairing the old or pour the new into old forms. The things which have happened in Jesus free us from all patchwork. Thus the entire section asks whether we will understand Jesus' presence so radically that we can recognize in him God's eschatological intervention which frees us from any reliance on works because it grants us the fullness of joy.

The Freedom from Law 2:23-28;
cf. Matt. 12:1-8; Luke 6:1-5

[23]Jesus was walking through some wheat fields on a Sabbath day. As his disciples walked along with him, they began to pick the heads of wheat. [24]So the Pharisees said to Jesus, "Look, it is against our Law for your disciples to do this on the Sabbath!" [25]Jesus answered: "Have you never read what David did that time when he needed something to eat? He and his men were hungry, [26]so he went into the house of God and ate the bread offered to God. This happened when Abiathar was the High Priest. According to our Law only the priests may eat this bread—but David ate it, and even gave it to his men." [27]And Jesus said, "The Sabbath was made for the good of man; man was not made for the Sabbath. [28]So the Son of Man is Lord even of the Sabbath."

(Vs. 25 f.: Lev. 24:5 ff.)

It is difficult to determine the origin of this section. Controversies concerning the Sabbath are a part of Jesus' life. But this story appears to be fictitious. Where do these Pharisees come from, since one is permitted to go only about half a mile on the Sabbath? Are they farmers who think like Pharisees? Why do they reproach the disciples for picking the heads of wheat but not for walking on the Sabbath, which was a more serious transgression? Moreover, there is no definite statement as to when or where all of this happened. Accordingly, we must reckon with the fact that a saying of Jesus has been inserted later into an incident which lent itself to making the Pharisees appear to be the ones who most frequently entered into argument with Jesus. In that case the plucking of wheat would be censured either because it is more in keeping with vss. 25 f. than is the censuring of walking, or because this particular reproach exposes an especially narrow-minded legalism. To be sure, vss. 25 f. can hardly be attributed to Jesus. The Pharisees used such Scripture references in their disputes, but Jesus' customary method of arguing was entirely different. The main objection to attributing vss. 25 f. to Jesus is that they contain no reference to the fact that he has brought about a completely new state of affairs. On the other hand, the church may have disputed in this way if it allowed itself to be drawn into arguing on the level of its opponents and was not sufficiently mindful of the new conditions Jesus has created.

Vss. 27 f. begin with a new introduction, which shows that originally they were independent. Some have supposed that vs. 28 may have arisen from a misunderstanding of vs. 27, since "Son of Man" is simply the equivalent of "man" in Aramaic. This is not very likely because vs. 28 contains an entirely different saying. Furthermore, it is clear that the saying in vs. 27 was translated with "man," not "Son of Man." In this connection, consideration must be given to the fact that vs. 28 was the real point of the story in its original form. In spite of the fact that it contradicts his concept of the Messianic secret (see 1:34), it has been included here by Mark because it was part of the story as it was passed on in the tradition. Both sayings may originate with Jesus, who supported the statement in vs. 27 (which is so liberal that it is almost frightening) with the subdued reference to the completely new state of affairs which has begun in his person. Vs. 28 may have been introduced originally with "because." This may have been changed to "so" in translation from Aramaic, since vs. 28 was viewed as the conclusion of the whole section. Therefore, three stages in development may be conjectured: (1) The saying in vs. 27, which was authenticated by the new situation that was provided by Jesus, whether this was expressed (vs. 28) or not. (2) Vss. 25 f. served as an argument in the discussion between the church and Judaism; it emphasizes merely David's situation of need and not the particular situation of the disciples of the "Son of Man." (3) In the time when the truth of vs. 27 had become obvious, vss. 25 f. were understood as referring to that truth and both were put into the incident related in vss. 23 f.; consequently, vs. 27 became the justification of Jesus' behavior (vs. 23) and the final answer to vs. 24. In conclusion, Matthew and Luke omit vs. 27 because, in contrast to vs. 28, it makes no mention of Jesus' special authority.

[23] The Greek word for "walked along" means "make a way for oneself." In order to do this one would have to trample the grain down; however, the reproof in this Sabbath controversy is not directed against this activity. **[24]** According to Deuteronomy 23:25 it is permissible to pluck the heads of wheat, presumably even on the Sabbath. Nevertheless, the Pharisees of Jesus' day considered plucking to be part of harvesting, and harvesting on the Sabbath was prohibited. **[25]** The companions of David are included in vss. 25 and 26 because it was not the conduct of Jesus alone that was being contested, but the conduct of the whole church. **[26]** The statement "when Abiathar was the High Priest" is a slip of the memory, according to 1 Samuel 21:2-7 and 22:20 ff. In those times, a complete Old Testament was so expensive that in the second century a bishop traveled from Asia Minor to Palestine before he found one in a church. Consequently, one could not simply check the reference in a Bible. The argument is rather subtle, because breaking the Sabbath is not mentioned either here or in the Old Testament. The only thing which is made clear is that the law may be broken in a time of great need. This is something to which even the Pharisees would agree; however, this is not relevant here to Jesus' disciples or to the Christian church. Perhaps in this way the church was merely confronting its opponents with the fact that they, too, were inconsistent and made exceptions. It is only when these verses are considered in their present connection with vs. 27 that they may be understood in a more profound sense and that an illustration may be found in them: Even in the Old Testament the law was not given to man to be a burden, but to be an aid.

[27] Jesus' attitude, however, is more radical: To him the law is a gift to man, not only in exceptional cases, but as a general principle. It is a gift comparable to a stair railing, which hinders no one from ascending without its help but keeps those who need help from plunging off the stairway. Accordingly, Jesus does not advocate that pharisaical reverence for God's law which does not dare to question the why or the wherefore of any command. A child may ask his father the reason for or the purpose of his commands. According to Jubilees 2:18 ff. (a pre-Christian Jewish writing) the Sabbath was first kept in heaven; afterward God created Israel in order to have a people to celebrate the Sabbath. A rabbi of the second century A.D. could say at one time: "The Sabbath has been committed to you, and not you to the Sabbath." Jesus, however, did not mean this to be a general statement. **[28]** It is the presence of the Son of Man (see 8:31) which makes such freedom possible, because in him God's will for man has been realized, namely, God's full and complete giving. Therefore, as Lord of the Sabbath Jesus gives the Sabbath back to man to be a help; he does not lay it on man as a burden. In Mark's time, of course, this more profound explanation was not clearly understood. The commandment concerning the Sabbath had not been binding for a long time. The new situation was distinguished by the fact that Sunday was celebrated (1 Cor. 16:2; Acts 20:7; Rev. 1:10). For this reason vs. 27 has increasingly become a self-evident truth, and vs. 28 its logical conclusion (see above).

The Stubbornness of the Pharisees 3:1-6;
cf. Matt. 12:9-14; Luke 6:6-11

[1]Then Jesus went back to the synagogue, where there was a
man who had a crippled hand. [2]Some people were there who
wanted to accuse Jesus of doing wrong; so they watched him very
closely, to see whether he would cure anyone on the Sabbath.
[3]Jesus said to the man with the crippled hand, "Come up here to
the front." [4]Then he asked the people: "What does our Law allow
us to do on the Sabbath? To help, or to harm? To save a man's
life, or to destroy it?" But they did not say a thing. [5]Jesus was
angry as he looked around at them, but at the same time he felt
sorry for them, because they were so stubborn and wrong. Then
he said to the man, "Stretch out your hand." He stretched it out
and it became well again. [6]So the Pharisees left the meeting
house and met at once with some members of Herod's party; and
they made plans against Jesus to kill him.

It is surprising that the persons who are not identified in vs. 2 appear as Pharisees in vs. 6. But vs. 2 itself is strange: Would the Pharisees really have considered Jesus capable of healing? Could the original statement have been the people were watching "whether he would really cure him"? In any event, Mark inserted vs. 6 here in order to conclude the stories of conflict which began in 2:1; or perhaps in order to conclude the entire first main section which began in 1:14. The mention of the Herodians (also 12:13; cf. 8:15) with the Pharisees may have originated in the tradition. Perhaps the political groups linked with Herod co-operated with the Pharisees in the time of Jesus for political reasons, because they considered Jesus to be dangerous. On the other hand, this statement may be an anachronism which really applies to the years 41-44 when Pharisees worked closely with Herod Agrippa. Therefore, Mark wants to declare: The ministry of Jesus which began with a summarized description of his preaching (1:14 f.), the call of the first disciples (1:16-20), and the demonstration of his authority over sickness and demons (1:21-45) as well as over sin and the law (2:1—3:6) ended in the complete blindness of the religious authorities. The cross comes into view for the first time. We cannot be certain how much of the story in vss. 1-5 is truly historical. We read in Luke 14:1-3 also that the Pharisees watch Jesus closely and that he responds in a very similar way. The saying in vs. 4 is well suited to Jesus in its radical nature and certainly presupposes an incident of healing on the Sabbath. It is not certain whether Mark's report or that of Luke is the correct one, or whether Jesus gave a similar answer on two different occasions. In the Gospel of the Nazarenes, which was used by Jewish Christians, the story has developed so that the man says he is a mason who is dependent for his livelihood upon the use of his hand (cf. comment on 5:25).

[1] Once again no details are given concerning the time or the place. We are simply told that the scene is the synagogue (see 1:21), where men sat on the floor. **[2]** A cure is considered to be the work of a physician, which is permitted on the Sabbath only in cases of life or death. The situation was different in 1:23-31. Consequently, one can see in II A (1:14-45) how Mark assembles the stories which describe Jesus' authority and his influence upon all the people; in II B (2:1—3:6), however, he brings together the stories which indicate the growing opposition. **[3, 4]** Since Jesus' reply is so radical, it is clear once more that a question is at stake here which primarily concerns the law. It is a matter of either-or: Failure to do good is the same as doing evil; failure to save a life is the same as destroying it. When good ought to be done there is no neutral ground where one does neither good nor evil. There is no escape, nor is there any justification for a legalism which merely for the sake of orthodoxy fails to do the good and therefore produces evil. **[5]** This is why Jesus' anger is resolute in response to the "hardening of the hearts" (this is the literal meaning of the Greek), the indifference which is no longer moved by need and arms itself against any compassion with correct dogmatic or ethical theories. That legalism by which man seeks to absolve himself makes him completely blind to the living God, since God always encounters man in a way which would never be expected by one who thinks he has God all wrapped up in his theories. **[6]** Of course, even the opponents understood this one thing: Everything depends on Jesus, and one must make a choice between Jesus and the law (cf. 10:17-22).

Mark's Gospel has reached a crucial point: The authority of God over sickness and demons, sin and law, which has become a reality in Jesus, exposes man's total blindness to the gift of God. The cross on which Jesus' ministry and the salvation of the world are accomplished has already appeared on the horizon.

Jesus' Attitude Toward the Pharisees' Observance of the Sabbath. In the time of Jesus, rigorous observance of the Sabbath was the hallmark of the segment of Israel which thought like the Pharisees. This was not hypocrisy on their part. Fine points were disputed, of course, such as whether a man might carry a handkerchief with him on the Sabbath, since all burden-bearing was forbidden; or whether he should bind it around his arm, since in this way it would be a piece of clothing. But even this was simply an expression of his earnest attempt to be absolutely obedient. Above all, the Israelites were willing to be massacred defenselessly on the Sabbath rather than to transgress this Sabbath commandment or diminish God's honor by their efforts to defend themselves (1 Macc. 2:36-38). Undoubtedly, Jesus' frequent transgressing of the Sabbath commandment in his preaching and in his conduct is historical. He did so not because he thought that it was possible to serve God with less dedication. No, it is the exact opposite: So far as Jesus is concerned, any obedience which simply follows the letter of the law is less than full obedience, because one can at times fulfill the letter of the law without his heart being in it. One may even fulfill the letter of the law while he would really like to do the opposite, so that his only concern is how far the law will permit him to go. This is how we treat traffic regulations. When, for example, the law forbids speeds of over 60 miles an hour, we may really wish to drive faster. Consequently, when we abide by the law we do so in such a way that we use our liberty to the maximum—the full 60 miles an hour. Jesus knows, however, that the commandment "Thou shalt not kill" is fulfilled only as our hearts are freed from everything which shows the slightest tendency in that direction—even from anger (Matt. 5:21 f.). In the second place, legalistic obedience leads to the keeping of accounts, because one depends upon his own merit in addition to the gift of God. This, too, runs parallel to the way we keep traffic regulations to avoid paying a fine. Certainly, an earnest Pharisee would agree that God's gift is the primary consideration and our obedience is merely a response to it. He could even say that the former is infinitely greater than the latter. Nevertheless, he is still inclined to keep an account of God's gifts as well as his own accomplishment. Moreover, Jesus knows that the obedience which has given up all keeping of accounts is the only genuine obedience (Matt. 20:1-16; cf. Mark 14: 6 f.). Therefore, he does not add anything to God's requirement, but in that freedom which shocked his contemporaries he follows a different principle. Man must receive everything from God as a gift without any consideration of merit, and must open his heart to the experience of joy. An open heart such as this will serve God for joy alone, like a child who no longer has an eye for rewards or fears spanking, but lives just to please his parents. God's law will help him in this—not as a fence restricting him, but as a guide pointing the direction. Such obedience may cost a great deal—to keep the Sabbath unencumbered for sheer delight in God can cost far more than mere abstinence from every kind of work. One cannot possibly rejoice in God so long as he is angry with his brother; thus delight is far more demanding than the mere satisfaction of the requirement to not kill. The obedience of those of whose works God does not keep any account demands the power of a love which goes far beyond the keeping of the law. Nevertheless, it always remains an obedience in freedom—an obedience which comes from the heart. It is to this kind of obedience that Jesus calls men by his word and by his conduct.

III

JESUS' MINISTRY IN PARABLES AND SIGNS AND THE BLINDNESS OF THE WORLD 3:7—6:6a

Jesus' Ministry to the Whole World 3:7-12;
cf. Matt. 12:15-21; Luke 6:17-19

[7]Jesus and his disciples went away to Lake Galilee, and a large crowd followed him. They came from Galilee, from Judea,
[8]from Jerusalem, from the territory of Idumea, from the territory on the other side of the Jordan, and from the neighborhood of the cities of Tyre and Sidon. This large crowd came to Jesus because they heard of the things he was doing. [9]The crowd was so large that Jesus told his disciples to get a boat ready for him, so the people would not crush him. [10]He had healed many people, and all the sick kept pushing their way to him in order to touch him.
[11]And whenever the people who had evil spirits in them saw him they would fall down before him and scream, "You are the Son of God!" [12]Jesus gave a stern command to the evil spirits not to tell who he was.

The third part of Mark's Gospel begins like the first with a summarized description of Jesus' ministry, followed by the appointment of the twelve. It ends with the rejection of Jesus (6:1-6). As in 1:14 f. we discover here the formative hand of Mark in the more important features. Of course, he made use of traditional material, as is evident in vs. 9. It would be impossible for Jesus to drive out the demons while sitting out in the boat. The very next story takes place on the mountain; then the boat reappears in 4:1 and 36. 4:1 is the only passage where the mention of the boat is really appropriate. This is evidence that Mark is relying on a tradition which contained at least the teaching in parables from the boat (4:1-9) and the concluding sign of the stilling of the storm (4:35-41). It is possible that vss. 9 f. are from the tradition, so that the "kept pushing" would have been resumed by Mark with the words "fall down" in vs. 11.* In this case the events in vs. 10 would have happened before Jesus entered the boat, and then he taught from the boat afterward (4:1 ff.). Perhaps the expression "large crowd" in vs. 7 as well as all of vs. 7a belonged to the original introduction, so that Mark takes up the very same expression when he adds vss. 7b and 8. However that may be, Mark wants to re-emphasize the Messianic secret before he continues his narration (3:11 f.). After this he wants to present the choice of the twelve, for whom the parables of Jesus are specially explained (3:13-19; cf. 4:10), and then point out why it is necessary as a general principle to speak in parables. For this reason he abandons the theme of the boat and does not take it up again until 4:1. The very fact that Mark has tolerated so many unhistorical details shows that he has a special interest in the section which has been inserted between them. Accordingly, this is where we need to be particularly attentive.

[7, 8] This long list of geographical areas is a somewhat awkward addition to the narrative which may have been intended to emphasize the special position of Galilee. All these people have gathered around the Savior of the world by the Sea of Galilee. This enumeration is meant to portray the impact of Jesus as worldwide. At the same time, emphasis is placed on the fact that he "went away," which shows that he had no desire to cause this influx of people. To some extent, the locations named form an outline of the Gospel of Mark, since Jesus is active in Galilee (chs. 1-6); Tyre, Sidon, and Decapolis (ch. 7); and finally beyond the Jordan and in Jerusalem (chs. 10 ff.). **[9]** The very fact that the boat was standing in readiness illustrates Jesus' dynamic power which sets everything in motion. **[10]** In addition to this, the power of God is mediated by the physical proximity of Jesus—

* These two expressions are based upon the same root in both Greek and German.

yes, by his very touch, as in 1:41 (see comment on 1:41 f.). **[11]** The recognition of Jesus' true nature by supernatural powers shows that "heaven" has come to earth. In contrast to 1:24, Mark uses the more distinct title "Son of God" (see 15:39), since he is working independently here. **[12]** He makes it very clear, however, that the time has not come for this title to be proclaimed publicly (see comment on 1:34).

By this means the text proclaims that in Jesus we are confronted by God who transforms everything, and that we will not be helped in any way if all we do is simply adopt this doctrine of the divine sonship of Jesus.

The Calling of the Twelve 3:13-19;
cf. Matt. 10:1-4; Luke 6:12-16

[13]Then Jesus went up a hill and called to himself the men he
wanted. They came to him [14]and he chose twelve, whom he
named apostles. "I have chosen you to stay with me," he told them;
"I will also send you out to preach, [15]and you will have authority
to drive out demons." [16]These are the twelve he chose: Simon
(Jesus gave him the name Peter); [17]James and his brother John,
the sons of Zebedee (Jesus gave them the name Boanerges, which
means "Men of Thunder"); [18]Andrew, Philip, Bartholomew, Matthew, Thomas, James the son of Alphaeus, Thaddaeus, Simon the
patriot, [19]and Judas Iscariot, who became the traitor.

This list of the twelve disciples was received by Mark from the tradition. The names are given in a different sequence in Matthew 10:2-4; Luke 6:14-16; and Acts 1:13. Nevertheless, they are the same except Thaddaeus, in whose place Judas the son of James is found in Luke 6:16 and Acts 1:13. Thaddaeus is called Lebbaeus in Matthew 10:3 and Mark 3:18 in many manuscripts. Nathaniel appears in John 1:40 ff., together with Andrew, Simon, and Philip (in 21:2 also). Thomas appears in John's Gospel in 11:16; 14:5; 20:24 ff.; and 21:2; Judas Iscariot in 6:71; 12:4; and 13:2, 26, and another Judas in 14:22. John is included in John 21:2 and apparently should be equated with the "disciple whom Jesus loved." A completely different list of disciples from the second century is found in the Epistle of the Apostles, and additional names of disciples of Jesus appear in Jewish sources (Aboda Zara 16b, 17a; Sanhedrin 43a). With reference to the historicity of the band of the twelve, see the excursus on 6:7-13. Each of the Gospel writers includes the calling of the twelve at a different place within his composition. Mark includes it at this point, against the background of the blindness of the world which hailed Jesus and then so quickly rejected him. This emphasizes the fact that even a beginning of understanding can be produced only by Jesus' sovereign choice and by his acts of loving concern on behalf of his chosen ones (cf. 3:7-12).

[13] No particular mountain is specified. A mountain is a place of retreat where God's revelation is most likely to occur (cf. Exod. 19:20; 1 Kings 19:8; Mark 6:46; 9:2). **[14]** The sovereign authority of Jesus is accentuated by the insertion of "he wanted" and the expression "he chose." The latter is somewhat strange in Greek: literally, "he made." This expression is used in a similar way in the Old Testament (1 Kings 12:31; 2 Chron. 2:17). It is surprising that the real goal is their "staying with Jesus." This expresses very clearly the significance of discipleship. On the other hand, their being sent out has been added as if it were not as important. This addition has made the structure so difficult grammatically that it is necessary to repeat the beginning of vs. 14 in vs. 16 (see 6:7-13). Accordingly, the choosing of the twelve seems to indicate Jesus' desire to establish the new people of God—the Israel of the end-time. This makes it clear that Jesus does not intend to form a select group such as the Pharisees or the people of Qumran; he is calling all Israel. When Mark inserts the sending out he is underscoring, from his historical perspective, what Jesus expressed by his choice: The new Israel is not fulfilled simply in the band of disciples as if a little band of Christians were all that was required. These men are merely the messengers who call everyone to come. **[15]** The authority of their preaching is exemplified by their authority over demons, as Jesus' authority is in 1:21 ff. **[16]** The conferring of new names by Jesus manifests his sovereign ability to create something new. Peter is called "rock," a name which does not suit his character but designates him as the first one whom God had chosen (see Matt. 16:18 f.; 1 Cor. 15:5), and the one upon whose apostolic preaching the church is built. **[17]** The correct interpretation of the name "Men of Thunder" is no longer known; it could hardly refer to their character (Luke 9:51 ff.; Mark 9:38 f.; 10:35 ff.). Perhaps it refers to the manner of their preaching, which may have reminded one of the thunder of the apocalyptic wrath of God. **[18]** "Canaanite" (the Greek word translated here "patriot") is more properly rendered "Zealot" in Luke (Greek). This name indicates that Simon was one of the revolutionaries who wanted to win Israel's independence from Rome through armed rebellion. Among those who are Jesus' disciples there is one who wants to fight against Rome, and at the same time another who is an official of the Roman tax administration, or of the Herodian tax administration in league with Rome. **[19]** "Iscariot" probably means "man from Kerioth"; or it might be a garbling of the Latin *sicarius* which means "assassin" or "Zealot." Jesus' band of disciples, therefore, is anything but a "pure church."

The Blindness of Man and the Parables of Jesus 3:20-35;
cf. Matt. 12:22-32, 46-50; Luke 11:14-23; 12:10; 8:19-21

20Then Jesus went home. Again such a large crowd gathered
that Jesus and his disciples had no time to eat. 21When his family
heard about this they set out to get him, because people were saying, "He's gone mad!"

22Some teachers of the Law who had come from Jerusalem
were saying, "He has Beelzebul in him!" Others said, "It is the
chief of the demons who gives him the power to drive them out."
23So Jesus called the people to him and told them some parables:
"How can Satan drive out Satan? 24If a country divides itself into
groups that fight each other, that country will fall apart. 25If a family divides itself into groups that fight each other, that family will
fall apart. 26So if Satan's kingdom divides into groups, it cannot
last, but will fall apart and come to an end.

27“No one can break into a strong man's house and take
away his belongings unless he ties up the strong man first; then he
can plunder his house.

28“Remember this! Men can be forgiven all their sins and all
the evil things they say, no matter how often they say them. 29But
the person who says evil things against the Holy Spirit can never
be forgiven, for he has committed an eternal sin.” 30(Jesus said
this because some had said, “He has an evil spirit in him.”)

31Then Jesus' mother and brothers arrived. They stood outside the house and sent in a message, asking for him. 32A crowd
was sitting around Jesus, and they told him, “Look, your mother
and brothers are outside, and they want you.” 33Jesus answered,
“Who is my mother? Who are my brothers?” 34He looked over the
people sitting around him and said, “Look! Here are my mother
and my brothers! 35For the person who does what God wants him
to do is my brother, my sister, my mother.”

There is scarcely any other passage where Mark's pen is as evident as it is here. The reference to the “family of God” in vss. 31-35 is in response to the blindness of Jesus' relatives in vss. 20 f. The reference to the unpardonable sin in vss. 28 f. (cf. vs. 30) is in response to the blindness of the teachers of the law in vs. 22. Jesus' first parable intervenes between them, enclosed within a double framework (with reference to this technique of framing see the introduction to 5:21-43). The fact that Mark is deliberately forming this structure is shown by the simpler form of the story which is still retained in Luke 11:14 ff. (Q). Mark doesn't mention the incident which provoked the censure by the teachers of the law (Luke 11:14); consequently, the reproof in Mark 3:22 comes immediately after the rebuke in vs. 21. Furthermore, he has reworded it (cf. Luke 11:15) in such a way that it now runs parallel to the statement of the relatives: both say that Jesus is insane. The relatives exercise a little more reserve; the teachers of the law from Jerusalem, who are the highest authorities in Israel and have been introduced into the story by Mark, speak somewhat more theologically and more maliciously. That vs. 23a has been added to the ancient account by Mark is very clear, because it is not a part of the story in either Matthew or Luke, and because the inappropriate introduction shows typical Markan style: "Jesus called the people to him." Mark is the one who considers it important to relate that Jesus began to speak in parables as a response to the blindness of man (the Greek verb expresses an action of long duration). Consequently, we must pay careful attention to this (see 4:33 f.). Perhaps the original story in Luke 11:19 f., which speaks of Beelzebul and not of Satan as does Mark 3:23-26 (Luke 11:17 f.), formed the reply to the charge of the opponents; other words on the same theme were added later. Vs. 27 may be a separate traditional saying of Jesus which was linked to the catchword "house" (translated "family" in vs. 25) because it has some relevance to the point in question. The difficult saying in vss. 28 f. has a different form in Matthew 12:32 (Luke 12:10 [Q]; cf. Gospel of Thomas 44), where "the Son of Man" apparently designates the earthly Jesus (see Mark 8:31). What this passage is saying, then, is that things that were pardonable before Easter cannot be forgiven in a time when the witness of the Holy Spirit is predominant. Perhaps the far more general form in Mark 3:28 arose later when men saw the Son of Man as the exalted One and would therefore no longer pardon any blasphemy against him. It is possible that this saying arose after Pentecost, since there is very little mention of the Holy Spirit in the other sayings of Jesus. Finally, vs. 35 is actually a further qualification of vs. 34, so it is logical for Luke to omit the first statement (the same is true in Gospel of Thomas 99; 2 Clement 9:11), while the Gospel of the Ebionites goes so far as to restrict the reference to the disciples. One may wonder whether originally Jesus made only the first statement, since it emphasizes in a surprising way Jesus' openness to all men. The church, then, by adding the second statement accentuated its own response to the first one.

[20] The extraordinary influence of Jesus is contrasted with the blindness of his own family ("friends" is another possible translation). **[21]** With reference to the word "home," see comment on 2:1. Jesus' brother James had been referred to already in Galatians 2:12 f. and Acts 21:18-24. The church fathers supplied the information that he kept the requirements of the law rigidly, and on this basis one may assume that Jesus' family either belonged to the order of the Pharisees or was connected with it. Naturally, the statement of the people refers to Jesus, and not to the large crowd as the Apologists have suggested. Even the acts of God may be accounted for by attributing everything to some well-known spiritual phenomenon. **[22]** The authorities from Jerusalem, who represent the real core of the hostility toward Jesus, give an interpretation which is far more harsh. The fact that they have come from such a distance indicates how widespread Jesus' influence has been. "Beelzebul" was originally the name of an ancient Syrian god, and apparently means "Lord of the house (the Temple?)," cf. Matthew 10:25. The form "Beelzebub," which means "Lord of the flies," first occurs in 2 Kings 1:2 where, presumably, it was deliberately corrupted by the Israelites as an expression of contempt. The name of this heathen god gradually became a designation for the devil.

[23] Jesus began to teach in parables in view of the blindness of his family and the blindness of the teachers of the law. It is significant to Mark that his discourse is entirely in the form of parables (4:11, 34). Up to this point there has been no mention whatever of the content of Jesus' preaching, with the exception of the brief statement in 1:14 f. This indicates that Mark places more importance on the nature of his preaching than on its content. Why is this? When someone tells us, "Dinner is at seven o'clock," this is a direct statement which can be understood by everyone. It can even be translated by machine. As soon as figurative language is used, as, for example, in the language of love, a certain relationship between speaker and hearer is required in order for it to be understood. It is similar to the way married couples use certain metaphors which are not understood by anyone other than the two who are related to one another in a common experience. Therefore, figurative language has a force more binding than that of direct speech, since it requires that the hearer be ready to enter into a special relationship with the speaker. According to Mark, Jesus must speak about God in a way that reaches hearers who will permit themselves to become involved, and who learn to know the reality which is paraphrased in his metaphors by association with Jesus and through discipleship. Consequently, his speech remains incomprehensible to the "average man" and becomes intelligible only to the one who is willing to enter this relationship. (Cf. 4:1.)

[24-26] In terms of pure logic this parable is not thoroughly convincing. It is taken for granted in the Old Testament (Exod. 7:11; 8:7), as it is in the New (2 Thess. 2:9; Rev. 13:13), that even those powers which are opposed to God are able to work miracles. Here, however, Satan would be fighting against those very demons who have gone out from him. **[27]** Accordingly, the parable is designed to raise the question of whether Jesus has come as the "stronger one" (cf. 1:7), of whom many had spoken (Isa. 49:24 f.; cf. Pss. of Sol. 5:4; Isa. 53:12 LXX). Luke 11:19 f. leads us one important step further, but even in that place the final answer is left open, because the reader is the only one who can give that answer. The very fact that this parable is a summons to faith demonstrates that it is a genuine saying of Jesus. Therefore, this is the meaning of the mighty acts of Jesus: Man should take courage to live in the presence of the almighty God and under his promise, because God's presence has already become a reality in the acts of Jesus and has been granted to those who follow him. When one understands the parable in this way, then, as in all true parables of Jesus, one must abstain from any such interpretation of details as saying that the "tying up" is described in 1:21 f. and the "plundering" in the exorcising of demons. A form of this parable which shows further development is found in the Gospel of Thomas (98): "The Kingdom of the Father is like a man who wishes to kill a powerful man. He drew the sword in his house, he stuck it into the wall, in order to know whether his hand would carry through; then he slew the powerful (man)" (an abbreviated version of Mark 3:32-35 follows). **[28]** In vs. 28 we must first of all see and take seriously the unbelievable breadth of the grace of God from which nothing is excluded. **[29]** What then is the meaning of vs. 29? According to vs. 30 this saying is directed against men who have been fully convinced by Jesus' mighty miracles that supernatural powers are at work, yet who do not leave the question open as to the kind of powers these are but declare unequivocally that they are diabolical and in so doing absolve themselves from the necessity of believing. These persons, therefore, are not skeptics or inquirers; the latter are blessed (4:41) in contrast to those who know all the answers (cf. 8:29). The church which formed this saying (see above) is thinking of men whose doubt has been conquered by the power of the Spirit of God, but who through their blasphemy still misrepresent faith in God as faith in the devil. This saying is an extremely serious warning against that most demonic and scarcely conceivable potential in man: To declare war on God. This is not done in weakness and doubt, but by one who has been overcome by the Holy Spirit and who knows very well on whom he is declaring war. For that very reason, those whose consciences are troubled for fear that they may have committed this sin are not the ones to whom this saying applies. It is meant for that antichrist who is hard as steel, who does not desire God's grace, and who makes himself God. Nor is it possible to say that this word of judgment is meant for some other person without making ourselves God. Jesus himself, according to Mark, does not even assert that the teachers of the law had committed this sin; but he warns them because they have accused him.

[31, 32] Joseph is not mentioned anywhere except in the stories of Jesus' childhood (except for being mentioned as the father of Jesus, Luke 4:22; John 1:45; 6:42). Did he die early? Brothers and sisters of Jesus are mentioned in 6:3 also (see comment). **[33]** Jesus' question caused great difficulty for the ancient church, but all that it says is that any blood relationship is of little consequence when compared to the real relationship with Jesus which grows out of seeing his deeds and hearing his words (as in 10:28-30). Perhaps in back of this passage there is a polemic against a kind of caliphate. Eusebius states that other relatives of Jesus held places of leadership in the Palestinian church after James, the brother of the Lord. **[34]** As is true of 2:15-17, this passage shows to an unprecedented degree that grace is bestowed on those who are simply in the presence of Jesus—where Jesus is, there is salvation. Blessed is the one who sees and hears him

(Matt. 13:16 f.; Luke 10:23 f.; 11:27 f.). **[35]** The last statement nearly cancels the startling comprehensiveness of the previous saying. It is meant as a summons to the readers to live as persons who in Jesus have been in the presence of God. Surely something never before dreamed of is promised to such a life: brotherhood with Jesus himself. Thus, to belong to God is the greatest of promises. The fact that 14:36 is the only other passage which speaks of God's will most likely indicates how Mark visualizes disciples—men who are open to God's will.

The Parable of the Troubled Farmer 4:1-9;
cf. Matt. 13:1-9; Luke 8:4-8

1Again Jesus began to teach by Lake Galilee. The crowd that
gathered around him was so large that he got into a boat and sat
in it. The boat was out in the water, while the crowd stood on the
shore, at the water's edge. 2He used parables to teach them many
things, and in his teaching said to them: 3"Listen! There was a
man who went out to sow. 4As he scattered the seed in the field,
some of it fell along the path, and the birds came and ate it up.
5Some of it fell on rocky ground, where there was little soil. The
seeds soon sprouted, because the soil wasn't deep. 6Then when
the sun came up it burned the young plants, and because the roots
had not grown deep enough the plants soon dried up. 7Some of
the seed fell among thorns, which grew up and choked the plants,
and they didn't bear grain. 8But some seeds fell in good soil, and
the plants sprouted, grew, and bore grain: some had thirty grains,
others sixty, and others one hundred." 9And Jesus said, "Listen,
then, if you have ears to hear with!"

The Parables. In academic circles a distinction is made between a parable and an allegory. A parable shows by a well-known, everyday occurrence what is the nature of something not generally known but comparable. In a given parable only one point of comparison is being made and every detail must support this point. Therefore, a parable follows a formula, such as: *a* is related to *b* as *A* is to *B*; for example, the sowing is related to the harvest as

Jesus' preaching is to the future Kingdom of God. A parable is designed to make something so clear that it will be obvious to everyone. An allegory, on the contrary, is a story which frequently contains very strange features, every one of which must be interpreted. The formula is like this: $a = A, b = B, c = C;$ for example, in vs. 15 the beaten path = the hardened heart, the birds = Satan, the eating = the destroying of the effectiveness of the Word. An allegory camouflages and frequently deliberately conceals so that only an initiated person can recognize what is meant (e.g., in times of great political stress; cf. Rev. 17:5-13). Jesus' parables, obviously, belong to the first type. The church was the first to see them as allegories and to interpret them as such. This was partly due to the fact that the parables were handed down without any description of the original situation or conversation in which they were given, and consequently had become incomprehensible. This much has been established, and research can go no further back. However, it is clear that this distinction is too simple. Jesus' parables are not mere pedagogical aids; he uses this method because there is no other appropriate way to speak about the Kingdom of God (see 3:23). Because the Kingdom of God is so mysterious that it can only be proclaimed in figures of speech to one who is willing to listen, the subject often strains the metaphor (cf. the strange dealings of the owner in Matthew 20:8-15, and the abundant joy in Luke 15:9, 20-24). Accordingly, the unsuccessful sowing is described in vss. 4-7 with surprising detail, and the later success in vs. 8 is exaggerated, if not absolutely impossible. In this description of an everyday occurrence Jesus is pointing to the miracle of God's action. It must be clearly stated that in the parables Jesus is following a train of thought which he wants his hearer to share. For this reason, he accommodates himself to his hearer's way of thinking in order to lead him step by step until that hearer arrives at a frame of mind in which he allows God's action to become vital to him, and in which he is given the ability to make the right decision (cf. 3:23).

Vss. 1 f. are Mark's introduction, even though the detail about Jesus' sitting in the boat comes from the tradition (see 3:9 and

4:35-41). In his characteristic manner Mark introduces a parable as the first example of Jesus' authoritative teaching (see 3:23). Probably in vss. 3-9 we have the ancient parable of Jesus which we must, first of all, interpret by itself.

[1] Here again Mark describes Jesus' teaching in a way intended to help the hearer perceive that he taught in the power of God (see 1:22). **[2]** What follows is simply an example of his teaching (according to Mark, vss. 21 ff. were spoken on a different occasion). **[3]** The command to listen (Gen. 23:6, 13; Deut. 6:4, et al.) is a summons to awaken to a manner of listening which leads to involvement and decision. Superficial listening which gives its attention to any illuminating instruction is not desirable. Sowing had been used as a metaphor by many individuals since the time of Plato. Accordingly, its use here is not original, but the very detailed description of the unsuccessful sowing is. **[4-7]** In Palestine a field is plowed after it is sown. One sows along the beaten path (Gospel of Thomas 9 and the church father Justin describe it more precisely as "upon the path") and "among the thorns," since both will be plowed up afterward. This explanation also accounts for the fact that those areas which are covered with only a little topsoil are not detected. **[8]** Nevertheless, the description of this farmer's misfortune seems rather lengthy compared with the brief statement telling of the seed which fell in good soil; moreover, it gives no indication whatever that the amount of seed which fell into good soil was greater than that which fell elsewhere. The yield, to be sure, is superabundant (the Gospel of Thomas has as much as 60 and 120 fold). Here the interpretation becomes part of the metaphor, not only because a yield of one hundred fold is very rare, but particularly because the Greek verb indicates a continuous productivity which is repeated over and over. **[9]** Finally, as was true of the beginning, the concluding verse summons men to listen with genuine involvement. In this verse, however, the fact that the achievement of proper hearing is a gift is emphasized by the phrase "if you have ears to hear with!"

Our task, then, is to listen to this account of an everyday experience in such a way that we may see in it what Jesus sees. This we can do most easily in the conclusion of the parable. The harvest is wonderfully glorious; God achieves his objective: his Kingdom, which is blessing and fullness. The Jewish apocalyptists, who waited for the final glorious age, might speak in this way also, and so might the Pharisees, who expected eternal reward as the result of God's judgment. The harvest is portrayed as being unusually glorious—but the work of sowing is described as unusually difficult, and the opposition against achieving that reward as unusually pronounced. The apocalyptist might speak of opposition also, but he eagerly awaits the annihilation of all his enemies. The Pharisee might speak in the same way, but he would emphasize the protection and final reward of the godly. In this passage, however, there is no mention of the annihilation of the evil birds and thorns; nor is there any indication that the soil or the seed fought against them. Birds, thorns, and rocks are treated more objectively and naturally. This, according to Jesus, is precisely the way God works: The field that has been sown, but appears to be no more than stones, thistles, and rocks, will some day produce a glorious "harvest." Jesus' message is strange: The Kingdom of God is here already, and opposition has broken out against it everywhere (see Matt. 11:12). The one who has ears to hear, however, can so listen to Jesus that he actually sees God at work in the outbreak of opposition. Therefore, he will not confront the cross and resurrection of Jesus without understanding. Jesus' parable makes it obvious that this is the situation with God and his Kingdom.

The Nature of the Parables 4:10-12;
cf. Matt. 13:10-15; Luke 8:9 f.

[10]When Jesus was alone, some of those who had heard him came to him with the twelve disciples and asked him to explain the parables. [11]"You have been given the secret of the Kingdom of God," Jesus answered; "but the others, who are on the outside, hear all things by means of parables, [12]so that,

'They may look and look, yet not see,

They may listen and listen, yet not understand,
For if they did, they might turn to God
And he would forgive them.' "

(Vs. 12: Isa. 6:9 f.)

[10] Many things about these two statements are surprising. The continuity from vs. 1 through vs. 35 is broken. The mention of the "twelve disciples" is appended in a strange way. The question is asked concerning "the parables" although only one parable has been mentioned. **[11, 12]** But the strangest thing is the assertion that the parables are riddles designed to keep men from seeing. 4:35 shows that it was still remembered at the earliest stages of the narration that Jesus had not yet left the boat from which he told the parable of the Sower. This indicates that the discussion with the disciples in vss. 10-12 and the explanation of the parable in vss. 13-20 are later additions. The unusual wording of vs. 10 makes it likely that the explanation of the parable was the only part which was added in the second stage. Perhaps it was introduced with a transitional statement such as, "And when he had withdrawn, those who were with him asked him about the parable." In a third stage the twelve disciples were added, and the question concerning the explanation of this one parable was revised to make it a basic question about parables in general. The answer to this question was then given in vss. 11 f. by means of an Old Testament quotation. The discussion of vss. 13-20 will show that even the second stage did not originate with Jesus, but with the church. It is not clear whether or not the third stage should be attributed to Mark. This saying certainly originated in the Aramaic-speaking church, because the Hebrew or Aramaic word for "parable" is synonymous with "riddle" (Ezek. 17:2; Hab. 2:6; Pss. 49:4; 78:2; Prov. 1:6; et al.), and it is only when a parable is viewed in this way that it forms a contrast to the revelation of the secrets to the disciples. In Palestine the Gentiles or unbelievers were called those "who are on the outside." Since Aramaic has no word for "to be" and no adverbs, one must say, "everything comes to them by means of riddles," instead of "everything is enigmatical to them." Finally, the details of vs. 12 correspond better with the Aramaic version of Isaiah 6:9 f., which was probably used in the worship services of the synagogue, than it does with either the Hebrew or the Greek text. Moreover, the words "in order that" and "lest" would have had a different meaning in Aramaic. Acts 28:25 ff. (cf. John 12:40) shows that on other occasions this same passage was used by the church to explain Israel's unbelief. Apparently the Aramaic form read as follows: ". . . to the unbelieving, however, everything is a riddle; to those who look and look and yet do not see, who listen and listen and yet do not understand, unless they repent and be forgiven." The saying has become much more harsh in the process of translation into Greek. The church wanted to make it very emphatic that all knowledge of God is pure gift—a divine miracle. The fact that the revelation was not given to the whole world, but only to the church which is able to understand and interpret the parables of Jesus, must be viewed by the church as the will of God. Therefore, it is actually God's will for these parables to create a division: To some they give complete understanding of God's secrets, but to others they seal these mysteries.

Is Mark the one who translated the quotation or, at least, the one who inserted it in this place? The concept "mystery," which played a large role among Jewish apocalyptists, in Qumran, and with Paul and his pupils (1 Cor. 2:7; 4:1; Rom. 16:25; Col. 1:26 f.; 2:2; Eph. 3:3 f., 9; 6:19; 1 Tim. 3:16), is not found anywhere else in Mark. He sees an entirely different significance in the parables. The concept which is predominant in all these passages is that of a small band to whom insight is given into God's plan, in contrast to the rest of the world. This point of view was typical of the church, which regarded the explanations of the parables as the key to their mystery, but it was not typical of Mark, who held that the parables of Jesus were meant for everyone. This fact is made clear by the scene in 4:1, which Mark has developed in conformity with certain other passages (2:13; 6:34). It is made clear by 3:23 where everyone is called, and by the summons to listen in 4:3 and 9; but it is made most clear in vss. 21-25 and 33. How then is it possible for Mark to appropriate the harsh saying in vss. 11 f.? He knows that the ability to hear is always a gift (cf. vs.

9). This is demonstrated by Jesus' special efforts on behalf of the disciples (4:13, 34). Consequently, if one really hears, it is a divine miracle. But Mark is the first one to carry this thought to a radical conclusion.

The criticism of the stubborn Pharisees in 3:5 and of "those who are on the outside" is applied to the disciples in 8:17. But Jesus has said this already in 4:13b: Even the disciples do not understand the parables; they, too, are blind and deaf to God's mystery. Therefore it is not enough to simply append an explanation to the parable which solves the riddle in such a way that it ceases to be a divine mystery. Just as he explains the parables to the disciples in 4:13-20 and 4:34, Jesus must continue to explain them again and again all the way to the cross and the resurrection, and afterward the exalted One must explain them to his church. This means that everyone stands under the judgment of vss. 11b, 12, and the miracle of vs. 11a is promised to every reader. The disciples, according to 8:17-21, have eyes and yet do not see; they have ears and yet do not hear. Therefore, they are not able to turn about in order to receive forgiveness; nevertheless, their hearts will be opened at Easter. In all of this they are merely an example of all those with whom Jesus has a special desire to speak. And so it is that what is impossible for man becomes possible for God (10:27). In his loving concern for the disciples Jesus represents God who is seeking all mankind. For this reason his parable must continue to be a riddle for all men, in order that no one will glory in his own knowledge and everyone will live by the miracle of God's grace alone (Jer. 9:23; 1 Cor. 1:18 f., 31; et al.).

But what relevance does this have for us? The church reflected on the fact that Jesus spoke in parables and in this way it gained insight by various stages, each of which emphasizes part of the truth. Mark is the one to whom we want to listen most carefully; however, it is possible that one of the earlier stages of insight will become especially important in a specific situation. We can discern four stages in the text: (1) Jesus speaks in parables because metaphorical language which compels men to become involved is the only language that can be used to describe the ways of God. (2) The church recognizes this fact and tries to respond appropriately when it declares the meaning which these metaphors have in the church's own particular situation (see 4:13-20). (3) The church is able to understand the parables and does not belong to "those who are on the outside" for whom the metaphors continue to be nothing more than nonsense. In vss. 11 f. the church is confessing that it recognizes this ability to be pure gift—a miracle which has happened in accordance with the will of God. (4) Mark interprets this statement—and by means of it Jesus' purpose for speaking in parables—in a radical fashion: The special instruction and the explanation of the parables do not even help the disciples. Thus the parables of Jesus reveal man's total blindness to the ways of God, and this includes the community of disciples. If, in spite of this, the community of disciples is promised "You have been given the secret of the Kingdom of God," then it is a far greater miracle than could possibly be described in vss. 11 f. Even if this miracle has been alluded to already in vs. 8 by the harvest which is superabundant in spite of all the failure described in vss. 4-7, it is not until 8:31, 34 that we are told how such a thing can come about.

The Explanation of the Four Kinds of Fields 4:13-20;
cf. Matt. 13:18-23; Luke 8:11-15

13Then Jesus asked them: "Don't you understand this parable?
How, then, will you ever understand any parable? 14The sower
sows God's message. 15Sometimes the message falls along the
path; these people hear it, but as soon as they hear it Satan comes
and takes away the message sown in them. 16Other people are
like the seeds that fall on rocky ground. As soon as they hear the
message they receive it gladly. 17But it does not sink deep into
them, and they don't last long. So when trouble or persecution
comes because of the message, they give up at once. 18Other people are like the seeds sown among the thorns. These are the ones
who hear the message, 19but the worries about this life, the love for
riches, and all other kinds of desires crowd in and choke the

message, and they don't bear fruit. [20]But other people are like the seeds sown in good soil. They hear the message, accept it, and bear fruit: some thirty, some sixty, and some one hundred."

A host of words appear in this section which are found in the Epistles but nowhere else in the first three Gospels. The church often speaks of the "Word" in the absolute sense (translated "message" here), but Jesus never does. Moreover, it is presupposed here that a Christian church is in existence. It is very significant that there are many similar examples which clearly indicate how the church took sayings of Jesus which deal with the specific time of Jesus' ministry or which deal with the future judgment and the Kingdom of God and transformed them into sayings about the psychological attitude of the church's own members. Thus the parables in 4:26-32 and Matthew 13:33 refer only to the Kingdom of God and say nothing at all about the man who receives that Kingdom. In other parables where this man does play a part, he does so only in terms of his "yes" or "no" which still are not accounted for or differentiated psychologically. Jesus is concerned principally with his own ministry and the coming of the Kingdom of God. In the development of the tradition, however, the godly or ungodly man has assumed this central position. A later adaptation is apparent even in the wording itself. According to vs. 14 the seed is the message; according to vss. 16-20 it is the fickle, unstable, or fruitful man. At the beginning of vs. 15 (Greek) the seed is the one who hears the message, but the end of the verse upholds the equation: the seed = the message. This, of course, has resulted from the fact that it is natural to compare the man with the field. Nevertheless, it is not possible to attribute either good or bad behavior to the soil. The most one can do is to speak of the nature of the soil, which cannot be changed. This is another evidence that the parable in vss. 3-9 was told at first without the explanation found in vss. 14-20. Although this later exposition lacks the uniqueness and power of the original parables of Jesus, the situation of the church is much more similar to ours. It will be to our advantage to pay careful attention also to what the church heard in this saying of Jesus that applied to its own particular situation.

[13] In the first verse attention is directed again to the parable in vss. 3-9. The concern of the second half of the verse is broadened so as to include the basic question about parables in general, but the treatment of the question is different from that in vss. 10-12 (*q.v.*). In this passage the matter to which Mark attaches special importance comes into view, the matter which he will express more clearly in 8:17-21: The blindness of man is so universal that the disciples are not even exempt from it. Consequently, it is very difficult for God to make himself known to men, and it is a wonder that faith ever arises. **[14]** The interpretation of the church holds that although the preaching of Jesus is something which happened in a particular time, it continues to have contemporary relevance. When used without qualification, the concept "Word" (TEV: "message") means the preaching which is an ongoing process. Today Jesus' message, of which the parable was speaking, encounters the church in that preaching. **[15]** One cannot speak of the matter of opposition to preaching in the present as merely past history from the time of Jesus; such opposition must be exposed as something that exists in one's own congregation. **[16-19]** For this reason those who do not receive the message at all are mentioned first; then those who are not steadfast during persecution—an experience which had come to the church already; finally those whose faith is choked by the troubles and joys of everyday living. **[20]** It is no longer necessary to interpret the concept of fruitbearing, because it is a common way of speaking about Christian obedience which is always producing and fostering new life. In the New Testament the "Word" must be viewed as something living; something which always produces life, impels one to faith, love, hope; something which comes to maturity and bears fruit in the total life of the church.

Moreover, in contrast to vss. 15-19, the form of the verbs in this verse describes the sowing as a completed action that has fulfilled its purpose. The hearing, on the contrary, is pictured as an action which goes on and on. Of course, the men of vss. 15-19 are the only ones who are described in concrete terms. Certainly this has not resulted simply from the fact that it is easier to preach a critical sermon than to give a positive description of faith. Rather, it is because the church is primarily interested in warning men against refusing the gift of God. There are many who have viewed the explanation of the parable as constituting a consolation for the church in times when its mission has been unsuccessful. It is conceivable that Mark might have made such a consolation of it, but the idea is contradicted by the fact that the last group is the very one which is not accentuated in the explanation that Mark has received from the tradition. It is true that the explanation is given in the form of a statement of fact and not in the form of a summons. However, an examination of certain other passages shows that there was a tendency to interpret things in the parables of Jesus as exhortations that were originally proclamations of salvation. Consequently, a proclamation of this kind may well have been the basis of vss. 13-20.

Is such an interpretation binding on us? It certainly does not get at the real essence of Jesus' parables. Therefore we must not permit vss. 13-20 to obscure vss. 3-9 or to rob us of their message. Nevertheless, the exhortation of the church must be taken just as seriously as, for example, the exhortation of Paul in his Epistles. After we have listened to the parable of Jesus, we must go one step further and allow the exposition of the church to protect us from studying the time of Jesus in a manner which does not involve any commitment. Therefore, just as we must not read vss. 13-20 without recognizing that they are deeply rooted in the proclamation in vss. 3-9 (that the Kingdom of God has come in the ministry of Jesus), so we must not listen to this proclamation of salvation without permitting the church to show us the danger in any opposition which could cheat the church of the gift of Jesus' message.

Listen, Then, If You Have Ears to Hear With! 4:21-25; cf. Luke 8:16-18

[21]And Jesus continued: "Does anyone ever bring in a lamp
and put it under a bowl or under the bed? Doesn't he put it on
the lamp-stand? [22]Whatever is hidden away will be brought out

into the open, and whatever is covered up will be uncovered.
[23]Listen, then, if you have ears to hear with!"
[24]He also said to them: "Pay attention to what you hear! The
same rules you use to judge others will be used by God to judge
you—and with even greater severity. [25]The man who has something will be given more; the man who has nothing will have
taken away from him even the little he has."

All four of these sayings are found scattered in Q. Matthew omits them from this context, because he has used them already in their context in Q (5:15; 10:26; 7:2; 25:29), except for the last one which he repeats in 13:12. Luke presents them twice: once in this context following Mark, and again in 11:33; 12:2; 6:38; and 19:26 following Q. A comparison of vs. 24 with Matthew 7:2 shows how the same sayings were put into completely different contexts and in that way were given entirely different meanings (see vs. 24). Perhaps originally this was a reference to the judgment of God; the same might apply to vs. 22, unless it was at one time identical in meaning to the parable of the Mustard Seed. Vs. 21 may have referred at first to the mission of Jesus, emphasizing that he could not hide in order to save himself, but must fulfill his commission in the same way that light exists only so that all may see (Matt. 5:15). Finally, vs. 25 could have been a proverb of resignation—the rich man becomes richer and richer, the poor devil is ruined—which was appropriated in a new sense by Jesus or by the church. But this is only supposition. Consequently, we must ask what message Mark wants to convey by means of these proverbs. We do not know whether he was the first to assemble them or whether this had been done previously. It is likely that he has placed them here in order to provide another opportunity to present his view of the significance of the parables. The proverbs in this passage portray God's efforts to give spiritual light to men. This is why he is seeking men who are willing to become involved in these efforts. Mark is probably thinking of the time of the world-wide proclamation of the gospel (cf. vs. 32), not the time of God's Kingdom after the final judgment.

On the basis of form, two groups of proverbs may be detected, with a transitional section between them. Vss. 22 and 25 which in the Greek text are introduced by "for" give the reasons for vss. 21 and 24. The transitional section in vs. 23 and the introduction of vs. 24 are likely an appeal to the reader, added by Mark, in which his objective becomes especially clear.

[21] If Matthew 5:15 is the older form of vs. 21, one might think of the bowl which was placed over the light to extinguish it. This was the customary procedure in Palestine, since the rooms had no windows and the smoke generated by the lamp would be annoying. Then the proverb would read: One does not light a lamp and immediately extinguish the flame. Perhaps the more paradoxical form which Mark uses is older: One does not put a light under a tub or—as was later added picturesquely—under the bed. In this regard perhaps the curious statement about the "coming" (the literal translation of the Greek) of the light is influenced by the association of the proverb with the coming of Jesus. Mark does not consider the saying in its present context as merely a review of past history, but as a statement about the parables of Jesus. **[22]** The explanation in vs. 22 shows that he interprets the metaphor as a promise: Even if a parable is not understood it will still fulfill its purpose, and that purpose is to reveal God. **[23]** By repeating the command to hear, Mark re-emphasizes the fact that the parables of Jesus are meant to be understood; there is nothing Jesus desires more fervently. He also stresses the fact that the ability to undertand presupposes God's gift—"if you have ears to hear with!"—and the miracle of a man's willingness to receive the gift—"Listen!"

[25] It is not easy to understand vs. 24; therefore, we will begin with the explanation in vs. 25 which describes the hearing and understanding of the parables as a continuing gift that constantly increases in value. **[24]** This statement, then, gives the reason for only the conclusion of vs. 24: "with even greater severity." This conclusion is missing from the parallel passage in Matthew 7:2. Originally it may have been part of a description of the judgment (it is well suited to the context in Matthew 25:29). Perhaps Mark added these words to vs. 24, and by so doing has expressed his interpretation of that verse. At the same time he indicates by his introduction who it is to whom God will "give more." It is the one who pays attention to "what" he hears, so that he hears God's Word in the parable which outwardly appears to deal simply with everyday affairs. The promise that God's grace will give him more and more understanding is given to the one who listens attentively. This is how the phrase "the same rules you use" (Greek: "in the same measure") is to be understood. Greater discernment will be granted to the one who is able to recognize the secret of the Kingdom of God in Jesus' parable.

This whole passage is a single promise: The figurative language which Jesus uses to speak about God will not remain obscure but will become clear. And consequently it is a single appeal to the reader: Let yourself be involved in the fulfillment of this promise. So the text calls on us to respond. How? By "hearing," that is, by a passive receptivity that corresponds to an attitude toward the light that shines without our action, so that nothing can remain hidden where God is breaking through. Fullness produces more fullness. Faith can be established only by calling on men to experience it and let themselves be overwhelmed by the fullness given them. The parable that follows is speaking about the same thing.

The Parable of the Seed Which Grows Without Any Help from the Farmer 4:26-29

26Jesus went on to say: "The Kingdom of God is like a man
who scatters seed in his field. 27He sleeps at night, is up and about
during the day, and all the while the seeds are sprouting and
growing. Yet he does not know how it happens. 28The soil itself
makes the plants grow and bear fruit: first the tender stalk appears,
then the head, and finally the head full of grain. 29When the grain
is ripe the man starts working with his sickle, for harvest time has
come."

(Vs. 29: Joel 3:13.)

This is the only section of Mark which has no parallel whatever in the other Gospels. It is possible that Matthew 13:24-30 is a later development of the same parable, since it comes after the explanation of the parable of the Sower and before the parable of the Mustard Seed as Mark 4:26-29 does, and it contains a whole series of the same expressions. It may be that it was omitted or changed by the later Gospel writers because it was not possible to give it a moralistic interpretation.

[26] This very difficult expression is based upon the realization that the Kingdom of God is so completely different from anything else known to man that the similarity can only be paraphrased: It "is like a man who . . ." **[27]** The change of the Greek tense in vs. 27 in contrast to vs. 26 emphasizes the continuous inactivity—sleeping and awakening—after the single operation of scattering the seed. Night is mentioned first because special emphasis is placed upon the passive nature of sleeping, or, perhaps, because in Judaism the day begins with the evening. **[28]** The first verb in the Greek text which is in the indicative mood is the one which expresses the bearing of fruit by the land. All the actions of the man in vss. 26 f., however, are expressed by verbs in the subjunctive mood. **[29]** The last statement is a quotation of Joel 3:13, which in its original context describes the day of God's final judgment.

It is surprising that in this description of the very familiar process of raising a crop there is no mention of the man's plowing, harrowing, or cultivating. Neither is there any reference to his struggle against drought and storm. Instead, the carefree manner in which he awaits the harvest is stressed. Is this an exhortation to carefree living, similar to Matthew 6:25 ff.? Or does it emphasize the fact that we are given a time in which we may live without anxiety, through faith that the future is in God's hands? But the final statement clearly points to the fulfillment of God's Kingdom for which the "harvest" is the customary figure. Therefore, the message of this parable is similar to that of vs. 8: The harvest is sure to come. Jesus has not been commissioned to do more than the sowing. Everything else is God's concern. It is true that vss. 27 f. strongly emphasize this confident attitude. What this means is: The parable with its assurance that the harvest will come stands in opposition to any form of doubt or care which, instead of waiting for God to fulfill his promise, endeavors to force the coming of the Kingdom or to build it—by a revolution like the Zealots, by exact calculations and preparation like the Apocalyptists, or by complete obedience to the law like the Pharisees. Thus the parable is asking if we are willing, for Jesus' sake, to wait with him for God to do what he is sure to do, and if we are willing to wait with the carefree attitude which is becoming to the children of God, without any spiritual maneuvering or misguided efforts. To build one's life in this way—entirely upon God's promise and no longer upon one's own ability or inability—demands all the feeling, thinking, doing, and speaking of which we are capable.

The Parable of the Mustard Seed Which Becomes a Great Bush 4:30-32;
cf. Matt. 13:31 f.; Luke 13:18 f.

[30]"What shall we say the Kingdom of God is like?" asked Jesus. "What parable shall we use to explain it? [31]It is like a mustard seed, the smallest seed in the world. A man takes it and plants it in the ground; [32]after a while it grows up and becomes the biggest of all plants. It puts out such large branches that the birds come and make their nests in its shade."

This brief parable is found in Q also, together with the parable of the Leaven which conveys the same message. Luke presents it in the form found in Q, whereas Matthew combines the forms of both Mark and Q. We cannot be sure if the last short statement ever was part of the parable, although it is contained in both versions and in the Gospel of Thomas (20). None of the other parables of Jesus contains allusions to Old Testament passages (see below).

[30] The introduction conforms to Semitic custom, but for Mark, at least, it emphasizes the difficulty of speaking appropriately about the Kingdom of God (cf. vs. 26). **[31]** Vs. 31 is redundant and grammatically difficult. (A literal translation would be: "which is smaller than all seed.") This reference to the small size of the mustard seed is not found in Q, probably because this saying was commonplace in Palestine. **[32]** Very likely it was not added until the parable was repeated outside of that country. The same thing applies to the reference to the size of the mustard bush. The story is told, for example, of a certain rabbi who climbed up the mustard bush in his garden as one would climb up a fig tree. This is why Q simply states that a "tree" grew.

It is no longer possible to say with certainty what significance this parable had for Jesus in its original form. Since the contrast between the proverbially small mustard seed and the "tree" is stressed in Q also, it is clear that this parable has the same meaning as the two preceding ones. They are expressions of the kind of confidence which catches sight of God's ultimate fulfillment even in a very unpromising beginning; right in the midst of opposition and enmity it is able to perceive the inbreaking of the Kingdom of God. There must have been a slight change in the meaning when the church first related Jesus' parable, because the church did not live with Jesus in the time of the first sowing, but was viewing it in retrospect. Therefore, the time which elapses between sowing and harvest must move into the foreground. Of course, in those days people were not taught as we are to understand growth as a development which can be explained by natural science. Therefore, the astonishment at the miracle of the mighty plant which grew from a tiny seed is predominant in the parable. Nevertheless, even in those days a Palestinian farmer understood something about the process of growth. The primary emphasis is still upon the contrast between a small beginning and a wonderfully glorious conclusion which God has produced. Thus the time between "sowing" and "harvest" is designated, in this way, as the time of the coming Kingdom: The field is no longer empty; the glory of the Kingdom of God is sure to come. At this stage, presumably, the parable was transformed into a double parable by being combined either with the parable of the Seed Which Grew by Itself (Mark's version), or with the parable of the Mustard

Seed (see Matt. 13:31 f.). One of these two combinations may have originated with Jesus. In the first instance, the waiting of the church receives the primary emphasis, while in the second instance the accent is on the secret working of the Kingdom of God which will embrace everything. The last step is completed by Mark. Although the concluding statement might be understood as a mere embellishment as in Psalm 104:12, or as a reference to the glory of Israel in the end-time as in Ezekiel 17:23 (as Jesus himself may have understood it), Mark apparently interprets it in keeping with Daniel 4:21 (or Ezek. 31:6) as a reference to something which he considers very important (see 13:10), that is, the incorporation of all nations into the community of Jesus. Even the Hellenistic-Jewish writing, Joseph and Asenath (15:7), speaks of the abode of Gentiles in the city of God. Even if Mark saw this parable as a picture of the ultimate consummation which as yet had not come (cf. 13:10), he was closer to an interpretation which saw the final fulfillment of the parable in the church which includes all nations. In this interpretation the great hope of the future Kingdom retreats into the background. Therefore, each has interpreted his own time on the basis of this parable, whether the emphasis lay upon the inauspicious beginning and the glorious end, on the time of waiting and hope, or on the signs of the coming harvest which were already visible. Hence, we are asked by the text if we are willing to understand our time as a time upon which, ever since Jesus sowed the seed, the light of the coming Kingdom has been shining.

Why Jesus Taught in Parables 4:33-34;
cf. Matt. 13:34 f.

[33]Jesus preached his message to the people, using many other parables like these; he told them as much as they could understand. [34]He would not speak to them without using parables; but when he was alone with his disciples he would explain everything to them.

Mark is writing on his own here, and presents his own theology of Jesus' parables at the conclusion of the section. It has been suggested that vs. 33 is the original conclusion and that the Markan interpretation appears only in vs. 34. This corresponds to the situation where in vs. 13 we have the ancient transition and in vs. 11 f. the Markan transition (*q.v.*). This suggestion is contradicted by the fact that the expression "Jesus preached his message to the people," which is found also in 2:2 and 8:32 (Greek; *q.v.*), reveals Mark's viewpoint very definitely. If this expression marks the beginning of the controversy about sin and the law which leads to the sentence of death in 3:6, then in this passage it indicates that Jesus' teaching in parables is the form which, as a general rule, is appropriate for the message. In subject matter, at least, vs. 34b corresponds more closely to the tradition which has come down to Mark. The reference to "many other parables" re-emphasizes the fact that only a few examples have been given.

[33] Once again the fact that Jesus taught in parables is more important than the content of those parables. In them "the Word" comes, which since Genesis 1:1 has described God's turning toward his creation, and toward man, in the following manner: "as much as they could understand." Direct speech is impossible, because God is not a "thing" that can be taught to others. From the viewpoint of Old Testament presuppositions anyone who sees God or hears him directly must die. Therefore, it cannot be said that God is involved in the acts of Jesus; one has to speak about it metaphorically (cf. 3:23), and this is the reason why everything Jesus says must be interpreted figuratively. **[34]** The concluding statement seems to contradict this assertion. Actually, however, in Mark's terms it is another reinforcement of what has been said. If metaphors are the appropriate form for man to use in speaking of God's Kingdom, then for that very reason Jesus' help is needed to understand them. Only in association with Jesus can one learn to understand the language about God. Consequently, the metaphors are not simply rhetorical, pedagogical aids; they draw one into that fellowship with the speaker which alone makes understanding possible. 8:17-21 and 34 will re-emphasize this. This is why Mark gives no explanation of the parables except in 4:13-20, where the explanation had been added already in the tradition.

Therefore the text is saying to us: Understanding is possible only in association with Jesus; but certainly not with the Jesus who might be reconstructed by means of historical research—to accomplish this it would only be necessary to report the explanation which Jesus gave the disciples in private conversation. This association must be with the living Jesus who speaks to the church today, and who alone can "explain everything."

The Authority of Jesus over the Wind and the Waves 4:35-41;
cf. Matt. 8:18, 23-27; Luke 8:22-25

35On the evening of that same day Jesus said to his disciples,
"Let us go across to the other side of the lake." 36So they left the
crowd; the disciples got into the boat that Jesus was already in,
and took him with them. Other boats were there too. 37A very
strong wind blew up and the waves began to spill over into the
boat, so that it was about to fill with water. 38Jesus was in the
back of the boat, sleeping with his head on a pillow. The disciples
woke him up and said, "Teacher, don't you care that we are about
to die?" 39Jesus got up and commanded the wind: "Be quiet!"
and said to the waves, "Be still!" The wind died down, and there
was a great calm. 40Then Jesus said to them, "Why are you
frightened? Are you still without faith?" 41But they were terribly
afraid, and began to say to each other, "Who is this man? Even
the wind and the waves obey him!"

Mark has received this story from the tradition. In vs. 36 "other boats" are mentioned. At an earlier stage of the story this detail probably had a function which it no longer possesses. Perhaps at one time the people in the boats served as witnesses of the miracle. The situation in 4:2 is taken for granted, since Jesus is still seated in the boat. Apparently this story had been told in connection with the parables of Jesus before 4:10a was added. This is why Mark brings it into the Gospel in this place.

Miracle Stories. Miracle stories were told about the Old Testament prophets, including stories about the raising of the dead (2 Kings 4:35; 13:21) and the sudden stilling of a storm (Jonah 1:15 f.), and such stories about Jewish and Gentile wonder-workers were quite common at the time of Jesus. In this way a definite narrative pattern was developed (cf. Introduction 4), which is followed in the miracle stories of the Gospels also. Even at that time, then, it was not possible to view them simply as proof of the uniqueness of Jesus. But surely they are indications of the secret which is behind Jesus' authority. There should be no doubt about the fact that Jesus performed miracles, and particularly acts of healing. Nevertheless, it is no longer possible to determine which specific details are historical and which are not, since the stories have passed through a long process of development in the course of the decades. We can observe this process of growth within the Gospels, but even more easily in the literature of the period after the New Testament. So in all of these accounts the impression of the authority which Jesus actually exercised still echoes clearly, but not in a way which provides such positive proof that faith is no longer necessary. What we still know of Jesus' actions poses the question, but it does not relieve us of the necessity of giving an answer. This is exactly the position in which the contemporaries of Jesus found themselves.

Apart from these considerations there is a twofold distinction between their situation and ours. In the first place, it is no longer possible for us to separate on principle the miraculous events from the nonmiraculous. A modern scientist will readily accept as factual strange occurrences which as yet have not been explained, since his world view is open to events which may be extremely unlikely but are not impossible in principle. On the other hand, we have learned that it is not the unusual nature of an event which makes it a miracle. An event is a miracle only if God speaks to us in it; therefore, whether God speaks in the form of the miraculous or the nonmiraculous is immaterial. Nevertheless, it cannot be disputed that even an event which was extremely unlikely—such as the healing of a man for whom there was scarcely any hope—does not really provide any proof of God's action. It does, however, pose the question about God more urgently than other events. Occasionally God has to wave a flag before our faces, so to speak, in order to make us sit up and take notice. Therefore the second difference is, in essence: the story is transmitted to us, who are readers of the Gospel, simply as the testimony of a believer. This means that the narrator, in the process of narration, vouches for that which he cannot prove and to which he can only bear witness. It means that in this event God is addressing men and seeking their faith, and that he continues to do so today. (Cf. 5:43; 6:5; 8:11.)

[35] The evening hour is an appropriate time for Jesus to sleep, but not for the continuation of the story in 5:1 ff. **[37]** Strong gales which arise unexpectedly are still feared today on Lake Galilee. **[38]** The detailed description in vs. 38a may originate from an eyewitness account, although such details are frequently added in the process of telling a story (see the comments on 3:1-6; 5:25; and the conclusion to the Introduction). The reproachful question of the disciples reveals that their anguish contains something of the distress experienced by a supplicant bewildered by the silence of God. **[39]** Jesus commands the lake (Greek: "the Sea"; cf. Ps. 106:9) and in his call his sovereign authority is revealed, as in 1:25. Moreover, the calm which ensues is a sign of the divine victory over all hostile powers. In this connection we should recall that in the Old Testament, creation is described in terms of a struggle between God and the sea, which is portrayed as a monster. God's victory consists in his confining of the sea within definite boundaries forever (cf. Pss. 74:13 f.; 89:9-13; 104:5-9; Job 38:8-11; Jer. 5:22; 31:35; Prayer of Manasseh, vss. 2-4). But the Old Testament background may be seen in other aspects of this story as well: Storm and water represent the trials of the believer (Pss. 69:1 f., 14 f.; 18:15 f.). In these trials he can trust only in God (Isa. 43:2; Pss. 46:2 f.; 65:7; especially 107:23-32), and peaceful sleep is a symbol of that trust (Prov. 3:24; Pss. 4:8; 3:5; Job 11:18 f.; Lev. 26:6). **[40]** In contrast to all the parallel passages, this story reaches its climax in the question about faith. Here is where we find the purpose of the storyteller. He places believing in contrast to faintheartedness, so that believing is not simply intellectual agreement to certain statements; it embraces the whole of life. Therefore, to believe means to rely upon God and his might in such a way that one positively expects to encounter this might again and again in Jesus (cf.

2:5). **[41]** The fear which breaks out is not mentioned until after the deliverance. This is a fear which is greater than any fear of a storm. It must not be confused with anxiety, but can be combined with a complete trust in the grace of God (Ps. 33:18), because there is only one thing which man fears: the possibility that he might not be really laid hold of by this grace—that he might not confront it properly. It is, therefore, as has been described in many passages of the Old and New Testaments, the fear of God's presence, or, more precisely, the fear of God's coming to us, the fear of his acting, not in some theoretical realm, but in the realm in which we actually live. Therefore, the disciples' question, "Who is this man?" is the question which is being asked in the entire section.

The most important things are those which differ from the regular scheme of the parallel miracle stories: In this place Jesus does not call upon God, but acts on his own as if he were taking God's place. The main point, then, is the question of faith: "Who is this man?" The answer cannot be comprehended in a concept or title (see 8:29 f.); consequently, the reader is not spared the necessity of giving an answer. Jesus might even be a charlatan (3:22) or merely a prophet (8:28). According to Mark, however, it is this question of the disciples which shows that God is at work among them, and that too much certainty would be suspicious (6:3; 8:29-33). Faith can only be perfected in discipleship, and in such a way that one has to say "yes" again and again to the acts of Jesus. Thus the Gospel writer dismisses us with the question: Do we expect God to act in connection with Jesus in such a way that authoritative commands are given and that a new creation results (see vs. 39)?

The Authority of Jesus over Demons 5:1-20;
cf. Matt. 8:28-34; Luke 8:26-39

1So they came to the other side of Lake Galilee, to the territory of the Gerasenes. 2As soon as Jesus got out of the boat he
was met by a man who came out of the burial caves. 3This man
had an evil spirit in him and lived among the graves. Nobody

could keep him tied with chains any more; 4many times his feet
and hands had been tied, but every time he broke the chains, and
smashed the irons on his feet. He was too strong for anyone to stop
him! 5Day and night he wandered among the graves and through
the hills, screaming and cutting himself with stones.

6He was some distance away when he saw Jesus; so he ran,
fell on his knees before him, 7and screamed in a loud voice, "Jesus,
Son of the Most High God! What do you want with me? For God's
sake, I beg you, don't punish me!" 8(He said this because Jesus
was saying to him, "Evil spirit, come out of this man!") 9So Jesus
asked him, "What is your name?" The man answered, "My name
is 'Mob'—there are so many of us!" 10And he kept begging Jesus
not to send the evil spirits out of that territory.

11A large herd of pigs was near by, feeding on the hillside.
12The spirits begged Jesus, "Send us to the pigs, and let us go into
them." 13So he let them. The evil spirits went out of the man and
went into the pigs. The whole herd—about two thousand pigs in
all—rushed down the side of the cliff into the lake and were
drowned.

14The men who had been taking care of the pigs ran away and
spread the news in the town and among the farms. The people went
out to see what had happened. 15They came to Jesus and saw the
man who used to have the mob of demons in him; he was sitting
there, clothed and in his right mind—and they were all afraid.
16Those who had seen it told the people what had happened to the
man with the demons, and about the pigs. 17So they began to ask
Jesus to leave their territory.

18As Jesus was getting into the boat, the man who had had the
demons begged him, "Let me go with you!" 19But Jesus would not
let him. Instead he told him, "Go back home to your family and
tell them how much the Lord has done for you, and how kind he
has been to you!" 20So the man left and went all through the Ten
Towns telling what Jesus had done for him; and all who heard it
were filled with wonder.

This is one of the strangest stories in Mark. One suspects that an account of a healing by Jesus has been combined with a popular fairy tale about a "defrauded devil." This is suggested particularly by the feature of the two thousand pigs. The devil thought the pigs would be an appropriate dwelling place for his mob of spirits. A Jew might experience a certain pleasure in relating the story of how a tremendous herd of pigs was destroyed when some spirits were sent to live in them, since pigs were an abomination to the Jews. Furthermore, vs. 9 may be explained the same way. In boasting of his mighty power the devil disclosed his name, which gave the exorcist power over him (cf. 1:24). This, of course, is not a likely interpretation. Vs. 9 merely describes the enormous number of demons, and vss. 10-13 are the proof of their being driven out such as is found in a similar Jewish story where the demon, as he is driven out, upsets a basin of water. From the way in which the mention of the pigs has been added to vs. 16 one might be led to suspect that there was an older form of the story which did not have this feature. If so, an ancient story about Jesus casting out a demon has been enlarged by the addition of various legendary features, but primarily through the addition of the folksy description of the pigs which rushed into the water. The other story about the two thousand pigs may have suggested giving the name "Mob" to the demon. These additions were intended merely to present a particularly impressive proof of the miracle, or they were chosen with deliberate humor by the Jewish storyteller, who saw an appropriate dwelling place for demons in the pigs which were an unclean animal according to the law (Deut. 14:8; Lev. 11:7) and who was delighted by their destruction. A few inconsistencies probably indicate that in the development of the tradition some things were either added or changed. Vs. 2 says, literally, "he met him," and yet in vs. 6 the sick man is still "some distance away." It is possible to attribute the inconsistencies to the narrator's lack of skill, so that the translation of vs. 2 might be refined as follows: "he ran to meet him." Furthermore, vs. 6 could be accounted for as a rather unskillful resumption of the story after the digression in vss. 3-5. Vs. 8, on the other hand, is a clumsy insertion, in the course of transmission, by some narrator who did not understand that demons experience agony by merely being in the presence of Jesus (as in 1:24) and not only at the command to come out. Certainly vs. 18a can be traced to the one who added this story to 4:36 (which see, and cf. 3:7-12; 4:1-9). He has added vss. 18 f. as a primary point. Vs. 20 is more difficult to appraise. Does it point to the fact that this story was told originally in the churches of the "Ten Towns" as the history of the beginning of the Christian mission in that region? But the similarity with 1:45 ("began to spread the news" [translated "telling" here]) and the change from "Lord" (Luke 8:39 has "God") to "Jesus" indicate instead that this verse originated with Mark (who returns to the Ten Towns in 7:31), who adds the conclusion which is very important to him: Jesus' power cannot be concealed in spite of Jesus' reserve (cf. 1:44 f.). Mark may have viewed this as the beginning of a mission to the Gentiles, in contrast to the mission in Jewish territory (6:12 f.). It is possible that Psalm 67:7 LXX (Psalm 68:6 in English) has had an effect upon the story in the course of its narration: "God makes the solitary dwell in houses, he leads forth in strength those who are bound, just as he calls the rebellious ones who live among the graves."

The Old Testament was the church's only Bible, and the church eagerly read into it the work and suffering of Jesus (cf. Isaiah 65:2, 4). Be that as it may, we must pay particular attention to the features which break away from the established pattern of a fairy tale or of the popular description of a miracle. It is obvious that these deviations reveal the message which was of greatest importance to the earlier narrators and which is also important to Mark who made use of the story.

[1] Since Gerasa is more than thirty miles away from the lake, it is hard to believe that its territory would have extended that far. For this reason Matthew has transferred the story to Gadara, which is situated about six miles from the shore. It seems that Mark no longer had any firsthand knowledge of the geography of Palestine. In any case the story takes place in the semi-Gentile region of the Ten Towns, which were under direct Roman rule. **[2-5]** The ghastly and shocking power of the illness, the complete hopelessness of the disease, is illustrated by the fact that the afflicted man lived in the realm of the dead, among the graves which were unclean to Jews; by the fact that the sick man had "an evil spirit" (literally: an unclean spirit) in him; and by the fact that it was futile to bind him with chains. **[6, 7]** Worship and entreaty follow as they do in 1:24 except that the title Son of God appears here as it does in 3:11 (perhaps Mark has inserted it to replace an older formula). **[8]** The clear command of Jesus which orders the enemy to his own domain is restored, whereas the ancient version was interested only in the conversation between Jesus and the demon. **[9]** In the same way, as far as Mark is concerned, Jesus' simple question is so compelling that the irresistible majesty of Jesus is expressed through it, whereas the ancient storyteller was probably thinking of an unintentional disclosure of the demon's name. **[10-12]** For the Jewish storyteller it is clear that the demons are well-off in Gentile territory and for this reason do not want to leave it; accordingly, the herd of pigs is a very desirable dwelling place. **[13]** Now, for Mark the unprecedented authority of Jesus is manifested in what was once the conclusion of a popular tale. **[14]** Those who cared for the pigs, and the other residents, are important not simply as witnesses to the miracle, but in Mark's estimation they are primarily important as examples of what a miracle can accomplish. **[15]** They acknowledge the miracle, and are even overcome by fear (cf. 4:41). **[16]** Accurate eyewitness accounts may be helpful—but all this does not result in the understanding of faith. **[17]** On the contrary, the people do all they can to prevent any disturbance of their peace. **[18]** There is only one who has really understood. The desire "to be with him" (literal translation) is the only proper response to what has happened (cf. Matt. 8:19). **[19]** Jesus' answer shows how impossible it is to have a stereotyped definition of discipleship. One person is taken away from home and family (1:16-20), another is sent back to them contrary to his own wishes. Discipleship is not a way of salvation by which the individual can secure his own happiness. The concern of discipleship is always how the Good News can best be proclaimed and passed on to others. **[20]** Vs. 20 conforms to Mark's concept of the outbreaking of the Messianic secret (cf. 1:34, 43). For one thing, the influence of Jesus' action cannot be confined to a single family; also, the man who was healed fulfilled Jesus' command by proclaiming what Jesus had done for him. The "Lord" (vs. 19) did not remain a general idea or theoretical truth for him; he became a reality. And where else but in Jesus would this be possible?

The passage we have before us contains a popular story which describes at length the power of the adversary and the power of God. It has become important to the church because it sets forth the recognition of Jesus by supernatural powers, Jesus' clear exorcizing command, and his authority which extends to the material-physical world; and above all because it portrays a false faith based on the miraculous and the appropriate response of the disciple. Thus it is a call for men who are ready to proclaim "what Jesus has done for them."

The Authority of Jesus over Sickness and Death 5:21-43;
cf. Matt. 9:18-26; Luke 8:40-56

[21]Jesus went back across to the other side of the lake. There at the lakeside a large crowd gathered around him. [22]Jairus, an official of the local synagogue, came up, and when he saw Jesus he threw himself down at his feet [23]and begged him as hard as he could: "My little daughter is very sick. Please come and place your hands on her, so that she will get well and live!" [24]Then Jesus started off with him. So many people were going along with him that they were crowding him from every side.

[25]There was a woman who had suffered terribly from severe bleeding for twelve years, [26]even though she had been treated by many doctors. She had spent all her money, but instead of getting better she got worse all the time. [27]She had heard about Jesus, so she came in the crowd behind him. [28]"If I touch just his clothes," she said to herself, "I shall get well." [29]She touched his cloak and her bleeding stopped at once; and she had the feeling inside herself that she was cured of her trouble. [30]At once Jesus felt that power had gone out of him. So he turned around in the crowd and said, "Who touched my clothes?" [31]His disciples answered, "You see that the people are crowding you; why do you ask who touched you?" [32]But Jesus kept looking around to see who had done it. [33]The woman realized what had happened to her; so she came, trembling with fear, and fell at his feet and told him the whole

truth. [34]Jesus said to her, "My daughter, your faith has made you
well. Go in peace, and be healed from your trouble."

[35]While Jesus was saying this, some messengers came from
Jairus' house and told him, "Your daughter has died. Why should
you bother the Teacher any longer?" [36]Jesus paid no attention to
what they said, but told him, "Don't be afraid, only believe."
[37]Then he did not let anyone go on with him except Peter and
James and his brother John. [38]They arrived at the official's house,
where Jesus saw the confusion and heard all the loud crying and
wailing. [39]He went in and said to them, "Why all this confusion?
Why are you crying? The child is not dead—she is only sleeping!"
[40]They all started making fun of him, so he put them all out, took
the child's father and mother, and his three disciples, and went into
the room where the child was lying. [41]He took her by the hand and
said to her, *Talitha koum,* which means, "Little girl! Get up, I tell
you!" [42]She got up at once and started walking around. (She was
twelve years old.) When this happened they were completely
amazed! [43]But Jesus gave them strict orders not to tell anyone,
and said, "Give her something to eat."

Possibly this story of the raising of a dead person was already connected in the tradition with the journey back from the east shore (vs. 21) and, consequently, with the entire collection found in 4:1—5:20 (see comment on 4:35-41). It is also possible, however, that Mark was the first to include it here, because the singling out of the few intimate disciples and the lack of understanding on the part of the people become especially vivid in it. Apparently the insertion of the story of the woman with the severe bleeding (which appears to be composed in better Greek than the rest of the passage) should be attributed to Mark, since he likes to use such insertions to fill time lapses (cf. 3:22-30; 6:14-29; 11:15-19, which Matthew places in a different sequence; 14:1-11, 53-72). Finally, Mark's editing is evident in vs. 43 where the Messianic secret emerges once more (see 1:34).

[21] Mark is not concerned about where Jesus reaches the shore or when the night begins (4:35). The customary scene is the only thing which is important to present to the reader—Jesus is on the lakeshore, thronged by the people. This reveals the great influence that emanates from him. **[22]** The chief official of the synagogue is the leader of divine worship and is held in high esteem. There was in addition a three-man or at most a seven-man board of "officials of the synagogue"—a title which is used also in Gentile religious fellowships. The chief official of the synagogue may belong to this board, but membership is not required of him. The titles are used interchangeably in Luke 8:41, 49 (Greek), and Acts 13:15 speaks of several officials in the same synagogue. The name, Jairus, is omitted in a few manuscripts and in Matthew; a copyist may have added it here on the basis of Luke 8:41. **[23]** The laying on of the hands is a common gesture used in connection with sacrifices, punishment of a criminal, blessing, healing, commissioning, ordination, etc. Vss. 30-34 show that Mark considers the matter of physical contact to be important. **[25]** Later witnesses record that the woman's name was Bernice or Veronica and that she was a princess from Edessa. So the tradition continues to grow without any historical evidence whatever (see introduction to 3:1-6). **[26]** It is affirmed explicitly that human skill had been exhausted. This is a regular feature in miracle stories, which usually indicates the severity of the illness (see Introduction 4) and does not say anything about the Christian's attitude toward physicians. **[27-29, 34]** It is amazing that the cure is described in such a concrete manner; and what we would view as superstition Jesus calls "faith." **[30-31]** In this account Mark is not endeavoring to present Jesus simply as some superman who possesses supernatural knowledge; after all, Jesus asks questions. Surely Mark has no concept of an inner nature which belongs especially to God and is distinguished from a world of external objective events which is more or less separated from God. This is why the word and physical contact always belong together. When Jesus heals, the power proceeds from him, not from the soul of the sick one, and it does not affect merely the thoughts and feelings but the body also. Of course, it must be affirmed immediately that in the act of healing itself nothing important has happened unless there is a personal encounter with

Jesus, which can only result from the word, i.e., from dialogue. **[32]** In this process the "looking" which seeks and establishes fellowship originates from Jesus alone (cf. 1:16). If the healing, which is already completed and capable of objective verification, is a transaction in which Jesus is the only participant and if it continues that way, then Jesus has not really reached the human being whom he is seeking. **[33]** The experience must lead to that confession and fear (cf. 4:41) which express an awareness of Jesus' overwhelming greatness and power and consequently of one's own insignificance. **[34]** And so we arrive at Jesus' ultimate response by which he dismisses the person in peace. "Go in peace" is an Old Testament expression (Judges 18:6; 1 Sam. 1:17; 2 Sam. 15:9); but in Luke 7:50; 10:5 f.; John 14:27; 16:33; 20:19, 21, 26, the word "peace" is synonymous with "salvation." It does not indicate peace of mind, but the objective standing of a man who, although he may be in the midst of storm and strife, has been restored to a proper relationship with God. To be sure, it was the woman's manner—"a little craftiness, a little modesty, a little shyness due to her own uncleanness, and through it all an unlimited confidence in him" (Lohmeyer)—which expressed the faith that made her well. The word translated "made you well" can also mean "save" or "make blessed," and the title "Savior" contains the same root. There are two other words which could have been used to describe the healing of a disease and that have no other meaning. Mark uses these in 1:34; 3:2, 10; 6:5, 13; and particularly in 5:29. Consequently, Jesus' answer has a broader meaning: The faith which grew in vs. 33 has brought healing to her in a far more comprehensive sense. This passage, like 1:15; 4:40; 9:23 f.; 11:22 ff., shows that faith is more than confidence in a miracle-worker, even though it may begin that way. For this reason the woman had to be made aware of what had taken place in the depths of her heart. **[35]** The question of faith is put to the official of the synagogue also. Human judgment would have advised him to give up in the attempt. **[36]** But into this situation comes the consolation "Don't be afraid" which banishes all anguish in spite of the "reality" which seemed to make all hope impossible. The accompanying demand, "only believe," is meant to help him hold on to the confidence which he had manifested. So it is that the word of Jesus confers the very thing which it requires. The word translated "paid no attention" probably was used to indicate that Jesus ignored the report which suggested that they give up; in other words, he refused to take cognizance of the voice of the tempter. Here again faith does not describe intellectual assent, but a reliance upon God that expects him to take concrete action in Jesus and persists in this confidence even in spite of the reality of death. **[37, 40]** This is the kind of faith which is needed; no other will do. Probably the statement that only a few intimate friends are taken along is part of the original story. It seems likely, however, that Mark interprets it in the sense of his Messianic secret (see 1:34). **[38]** The mourning rites are in conformity with Palestinian custom. "Even the poorest in Israel provide no fewer than two flutists and one female mourner" (Josephus). **[39]** Jesus' response to these rites flatly denies the fact of death, because the word "sleeping," which is used to describe death in both the Old and the New Testaments (although it is usually a different Greek word), is clearly used in this place to indicate life. Jesus' statement is an expression of the fact that he views the child in the same way that God does. For him the coming resurrection is so certain that even now it is more real than the testimony of human eyesight. In the same way Jesus views the future kingdom as already active in the present. Naturally, however, everything depends on the "validation" of this point of view, and this validation has not been carried out as yet. **[40]** For the time being this point of view only arouses the ridicule of the crowd, which, like the funeral observances, shows how little they expected the intervention of God. **[41]** Formulas in a foreign language such as Jesus uses here are found in many miracle stories. It is likely that the story has preserved the old expression from Aramaic tradition because it conveys an impression of mysterious power. Presumably Mark has simply appropriated this expression without intending any particular emphasis, as he has done in other places (7:11; 15:22, 34). This is another instance where a clear command of Jesus produces its own fulfillment. **[42]** The features whereby the girl authenticated the miracle by walking and eating, and the acknowledgment of the miracle by the bystanders, are part of the regular pattern for such stories. The fact that God became a concrete reality within the experience of these human beings immediately produced fear. This shows how uncomfortable the presence of God is, because it disturbs the status quo in which man feels more or less at home. Yet it is clear in this verse, as in vss. 32-34, that such fear does not in itself lead to spiritual progress, because it can even lead to error if it does not result in a real encounter with Jesus. **[43]** The very fact that it is impossible to be silent here—the mourning was already in process—emphasizes clearly the great importance Mark attributes to this statement which warns against merely being astonished by the miracle.

Thus Mark has produced this story within a story in the expectation that faith will be created in the reader. The physical nature of Jesus' action is portrayed in such an amazing manner that we cannot escape the question whether we will take into consideration that God acts even in the physical world or whether we will deny him that possibility. At the same time the point is clearly made that faith comes to fulfillment only in a personal encounter with Jesus, in dialogue with him. Without this there is no value in the experience of miracles which stagger the imagination, although such experience may help us to reach a proper understanding. Mark presents the raising of this dead person as a single exception, which, although it demonstrates Jesus' authority, does not solve man's problem of death. The fact that in a particularly tragic case Jesus restored a dead person to his family for a few more years does not mean that he had overcome death. Accordingly, the following sequence is the only one in which the story is understandable: In the midst of every conceivable circumstance faith arises which leads from the "looking" on the part of Jesus that seeks and establishes fellowship, to dialogue with Jesus and then to his word by which one is dismissed in the peace of God (vss. 32-34). In this experience the believer learns that this indicates God's acceptance of him, and that God has entered into a fellowship with him which death will not terminate. From this beginning he can trust that God possesses the concrete creative power by which he can even raise people from the dead. This power appears in the story in a symbolic manner. The believer can also learn through Jesus to take the reality of the God who raises the dead more seriously than the apparent reality of death. Then, by the side of a casket or on his own deathbed he will be able to believe in life which is more concrete and real than anything on earth which is called personal life.

Raising the Dead. The fact that it is far more difficult for us than it was for Mark's contemporaries to accept the truth of the resurrection of a dead person, such as is described here, opens one's eyes to the message of this story. Surely the explanation is not to be sought in the supposition that the girl only appeared to be dead. Even if this really were the origin of the story—which is very unlikely—neither Mark nor the narrator before him had any interest in it. Undoubtedly, they are reporting a straightforward miracle of resurrection. Of course, a thing like this might seem almost natural to them, since such miracles were attributed to Greek wonder-workers and even were authenticated by the testimony of physicians. We, however, live in a completely different situation. The story presented no special intellectual problems for them. Thus they were able to focus their attention on the faith which believes that nothing is impossible for God—not even victory over death. Of course, such faith was not possible until after the resurrection of Jesus—a resurrection which surpasses the Jewish and Greek ideas. The situation of man today is so different that his attention becomes fixed upon the miracle itself—whether or not he believes it to be true. In the process the story loses its "symbolic" meaning. It must be recognized that the resuscitation of a corpse and the person's return to what for all practical purposes is the same kind of an earthly life, as is presented in Dürrenmatt's *Meteor,* is the exact opposite of what the Bible calls resurrection—re-creation by God to an existence which is entirely new. It is life in a manner that is inconceivable, because it is existence in fellowship with God. To be sure, God provides signs for this. But to transfer the question of faith from the thing itself to the sign would be fatal. Whoever simply requires modern man to believe this story to be true conceals from him the fact that the real miracle in this story is the emergence of faith which believes God is able to triumph over death; he also leads modern man into the error of seeing the resurrection of the dead merely as a return to an earthly life under improved circumstances. It would be equally unreasonable to state the opposite, that under no circumstances could God work a miracle like this which surpasses all experience. In making such a statement he would presume to know enough about God to be able to prescribe for him what he is capable of doing, what would be prudent for him, and whether or not the time is right for such signs. In this way the story points forcefully away from itself and asks the reader whether he considers God able to triumph over death in the hour of his own death when, presumably, no "miracle" may be expected. (See comments on 4:35-41; 16:1-6.)

The Rejection of Jesus by His Fellow Citizens 6:1-6a;
cf. Matt. 13:53-58; Luke 4:16-30

1Jesus left that place and went back to his home town, followed by his disciples. 2On the Sabbath day he began to teach in
the synagogue. Many people were there, and when they heard him
they were all amazed. "Where did he get all this?" they asked.
"What wisdom is this that has been given him? How does he perform miracles? 3Isn't he the carpenter, the son of Mary, and the
brother of James, Joses, Judas, and Simon? Aren't his sisters living here?" And so they rejected him. 4Jesus said to them: "A
prophet is respected everywhere except in his home town, and by
his relatives and his family." 5He wasn't able to perform any miracles there, except that he placed his hands on a few sick people
and healed them. 6He was greatly surprised, because they did not
have faith.

Mark concludes his third section with the rejection of Jesus in the same way as he concluded the second section at 3:6. Only now it is Jesus' fellow citizens who reject him and not the authorities, who were never his close associates. In the formation of the whole section emphasis is laid upon the blindness of the world to God's revelation. It can be pointed out in this connection that in John 11:45-50 the rejection of Jesus also followed the raising of a dead person. Mark is not aware of the fact that Jesus would have been rescued miraculously from any attempt upon his life (according to the arrangement of Luke's Gospel, this fact is declared at the beginning of Jesus' ministry [4:16-30]). Some have even suspected that the entire scene might have developed from the proverb which is found in vs. 4. Nevertheless, the church considered Jesus to be more than a prophet, so it is not very likely that the church would apply such a proverb to him unless there were some special reason for doing so. Furthermore, vs. 3 contains details which are not given simply to fill up space, and it is unlikely that vs. 5a has been fabricated without historical evidence. It is possible that the story was transmitted orally at first, so that not much more than the fact of Jesus' rejection is certain. In vss. 1 f. the statements that the disciples followed Jesus and that Jesus taught in the synagogue are typical signs of Mark's editing; and vs. 5b appears to be the kind of general summary of Jesus' healing activity which Mark frequently inserts, except that here it has taken a rather negative turn. It would be better, then, to assume that the very general, proverb-like statement in vs. 4 has been added in oral transmission as a summarizing slogan (cf. the way in which the summary statement cited in Mark 10:31 is a later addition in Matthew 20:16 and Luke 13:30).

[1] The name Nazareth which is mentioned in 1:9 (so that in 1:14a Jesus would not appear to be fleeing?) is missing here because it is not vital to the point of the story. The "following" of the disciples is another indication of the special position which they assume in this part of the Gospel. **[2]** "He began to teach" is one of Mark's typical expressions; it is the more striking, since the end of vs. 2 presupposes Jesus' mighty deeds. For Mark, however, the decisive acceptance or rejection is made in response to Jesus' teaching. It is not in response to some particular point in his teaching—nothing is reported of the content—but simply in response to the fact that in Jesus' teaching God addresses man with an authoritative word. **[3]** A question is the appropriate response and, also quite appropriately, the response is a question about Jesus himself. But the question is not left open; it is met with a ready-made answer in which Jesus is classified according to familiar categories. Moreover, this is the only place where Jesus' occupation is mentioned. Matthew says it is Jesus' father who is a carpenter and Luke omits this detail entirely. The Greek word can also mean a builder who works with stone. In the second century, Justin recorded that Jesus had made (wooden) plows and yokes. It is strange that only Jesus' mother is named, at least so far as the original form of the story is concerned, because it was still rooted in Judaism; therefore, it is necessary to assume that his father had been dead for some time. The brothers of Jesus are mentioned also in 3:31; John 2:12; 7:3, 5, 10; Acts 1:14; 1 Corinthians 9:5; Galatians 1:19. This demonstrates that the New Testament knows nothing of the perpetual virginity of Mary. The Greek word, *skandalizein,* from which our term "scandal" comes, is really translated too mildly with "be offended" (KJV) or "take offense" (RSV); in 4:17 it is translated "they give up," and here, "they rejected him." **[4]** Vs. 4 is preserved as a saying of Jesus also in a papyrus and in the Gospel of Thomas 31: "No prophet is acceptable in his village [Luke 4:24], no physician heals those who know him." Passages which are parallel in content may be found in Greek writers also. **[5]** Vs. 5a is milder in Matthew and is omitted by Luke; it contradicts the later concept of Jesus' unlimited power. It was still known in the older tradition, however, that a genuine miracle (see comment on 4:35-41) always establishes fellowship between God and man in that it seeks faith, arouses questions, and gives answers. It was known, moreover, that Jesus did not work miracles unless the miracle would lead to such "dialogue." The concluding statement reaffirms that the pivotal point is the question of faith.

Thus in the last section of the third division the real hindrance to faith is revealed once more: it is the fact that God is invisible, i.e., he is concealed in the commonplace. This hindrance is more serious today—because, on the one hand, we recognize the possibility of error in the transmission of miracle stories and, on the other hand, we explain many things psychologically. Nevertheless, the situation has not been changed fundamentally. The choice is still between a "discipleship" which even in the case of the disciples is simply a matter of indecision at first, a question (see 4:41), a misunderstanding (see 8:12-21), or a premature answer which finishes the matter. The disciples live with Jesus and yield themselves to him, often without understanding him, because they have noted that the answer is not as simple as the unbelieving residents of Nazareth or the "orthodox" demons (1:24; 3:11; 5:7) think, and is not supplied by simply affirming correctly "he is the son of Mary" or even "he is the Son of God." Moreover, the story frequently may have consoled the church when it was troubled because of the ineffectiveness of its preaching.

IV

JESUS' MINISTRY TO THE GENTILES AND THE BLINDNESS OF THE DISCIPLES 6:6b—8:26

Jesus' Teaching Ministry 6:6b;
cf. Matt. 9:35a

[6]Then Jesus went to all the villages around there, teaching the people.

The concluding section in each of the divisions II-IV reports a rejection of Jesus (3:1-6; 6:1-6a; 8:14-21). The beginnings of these divisions also correspond to one another (1:14 f.; 3:7-12; 6:6b). Each begins with a brief editorial note about the ministry of Jesus. In this passage the editorial note is especially concise, because the description of Jesus' ministry has actually begun in vs. 5. Here again it is only the "teaching" of Jesus and not his healing which is stressed (see 1:21). This is typical of Mark.

The Sending of the Disciples 6:7-13;
cf. Matt. 10:1-42; Luke 9:1-6; 10:1-16

[7]He called the twelve disciples together and sent them out two by
two. He gave them authority over the evil spirits [8]and ordered
them: "Don't take anything with you on the trip except a walking
stick; no bread, no beggar's bag, no money in your pockets. [9]Wear
sandals, but don't wear an extra shirt." [10]He also told them:
"When you come to a town, stay with the people who receive you
in their home until you leave that place. [11]If you come to a place
where people do not welcome you or will not listen to you, leave
it and shake the dust off your feet. This will be a warning to
them!" [12]So they went out and preached that people should turn

away from their sins. [13]They drove out many demons, and poured oil on many sick people and healed them.

As the choosing of the disciples follows a brief summary account of Jesus' ministry at the beginning of divisions II and III, so the sending out of the disciples follows here (cf. 1:16-20; 3:13-19). The historicity of this section has been particularly contested.

The Circle of the Twelve. There is some doubt whether Jesus chose a more limited circle of twelve disciples. 1 Corinthians 15:5 mentions the "twelve" in spite of the fact that after the exclusion of Judas there would have been only eleven. Consequently, it is more likely that twelve are mentioned from the wider circle of disciples who, because they had witnessed an appearance of the risen Jesus, would become the leaders in the early church. It has been observed that the twelve are seldom connected with the stories which have been transmitted to us, and that they usually appear in editorial statements. Peter and the sons of Zebedee are the only ones of whom we hear occasionally; the others remain inconspicuous. This applies equally to the time after Easter. It is not at all certain that the twelve were the leaders of the early church (Acts 6:2) because Peter and John are the only ones concerning whom any details are given. In Galatians 2:9 the leadership of James, Peter, and John is implied, while the apostles in Galatians 1:19 appear to be a wider circle (see below). Moreover, a circle of twelve leaders is almost without parallel in Jewish fellowships; there are only two examples for Caesaria; and newly discovered texts show that 1QS 8:1 f. presupposes a total of 15 officials, not 12. The expression "the twelve" in 1 Corinthians 15:5 is presumably a fixed expression for the narrower circle of Jesus' disciples and does not necessarily indicate the exact number. There is in addition the regular expression "Judas, one of the twelve" (cf. 14:10 f.). If the twelve first appeared as the leading group within the early church, it would be difficult to conceive that the tradition would have put the betrayer into this innermost group of the disciples without any historical justification, especially since it would have been necessary, in that case, to strike another name from the list of Jesus' disciples. Furthermore, Paul never questioned the fact that his discipleship was an exceptional circumstance clearly distinct from that of the twelve. This distinction implies more than simply a difference in the time when they witnessed an appearance of the resurrected One. Whether Jesus ever sent out the twelve is another question. Outside of the writings of Luke, the name "apostle" ("he who is sent," "missionary") is used for the twelve only in Mark 6:30; in Matthew 10:2 as an editorial note; and in Revelation 21:14. John 13:16 uses the word in a very general sense. With the exception of Peter, and possibly John, those who are specifically called missionaries are men outside the circle of the twelve (1 Cor. 9:5 f.; Acts 8:4 f., 26, 40; 15:39 f.; cf. Acts 11:19 f.). Paul's much broader concept of apostle (1 Cor. 15:7; Rom. 11:7; 2 Cor. 8:23; Phil. 2:25) persisted even into the post-New Testament period. According to Matthew 19:28 (Luke 22:30) the early church expected that the twelve would have a special place in the future Kingdom of God as judges or rulers of the perfected Israel. Presumably Jesus has called the twelve as a special inner group of his followers and has viewed this call as evidence of the future completion of the people of God. Perhaps the twelve were already called Jesus' *šeluḥim* ("sent ones" in the sense of "authorized agents") in the Aramaic-speaking church. It was Paul's claim that he was an "apostle of Jesus Christ" in a special sense which first brought about the situation where together with him or in contrast to him the twelve were called the real apostles, since in the beginning every missionary was called an "apostle" in the Greek-speaking church.

Then the question arises whether the sending in this instance is not a later view which has been transferred back into the life of Jesus. Vss. 8-10 resemble a code of conduct which might have been set up in the church and used for missionaries. Did the twelve in the time of Jesus have more possessions than permitted in vss. 8 f.? And if so, what should they do with them? Moreover, the introduction and conclusion (vss. 7, 12 f.) show the typical Markan style and concepts, e.g., the preaching of repentance and the word "apostle" in vs. 30, which is a title that was developed later. On the other hand, vs. 11 no longer corresponds to the situation of the church, since the statement implies that a brief call to repentance is given but once, and that after it has been rejected the judgment begins. Luke 10:3-11 shows that the same order was found in Q: sending, regulations about outfitting, proper conduct in houses and in towns, the combination of miracle-working and preaching (cf. Luke 9:1-6 which corresponds to Mark 6:6-13). Luke has preserved some additional ancient features: the prohibition of shoes and of greetings on the road (to avoid the loss of any time) in 10:4; the expression "peace-loving man" and the concept of the greeting of peace remaining on a man or of its being withdrawn by the disciples in vs. 6; the reference to the Kingdom of God in vss. 9, 11; and the conclusion in vs. 17, according to which the disciples do not discover their power over demons until later. For the most part this seems to be the older form of the instructions. Mark 6:8 f. also appears in Q in a form which is fully appropriate for Jesus' situation: "Do not acquire for yourself . . ." (therefore, it appears to be the oldest form, Matt. 10:9-10a). Moreover, the eschatological tension and the extreme seriousness in vs. 11 could have originated with Jesus (cf. Luke 10:11). Apparently certain individual sayings which were already formulated and in common usage have been collected and augmented to form a kind of missionary code which the church needed for the instruction of its missionaries. If vs. 11 originated with Jesus, then of course we must grant that Jesus did send out the twelve. This is not unlikely since Jesus did not intend to form an exclusive group, but looked upon the twelve as a symbol of his claim upon all Israel.

[7] Service for Jesus is always service in the church and can never be done by only one person. The teamwork of at least two is a symbol of this truth. This is in conformity with the practice of the church also (1 Cor. 9:6; Acts 8:14; 15:36-40; etc.; cf. the arrangement of the names in pairs in Matt. 10:2-4). Authority is emphasized again; preaching is not theoretical instruction, but exhortation in which God's power is expressed and every hostile power is assailed. **[8, 9]** The poverty of the messengers who travel without provisions, without money in their pockets, and without additional protective clothing is the sign of a life like that of the "birds" and the "wild flowers" (Matt. 6:25-34), in which there is no reliance upon one's own means. Messengers who wish to provide for every emergency do not have faith. Messengers are not to be believed if they rely upon their own resources (material or spiritual) rather than on the One whom they proclaim. On the other hand, they should make use of whatever they need without hesitation and not fanatically regard asceticism as something worthwhile in itself. Actually, it is not the possession of an extra shirt that is warned against, but only burdening oneself with it on the mission. One must not be so fanatical as to think that he is permitted to use only his faith in the miraculous against wild animals and snakes, and not to use a stick or a shoe (in contrast to Matt. 10:10; Luke 9:3; 10:4). Furthermore, the fact that in every Jewish city a social welfare worker provided food and clothing for wanderers must not be forgotten (Josephus, *Wars* II. 125). **[10]** There was a great deal of discussion as to how long one might expect to receive hospitality. While individual rabbis thought a guest might stay until his host strikes him (if the host strikes only the guest's wife it is not so bad) or until he throws the guest's belongings out after him, an early regulation of the Christian church establishes that anyone is a false prophet who stays more than two days (Didache 11:4 f.). The warning given here is against a change to more pleasant quarters in the same locality. **[11]** The situation is different in vs. 11, which is referring to a preaching mission which requires only an acceptance or a rejection and leaves no room for any more extensive pastoral endeavor. This verse is based upon the awareness that the rejection of the message must not be considered so innocuous that the results of such a rejection are ignored. With every authoritative proclamation, judgment is also pronounced. For this reason the messengers of Jesus have "a task but no goal"; i.e., they must proclaim the message and with all their being, even with their outward behavior, but the responsibility for the outcome must be left to God. The gesture of shaking off the dust was performed by Jews when they returned to the Holy Land from a Gentile region and wished to leave everything unclean behind them. It might be a "sign" (translated here as "warning") for those who were not ready to repent, so that they might recognize the seriousness of their action and perhaps repent even yet, or it may be a sign against them, namely, on the Day of Judgment. **[12, 13]** The content of the call is summarized similarly as in 1:4, 14 f., but at the same time their work of healing is mentioned also. Oil was used frequently as a salve (Luke 10:34); in this instance, however, it is something objective which may be interpreted as the sign reinforcing the word which announces the healing.

This brief description reveals the importance of authenticity in preaching. Everything done, all the way from the poverty and unpretentiousness of the messengers to the courage to make clear the judgment which will follow the rejection of the message, must concur with the word which declares that God will always be more important than everything else.

The Destiny of the Baptist as Prophetic of the Destiny of Jesus 6:14-29;

cf. Matt. 14:1-12; Luke 9:7-9; 3:19-20

14Now King Herod heard about all this, because Jesus' repu-
tation had spread everywhere. Some people said, "John the
Baptist has come back to life! That is why these powers are at
work in him." 15Others, however, said, "He is Elijah." Others
said, "He is a prophet, like one of the prophets of long ago."

16When Herod heard it he said, "He is John the Baptist!
I had his head cut off, but he has come back to life!" 17Herod himself had ordered John's arrest, and had him tied up and put in
prison. Herod did this because of Herodias, whom he had married even though she was the wife of his brother Philip. 18John
the Baptist kept telling Herod: "It isn't right for you to marry your
brother's wife!" 19So Herodias held a grudge against John and
wanted to kill him, but she couldn't because of Herod. 20Herod
was afraid of John because he knew that John was a good and
holy man, and so he kept him safe. He liked to listen to him,
even though he became greatly disturbed every time he heard him.

21Finally Herodias got her chance. It was on Herod's birth-

day, when he gave a feast for all the top government officials, the
military chiefs, and the leading citizens of Galilee. 22The daughter
of Herodias came in and danced, and pleased Herod and his guests.
So the king said to the girl, "What would you like to have? I
will give you anything you want." 23With many vows he said to
her, "I promise that I will give you anything you ask for, even as
much as half my kingdom!" 24So the girl went out and asked her
mother, "What shall I ask for?" "The head of John the Baptist,"
she answered. 25The girl hurried back at once to the king and demanded, "I want you to give me right now the head of John the
Baptist on a plate!" 26This made the king very sad; but he could
not refuse her, because of the vows he had made in front of all his
guests. 27So he sent off a guard at once with orders to bring John's
head. The guard left, went to the prison and cut John's head off;
28then he brought it on a plate and gave it to the girl, who gave it
to her mother. 29When John's disciples heard about this, they
came and got his body and laid it in a grave.

A considerable period of time elapsed between the sending of the disciples and their return. Consequently, Mark must fill in the interval (cf. 5:21-43). For this purpose he selects the reference to Herod's opinion about Jesus (vs. 16), an item that probably had come to him from the tradition. He enlarges it with the addition of vs. 15, which originally must have been connected with 8:27 f., and then adds vs. 14 to serve as an introduction. Vs. 16 provides an opportunity for him to return to the execution of the Baptist. It is at the same time a prophecy of man's opposition to Jesus and of Jesus' future destiny. It is the only story in Mark which is not directly a story about Jesus, and it is written in a cultured style which shows that it must have been established in written form before Mark. The execution of the Baptist by Herod was reported also by the Jewish author Josephus, although he states that it took place in the fortress Machaerus which lay east of the Dead Sea. The number of guests described here (end of vs. 21), however, is only conceivable at the Herodian Palace in Tiberias, the capital of Galilee. Moreover, Josephus reports that Herodias was the former wife of a half-brother of Herod, who was also named Herod, and not the former wife of Philip, who married a daughter of Herodias. Finally, a public dance by the king's daughter is almost unbelievable. Accordingly, an historical event has been adorned with legendary elements, most likely by someone belonging to the circle of John's disciples (vs. 29), who viewed their master as the returning Elijah (1 Kings 21:17 ff.).

[14] The story is about Herod Antipas, who reigned over Galilee and Perea (east of the Jordan) as tetrarch from 4 B.C. to A.D. 39; the people may have called him king. **[14, 15]** His opinion is not presented until vs. 16, since vss. 14b, 15 speak of the opinion of the people in general. This shows that it is the question about Christ which interests Mark, and not Herod's uneasy conscience. This is how Mark prepares the way for 8:28. One could be fully convinced of the possibility of John's resurrection and yet not honor him as the Messiah. The statements of the people imply that Jesus did not begin his ministry until after the death of the Baptist (see 1:14). Others guess that he is Elijah; accordingly, Elijah is not identified with John here as in 9:13. Malachi 4:5 and Ecclesiasticus 48:10 f. speak of Elijah's reappearance, and Deuteronomy 18:15 describes the coming prophet (cf. 1 Macc. 4:46; 14:41; John 1:21). **[16]** According to this saying, Herod himself interprets Jesus' person in the light of his own guilty conscience. It is not certain whether this statement should be understood as referring to a real resurrection of John, as in vs. 14. Since it had been known for a long time that Jesus was about thirty years old when John was killed (Luke 3:23), perhaps it is simply saying: John cannot be killed; his call to repentance will merely come again through some other person. Mark interprets it in the first sense. In general, what is striking about Jesus are his mighty deeds. The fact that he acts with authority is not contested; it is only the significance of those actions which is in dispute. Is it a phenomenon which can be explained psychologically (3:21), or as malicious deceit (3:22)? Can it be explained perhaps in terms of religious phenomena which are already known (6:14 f.)? No consideration is given to the possibility that more than this may have happened—the possibility that God might be met here in a special way.

[17] According to Luke 3:20 John was imprisoned before the baptism of Jesus. Mark refers to this imprisonment in 1:14. He chose to include the story of John's arrest and execution here instead of at that place, because in this division he wants to present particularly the ever-increasing blindness of the world to God's revelation. **[18]** Herodias was the granddaughter of Herod the Great; therefore, she was the niece of Antipas and it was not legal for Antipas to marry her (according to Leviticus 18:16; 20:21; cf. Deuteronomy 25:5 f.). Furthermore, he had divorced his own wife and had enticed Herodias away from his half-brother Herod. The mention of Philip here is an error. This name is omitted in Luke 3:19 and a later copyist omitted it from Matthew 14:3 and from this passage. **[19, 21]** Herodias resembles Jezebel (1 Kings 19:2), and Herod resembles Ahab (1 Kings 21:4 ff.). **[20]** Herod is not the victim of circumstances which made it impossible to distinguish between right and wrong. He stands under the terrible pressures of the consequences of a wrong decision made previously. The reading "he became greatly disturbed," i.e., in view of the prophetic word of the Baptist, is not certain; other texts read something like this: "he did so often." **[22]** It is almost inconceivable that the princess would dance in this way; undoubtedly the story is intended to say: Herodias goes so far that she will even sacrifice the honor of her daughter to gain her objective. **[23]** Herod's promise is formulated according to Esther 5:3; 7:2; moreover, this petty prince, ruling by the grace of Rome, could not give away one handsbreadth of his territory. **[24]** The conversation between the girl and her mother increases the suspense. **[25-27]** The story of the execution is given without any exaltation of the martyr, because the theme is not John's role as an example but the opposition of the world to God. Legalism and a passion for the miraculous, adultery and an evil conscience, weakness and a spirit of intrigue, oppose God. **[28]** The presentation of John's head is purposely portrayed in a hideous manner. **[29]** The love of John's disciples at the end is the only thing which brings a little ray of light.

In the formation of the Gospel a legendary account of the death of the Baptist, which has been embellished with details from Old Testament stories, serves here to illustrate the opposition and the blindness of the world; in this connection, however, the weakness and ineffectiveness of God's prophet and of his few disciples are not concealed. In this way the story is made into a question aimed at the reader and prepares him for 8:31, 34.

The Return of the Disciples 6:30-31;
cf. Luke 9:10a; 10:17-20

[30]The apostles returned and met with Jesus, and told him all they had done and taught. [31]There were so many people coming and going that Jesus and his disciples didn't even have time to eat. So he said to them, "Let us go off by ourselves to some place where we will be alone and you can rest a while."

This is an editorial transition which clearly shows the style of Mark. Moreover, it shows that Mark knew nothing more about the mission's success or failure, since he presents a situation which is essentially unchanged. In addition there is no mention of what Jesus did in the meantime. As in 4:34; 9:2, 28; and 13:3, where the same expression is found in Greek, Jesus desires to be alone with his disciples. In this way emphasis is put upon the private instruction of the disciples by Jesus, which shows how God does everything he can in order to reach man. Emphasis is also put upon the efficacy of the power of God which is visible in the works of Jesus; it is effectual beyond all imagination. At the same time the transition is made skillfully to the following story, which in the tradition already presupposed a setting in a lonely place with a great crowd.

[30] This is the only place where the twelve (6:7) are called apostles (i.e., "ones sent out"); it is still clearly a designation of their ministry and not a regular title. Their deeds predominate while their teaching is of secondary importance and mentioned only once (see comment on 1:21). **[31]** It is strange that the motive for withdrawal is the desire to rest a while; perhaps what is meant is solitude and rest from all the commotion, similar to the withdrawal mentioned in 1:35. Nevertheless, Mark's primary need is a basis for vs. 32b. The great crowd is portrayed here in the same way that it is in 3:20.

The Authority of Jesus to Feed Five Thousand 6:32-44; cf. Matt. 14:13-21; Luke 9:10-17

[32]So they started out in the boat by themselves to a lonely place.

[33]Many people, however, saw them leave and knew at once who they were; so they left from all the towns and ran ahead by land and got to the place ahead of Jesus and his disciples. [34]When Jesus got out of the boat, he saw this large crowd, and his heart was filled with pity for them, because they looked like sheep without a shepherd. So he began to teach them many things. [35]When it was getting late, his disciples came to him and said, "It is already very late, and this is a lonely place. [36]Send the people away, and let them go to the nearby farms and villages and buy themselves something to eat." [37]"You yourselves give them something to eat," Jesus answered. They asked, "Do you want us to go and buy two hundred dollars' worth of bread and feed them?" [38]So Jesus asked them, "How much bread do you have? Go and see." When they found out they told him, "Five loaves, and two fish also."

[39]Jesus then told his disciples to make all the people divide into groups and sit down on the green grass. [40]So the people sat down in rows, in groups of a hundred and groups of fifty. [41]Then Jesus took the five loaves and the two fish, looked up to heaven, and gave thanks to God. He broke the loaves and gave them to his disciples to distribute to the people. He also divided the two fish among them all. [42]Everyone ate and had enough. [43]Then the disciples took up twelve baskets full of what was left of the bread and of the fish. [44]The number of men who ate the bread was five thousand.

In 8:1 ff. a similar story is told. Moreover, the feeding of the five thousand is reported in John 6 in a form which most likely is independent of Mark. The crossing to the eastern shore, the feeding of the five thousand, Jesus' withdrawal, the journey back, and the walking on the water follow one another in that passage as they do here. What is more important is that the demand for a sign (Mark 8:11-13; cf. 6:53-56), the misunderstanding of Jesus' symbolic language about bread (Mark 8:14-21; cf. 6:52), and Peter's confession (Mark 8:27-30) are added in John. Obviously, these stories were regularly associated with one another before Mark. Furthermore, the same story was told over again with somewhat different details, so that one version reported four thousand and another reported five thousand (see 8:1-10). Mark has understood these two versions as two separate events. To keep them from appearing in immediate succession he has inserted between them the material in chapter 7. In constructing his Gospel, Mark chooses to include this collection of stories in this place because in the tradition these stories led to Peter's confession, but primarily because they clearly demonstrate how blind man can be to God's message even in the light of Jesus' amazing miracles (6:52; 8:17-21). In chapter 7 the faith of a Gentile woman is contrasted with this blindness. What makes her faith so conspicuous is the contrast with the blindness of a legalistic Judaism in which even the disciples are somewhat involved.

Various events have been proposed as the ultimate origin of this story: a Messianic sacrament, through which Jesus consecrated his followers for the future kingdom, in which case the only erroneous part would be the report that everyone had enough; a band of revolutionaries who gathered in the wilderness and wanted to choose Jesus as their political leader, but he withdrew from them; or a peaceful gathering where the problem of insufficient food was solved by Jesus' exhortation to share with others. However, the narrative bears so clearly the distinctive marks of a miracle-story that it must have been recounted as one from the very beginning. There are many parallels to it (1 Kings 17:8 ff.; 2 Kings 4:1 ff., 42 ff.; and stories among the Jews and Greeks and all over the world), which show that we are dealing with a roving legend which has been transferred to Jesus. The crucial question is: What was it that happened to Jesus in such an impressive way that a legend like this was transferred to him and was reformulated, in the process, according to the regular pattern? One must keep this question in mind while explaining the details. To be sure, in the course of transmission the story was interpreted as an allusion to the Lord's Supper. It has even been supposed that originally vs. 41 simply stated: "And he took the five loaves and the two fish and divided them among all." Since vs. 41 does not agree exactly with either 8:6 or 14:22, it is likely that the assimilation to the Lord's Supper occurred before Mark. Markan composition is seen particularly in vss. 32 f., where Jesus' desire to be alone with his disciples forms a contrast to the massive crowd of people, and in the concluding statement of vs. 34.

[32] Luke 9:10 indicates that the feeding took place in Bethsaida. According to Mark 6:45 (and 8:13, 22) this city is situated on the other side of the lake and, presumably, this is in agreement with the tradition. **[33]** Apparently Mark conceives of the feeding as taking place on the western shore, so that Jesus travels only a little way along the shore and the crowd can easily overtake him. Bethsaida is located north of the lake and east of the Jordan so that from the west one actually travels "across" the lake to this city. In John 6:1, 17 the feeding occurs on the eastern shore, because afterward the disciples go back across the lake to Capernaum on the western shore. **[34]** As 8:2 shows, originally Jesus' pity (found elsewhere in the tradition only in 9:22) had reference to the physical hunger. But even here Mark stresses that the concern of this story ultimately is something entirely different—it is Jesus' teaching in which God reveals himself. In this divine pity is manifested, and this is what men need. The figure of the sheep occurs in Numbers 27:17 f. (where LXX speaks of Jesus-Joshua as Moses' minister); Ezekiel 34:5; cf. 1 Kings 22:17; Zechariah 13:7. It is used with a different meaning in Matthew 9:36 (here the figure is used in connection with preaching, which explains its omission from Matthew 14:14) and in Mark 14:27. **[35-37]** Probably the challenge to the disciples is inserted only because it shows their lack of understanding (cf. Num. 11:22). The specific task which will bring faith to fulfillment also exposes this lack of understanding. Surely their counter-question is meant only to show the impossibility of Jesus' proposition, since the amount of money mentioned is far more than they had. **[38]** The loaves of that time were as large as a plate and the thickness of a thumb. They were made of wheat or of barley, which was less expensive (John 6:9), and were broken when eaten. **[39]** The word of the master ends the discussion. It is doubtful whether the mention of the "green grass" reveals a glimmer of the hope of the Apocalyptics who believed that in the end-time the wilderness would become a fruitful land. **[40]** The arrangement in groups may be reminiscent of the arrangement of the hosts of Israel in the wilderness. **[41]** The description of the distribution probably has been deliberately made to agree with Mark 14:22, which explains why the distribution of the fish is not mentioned until the end. The customary Jewish blessing reads: "Blessed art thou, O Lord, our God, King of the world, who causest bread to grow from the earth." The tense of the verb "he gave" implies that Jesus passed bread to the disciples again and again. It was the disciples, and not Jesus himself, who passed the bread to the people. This is a reasonable arrangement considering the size of the crowd; consequently, it is not likely that it refers to the subsequent role of the deacons in distributing the bread at the Lord's Supper, or that it refers in a symbolic way to the apostles who proclaim the gospel to all nations. **[42, 43]** The lavishness of the gift is particularly accentuated (cf. 2 Kings 4:44); this impression grows until the very end where the number of persons fed is stated. It is not clear whether "men" should be interpreted as excluding women and children in agreement with Matthew 14:21. The expression may simply be another way of saying "human beings" or may, indeed, have been suggested by the memory of the hosts of Israel.

In seeking the meaning of the whole story it is necessary to distinguish between the tradition and Mark. Certainly it does not describe a Messianic banquet. It is an ordinary everyday meal—rather simple and without wine (in contrast to Mark 14:22 f.; 1QS 2:21 ff.). There is nothing which points to a special sacramental gift or to a new fellowship with God. Jesus is the one who cares for the physical needs of the people. John 6:31 refers to the manna in the wilderness, and a few details in this story might suggest that the tradition which Mark had at his disposal also portrayed Jesus as the redeemer of Israel in the end-time; in him the salvation-time of the exodus from Egypt finds its eschatological fulfillment. Although this is uncertain, it is quite clear that he is presented as the one who excels all the prophets and is, therefore, the one who brings salvation in the end-time. Probably the tradition is responsible for the assimilation of this story to the Lord's Supper. In later times bread and fish appear frequently as symbols of the Lord's Supper in figurative representations. It is certain that in 6:52 and 8:19 Mark returns to this story and discerns the incomprehensible blindness of the disciples in it. From this point of view the editorial change in vs. 34 becomes intelligible: As on a previous occasion (see 1:21-28), Mark sees the miracle as another concrete manifestation of the authority of Jesus, who wants to lead men back to God by his teaching. The bread—perhaps the bread of the Lord's Supper also—is a symbol of God's gift of the revelation which is contained in Jesus' teaching. As in 4:35-41, this is a miracle of creation which is seeking to arouse the faith of man (4:40; cf. 5:32-34; etc.). In this account the lack of understanding on the part of the disciples is revealed in a new way. Thus the presentation of the blindness of the world is intensified as is the description of the care and the trouble which God has to take upon himself in order to reveal himself to the world. Both of these elements will reach their climax in 8:27-33. This is confirmed by the form of the narrative, because, in contrast to the other miracle stories, the astonishment of the crowd and the verification of the miracle by the spectators is missing here. Therefore, the story is asking the reader whether he will be guided by this one miraculous sign (and his willingness or unwillingness to accept this story as being true) to the question which confronts him in it about Jesus' authority over him.

The Authority of Jesus in Walking on the Water 6:45-52; cf. Matt. 14:22-33

45At once Jesus made his disciples get into the boat and go ahead of him to Bethsaida, on the other side of the lake, while he sent the crowd away. 46After saying goodbye to the disciples, he went away to a hill to pray. 47When evening came the boat was in the middle of the lake, while Jesus was alone on land. 48He saw that his disciples were having trouble rowing the boat, because the wind was blowing against them; so sometime between three and six o'clock in the morning he came to them, walking on the water. He was going to pass them by. 49But they saw him walking on the water. "It's a ghost!" they thought, and screamed. 50For when they all saw him they were afraid. Jesus spoke to them at once, "Courage!" he said. "It is I. Don't be afraid!" 51Then he got into the boat with them, and the wind died down. The disciples were completely amazed and utterly confused. 52They had not understood what the loaves of bread meant; their minds could not grasp it.

With reference to the pre-Markan tradition see the introduction to 6:32-44. Greek writers asserted that supermen and demons could walk upon the sea. The fact that in Job 9:8 (cf. 38:16) this ability is ascribed to God is more significant (in a similar way this ability is ascribed to "wisdom" in Ecclus. 24:5 f.). It has been suggested that originally this story described an appearance of the resurrected One (cf. John 21:1-14). It must be admitted that two entirely different themes have been fused in this story. The fact that Jesus intends to go on past the boat shows that he has not come to help them in the storm. Consequently, the stilling of the storm at the end of vs. 51 is a later addition. At the very most, the stilling of the storm is only hinted at in John 6:21 (cf. John 6:22-24, where the crossing of the lake by Jesus is all that is substantiated). This theme may have been brought in here from some story such as 4:35-41 and then it led naturally to the additions found in 6:48a. The actual story included these features: Jesus' lingering behind, Jesus' walking by during the night, the terror of the disciples who thought they were seeing a ghost, Jesus' entering the boat and his exhortation. At one time this may have been the description of an appearance of the risen Jesus, but it is more likely a story which pictured the divine power Jesus possessed during his earthly life. The meaning which this section has for Mark becomes clear in vs. 52. His editing can be seen in the theme of the blindness of the disciples as well as in the statement "their minds could not grasp it" (cf. 3:5a; 8:17b).

[45] The geographical notations are confused (cf. vss. 32 f.). The disciples are instructed to go to Bethsaida, but they don't land there until 8:22, and according to vs. 53 they disembark south of Capernaum. **[46]** The reason for Jesus' parting from the disciples is not quite clear. As in 1:35 Mark explains that he wanted to be alone to pray (in contrast to John 6:15). In this way Mark wants to show where the source of Jesus' authority is to be found. **[47]** The statement that the disciples are "in the middle of the lake" is not meant to convey geographical information, but to present the fact that the disciples are lonely and at the mercy of the storm. **[48]** This is further emphasized by the fact that they made scarcely any progress from evening until three o'clock in the morning. Usually the lake could be crossed in six to eight hours even under adverse circumstances. Perhaps Mark has understood Jesus' passing them by as a test of faith, which they failed immediately. **[49]** One can see Jesus and yet not see him (4:12), so that the result is a frightened scream. **[50]** This is because not until there is understanding of the Word, not until there is fellowship in dialogue with God, will one perceive the real miracle in those miraculous things which he sees. **[51]** The stilling of the storm is a picture of the peace in which Jesus dismisses a person (5:34) when he enters that person's life. The inbreaking of God, which shatters all customary standards, causes utter confusion. This is a sign of how little man actually believes in the reality of God (see 4:41). **[52]** This very thing is what Mark calls the "stubborn heart" (translated: "their minds could not grasp it"). In so doing Mark has put the disciples on a level with the Pharisees of 3:5.

And so this is another story which is seeking to arouse faith, this time in a manner which accentuates the marvel of God's condescension despite the incomprehensible blindness of man. For this reason the parallel to the feeding of the five thousand is reemphasized at the conclusion.

The Pursuit of Miracles 6:53-56;
cf. Matt. 14:34-36

[53]They crossed the lake and came to land at Gennesaret, where they tied up the boat. [54]As they left the boat, people recognized Jesus at once. [55]So they ran throughout the whole region and brought the sick lying on their mats to him, wherever they heard he was. [56]And everywhere Jesus went, to villages, towns, or farms, people would take their sick to the market places and beg him to let the sick at least touch the edge of his cloak; and all who touched it were made well.

This section may be the editorial work of Mark (cf. 1:32-34; 3:7-12; 6:33), in which he used the descriptions found in 2:3 f. and 5:28 as patterns (the parallels to 5:28 in Matthew 9:20 and Luke 8:44 mention "the edge of his cloak"). Perhaps Mark's summary serves a purpose similar to that of 8:11-13. In any case it is not Jesus' healing which is stressed—even though more healings are reported here than in 3:10 or 5:28 (which see). What is stressed is the coming of many people, which, while it manifests the tremendous influence of Jesus, indicates even more the blindness of those whose only interest is in the miraculous.

The Question about the Law 7:1-23;
cf. Matt. 15:1-20

[1]The Pharisees and some teachers of the Law who had come from Jerusalem gathered around Jesus. [2]They noticed that some of his disciples were eating their food with "unclean" hands—that is, they had not washed them in the way the Pharisees said people should.

[3]For the Pharisees, as well as the rest of the Jews, follow the teaching they received from their ancestors: they don't eat unless they wash their hands in the proper way, [4]nor do they eat anything that comes from the market unless they wash it first. And they follow many other rules which they have received, such as the proper way to wash cups, pots, copper bowls, and beds.

[5]So the Pharisees and the teachers of the Law asked Jesus,
"Why is it that your disciples do not follow the teaching handed
down by our ancestors, but instead eat with unclean hands?"
[6]Jesus answered them: "How right Isaiah was when he prophesied about you! You are hypocrites, just as he wrote:

'These people, says God, honor me with their words,
But their heart is really far away from me.
[7]It is no use for them to worship me,
Because they teach man-made commandments as though
they were God's rules!' "

[8]And Jesus said, "You put aside the commandment of God and
obey the teachings of men."

[9]And Jesus continued: "You have a clever way of rejecting
God's law in order to uphold your own teaching! [10]For Moses
commanded, 'Honor your father and mother,' and, 'Anyone
who says bad things about his father or mother must be put to
death.' [11]But you teach that if a person has something he could use
to help his father or mother, but says, 'This is Corban' (which
means, it belongs to God), [12]he is excused from helping his father
or mother. [13]In this way you disregard the word of God with the
teaching you pass on to others. And there are many other things
of this kind that you do."

[14]Then Jesus called the crowd to him once more and said to
them: "Listen to me, all of you, and understand. [15]There is nothing
that goes into a person from the outside which can make him unclean. Rather, it is what comes out of a person that makes him
unclean. [[16]Listen, then, if you have ears to hear with!]"

[17]When he left the crowd and went into the house, his disciples asked him about this parable. [18]"You are no more intel-
ligent than the others," Jesus said to them. "Don't you understand? Nothing that goes into a person from the outside can really
make him unclean, [19]because it does not go into his heart but
into his stomach and then goes on out of the body." (In saying this
Jesus declared that all foods are fit to be eaten.) [20]And he went
on to say: "It is what comes out of a person that makes him unclean. [21]For from the inside, from a man's heart, come the evil
ideas which lead him to do immoral things, to rob, kill, [22]commit

adultery, covet, and do all sorts of evil things; deceit, indecency, jealousy, slander, pride, and folly—[23]all these evil things come from inside a man and make him unclean."

(Vss. 6-7: Isa. 29:13. Vs. 10: Exod. 20:12; 21:17; Deut. 5:16.)

The hand of Mark is found first in vss. 3 f. These verses interrupt the statement which begins in vs. 2 and continues in vs. 5. Mark is concerned over the excessive number of regulations about purification, which seemed superstitious to the enlightened Hellenists of that day. In this way the Gospel writer emphasizes the fact that the question in vs. 5 does not apply to a single incident, but to legalism as a general principle which molds the whole of life. The answer to vs. 5 is given in vss. 6-8. Of course, the quotation from Isaiah is not altogether appropriate, since it is not really a matter of honoring God with words. Nevertheless, as is declared in vs. 8 in a summary fashion, the passage does set the divine law in opposition to human ordinances which are later additions. This contrast is found only in the Greek text of Isaiah 29:13 and not in the Hebrew original which was known to Jesus and to Palestinian Judaism. Thus we find here the attitude typical of liberal (Hellenistic) Judaism, which wants to adhere to the law, but not to the elaborate practice of the Pharisees which could not be carried out in foreign lands. Very likely the church appropriated this argument from liberal Jewish circles in a time when the boundary between the church and the Jewish community was still in a state of flux. Jesus himself, to be sure, did not say anything like this; his struggle is far more profound. In 2:23 ff.; 3:1 ff.; particularly in Matthew 5:21 ff.; and in Luke 18:9-14, it is not against some unusual abuse that Jesus sets himself, but against a legalistic understanding of the chief commandments; indeed, Jesus is opposed in general to the legalistic attitude which eagerly seeks honor in the sight of God. In vss. 9-13 another example is added which Mark certainly appropriated from the tradition, because he had no firsthand knowledge of such practices. Moreover, it deals with a very extreme case, the absurdity of which must be clear to everyone, since a particular minute regulation leads to a violation of one of the principal commandments. There is not even the suggestion that a genuine problem might be involved. To a Pharisee the issue was that obedience to God is considered even more important than love to father and mother, and this agrees in principle with Matthew 10:37 and Luke 14:26. The only part which is a basic principle and, therefore, consistent with Jesus' attitude is vs. 15 which, at best, is appropriate as an answer to vss. 1 f., 5. Presumably vs. 15 is the oldest kernel and may have been formulated originally as an answer to the problem of unclean food (see vs. 15). Furthermore, it may be assumed that, as a first step, the church in a very rationalistic manner added an exposition of the saying, first in vss. 18b, 19 and then in 20-23. In so doing the church made use of one of the current lists of vices (see comment on vss. 21 f.). As a second step, in vss. 1 f., 5 it has provided a suitable situation to illustrate the saying. Then, in the development of the tradition, the argument of liberal Judaism may have been added in vss. 6-8. Colossians 2:22 and a papyrus manuscript show that at other times the Christian church used this saying in a polemical way. This papyrus has Jesus use the same quotation in speaking to a man who called him "Lord" but did not believe in him (which, after all, is more nearly a "service of words" than is the question of the Pharisees found in this passage). Vss. 9-13 are then an additional example of this distinction between an ancient command of God and the newer human ordinances of Pharisaic custom. Mark probably took this example from the tradition and inserted it here. That this passage is a later insertion is evident also in that it speaks of "your teaching" (vss. 9, 13) instead of the teaching of the ancestors or "of men" (vss. 5, 8) and in that the words "how right," used in an ironical sense, are added to vs. 6 where they are meant seriously. Vss. 17, 18a, which are clearly Markan both in language and in content, show that what Mark considers the real point of the passage is the disciples' lack of understanding in spite of the clarity of Jesus' statement (vs. 15). Accordingly, he has to conclude the controversy with that lack of understanding and with Jesus' reprimand. This is why it was necessary for him to insert the illustration of their teaching in vss. 9-13, instead of at the end of the disputation. What is primarily important to Mark is this absurd Jewish legalism and Jesus' victory over it—a victory which is evident to everyone. This is the situation which prevailed in the post-Pauline era. Jesus had to carry on the real battle against the problem of legalism in an entirely different manner, as did Paul in the same way after Easter. They had to take the question seriously and expose the deepest root of legalism, which is man's desire to justify himself before God in order that he may be able ultimately to maintain his claim against God. This time was long gone and had given way to a far more rationalistic view. In the church of Mark's time the law was a temptation no longer; to the enlightened mind it seemed outdated and ridiculous. Accordingly, a papyrus states that Jesus proved the futility of ceremonial washings by pointing out that water cannot cleanse, since even dogs and pigs roll in it; and although prostitutes bathe and anoint themselves, they are not made clean inwardly. So Mark also stresses the absurdity of such a system of legalism with vss. 3-4 and the insertion of vss. 9-13 from the tradition. However, he is not concerned simply to present a rational explanation, because all this merely serves to reveal the incomprehensible blindness of even the disciples (vss. 17, 18a): to such a degree is man's heart hardened to the revelation of God; so difficult is the way of Jesus. From this standpoint it is easy to understand why Mark placed this passage where he did in the composition of his Gospel (cf. introduction to 6:32-44). The legalism which is described here and especially the blindness of the disciples contribute to the ever-increasing emphasis upon the rejection of Jesus by the world, and lead to the result given in 8:31. At the same time the blindness of the disciples stands out in contrast to the faith of the woman in 7:24-30, which is the first example of a glimmer of faith on the part of a Gentile.

[1] The rabbis exercised a kind of inspectorate over Galilee; but Mark mentions Jerusalem as the center of the opposition to Jesus (see 3:22), while he portrays Galilee as being more tolerant—somewhat like the Gentile church of the future (see 15:41). **[2, 5]** It is the church's attitude and not the attitude of Jesus which is under discussion. "Unclean" signifies secular—not sacred, not set apart for God. It is this separation of life into a religious or sacred sphere and a secular sphere, which does not belong to God, that was completely eradicated by Jesus. **[3]** "In the proper way" may be translated "with a handful of water" (the Greek is literally: "with the fist"). Is this referring to a symbolic rubbing by rotating the fist in the hollow of the hand, or does it mean: only the hand, as far as the wrist? The "teaching they received from their ancestors" refers to the Jewish exposition of the commandment of God as distinct from the commandment itself. **[4]** One is most likely to be unclean as the result of contact with others when he returns from the market. The word translated "to wash" can also be translated "to baptize." The detailed itemization indicates the scorn of the non-Jew for such absurd practices. **[5]** The question of vs. 2 is expanded to become a general principle; it does not apply merely to this one example, but applies in general to the attitude of freedom from law held by the community of Jesus. The question is tempered inasmuch as it is the exposition of the law which is discussed and not the law itself. **[6]** In Psalms of Solomon 4:7 the Pharisees reproved their opponents for "hypocrisy" (cf. Matt. 6:2, 5, 16; 23:13-29; etc.). Here the reproach is not directed against individual persons, but against basic principles. Legalism is a pseudo-holiness. Matthew uses the term "hypocrite" rather freely, and it is taken over in Didache 8:1 f. By this means an important point is clarified. Any piety which is striving for something measurable, whether the tribunal is one's own conscience, other men, or God, remains nothing more than a piety based upon appearances, because the externally visible is all that can ever be measured—the innermost person is inaccessible. Nevertheless, this is not the end of the matter. The situation was radically different for Paul in his earnest obedience to the law; consequently, he can reason more profoundly about the conquest of legalism by means of an ethic which, although it is not striving for approval, is no less demanding (cf. Gal. 5). **[7]** The quotation which follows merely presents the prophetic criticism of superficial piety. This criticism is enlightening, but it does not point out, as Paul did, the danger that instead of being humble before God, a man might demand recognition from him on the basis of such a piety. **[8]** Vs. 8 is illustrated in vss. 9-13. **[11]** "Corban" is what one says when he wants to dedicate an object to God, i.e., to withdraw it from ordinary use, but without handing it over directly to the temple treasury. **[9-13]** This example, which is shockingly clear to every Gentile, does not settle the question of the law, because in this case, at least, the later Jewish teachers are fully in agreement with Jesus. The only thing important about it is Jesus' attitude, which is continually and unconditionally oriented toward the needs of man (3:4). **[14]** With a common editorial expression Mark leads back again to the decisive saying in vs. 15, and emphasizes the significance that this saying has for the whole church beyond this particular controversy. As in 4:3, 23 f., the call to listen accentuates the figurative nature of the saying, because it can only be understood with "listening ears." **[15]** Vs. 15 is found slightly simplified in the Gospel of Thomas (14). With the declaration that the "things" of the world are never unclean, but are only made unclean by the heart of man, the fellowship of Jesus has affirmed faith in the goodness of creation as opposed to an asceticism which puts God's creation under suspicion. Therefore, this does not assert in any way that the inner life is more valuable than the external; the heart itself can be evil (vs. 21). These considerations frequently entered into discussions of the problem of table fellowship between Jews and Gentiles (Acts 10:14; 15:28; Gal. 2:11-17; Rom. 14:14; Col. 2:20-22). Paul clearly states that abstinence is wrong if by this means a man wants to acquire merit in the sight of God, man, or himself. It brings a blessing only when he practices abstinence as a part of his service to others. **[16]** "Listen, then, if you have ears to hear with!" (vs. 16) is missing in a few manuscripts. If Mark wrote this verse (like 4:9 before Jesus' teaching of the disciples, and 4:3 also), he did so because he desired another opportunity to emphasize the figurative nature of Jesus' teaching—a matter which was especially important to him (cf. vs. 14b). **[17, 18]** The blindness of the disciples is described here in stronger terms than in 4:13 (with respect to "house" cf. 2:1). Accordingly, the church is not a holy band separated from the world. If they are able to understand, it is a matter of pure grace—a miracle of God. **[19]** The conclusion of vs. 19 is strange; is it an ironical remark which states that ultimately any distinction in foods is lost in the process of elimination? Could it be a marginal gloss which asserted that Jesus declared that all foods are fit to be eaten? The second suggestion is more likely, because the passage reads literally: "in the excrement, cleansing . . ." not: "in the . . . cleansing excrement." **[21, 22]** This list of vices corresponds with similar compilations which probably arose in Hellenistic Judaism (cf., e.g., Rom. 1:29-31; Gal. 5:19-21; Col. 3:5, 8; 1 Tim. 1:9-10; 2 Tim. 3:2-5). The doing of "evil" is put alongside "covetousness" ("greed") in Romans 1:29 also, although it is likely that the words appeared there in the opposite order. This traditional combination probably explains the inclusion of such a general term. "Jealousy" (literally: evil eye) means envy or insinuation with evil intent, but it is not likely that it refers to magical practices. **[23]** In all of this it is no longer possible to make any neat separation between thought and action.

If one reflects on this section, the thing which is most striking is that in the name of common sense an ironical polemic is conducted against nonsensical legalistic practices. Naturally, there is nothing wrong about this; but the fact that this polemic is rooted in the Gospel, thus in the freeing of man from "works"—from everything whereby he thinks he must justify himself—can be seen only in the light of Mark's entire Gospel. However, the new orientation found here—away from any external deeds and to the inner life—points in this direction. The fact that the discussion here adds nothing important to the prophetic criticism which had already been appropriated by Hellenistic Judaism, is related to the fact that Mark is interested primarily in vs. 18a. In this verse he arrives at the Pauline position of "by grace alone" from an entirely different direction—from the problem of understanding God. With respect to the blindness of the disciples he points out the same thing that Paul indicates about the legalism of all men in general and not of the Jews alone—that man is so intent upon justifying himself that he cannot forget himself and, for once, let God be the only one who counts. What Mark presents in terms of discipleship (see 8:34 f.) is what Paul means by the freedom of faith in which man, just because he no longer has to assert himself, is able to live for God by grace and, consequently, to live from the heart.

The First Example of the Faith of the Gentiles 7:24-30;
cf. Matt. 15:21-28

[24]Then Jesus left and went away to the territory near the city
of Tyre. He went into a house, and did not want anyone to know
he was there; but he could not stay hidden. [25]A certain woman,
whose daughter had an evil spirit in her, heard about Jesus and
came to him at once and fell at his feet. [26]The woman was a
foreigner, born in Phoenicia of Syria. She begged Jesus to drive
the demon out of her daughter. [27]But Jesus answered, "Let us
feed the children first; it isn't right to take the children's food and
throw it to the dogs." [28]"Sir," she answered, "even the dogs under
the table eat the children's leftovers!" [29]So Jesus said to her, "For
such an answer you may go home; the demon has gone out of your
daughter!" [30]So she went back home and there found her child
lying on the bed; the demon had indeed gone out of her.

With reference to the position of this story in the composition of the Gospel, see the introduction to 6:32-44. In the immediate context the faith of the Gentile woman, who is free from the law, stands out against the background of Jewish legalism, the absurdity of which is not recognized even by the disciples. Apart from the transition in vs. 24 and the slight alteration of vs. 27a (see comment), this section is a single story organized entirely around the saying in vss. 27 f. One may wonder whether Jesus made some statement similar to Matthew 15:24 and in this way provoked the humble reply of the Gentile woman. In any case, like Matthew 8:5-13, the story must have been directed from the very beginning to the problem of the relation of the Gentiles to the Jews. Here, as in that passage, it is the faith of the Gentile which finds access to Jesus. In this experience the boundaries of Israel have been transcended, a feat which Jesus accomplished even though he seldom left the land of the Jews, encountered Gentiles only in exceptional cases, and did not launch any mission to them. If the decisive thing is no longer faithfulness to the law, but the attitude of faith to which Jesus is calling and which is presented here by way of an example, then the Gospel actually is offered to all nations. Without presenting anything like a mission to the Gentiles by Jesus, Mark has still emphasized in vs. 24a Jesus' crossing over to Gentile territory; because immediately in vs. 31 he has Jesus return to Lake Galilee even though it is to the semi-Gentile region on the eastern shore. Nevertheless, it is clear that the story had an important role in the discussions of the church concerning the mission to the Gentiles.

[24] Sidon is missing in a few manuscripts; probably it was eliminated later on account of vs. 31. The phrase "Tyre and Sidon" embraces all Phoenicia. The "house" helps to describe the large crowd which gathers even in Gentile territory (cf. 2:1). **[25]** In addition, the momentum of God's revelation is presented in this way. With reference to "evil spirit" see 1:23. **[26]** The supplicant is designated explicitly as a non-Israelite. She reminds one of 1 Kings 17:9, 17. **[27]** The word "first" (not found in Matthew 15: 26), which qualifies Jesus' reply, may have been added by Mark, who knew about the mission to the Gentiles which was conducted by the church in later years. The expression "feed" literally means "feed until full." It is uncertain whether Mark introduced this expression as an allusion to the two stories about the feeding of the multitudes and, therefore, has formed vs. 27a himself. The fact that the Jews call the Gentiles "dogs" has only indirect significance, if any, since the word chosen here indicates a household pet which was not greatly despised, and a dog is the only animal which would be suitable for the metaphor. **[28]** The salutation "sir" is typical of Gentiles, and is not found anywhere else in Mark (see comment on 11:9). **[29]** Matthew 8:5-13 records another breaching of the wall separating Israel and the Gentile world through Jesus' healing of a sick man, from a distance, on the basis of an extraordinary faith. **[30]** It is apparent in this passage also that the interest is focused upon this breakthrough, inasmuch as there is no proof of the healing nor is it applauded by a group of men—features which are part of the regular plan of miracle stories.

Although the word "faith" does not occur in it, this story about the problem of the relationship between Jew and Gentile exemplifies what faith is, because it portrays the humility and persistence of this woman who takes for granted that God will be merciful in Jesus, and who will not give up. She will not see or consider anything other than the promise for which she is hoping. In this way it is maintained that the gospel has no prerequisites on the basis of which one might claim personal merit. It is not the fulfilling of the law which saves (7:1-23), but the "heart" which expects everything from God and, to be sure, in Jesus. This does not mean that faith is salvation, because Jesus' promise alone is salvation—the promise which turns toward the difficulty in a very concrete manner so that faith is fulfilled in experience. That this has happened through Jesus is the important thing in this section and not the question of what function, if any, entreaty and healing had in the earthly life of Jesus.

The Miracle of the Opening of Deaf Ears 7:31-37; cf. Matt. 15:29-31

[31]Jesus then left the neighborhood of Tyre and went on through
Sidon to Lake Galilee, going by way of the territory of the Ten
Towns. [32]Some people brought him a man who was deaf and
could hardly speak, and begged Jesus to place his hand on him.
[33]So Jesus took him off alone, away from the crowd, put his fingers
in the man's ears, spat, and touched the man's tongue. [34]Then
Jesus looked up to heaven, gave a deep groan, and said to the man,
Ephphatha, which means, "Open up!" [35]At once the man's ears
were opened, his tongue was set loose, and he began to talk without any trouble. [36]Then Jesus ordered them all not to speak of it
to anyone; but the more he ordered them, the more they told it.
[37]And all who heard were completely amazed. "How well he does
everything!" they exclaimed. "He even makes the deaf to hear and
the dumb to speak!"

7:14 has summoned all to listen and understand. Nevertheless, even the disciples did not understand the principle of victory over the law; but the fact that a Gentile woman had realized something of that victory was a symbol of things to come. At this point Mark inserts the miracle of the healing of a deaf-mute and brings the division to a close in a way that is reminiscent of Isaiah 35:5, which declares that the opening of the ears of the deaf and the eyes of the blind is expected in the future salvation-time. Therefore, by simply rearranging the material, Mark has given an entirely new meaning to a miracle-story which already was a part of the tradition. Mark is responsible for the strange information about the route in vs. 31, as well as the intensification of the Messianic secret and its disclosure (see comment on 1:34 and 1:45) in vs. 36, while vs. 37 probably presents the original conclusion of the story (at one time it may have been the conclusion of a series of miracle-stories).

[31] The impossibility of this route of travel must be illustrated by an example from closer to home, e.g., going from New York to Washington by way of Boston down the Mohawk Valley (see comment on 5:1). Apparently the naming of all the foreign lands around Galilee is a way of saying that the message is available to the Gentile world. **[33, 34]** That Jesus' work takes place in secret indicates that God works quietly and does not perform like a showman. The gestures are the only way in which Jesus can speak to the deaf-mute; consequently, even in this instance the fact is preserved that in his healing Jesus addresses the person. Surely Jesus' groaning is to be understood as in 1:41. With reference to the use of Aramaic words (*Ephphatha*) see comment on 5:41. **[35]** That "his tongue was set loose" (literally: "the bonds of his tongue were loosed") perhaps still indicates (like the deep groan in vs. 34) an original notion of demonic restraint. The speaking of the man who is healed is presented in Greek as a continuous activity in contrast to the previous actions which occurred only once. **[36]** The command to be silent (see 1:34) cannot be carried out in practice here either, and is promptly broken. This expresses the truth which Mark wants to present here: God's revelation breaks out with power and cannot be stopped, but nothing whatever is achieved either by the sensation caused by the miracle or by the astonishment over it. **[32, 37]** The allusion to the Isaiah passage from which, apparently, comes the rather unusual word for "dumb" in vs. 32 (translated "could hardly speak" but not used in vs. 37) which is used to refer symbolically to the activity of "wisdom" in Wisdom of Solomon 10:21, hints that this miracle marks the beginning of the special salvation-time. Probably this is the way the story was interpreted before Mark. But for him this special salvation-time comes with God's revelation which will be given openly in 8:31. In chapter 8 a miraculous feeding, the hostility of the Pharisees, the disciples' lack of understanding, and the miracle of the opening of blind eyes by Jesus are found following one another once more. After that Jesus' secret will be disclosed and through God's miracle the ears, mouths, and eyes of men will be opened to God, who will reveal himself in Jesus' path of suffering.

The Authority of Jesus to Feed Four Thousand 8:1-10;
cf. Matt. 15:32-39

1Not long afterward, another large crowd came together. When they had nothing left to eat, Jesus called the disciples to him and said: 2"I feel sorry for these people, because they have been with me for three days and now have nothing to eat. 3If I send them home without feeding them they will faint as they go, because some of them have come a long way." 4His disciples asked him, "Where in this desert can anyone find enough food to feed all these people?" 5"How much bread do you have?" Jesus asked. "Seven loaves," they answered.

6He ordered the crowd to sit down on the ground. Then he took the seven loaves, gave thanks to God, broke them, and gave them to his disciples to distribute to the crowd; and the disciples did so. 7They also had a few small fish. Jesus gave thanks for these and told the disciples to distribute them too. 8Everybody ate and had enough—there were about four thousand people. 9Then the disciples took up seven baskets full of pieces left over. Jesus sent the people away, [10]and at once got into the boat with his disciples and went to the district of Dalmanutha.

With reference to the incorporation of this passage into the total composition of the Gospel, compare the introduction to 6:32-44 and the conclusion of the exposition of 7:31-37. This story is a duplicate of the account in 6:32-44. The pity of Jesus, the conversation with the disciples, their perplexity, the inquiry of Jesus about the number of loaves, the distribution by the disciples after the blessing and the breaking of the loaves, the fish which are a later addition, the having enough to eat, the gathering of the left-over pieces, the dismissal, and the journey across the lake are reported here also. The fact that after the experience described in 6:32-44 the disciples now (vs. 4) have no idea whatever about what can be done cannot be explained psychologically. This very impossibility is what is important to Mark, who was the first to put the two variant accounts side by side. He wants to use this means to show how absolutely and unimaginably blind man is to the activity of God.

[1] As usual, no detailed information is given about time and place. Accordingly, it is not Mark's desire to stress that this feeding took place in Gentile territory, while the other occurred in Jewish territory. **[3]** Therefore, it is unlikely that the expression "a long way" in vs. 3 (cf. Joshua 9:6; Isa. 60:4; Acts 2:39; Eph. 2:11 ff.) contains a symbolic reference to the Gentile Christians. **[1]** Jesus' calling the disciples to him is reported with one of Mark's favorite expressions, although here it does have much significance. This expression is important to Mark because the disciples' lack of understanding is to be presented. In comparison with 6:35 f., it seems likely that this form of the account in which Jesus takes the initiative is the later of the two. **[2]** With reference to Jesus' pity compare 6:34. The power of attraction which proceeds from Jesus is made more impressive and the situation more urgent by the mention of the three days. **[3]** The deliberations of Jesus, who of course already knew what he would do, appear artificial in any psychological and historical examination, but this deliberation emphasizes the impotence and helplessness of man. It has been assumed that the crowd had gathered in a desert although it has not been mentioned until now (vs. 4). **[4]** Ever since 6:32, whenever the disciples make their appearance, Mark presents their lack of understanding. **[5]** Jesus' question agrees word for word with the account in 6:38-43, and the description of the distribution, of the having enough, and of the gathering of the pieces is almost identical. **[6, 8]** The statement "gave thanks to God, broke them, and . . ." is the same, word for word, as in 1 Corinthians 11:24. Did the church which handed down this narrative perhaps employ this as a liturgy for the Lord's Supper, and did the church which handed down 6:32-44 employ a somewhat different liturgy? The numbers are changed, so the increase does not seem to be quite as great; the reference to the green grass and the arrangement in groups is lacking; and the prayer of thanks instead of the blessing (however, cf. vs. 7 [Greek: "he blessed them"]) is more in accordance with Hellenistic usage. **[7]** Obviously the fish are a permanent part of the story, but they have been placed at the end. If they had been included earlier the parallel with the Lord's Supper would have been lost. **[9]** The word used for "basket" here is different from the one in 6:43. Some think this word designates a smaller basket, but that is unlikely since the same word is used in Acts 9:25. **[10]** No one knows where Dalmanutha is located.

The story was told first as a miracle-story designed to extol the unlimited divine power of Jesus. Surely the relationship to the Lord's Supper came to be associated with it very soon. What theological truth Mark wishes to express through this passage, in addition to that which he presented in 6:32-44, will not be clear until 8:17-21.

The Demand for a Sign 8:11-13;
cf. Matt. 16:1-4 (12:38 f.; Luke 11:29)

11Some Pharisees came up and started to argue with Jesus. They wanted to trap him, so they asked him to perform a miracle to show God's approval. [12]Jesus gave a deep groan and said: "Why do the people of this day ask for a miracle? No, I tell you! No such proof will be given this people!" [13]He left them, got back into the boat, and started across to the other side of the lake.

In the tradition this section was already associated with the story of the miraculous feeding (see 6:32-44), and in this context it is well adapted to Mark's purpose because it provides another illustration of the blindness of man. The saying of Jesus in vs. 12 is the nucleus and everything else forms the framework around it. This saying is preserved in Q also, which is the reason Matthew reports it twice (12:39; 16:4). The material in Mark 6:45—8:27 is not found anywhere in Luke except that Luke 11:16 contains the expressions "wanted to trap him" and "a miracle to show God's approval" which are found in Mark 8:11, while the saying of Jesus does not appear until Luke 11:29 in the Q version. The sign of Jonah is promised in Q, which has influenced Matthew 16:4. The strange formulation in Mark (literally: "if a sign will be given to this generation!") speaks in favor of its being the original wording. Additional support is found in the fact that in other places "the people of this day" is used almost exclusively in contrast to "the Son of Man," as is true in Luke 11:29 f. (Matthew 12:39 f., *q.v.*). Thus when Mark received the saying it was already polished and abbreviated, since the reference to Jonah was no longer understood (this is confirmed by the attempt to give the saying a new meaning in Matthew 12:40). This saying was connected with the story of the miraculous feeding before Mark, because he speaks nowhere else of "signs" (the only exceptions are in 13:4, 22), but of "mighty deeds" (cf. John 6:30).

[11] The place from which the Pharisees came is not mentioned. The Pharisees were "wanting to trap him" in 10:2 and 12:15 also, but here the question is not the kind of controversial issue which the community of Jesus might have disputed with Judaism. The demand for a sign can only be granted or refused. So the issue here is not some specific problem, but the fundamental question of what faith is. "Heaven" (translated here: "to show God's approval") could be simply a paraphrase for "God," but it is more likely that it means a sign which no ordinary miracle-worker would be able to perform—a cosmic miracle of an apocalyptic nature. Such a demand, however, is a desire to trap. To be sure, it is the very earthly nature of God's activity to which Mark gives unusual emphasis. He knows, however, that everything becomes false as soon as a sign is demanded—as soon as faith becomes dependent upon visible proof. For then faith would be nothing more than a logical conclusion which anyone ultimately might draw without becoming involved. It is the same as in the case of a husband who hires a private detective to gather proof of his wife's faithfulness. He would not strengthen the love between himself and his wife; he would destroy it. Compare 4:35-41. **[12]** Jesus' groaning is mentioned as in 7:34 (see 1:41). In order to explain the way Jesus' refusal is worded in Greek, one must assume that the form normally demanded some expression such as, "may I be accursed." On the other hand, it could be interpreted as a question in the sense of "Should perhaps . . .?" **[13]** It looks as if Jesus is the helpless one; but actually he abandons them and they remain behind, bereft of God's presence.

The original saying of Jesus—it makes no difference whether the Markan form or the Q form is older—warns that before coming to know God, one must not form a priori a picture of God for himself by which he can test the actions of God and decide on the basis of his own standard whether or not God has really acted in a specific instance. The church which connected this saying to the story of the miraculous feeding wanted to distinguish at this point between the sign given freely by God, which summons man to ask questions and strengthens his faith, and the sign demanded by man, which destroys faith. Finally, by the inclusion of this story in his total composition Mark emphasizes again the blindness of men who misunderstand the sign of God in Jesus, and who would rather seek security than allow that sign to summon them to faith. In contrast to this, he is probably indicating in the brief concluding statement that the potentiality of discipleship is entirely different: faith comes when one steps into the boat with Jesus and does not prefer to remain in safety on the shore.

The Blindness of the Disciples 8:14-21;
cf. Matt. 16:5-12

14The disciples had forgotten to bring any extra bread, and
had only one loaf with them in the boat. 15"Look out," Jesus
warned them, "and be on your guard against the yeast of the
Pharisees and the yeast of Herod." 16They started discussing
among themselves: "He says this because we don't have any
bread." 17Jesus knew what they were saying, so he asked them:
"Why are you discussing about not having any bread? Don't you
know or understand yet? Are your minds so dull? 18You have
eyes—can't you see? You have ears—can't you hear? Don't you
remember 19when I broke the five loaves for the five thousand
people? How many baskets full of leftover pieces did you take up?"
"Twelve," they answered. 20"And when I broke the seven loaves
for the four thousand people," asked Jesus, "how many baskets
full of leftover pieces did you take up?" "Seven," they answered.
21"And you still don't understand?" he asked them.

(Vs. 18: Isa. 6:9 f.; Jer. 5:21; Ezek. 12:2.)

Mark has revised this section extensively. Since the misunderstanding of the disciples in vs. 16 does not depend in any way upon the one loaf, it is likely that Mark has taken the description of the situation in vs. 14 from the tradition. Vs. 15 also contains a saying which was part of the tradition. It appears in Luke 12:1 in an entirely different context and is a most unfortunate choice for presenting the cause of the misunderstanding in vs. 16. This is the clue which indicates the importance Mark attaches to this misunderstanding by the disciples for which there is no psychological explanation. If vs. 15 is put into parentheses, vs. 16 makes much better sense, because it then follows vs. 14 and presents a story in which the disciples are concerned about the lack of bread and are reproved by Jesus for their little faith: "Why are you discussing the fact that you do not have any bread? Don't you remember

. . .?" In keeping with his regular tendency, Mark has increased his emphasis upon the disciples' misunderstanding by inserting Jesus' severe indictment in vss. 17b, 18. Finally, this emphasis is made more impressive by the repetition of the reference to the miraculous feeding, something which could not have been done by anyone other than Mark (see 8:1-10). In this passage Jesus uses almost the same expressions as appear in the two stories and in the same combinations in which they are found, e.g., the same two words for "basket." This shows that Mark, who had both stories of the miraculous feedings with their exact wordings at his disposal, was the one who formed these sayings of Jesus in detail. These signs of editorial compilation reveal how unusually important this passage is to his proclamation. Moreover, this passage characterizes the entire fourth division: As divisions II (3:1-6) and III (6:1-6a) close with the stubbornness of the Pharisees and Jesus' fellow citizens, so this division closes with the stubbornness of the disciples. Now the point has been reached where the only thing which can open the blind eyes is the miracle of Jesus' self-disclosure in 8:27-32, which is announced symbolically in 8:22-26.

[15] To the rabbis "yeast" symbolized something evil, especially the evil desire of sin (cf. Lev. 2:11; 1 Cor. 5:7 f.). Perhaps it is also its infectious, continuous operation which is referred to here (cf. Matt. 13:33; Gal. 5:9; 1 Cor. 5:6). **[16]** The misunderstanding is almost absurd and is extremely striking for that very reason. "Because" is translated from a Greek particle which also means "that." Perhaps the simple meaning "they were worried, because (or that) they had no bread" has been altered by the insertion of vs. 15; so that now we ought to understand it this way: "(he says this) because they have no bread" or, following other manuscripts, "because we have no bread." **[17, 21]** The real point here is found in Jesus' rebuke. What applied to the Pharisees in 3:5 was stated concerning the disciples immediately after the first miraculous feeding in 6:52 (see comment). **[18-20]** In this passage the disciples are in addition accused of the charge which in 4:12 is directed against "the others, who are on the outside"—those who are lost. Yes, here the charge is really more severe: Hasn't God done all that he could—even fed thousands; has he not taken special pains on behalf of these disciples who still do not understand but remain blind and deaf? Man is so enmeshed in his own world and its cares that he always interprets God's metaphorical language in a crassly literal sense and is not drawn by that language to the kind of faith in which he surrenders himself to the one whom he can never capture in words and concepts, but can only experience (vss. 19 f.; see comment on 3:23). Faith knows that again and again it stands in the place where those who are "on the outside" stand. It is no virtue of its own which separates it from unfaith—it is only the divine miracle which is repeated over and over. This leads to an ultimate solidarity of the church with the "world."

The story concludes with a question which continues to be a question for the reader as well. Although originally this brief story may have reproved and sought to overcome their little faith by the reference to Jesus' miracle, Mark has transformed it into a description of the total blindness and deafness of man to God's metaphorical language. He has done this in order to accentuate the divine miracle which bestows faith. This truth will be presented again in the following section before Jesus reveals his pathway to the cross in 8:31 and the new possibility of discipleship in 8:34.

The Miracle of the Opening of Blind Eyes 8:22-26

22They came to Bethsaida, where some people brought a blind
man to Jesus and begged him to touch him. 23Jesus took the blind
man by the hand and led him out of the village. After spitting on
the man's eyes, Jesus placed his hands on him and asked him,
"Can you see anything?" 24The man looked up and said, "I can
see men, but they look like trees walking around." 25Jesus again
placed his hands on the man's eyes. This time the man looked
hard, his eyesight came back, and he saw everything clearly.
26Jesus then sent him home with the order, "Don't go back into
the village."

This is a brief miracle-story to which Mark has added only the first and last short sentences. He has, however, transformed the story in a very decisive manner by including it at this particular point (see 6:32-44 and 8:14-21). The wording of vss. 22-24a corresponds in large measure with that of 7:32-34a. There is agreement in much of the subject matter also: Jesus takes the man aside, he makes certain gestures, he spits and touches the affected member, he commands the man to keep silent. It is no longer possible to determine whether or not Mark has assimilated these two stories stylistically. It is more likely that the stories had already been assimilated in the development of the tradition. It is also possible that originally there was only one story which developed into two very different forms.

[22] Bethsaida is a city (Luke 9:10), but vss. 23, 26 speak of a village. Probably there was no indication of where this story took place and the first short sentence should perhaps be added to the end of vs. 21 (cf. 6:45). **[23-25]** Here for the first time the subject is a blind man. The healing by stages is unusual. Surely it does not mean that healing can be performed only in proportion to the amount of faith which a person has at a particular time. Apparently, in this popular narrative, it is merely a means of presenting more graphically the difficulty of the healing and the magnitude of the miracle. Afterward it may have become a picture of the growth of faith for Mark. **[26]** Probably he is the one who emphasizes the Messianic secret (see 1:34) once more in the last verse. In a number of manuscripts vs. 26b reads, "Don't speak about this to anyone in the village!" However, the English translation "Don't go back into the village" has good textual support. One may suspect that the unusual use in Greek of "into" with the meaning "in" is responsible for the change from the first reading to the second. Then it would have been one more warning against attributing too much importance to the miracle itself.

It is obvious that the only things which are described here are the healing and, in greater detail, the sight which is restored. Nothing is said about the reaction of the one who is healed or of the reaction of any others. For this reason Mark regards this story as a last clear reference to the divine miracle which alone can open the eyes of the blind. This forms a sharp contrast to vs. 18 which speaks of human potentialities. Consequently, Mark places this section immediately before the dialogue in Caesarea Philippi in which Jesus will reveal his secret openly.

V

JESUS' OPEN REVELATION AND THE MEANING OF DISCIPLESHIP 8:27—10:52

Peter's Misunderstanding,
Jesus' Teaching about the Suffering of the Son of Man,
and the Disciples' Lack of Understanding 8:27-33;
cf. Matt. 16:13-23; Luke 9:18-22

27Then Jesus and his disciples went away to the villages of Caesarea Philippi. On the way he asked them, "Tell me, who do people say I am?" 28"Some say that you are John the Baptist," they answered; "others say that you are Elijah, while others say that you are one of the prophets." 29"What about you?" he asked them. "Who do you say I am?" Peter answered, "You are the Messiah." 30Then Jesus ordered them, "Do not tell anyone about me."

31Then Jesus began to teach his disciples: "The Son of Man must suffer much, and be rejected by the elders, the chief priests, and the teachers of the Law. He will be put to death, and after three days he will be raised to life." 32He made this very clear to them. So Peter took him aside and began to rebuke him. 33But Jesus turned around, looked at his disciples, and rebuked Peter. "Get away from me, Satan," he said. "Your thoughts are men's thoughts, not God's!"

In spite of the tension between Peter and Paul (Gal. 2:11 ff.), Peter and James (in Gal. 2:9 James is mentioned before Peter; compare Acts 21:18), or Peter and the "disciple whom Jesus loved" (John 21:20 ff.), there is no evidence of any opposition to Peter in the church of the first century; therefore, vs. 33 could not have arisen in that kind of situation, but must be an authentic saying of Jesus. Peter must have said something prior to this which produced Jesus' reaction. Scholars who consider it impossible that Jesus designated himself as the "Son of Man" regard vs. 33 as the original reply to vs. 29, because the title of Messiah included the expectation of a king who would restore Israel's national glory. It must be admitted that it is hard to conceive of Jesus actually giving the detailed announcement of his suffering found in vs. 31. If he had told them, the complete helplessness of the disciples on Good Friday and their stubborn doubt despite the appearances of the resurrected One would scarcely be comprehensible. Perhaps this is another case where a brief saying of Jesus has later been expanded and embellished with details. This explanation is favored by the possibility that the beginning of the verse—"The Son of Man must suffer much [a common Jewish expression], and be rejected"—might be the ancient form of the saying (cf. Luke 17:25; Mark 9:12), which later was enlarged by the addition of the material that follows. As in many ancient formulas (e.g., Luke 22:15; Acts 1:3; Heb. 13:12; 1 Peter 4:1; etc.), "suffer" originally included "dying." In the present text, where it is distinguished from "be put to death," it can refer only to mistreatment, and mistreatment logically would come after the phrase "and be rejected." Vs. 30, then, where the Messianic secret (see 1:34) is introduced, is the work of Mark. Certainly the title of Christ is absolutely correct (cf. 1:1), but it cannot be understood apart from vss. 31 and 34. Probably at one time the beginning of vs. 31 simply stated, "Then Jesus said," but has been reformulated in this context with typical Markan expressions because he regards the following statements as the real content of Jesus' teaching (see comment on 1:21-28). Moreover, he clearly emphasized this same thing with the beginning of vs. 32. Jesus' questions in vss. 27, 29 may have been revised to a certain extent under the influence of catechetical instruction, although this would have happened before Mark. But, from the historical standpoint, could Jesus have spoken of the suffering Son of Man? This is widely contested.

The Son of Man. This title, which in Hebrew and Aramaic simply means an individual man (e.g., Ps. 8:4), appears in the Gospels:

(a) in the description of the Jesus who returns for judgment, (b) in the statements about the Passion, (c) as a description of the earthly Jesus. A number of scholars have considered the passages classified under (a) to be the oldest. If this is true, then three possibilities emerge. (1) The title might have been introduced by the church, because it expected the Kingdom of God to begin when Jesus returned in the near future. Gradually, however, they began to designate the earthly Jesus in the same way. Of course this suggestion is contradicted by the fact that "Son of Man" occurs only in sayings of Jesus, except for Acts 7:56, which may originally have read "Son of God" (in the Greek of Rev. 1:13 "Son of Man" is used without the article and is an Old Testament image). On the other hand, titles such as "Christ" or "Servant of God" appear very frequently in the church's statements about Jesus, but almost never in Jesus' own sayings. The explanation for this must be that prophets in the early church would have spoken in the name of Jesus (as is the case in Revelation, chapter 2) and would have spoken primarily about apocalyptic events, consequently about the coming of the "Son of Man" for judgment, while preachers and teachers would more likely have spoken in the third person of "Christ" or the "Servant of God." (2) On the basis of Mark 8:38 and Luke 12:8 f., one may come to share the opinion of other New Testament scholars that Jesus expected someone other than himself to appear soon as the "Son of Man." Of course, this seems very unlikely. Statements like Matthew 5:21 ff.; 11:11; Luke 11:20; 17:20 f. indicate that Jesus did not consider himself to be merely the messenger of a yet greater "Son of Man." His call to discipleship and the fact that he never introduced his sayings as the prophets did with "Thus saith the Lord" prove the exact opposite. The primary objection is that such an expectation is not in harmony with Jesus' attitude toward the future: he believed that the future was already impinging upon the present. Moreover, if Jesus had announced the coming of another, Easter would not have led the disciples to identify Jesus with that person. They would have had more encouragement than ever to wait for the coming One after God had confirmed his messenger (as, e.g., the people thought God had done in the case of the Baptist, Mark

6:14). It is hardly possible that Jesus, who avoided anything of an apocalyptic nature, would have used to denote the coming of a heavenly figure a title which at that time was familiar only to small separatist groups. The phrase "son of man" does occur in Daniel 7:13, but it is a symbolic representation of Israel, who after a long period of suffering has finally been justified and exalted. It is contrasted with the previously described animals which represent the world empires. Accordingly, the "son of man" comes to God, and not from God to earth. We do not know whether a heavenly Son of Man had been mentioned in any other Jewish writings. According to 2 Esdras 13:3 ff., the Son of Man will arise from the sea in the end-time and destroy his enemies; but the earliest date which can be assigned to 2 Esdras is the end of the first century A.D. In the Book of Similitudes (Ethiopian Enoch 37-71) the Son of Man, who now sits enthroned in heaven, is described as officiating in the future as judge. However, we cannot be sure when this was written, since fragments from every chapter of the other books of Enoch have been found in Qumran, but not one single fragment from this book. (3) If we assume that the use of this title originated with Jesus himself, since it occurs exclusively in the sayings of Jesus, it would then be conceivable that Jesus appropriated it from Daniel 7:13—a verse which already had been given an apocalyptic interpretation. In so doing Jesus would have designated himself as the one who is coming again for the final judgment—as the one who is being proclaimed on earth as the "Son of Man." All the objections to the second possibility apply here as well. There is an additional problem. If the Jesus who was living on earth had spoken of his own coming again, he would have had to state that he would die first and be raised again. But no such assertion is ever found in connection with the statements about his coming again; the announcements of Jesus' death and resurrection are always kept separate.

There is, however, another way in which this title is used in the Old Testament. Ezekiel is called "son of man" about 87 times. As the "son of man" he must be filled with the Spirit of God (2:1 ff.; 3:24 f.; 11:4 f.), be a watchman for Israel (3:17; 33:7), eat God's Word and deliver it to the people (3:1 ff.). He not only has to observe Israel's sins (8:5 ff.), but also must live in the midst of those who have eyes to see but see not, who have ears to hear but hear not (12:2 f.), who talk about Ezekiel and run after him, but do not obey his word (33:30 ff.), because they think the judgment is a long way off (12:27). Therefore, his preaching takes the form of riddles and allegories (17:2; cf. 20:49). He must proclaim disaster (6:1 ff.), pronounce judgment upon sinners (20:3 f.; 22:2; 23:36) and almost destroy them (11:4-13; 21:14 ff.). He must take upon himself privation and suffering as symbols of Israel's distress (4:9 ff.; 5:1 ff.; 12:6, 11, 17 ff.; 24:16 ff., 27). But he is privileged to announce the coming of the good shepherd (34:23 ff.), the cleansing by the Spirit in the end-time (36:25 ff.), the resurrection of the dead (37:1-14; for Ezekiel this was a metaphor, but it came to be interpreted literally), and the future glory (40:4; 43:7, 10; 47:6 ff.). Indeed, he is permitted to inaugurate the resurrection and world judgment (37:9 f., cf. 15 ff.; 39:17 ff.). Perhaps Jesus called himself "Son of Man" in the way Ezekiel did in order to describe the commission he had received from God to serve in lowliness and in suffering (cf. Matt. 8:20; 11:19, et al.). This means that the most original of Jesus' sayings would be the ones about the earthly Son of Man. This conclusion is confirmed by the fact that the statement that the Son of Man would be "handed over" appears frequently, and by the fact that the expression "the people of this day," which is typical of Jesus' preaching of repentance, is mentioned quite often in connection with the title "Son of Man." Sayings of this kind show more of the characteristics of genuineness than do the sayings about the Son of Man coming with the clouds of heaven. When Jesus applied the title "Son of Man" to himself it would be logical for him to expect to experience the destiny of the innocent sufferer. Ever since the time of Isaiah 53 the Israelites believed that the career of anyone who wished to be obedient to God would lead to suffering and death. But it was natural for that one to hope also to be exalted to the throne of God (Isa. 52:13, 15; 53:12) and to have a part in the final judgment (Jubilees 4:23; 10:17; Syriac Baruch 13:3; and primarily Wisdom of Solomon 2:10-20; 4:7, 10, 16; 5:1-5, where the career of

Jesus is described in detail). On the basis of these passages and of Ezekiel's experience, Jesus realized that his own destiny was to accomplish the ultimate fulfillment of the suffering of Israel and of her prophets and righteous men. If Jesus was to be granted a role in the future judgment in addition to the career of the innocent sufferer, then he did not consider himself to be just one of many witnesses (as in Wisdom of Solomon 5:1-5). He regarded himself as *the* witness, who in a unique way enters into the final judgment speaking for or against those who have received or rejected his call, because the manner in which men have received him will determine their judgment: Mark 8:38 (see comment). It is only in the church's concept of Jesus that he himself moves more and more into the position of Judge (cf. Rom. 2:3-11; 14:10 with 2 Cor. 5:10; 1 Cor. 4:4-5). Consequently, instead of speaking of the coming of the Kingdom of God (Mark 9:1; Luke 22:18), or of God's coming to judge (as in the Old Testament), the church spoke of the coming of the Son of Man. Probably this conception was then adopted by Jewish apocalyptic groups and transferred to the Jewish Messiah (Ethiopian Enoch 46:1 ff.; 48:2 ff.; 62:2-16; 69:26 ff.; 2 Esdras 13:3 ff.). Christians, on the other hand, used Jewish expressions and concepts in declaring their own beliefs. There is no material difference between what the church has said in this way and what Jesus said. He, too, asserted that the witness of the Son of Man would actually decide the outcome of the judgment. Yes, Jesus intended to say that the present attitude of men toward the earthly Jesus would decide their future judgment; consequently, it was no longer possible for them to postpone their "yes" or "no"—their believing in him or their hardening of heart. In vs. 38 Jesus declares that one's present conduct in relationship to the lowly and suffering One will be remembered on the day of judgment. In this sense the God who judges on the last day will be in fact none other than the Son of Man who stands before them now.

In any case Jesus is unique in that he does not compare himself with the prophets, with the righteous, or with the teachers of the Old Testament. He considers his career to be basically different from all other careers. For this reason he has called his disciples to follow him and has explained to them that their eternal life depends upon whether or not they listen to his call. If the last of these three explanations is correct, then "Son of Man" is, at one and the same time, a title of lowliness as well as a title of majesty. It describes a ministry of suffering exactly as it did in the case of Ezekiel, only now as the eschatological fulfillment. This ministry is carried out at God's command and will be the basis upon which salvation and destruction are apportioned some day. This lowly One who has been rejected by men will be exalted to the right hand of God in exactly the same manner as the innocent sufferer is exalted, but, once again, as the eschatological fulfillment. As the exalted One he will judge those who have received him and those who have rejected him. At the present time it is not possible to decide with certainty between this hypothesis and the first one, nor can we entirely eliminate the other explanations so long as we have no more evidence. Nevertheless, serious consideration must be given to the view that in Mark 8:27-38 an event in the life of Jesus has been reported accurately in all its essentials.

[27] Luke does not mention the location where this event occurred (he omits everything in Mark 6:45—8:27); consequently, for him the scene takes place in Bethsaida (Luke 9:10) and could be regarded as the conclusion of the preceding story. Mark's mention of Caesarea Philippi comes as a surprise, because it is not one of the more familiar places, nor is this merely a statement of general location. Nevertheless, it is a very appropriate place since, according to rabbinical statements, it is on the boundary between the Holy Land and Gentile territory. This is the place where Jesus must decide whether he will abandon Israel or do the exact opposite—set out on the perilous journey to Jerusalem. Probably the designation of the location is a part of the tradition. In any case, Mark is vague about many geographical details (cf. 5:1; 7:31; 10:1; 11:1), and it is well-nigh impossible to discover any motive for his introducing them. **[28]** With reference to vs. 28 compare 6:15. There are not many names more honorable than these which "people" ascribe to Jesus, but even these are inadequate. **[29]** With the words "What about you?" Jesus makes a distinction between his disciples and "people" in general. In this way he transforms a discussion which is more or less noncommittal into a dialogue in which the disciples must become personally involved and be held accountable for what they say. Accordingly, here is how genuine confession comes about: A man is interrogated and in response he attempts to express by means of a bold, new formula the philosophy by which he lives. For this very reason the form in which the confession is made is not the result of careful and leisurely reflection. According to the Gospel of Thomas (13) Peter called Jesus "a righteous angel" and Matthew called him "a philosopher." But here Peter calls him by the name which has been hallowed in the Old Testament, "the Anointed One" ("Messiah" in Hebrew and "Christ" in Greek). On the basis of Zechariah 4:14 the people of Qumran expected two messiahs—one a priest, and the other a king. The title indicates that Jesus is the one for whom Israel has waited throughout the centuries; but the nature of Jesus' career is so new and unusual that the old terminology (according to which the "Messiah" is an earthly king with supernatural power) is no longer adequate. **[31]** Jesus, therefore, coins a new name, "Son of Man" (see above), which can mean simply "a man" (as it does in Aramaic) and be understood as a humble designation of himself such as Paul uses in 2 Corinthians 12:2. At the same time this title can direct the hearer's attention to the prophetic ministry of Ezekiel and, through what is said about that "son of man," point beyond him. In any case, its meaning had not become fixed as yet through rigidly defined usage. God's revelation is given in this way: The one who is popularly acclaimed as the prophet, as the reappearance of Elijah, or as the Messiah, is defeated. This is further accentuated by the statement which the church has added declaring that it is the Sanhedrin with its seventy-one members which condemns the Son of Man. These members are the nobility who were eligible for the office of high priest; the "teachers of the Law," i.e., the trained theologians (who were also lawyers since the law of God was the law of the state, cf. 1:22); and the "elders," i.e., the laity. The rejection of the Son of Man is thus no accident; but a conscious, deliberate "No" to him. The world's rejection of God is so complete that even the church hierarchy, of all people, refused to accept him. This suffering is not explained (see 10:45); but God's holiness is such a contrast to the way of the world that his suffering becomes inevitable.

[30] The title of Messiah (Christ) had been familiar in the church for a long time. Consequently, it was only in terms of his theory of the Messianic secret (see 1:34) that Mark was able to explain Jesus' use of a different name in his reply in vs. 31. (The word translated in vs. 30 as "ordered" occurs also in 1:25; 3:12; 4:39; 8:32, 33; 9:25; 10:13, 48, and can be translated as "scold" or "denounce.") Apparently Jesus carefully avoided the title "Christ" during his entire ministry. Mark's situation is different, because after Easter the name Jesus Christ included the concept that a man who had been crucified was the Messiah, so the idea of a successful national king was excluded. Moreover, the very thing which hindered Jesus from using this title may have made it very appropriate for Mark and his Messianic secret: Man must be warned that if he simply adopts a traditional expression as a name for Jesus, he may not be able to encounter him authentically and without bias. When one is aware that he is talking to a clergyman, it happens frequently that a false notion of what a clergyman is prevents the man from really listening to the clergyman. On the other hand, one who is deeply impressed by another without knowing who he is can exclaim afterward: He is truly a clergyman! Mark is saying that this is why what is announced in vs. 31 must occur before the person who has met the crucified and risen One can attempt to tell what has happened to him in his own language, the language of the community. Mark stresses the importance of this occurrence by designating vs. 31 explicitly as Jesus' "teaching" (see 1:21 f.). **[32]** Its importance is most clearly emphasized by the statement "He [Jesus] made this very clear to them." A similar formula in 2:2 indicates the beginning of the controversy concerning the law and in 4:33 marks the conclusion of the parables. There it was asserted that it was necessary for Jesus to speak about God in metaphors because no other form of speech would have been intelligible to man. Now, however, this very open way of speaking about God signifies the end of all figurative speech. **[31]** What then is affirmed about God in these direct words? "The Son of Man must suffer much, and be rejected." God is God inasmuch as he can do what man cannot: He can permit himself to be rejected—to be lowly and insignificant. Man, however, would be plunged into an inferiority complex, showing that he wants with all his heart to be great. Whoever understands the suffering of the Son of Man has understood God. It is here and not in heavenly glory that he sees the heart of God. According to 4:35, Jesus drew his disciples apart from the people and went with them into the storm. This gave rise to the question: "Who is this man . . .?" (4:41). **[29]** Now Jesus, alone with his disciples, has asked them, "Who am I?" In spite of all its orthodoxy Peter's reply shows that he has no better understanding than the demons in 3:11 and 5:7, who gave a far better answer. **[33]** His response reveals that the disciples (vs. 33a includes all the disciples with Peter, cf. 14:37) belong to the world of "men" just like everyone else, and not to God's world. On this point Mark differs from the people of Qumran and other apocalyptic groups, who saw themselves as the exceptional few chosen out of the world.

In Mark's estimation the gulf between God and man can only be spanned when that which is announced in vs. 31 comes to pass—when the rejected and slain Son of Man endued with the power of the resurrection draws men into his discipleship and makes their hearts receptive to God. Therefore, the invitation in vss. 34 ff. is extended to everyone and not simply to the twelve. What the heart of the gospel is for Mark is formulated here in a manner entirely different from the way in which Paul writes in 1 Corinthians 1:18—2:9, and yet the content is very similar.

Discipleship 8:34—9:1;
cf. Matt. 16:24-28; Luke 9:23-27

34Then Jesus called the crowd and his disciples to him. "If anyone wants to come with me," he told them, "he must forget himself, carry his cross, and follow me. 35For the man who wants to save his own life will lose it; but the man who loses his life for me and for the gospel will save it. [36]Does a man gain anything if he wins the whole world but loses his life? Of course not! [37]There is nothing a man can give to regain his life. [38]If, then, a man is ashamed of me and of my teaching in this godless and wicked day, then the Son of Man will be ashamed of him when he comes in the glory of his Father with the holy angels."

[1]And he went on to say: "Remember this! There are some here who will not die until they have seen the Kingdom of God come with power."

In this passage five separate sayings of Jesus have been brought together. It is likely that this arrangement developed with the passing of time. The first two sayings appear in Matthew 10:38 f. in a slightly different form. They are separated in Luke (14:27 and 17:33). In both Matthew and Luke (as well as in the Gospel of Thomas 55) the first of these is joined to the saying about hating (or having less love for) one's father and mother. The fourth saying (vs. 38) occurs in Matthew 10:33 and Luke 12:9. The announcement of the suffering of the Son of Man (vs. 31) must have been associated with the call to discipleship (vs. 34) and the statement about saving the true life (vs. 35) long before Mark, since it is found also in John 12:24-26, although the individual sayings have assumed an entirely different form there. Jesus may have been the one who connected these sayings. The introduction to vs. 34 is typical of Mark. Nevertheless, in 3:23 he inserted a similar formula into a context which was available to him in finished form.

[34] Mark emphasizes that the sayings which follow apply to everyone and not merely to a select group. Vs. 33 indicated how impossible it is to separate the band of disciples from the world. At the same time vs. 34 shows how important these statements are to Mark, because in them the correct understanding of vs. 31 is achieved for the first time. It is no longer possible to assert with any certainty what the original form of the saying was. It would not have been possible to find "come with me" (literally: "come after me") and "follow me" side by side in Jesus' native tongue, since there is only one expression in Aramaic for both. It is likely that the ancient form has been preserved better in Matthew 10:38. One may wonder whether Jesus spoke only of "forgetting oneself" and then after his death the symbol of the cross was added by the church as an illustration of self-denial. But crucifixion was very common, and the figure of the condemned man who takes up his cross and starts out on the way to his execution is so full of meaning that it could have originated with Jesus. This is not very likely, however, since before Jesus' crucifixion, the figure would normally have been associated with a criminal. There are no Jewish parallels from the time of Jesus. The *carrying* of the cross is mentioned for the first time in Luke 14:27. The original picture describes one who is prepared to die—one who has surrendered his life and must manifest this fact in a concrete way. Self-denial is the same thing. In Mark 14:71 f. "denial" signifies "I do not know the man." It designates freedom from oneself and every security, whether the security be some earthly possession or the certainty of a claim upon heavenly reward. It indicates a freedom in which one no longer wills to recognize his own "I"—a freedom which is possible only when man commits himself completely to God. Paul calls it a crucifying of the flesh in a life of the Spirit (Gal. 5:24 f.). John designates it as being born from above and not of the flesh (3:5 f.). Something like this happened when the disciples forsook boat, family, tax office, to accept Jesus' invitation to a life of discipleship. Such is the attitude which one must have in order to understand this very plain way of speaking about God (vss. 31 f.).

[35] The next saying is preserved in four different forms: (a) Mark 8:35, (b) Matthew 10:39, (c) Luke 17:33, (d) John 12:25. Perhaps (a) is the oldest. Of course, Mark is the one who has added the words "and for the gospel." He wants to affirm, and rightly so, that the saying still applies after Jesus' death. Probably the words "for me" were added in the development of the tradition as an explanation. These words are not found in (c) or (d). Surely Jesus would have said "for the sake of the Kingdom of God" (Luke 18:29; cf. Mark 10:29). Nevertheless, there would be no need to add these words for those disciples who were already following Jesus. In discipleship to Jesus there is a reversal of values. To assert oneself leads to loss; to give oneself leads to the gaining of "life." Like the corresponding Semitic expression, the Greek word *psyche* means "soul" as well as "life." Consequently, it is clear that "natural" and "religious" life cannot easily be separated. Jesus' saying implies that one finds real life—even earthly, natural life—only in the giving up of self. He who desperately wishes to cling to life is the very one who sacrifices the possibility of life that is genuine and happy. Life, as the Creator meant it to be, can only be found in renunciation. This is the only way it can be an unfettered, free, open life which is receptive to God and one's neighbor. Such a life will not end with death, because it belongs to God already and he will stand by that life through every experience of death. This truth has already been indicated by the end of vs. 31. This does not mean, however, that one may exchange this life for a higher one—an eternal life—by means of ascetic practices as is affirmed in Jewish and Greek parallels, because this would permit man to cling to himself—and to his future. The saying signifies a life of discipleship which is possible only in following him who has given his life for all. It is a life in which Jesus has become predominant to the extent that one is no longer influenced by humiliation or by exaltation (Phil. 4:12). This is true because the one who is oriented toward God's Name, God's Kingdom, and God's will has become free from himself.

[36] At one time vs. 36 may have been a proverb which implied that riches have absolutely no value when death comes. In the present context it accentuates the exhortation in vs. 35: Whoever is determined to assert himself may even win the world; nevertheless, in the end he will lose himself and fail to attain the possibility of a truly fulfilled life. **[37]** There is nothing which can compensate for this loss.

[38] Vs. 38 is more difficult. The concluding statement is not found in the parallels in Matthew 10:33 and Luke 12:9. Nowhere else are "Son of Man" and "Son of God" (which is implied inasmuch as Jesus calls God "Father") found side by side in the same context. This statement must be an explanation which has been added by the church. Moreover, the bringing together of Father, Son, and holy angels (this is clearer in Luke 9:26) is found also in 1 Timothy 5:21; cf. 1 Thessalonians 3:13; Revelation 1:4 f. (Although for the author the seven "spirits" represent the Holy Spirit, they stand before God's throne in Rev. 4:5 as the "angels" do in Rev. 8:2.) Obviously this feature is typical of a church which has an apocalyptic orientation. Apparently the oldest form of the saying is preserved in Luke 12:8 f. The unusual distinction made between "I" and "Son of Man" can be traced to Jesus, since it was taken for granted by the church that these were equivalent terms. That Jesus by his choice of words did not intend to say that another Son of Man would come is discussed in the introduction to 8:27-33. This statement is clear if we emphasize that the final judgment will be determined now by the decision of the hearers as they confront the man Jesus. Jesus is speaking of that judgment in modest terms which portray his role objectively, just as in 2 Corinthians 12:2 Paul switches suddenly to the third person and speaks of "a man" (in Aramaic it would be "Son of Man") when he speaks of a mysterious divine experience. Moreover, Paul uses the objective language of Old Testament quotations to describe the wrath of God on the day of judgment (Rom. 2:6; 11:8-10; etc.). The phrase "this generation" (translated here: "this . . . day") is found frequently in connection with "Son of Man" and sets him apart from the human race which is no longer serving God. Compare the introduction to 8:27-33.

[1] Finally, the Markan formula "he went on to say" is used to introduce a saying about the nearness of the future Kingdom of God. Perhaps this is not the original context, since the saying deals with the coming of the Kingdom of God in power and not with the coming of the Son of Man. Of course, Mark is thinking only of the judgment described in 8:38. The phrase "will not die" (literally: "taste death," which is a common idiom for "die") requires an interpretation which implies that the end of the world is expected to come during the lifetime of a few of Jesus' contemporaries. This means that they had calculated on a rather short span of time between Jesus' death and the end. It is doubtful whether this saying may be traced to Jesus since he explicitly rejects any attempt to calculate the time of the end (Luke 17: 20 f.; cf. Mark 13:32). It may have arisen in the church because of the church's desire to dispel the growing impatience by referring to the imminence of the end. This creates difficulties for us since the fulfillment did not come in the way that was expected. But whenever a person reckons earnestly with God's intervention he cannot relegate it to the distant future, as if it were not as yet a very serious matter. For this reason the prophets expected the coming of the Day of the Lord in the very near future, in conjunction with contemporary events. This can be compared to looking at several mountain ranges which are separated by many miles, and yet one range appears to tower directly above another. 9:1 does not reflect Jesus' manner of speaking. The way in which he speaks clearly indicates that the future event will be decided at the precise moment when his word encounters man (8:38). Nevertheless, 9:1 is concerned about the same thing: Man should not be deceived about the imminence of the coming of God. But now it is no longer possible to repeat that message in the form which at one time was appropriate.

A review of 8:27—9:1 shows that Jesus announced the suffering of the Son of Man, something which ran counter to Peter's expectation, and that with all his might he checked every attempt to avert that suffering. Only one who is willing to be called as a disciple understands Jesus and, as a disciple, learns that real life is found in self-denial. This kind of "yes" to Jesus will be remembered in the future judgment. At that time God will keep his word of promise and, despite the earthly experience of death, the true life will be the sure possession of the one who has renounced his life to follow Jesus. In the figure of the Son of Man who is coming soon, the church on several occasions has clearly presented the nearness of God's approach to man. This nearness as it closes in on man was also proclaimed by Jesus (vs. 38c). Above all, the church made it even clearer that it is only on the basis of Jesus' death on the cross that a man can "carry his cross" and enter discipleship. Finally, at the very center of his Gospel Mark has accentuated the extreme importance of this saying by designating it as Jesus' "public" teaching which supersedes all his teaching in parables and by emphasizing that it applies to the whole world. What Mark says in this way, which applies to the whole world, is that all the promises and expectations, including those implied by the title "Christ," are fulfilled only in the suffering of the Son of Man and in man's acceptance of discipleship (8:27-38).

God's Response to the Clear Statement in Regard to the Suffering of the Son of Man 9:2-8;
cf. Matt. 17:1-8; Luke 9:28-36

[2]Six days later Jesus took Peter, James, and John with him, and led them up a high mountain by themselves. As they looked on, a change came over him, [3]and his clothes became very shining and white; nobody in the world could clean them as white. [4]Then the three disciples saw Elijah and Moses, who were talking with Jesus. [5]Peter spoke up and said to Jesus: "Teacher, it is a good thing that we are here. We will make three tents, one for you, one for Moses, and one for Elijah." [6]He and the others were so frightened that he did not know what to say. [7]A cloud appeared and covered them with its shadow, and a voice came from the cloud: "This is my own dear Son—listen to him!" [8]They took a quick look around but did not see anybody else; only Jesus was with them.

(Vs. 7: Ps. 2:7; Isa. 42:1; Deut. 18:15.)

It is no longer possible to explain the history of the tradition of this passage. Probably Mark has digressed in vs. 6 in order to emphasize once more how blind the disciples were to God's revelation. The statement is much more appropriate in 14:40. Vs. 7 is reminiscent of 1:11. Is it the memory of Jesus' baptism which has caused this feature to be incorporated here? It has been suggested that this is the altered version of an Easter appearance. This is unlikely because there is no Easter story which tells of a divine voice, heavenly companions, or the visible glory of Jesus. On the other hand, although every Easter account includes a saying of Jesus, there is none here; nor is there any reference to death and resurrection. Moreover, we know of a story in which the resurrected Jesus appears to Peter and the twelve (1 Cor. 15: 5) but none where he is seen by three disciples. Details of the description are closely akin to Jewish visions of the end-time. Perhaps this is the account of an experience of the three disciples (or even a vision) that was portrayed in apocalyptic colors by the church, which interpreted the coming of Jesus as the beginning of the end.

[2] The only other place where there is a specific statement about the time an event occurred is in the Passion narrative. Is this an attempt to emphasize the similarity to Exodus 24:16? Has Mark retained this statement because it links the transfiguration with the preceding section? With reference to the mountain, compare Exodus 24:13 where Moses and Joshua (Jesus in the Greek Old Testament) went up the mountain to receive the divine revelation. The same three disciples were selected also in 5:37; 13:3; and 14:33. These three were chosen whenever there was need for the utmost secrecy. **[3]** The transfiguration of Jesus is reminiscent of Exodus 34:29 ff. (In the biblical history as narrated for the people by Pseudo-Philo [11:15—12:1], who was nearly a contemporary of Mark, the events of Exodus 34:29 ff. are placed very near those of 24:15 f.) However, there is no reference here to any radiance on Jesus' face. Judaism was expecting the righteous to be transfigured with celestial glory and resplendent beauty in the end-time (Syriac Baruch 51:3 ff.; cf. Mark 12:25; 1 Cor. 15:51 f.). Paul too regarded the present life of the believer in this light (Rom. 12:2; 2 Cor. 3:18; and Phil. 3:21). White is the color of the angels (Mark 16:5; cf. the Son of Man in Rev. 1:13 ff., which resembles Dan. 7:9, 13). The wearing of new or white clothing as the symbol of life in the resurrection is mentioned also in Ethiopian Enoch 62:15 f.; Slavonic Enoch 22:8; Revelation 3:4; 7:9 (cf. Rev. 4:4; 1 Cor. 15:43, 49, 51-53). Things which men were expecting on the day of judgment have already occurred in Jesus, things similar to what happened in the case of Moses. **[4]** The glory of the end-time dawns upon Jesus. Ever since the announcement in Malachi 4:1-6 men had expected Elijah to reappear shortly before the end. Occasionally Enoch also was included, because according to the Old Testament he and Elijah were the only men who were translated to God without dying (cf. 2 Esdras 6:26, from the end of the first century A.D.). It seems that certain Jewish groups may have inferred from Deuteronomy 34:6 that Moses also was translated, because the Jewish writer Josephus takes issue with such speculation around A.D. 93/94 (*Antiquities* IV:326). In contrast to Revelation 11:3 ff., where the prophets of the end-time who are clearly identifiable as Moses and Elijah are considered equals, in this passage the old view is still dominant which regards Elijah as the decisive figure of the end-time (cf. 9:11-13). Moses appears as Elijah's companion because of the similarity between him and Jesus, to which reference has been made, and in vs. 5 he is even mentioned first. **[5]** Booths were built at the Feast of Tabernacles in memory of the wilderness wandering. Is this description based upon something which the disciples experienced at the Feast of Tabernacles? In that case the only strange element would be the extra booths for Moses and Elijah, since the building of booths was customary. It is more likely that, from the beginning, the story has served to emphasize Peter's mistaken notion that the eschatological rest in which God and his heavenly retinue would dwell upon earth had already begun (Rev. 21:3; cf. John 1:14. The same Greek root is used in each passage). **[6]** In any case, Mark lays special stress on Peter's mistake. **[7]** In Judaism, clouds played an important role in theophanies (e.g., Exod. 16:10; 24:18; 40:35; Ezek. 1:4) and in accounts of translation to heaven (Ethiopian Enoch 14:8; Acts 1:9; 1 Thess. 4:17; Rev. 11:12). The church expected Jesus to appear on a cloud when he returned in the end-time (Luke 21:27; cf. Mark 13:26; 14:62; Rev. 1:7). The message of the divine voice agrees with 1:11 except for the change from second to third person, which Mark considers to be very important: what is transacted there between Father and Son alone is now revealed to the three intimate friends. The words "listen to him!" are added as another designation of Jesus as the one who fulfills the ministry of Moses (Deut. 18:15). Probably they have special reference to Jesus' teaching in vs. 31. For Mark these words call the church away from fanatically longing for the end to come—back to listening—back to the Word, i.e., to the Good News. **[8]** This is why the appearance concludes so abruptly: Jesus is all that is given to the church. Any visions which could point to the dawning of the end are meant only to indicate the dimension in which one should view those things which will happen to Jesus in his Passion (vs. 12).

This story has united two expectations which were alive in Judaism: the coming of the prophet of the end-time who is like Moses and the appearing of Elijah at the dawning of the end-time. It has declared to every Jew that the fulfillment of the history of Israel and of every hope for the glorious end-time have already begun with the coming of Jesus. It is likely that Mark placed this section immediately after 8:27—9:1 not because he regarded it as an anticipatory fulfillment of 9:1 but because he wanted another opportunity to designate 8:31 as the center of his Gospel. Jesus' straightforward speech, which brings an end to all parables (8:32), corresponds to God's own clear declaration (9:7; cf. 3:11 f.). When Jesus' secret is revealed for the first time, it is revealed to a select three. Until now this secret has been betrayed only by the demons. Moreover, God's declaration dispels any fanaticism on the part of the disciples in which they might regard the glorious end-time as having come already upon earth. It points them to the Word—that very saying which presents the suffering Son of Man (8:31; 9:12). In 9:5 f. Mark emphasizes, as he does in 8:32b, that the disciples themselves lack understanding. The heavenly vision passes away; the message is all that abides. The vision can only underscore the importance of that message.

The Discussion Concerning the Coming of Elijah and the Suffering of the Son of Man 9:9-13;
cf. Matt. 17:9-13

[9]As they came down the mountain Jesus ordered them: "Don't
tell anyone what you have seen, until the Son of Man has been
raised from death." [10]They obeyed his order, but among them-

selves they started discussing the matter: "What does this 'rising
from death' mean?" 11And they asked Jesus: "Why do the teachers
of the Law say that Elijah has to come first?" 12His answer was:
"Elijah does indeed come first to get everything ready. Yet why do the Scriptures say that the Son of Man will suffer much and be
rejected? 13I tell you, however, that Elijah has already come, and that people did to him all they wanted to, just as the Scriptures say about him."

The continuity of this passage is obscure. The connection between vss. 9-10 and 11-13, which do not really deal with the resurrection, is very loose. Is it possible that formerly vss. 11-13 followed directly on vs. 1? If this is true, then Mark has inserted the narrative in vss. 2-8, after which he has made the transition back to vss. 11-13 by means of vss. 9-10, which undoubtedly are his own creation. Or are vss. 11-13 simply joined to the catchword "Elijah"? (See comment on 9:41-50.) If Jesus was identified with the reappearance of Elijah, vss. 11-13 might be viewed as dealing with a single theme: The expectation (vs. 11) is correct (vs. 12a), and reaches fulfillment in the activity of Jesus; nevertheless, the suffering of the Son of Man is announced (vs. 12b); in this way he is like Elijah, whose persecution is described in the Old Testament (vs. 13). This suggestion is not impossible, since the old expectation regarded Elijah as the forerunner of God when he comes for judgment, and not as the forerunner of the Messiah. The use of the past tense in vs. 13, while the present tense is used in vs. 12a, favors the application of vs. 13 to the Elijah of the Old Testament. If this was its original meaning, then it may have been formulated at first in a way that would not have been misunderstood so easily. "At that time when Elijah had come . . ." Vs. 13 seems to refer most naturally to 1 Kings 19:2, 10. Of course, it has been interpreted in a different way in Matthew 17:13. In any case, the Baptist had been identified with the reappearance of Elijah before Mark (see 1:6 and cf. Matt. 17:12 f.). Since presumably even contemporary Judaism expected Elijah to come as the forerunner of the Messiah, it is more likely that the text presupposed this identification from the very beginning. In this way two assertions are placed side by side. (a) Elijah has really come in the person of the Baptist; (b) the fate of the Baptist, which has given eschatological fulfillment to 1 Kings 19:2, 10, is prophetic of the fate of the Son of Man. Surely this is the way Mark interpreted it, whether Mark's view corrects an earlier misconception or is in conformity with the original meaning. The two themes are so intertwined that their relationship has become illogical.

[9] The scene of the descent from the mountain of eschatological glory into the depths of human insecurity and need has been portrayed very impressively in a well-known painting by Raphael in the Vatican. Once again Mark is emphasizing the Messianic secret (see 1:34). A proclamation of the majesty of Jesus would be possible only in the post-Easter church which knew of the crucifixion also (cf. 8:30). This is the only passage which refers to Jesus' coming resurrection without mentioning his suffering and death (with the exception of vs. 12!). Surely this is due to the fact that it was the resurrection and not the crucifixion which moved the disciples to begin preaching. This statement about the resurrection is worded in a way that is reminiscent of 8:31. Consequently, all the heavenly splendor of Jesus in miracles and visionary experiences can only signify that the cross and the resurrection are the center of the public proclamation which began after Easter. **[10]** A Jew would not have questioned what the resurrection might be. It is Mark's way of presenting the fact that the disciples were totally blind to God's revelation. **[11]** Probably the reason why the statement about the return of Elijah was important to the church is that the Jews contended that the Christians were wrong in asserting that the end was very near, since Elijah had not returned as yet. **[12, 13]** The destiny of "Elijah" as prophetic of the suffering of the Son of Man is far more important to Mark than the mere fact of his coming (in the person of the Baptist).

Whatever the original meaning of these verses may have been, they are for Mark another description of the transition from a theology of glory to the theology of the cross. Without these verses it would be impossible to gain a proper understanding of the transfiguration. Thus the declarations of triumph in 9:1 and 9:2-8 are bracketed by and interpreted by 8:31 and 9:12. No reason for the suffering is given which might make it easier to endure; no, there is only the statement that the suffering is imposed by God and is necessary, as was the fate of John the Baptist–Elijah.

The Healing of the Boy with Epilepsy and His Father's Lack of Faith 9:14-29;
cf. Matt. 17:14-21; Luke 9:37-43a

[14]When they joined the rest of the disciples, they saw a large crowd there. Some teachers of the Law were arguing with the disciples. [15]As soon as the people saw Jesus, they were greatly surprised and ran to him and greeted him. [16]Jesus asked his disciples, "What are you arguing with them about?" [17]A man in the crowd answered: "Teacher, I brought my son to you, because he has an evil spirit in him and cannot talk. [18]Whenever the spirit attacks him, it throws him to the ground, and he foams at the mouth, grits his teeth, and becomes stiff all over. I asked your disciples to drive the spirit out, but they could not." [19]Jesus said to them: "How unbelieving you people are! How long must I stay with you? How long do I have to put up with you? Bring the boy to me!" [20]And they brought him to Jesus. As soon as the spirit saw Jesus, it threw the boy into a fit, so that he fell on the ground and rolled around, foaming at the mouth. [21]"How long has he been like this?" Jesus asked the father. "Ever since he was a child," he replied. [22]"Many times it has tried to kill him by throwing him in the fire and in the water. Have pity on us and help us, if you possibly can!" [23]"Yes," said Jesus, "if *you* can! Everything is possible for the person who has faith." [24]The father at once cried out, "I do have faith, but not enough. Help me!"

[25]Jesus noticed that the crowd was closing in on them, so he gave a command to the evil spirit. "Deaf and dumb spirit," he said, "I order you to come out of the boy and never go into him again!" [26]With a scream the spirit threw the boy into a bad fit and

came out. The boy looked like a corpse, so that everybody said, "He is dead!" [27]But Jesus took the boy by the hand and helped him rise, and he stood up.

[28]After Jesus had gone indoors, his disciples asked him privately: "Why couldn't we drive the spirit out?" [29]"Only prayer can drive this kind out," answered Jesus; "nothing else can."

It appears that Mark may have known this story in two different versions. In vss. 14-19 and 28 f. the story is told in a way that centers the interest entirely upon the disciples and their ignorance. In vss. 20-27 the interest centers upon the father. The illness is described twice: in vs. 18 and in vss. 21 f. The people are already present, according to vss. 14 and 17, but according to vs. 25 they are just assembling. Mark has combined these two stories because he has found both versions helpful in defining what faith is in the discipleship of Jesus. This is why he has included the story at this point in his Gospel instead of putting it with the other miracles of Jesus. Moreover, this is the reason for the absence of the Messianic secret (see 1:34) from this passage—Jesus is not proclaimed by the demons or by the one who is healed, and Jesus does not insist that he keep silent.

[14] Strictly speaking it should say, "the other nine disciples." Perhaps the story referred merely to "the disciples" before Mark inserted it here. **[15]** The astonishment and fear of the people show, as does 1:27, that Jesus comes with an authority which is entirely different from that of the teachers of the law (1:22), and that this authority emanates from him even before he speaks or acts. **[16]** What follows has no relationship at all to any controversy between teachers of the law and disciples of Jesus. Yet the very fact that the introduction in vss. 14-16 does not really fit this specific situation makes the purpose of the introduction clear. That purpose is to give the story universal application and show that a fundamental issue is being considered here, not simply an individual case. In so doing, attention is focused on the band of disciples (consequently on the church) which is engaged in controversy with its enemies because of its faith. **[18]** In contrast to their master, the disciples' difficulty is their lack of authority due to their unbelief. Thus it is not easy to distinguish between the disciples and the teachers of the law on the basis of what they may or may not know. What distinguishes between them is the place to which they turn for help. **[19]** Jesus' saying (cf. Jer. 5:23; 1 Kings 19:14; Num. 14:27; Deut. 32:5, 20) shows that he does not belong to this "unbelieving generation" but stands diametrically opposed to it. He stands at God's side, grieving with God at the distress caused by such unbelief. The saying shows clearly that this unbelief is the primary cause of Jesus' suffering. It is impossible to read this text without submitting to the demands of the saying, which is the main point of this section. **[20]** The authority of Jesus is presented as something which forces itself upon us the moment Jesus meets us. There is no opportunity to postpone one's decision until there is time to reflect upon Jesus' words and actions. Accordingly, the evil spirit detects that authority before Jesus speaks to him. In response he offers resistance and challenges Jesus to combat. This indicates how the presence of God can produce storm and stress before anything constructive is accomplished. **[21]** The obstinacy of the disease is portrayed very dramatically. **[22]** As in vs. 18, all of the regular symptoms of epilepsy are evident. The expression "if you possibly can" has been formulated deliberately along the lines of the answer expected from Jesus; it is an excellent description of the father's superficial faith. **[23]** Strictly speaking, Jesus' answer refers to his own faith; however, it is clearly intended to portray the entire history of the distress of human unbelief and superficial faith (vss. 19, 22, 24) and to offer help for it (vss. 23, 28 f.). **[24]** The outcry of the father reveals his anguish. From this anguish is born the answer which is probably the finest ever given to this question. Whoever dares to say "I believe" must say, in the same breath, that he can make this assertion only as one who trusts God to help him again and again to believe. He must confess that the subject of that faith ultimately must be "God" and not "I." Only in the knowledge of his unbelief can one acknowledge the divine gift of faith joyfully and with assurance. It is impossible to be confident unless one is relying upon God's action. Therefore, faith is that unconditional receptiveness to the action of God—that constant expectation that as often as one looks to himself he will discover nothing but unbelief. In looking to God, however, he joyously and confidently confesses that God will continue to heal this unbelief. As in 2:5, it is not the faith of the sick man which is being discussed, but the faith of another. It is obvious that the narrator is not thinking of a healing through the power of suggestion. **[25]** On the contrary, the healing of the boy is described, as in 1:25 (cf. 4:39), as a challenge—i.e., a conflict with the enemy in which Jesus stresses his authority with a very emphatic "I." **[26]** The magnitude of Jesus' act is revealed in the description of the difficulty of the healing. **[27]** The expression used in connection with the cure is the Easter affirmation: "Jesus . . . helped him rise, and he stood up." If sickness and healing were already conceived of in terms of death and resurrection in the Old Testament (e.g., Ps. 30:3), then the significance of this mighty act of Jesus is clear also: On the surface it appears to be no more than the healing of a sick person; but underneath, the reader catches a glimpse of the one who someday will actually raise the dead. **[28]** The separation of the disciples from the masses indicated by the word "privately" (a typical Markan expression) and the teaching "indoors" (cf. 2:1), which preserves the significance of the story for the church, are typical of Mark. **[29]** The reference to prayer requires no explanation. Therefore the disciples have misunderstood the story if they seek for some special method by which they can overcome the misery of their impotence. Perhaps the truth that all power is found in God and not in the inner being of the believer is stressed more emphatically by Jesus' call to prayer than by his call to faith. There is no room whatever for human achievement; all that man can do is be receptive to the action of God. Of course, this was not understood by the copyists who added the words "and fasting" (which are found in many manuscripts), because to them prayer alone seemed too simple. They were not able to perceive that what is simplest and most taken for granted is really most important, since it causes one to cease looking at himself, and look to God.

In this particular passage there is a very urgent call to discipleship. By means of this story and its explanation, which is found in vss. 28 f. and to some extent in vss. 14 f., Mark wants to proclaim that this kind of discipleship does not result from the effectiveness of one's own piety but only from the action of God. For this reason the man who is called is that one who realizes the inadequacy of his own faith and continues to be entirely dependent upon God. This is the man who has learned to pray. So this story is in the proper place, between the first and second announcements of the suffering of the Son of Man.

Jesus' Second Teaching about the Suffering of the Son of Man 9:30-32;
cf. Matt. 17:22 f.; Luke 9:43b-45

30They left that place and went on through Galilee. Jesus did
not want anyone to know where he was, 31because he was teaching
his disciples: "The Son of Man will be handed over to men who will kill him; three days later, however, he will be raised to life."
32They did not understand what this teaching meant, but they were afraid to ask him.

[31] This is probably the oldest form of Jesus' announcement of his Passion: "The Son of Man will be handed over to men." The play on words gives a unique emphasis to the fact that he who is a man among men is still basically different from them and will be rejected by them. "Handed over" intimates that God himself is active in this event, although it does not say so explicitly. Consequently, the possibility remains that it refers to the action of man—for example, the action of the betrayer. The interrelationship between human action and the will of God is not dissolved. The statement invites us to believe, but this does not mean that it is a proposition which may simply be accepted as true. The reference to death and resurrection is a later explanation (cf. Luke 9:44). **[30]** Finally, the literary framework which Mark has supplied makes Jesus' statement stand out in bold relief. The primary emphasis is placed once more upon the Messianic secret (cf. 1:34), i.e., the inability of man to understand Jesus. The reason given for Jesus' withdrawal from public view is that he might announce his Passion. **[31]** He does not want any public acclaim because his path leads to the suffering of the Son of Man. This "teaching" of Jesus differs from all "preaching" done before or after (see 1:22); it is the real revelation of God. **[32]** It is so truly the revelation of God that it remains totally foreign to man, even to the chosen disciples who share in Jesus' instruction. God's world and man's world remain separate, as in 8:33. If faith comes at all, it will only be as an absolute and incomprehensible divine miracle (cf. 15:39).

The Ignorance of the Disciples and Discipleship 9:33-37;
cf. Matt. 18:1-5; Luke 9:46-48

33They came to Capernaum, and after going indoors Jesus asked his disciples: "What were you arguing about on the road?" 34But they would not answer him, because on the road they had been arguing among themselves about who was the greatest. 35Jesus sat down, called the twelve disciples and said to them: "Whoever wants to be first must place himself last of all and be the servant of all." 36He took a child and made him stand in front of them. Then he put his arms around him and said to them, 37"The person who in my name welcomes one of these children, welcomes me; and whoever welcomes me, welcomes not only me but also the one who sent me."

Just as in 8:33 ff., the announcement of the Passion is followed here by the story of the complete ignorance of the disciples and Jesus' call to discipleship (cf. the catchword in 9:38). This shows that Mark is responsible for the arrangement of the material (cf. 10:32-34), as well as for the scene "indoors" (see 2:1) which unites Jesus and the disciples and separates them from the rest of the crowd. He has also characterized the disciples in a way that accentuates their blindness to the career of Jesus. At one time, obviously, vs. 35 was handed down without the setting in vss. 33 f. According to vss. 33 f. Jesus would not have had to call the disciples. Jesus' answer consists primarily of an aphorism which was repeated frequently in the church without supplying any details about a particular setting. It has been preserved in several different versions: (a) Mark 9:35; (b) Mark 10:43 f. (Matt. 20:26 f.); (c) Luke 22:26 and Matthew 23:11; (d) Luke 9:48c. Surely the oldest version is (b), in which there is typical Jewish parallelism. The catchword "servant" occurs in each of these versions. The expression "the first" is probably older than "the greatest" (in c). The latter would be more appropriate here and is, therefore, a later adaptation. Moreover, vs. 37b appears in a different context in Matthew (10:40) but the form is similar. In this particular context Matthew replaces this aphorism with two others (18:3 f.), which appear similarly in Mark 10:15 and Luke 14:11; 18:14. It is obvious, therefore, that the Gospel writers included the individual traditional sayings of Jesus wherever they deemed them to be appropriate (cf. 10:35-45). The entire section has been compiled by Mark, who also constructed the scene in vs. 36. Consequently, we will have to be attentive to what Mark wants to tell us in this particular passage of his book.

[33] In asking this question Jesus takes the initiative, as he does in 8:1 (see comment) and 8:27. **[34]** The attitude of the disciples shows the human will diametrically opposed to Jesus' willingness to suffer, as is true in 8:32. Man's intense longing for greatness—expressed, e.g., in his inferiority complex—shows that he is separated from God, because God in Jesus affirms lowliness and he, himself, can be lowly too. **[35]** Certainly there can be no organization unless one is superior and another subordinate. It is easy to understand how the question of rank in the sight of God became the most important question in Judaism. Furthermore, Jesus' saying acknowledges that there is such a thing as rank in the sight of God; but he who is last and is servant to all is the one who is first in God's estimation. Hence it is the one who refuses to have a haughty spirit and assert himself in the sight of God or the world. This is very similar to what Paul writes in Philippians 3:7-9 and 1 Corinthians 1:18-31. **[36, 37]** The statement about the receiving of a child, which is illustrated by an appropriate action on the part of Jesus, implies something entirely different (and probably was added originally to the catchword "big/small"; see comment on 9:41-50). Mark, however, sees a connection here inasmuch as Jesus identifies himself with the little ones—the helpless ones (cf. Matt. 25:31 ff.); consequently, it is evident that for Mark vs. 37b is a part of the saying (although Matthew 18:5 no longer shows this). Furthermore, the child is a picture of the needy disciples (cf. vs. 41). Hence the saying does not promote the adoption of children as a meritorious work (as was done by the rabbis) or as a safeguard for the perpetuating of one's own religious community (as in the case of the people of Qumran); it simply impresses upon the disciples that Jesus—and even the Father—will be found in these little, helpless ones. A disciple, therefore, should not shy away from this status. As one who has heard vs. 31, he has been called to a discipleship in which he may dare to become one of the "last" and in this way witness to the world about Jesus—and about God. Matthew, by the arrangement of his material, has conveyed a different idea, which is probably included here as well—the idea that the one who himself is able to be small does not feel compelled to "go up into heaven" (Rom. 10:6). He does not have to carry out every conceivable kind of religious exertion and meditation in order to find God; but he is able to be, and must be, where his daily responsibilities require him to be, e.g., with the orphan who is dependent upon his practical assistance.

In this way Mark impresses upon us that all of Jesus' special teaching cannot impart the divine revelation to anyone who is not ready to enter into discipleship and there become "last" and "a servant." Men with their lust for greatness are blind to this truth, even those men whom God has chosen; consequently, they remain completely dependent upon the divine miracle which alone can bestow such discipleship (see comment on 16:7).

Who Is Truly a Disciple? 9:38-40;
cf. Luke 9:49-50

[38]John said to him, "Teacher, we saw a man who was driving out demons in your name, and we told him to stop, because he

doesn't belong to our group." [39]"Do not try to stop him," answered Jesus, "because no one who performs a miracle in my name will be able soon after to say bad things about me. [40]For whoever is not against us is for us."

There is no other place in this Gospel where John plays a special role. This makes it obvious that Mark has incorporated this section from the tradition without prefixing an introduction (cf. 9:41-50). The problem which is presented in this section had become very acute, because ecstatic prophets had arisen who performed all sorts of miracles—often by calling upon Jesus—but who did not belong to the Christian church. The expression "our group" is surprising, since the New Testament never speaks of any "discipleship" other than the discipleship of Jesus. Above all, the disciples could not have had this kind of attitude at the time of Jesus. Completely aside from the fact that there could hardly have been an independent group which functioned apart from Jesus, the fact that someone did not belong to "their group" would not have surprised the disciples, since Jesus at no time required everyone to join the circle of the twelve (cf. 5:19). All of this points to the time when this was a burning issue in the church, but not to the time of Jesus. Probably this brief story arose when the question was asked in the church: "What would Jesus say?" Then a Christian prophet in the name of the exalted Jesus (cf. Rev. 2:1) gave the answer found in vs. 40, which was then illustrated with vs. 39. A more emphatic statement of vs. 40 is found in Matthew 12:30; a papyrus states that Jesus justified the statement as found in Mark with the hope that these persons would affiliate with the church in the future.

[38] "In the name of . . ." is not a usual Greek expression; however, it is found in the Greek Old Testament and in Mark 16:17; Luke 10:17; Acts 3:6; 4:7, 10; and James 5:14 ("invoking the name of . . ."). John embodies man's natural attitude, since man is concerned with winning members and strengthening his own church group and, as a result, has little time for those who sit on the fence and do not wish to join. **[39]** The answer reflects the thinking of Jesus when it states that the church should never be anxiously concerned with its own external growth, but should be broadminded and receptive to outsiders. Of course, the expression "no one . . . will be able soon" shows that the problem has not been completely resolved, since this might happen occasionally. This question has arisen in the church again and again: Are all kinds of experiences—especially ecstatic ones—really signs that one possesses the Spirit and belongs to the church of Jesus? According to Matthew 7:16 and Didache 11:8-12 (end of the first century), ethical conduct is required. According to 1 John 4:2 it depends on a clear doctrinal confession, and according to the Shepherd of Hermas (beginning of the second century; *Mand.* 11:7-16), a wholesome relationship to the whole congregation is required. According to Pseudo-Clement (end of the second century; *Hom.* 2:10), the fulfillment of what has been prophesied is required. According to Pseudo-Paul (beginning of the third century; 3 Cor. 3 ff.), acceptance of the authority of the apostles is required. Paul has given the clearest answer in 1 Corinthians 12:1-11, where he states that there are many kinds of astonishing phenomena and experiences of "God" even in the heathen world (vs. 2), but that possession of the Spirit is shown by the acknowledgment of Jesus as Lord (vs. 3) and by a willingness to serve others (vs. 7). Accordingly, the mighty acts of the Spirit are always taken seriously, especially by Paul, but in themselves they are not adequate criteria by which to judge whether an individual is performing these acts to proclaim Jesus or is working against him. **[40]** The concluding statement affirms that one is a member of Jesus' church so long as he does not categorically separate himself from Jesus ("A curse on Jesus!" 1 Cor. 12:3).

Mark interprets these verses in connection with vss. 33-37 as a warning against arrogance on the part of the church (cf. Acts 19:15 ff.). At the same time, they explain that the call to discipleship demands not merely formal membership in the church, but a life in the power of the Spirit.

Proverbs for Disciples 9:41-50;
cf. Matt. 18:6-9

41"Remember this! Anyone who gives you a drink of water
because you belong to Christ will certainly receive his reward."
42"As for these little ones who believe in me—it would be better for a man to have a large millstone tied around his neck and
be thrown into the sea, than for him to cause one of them to turn
away from me. 43So if your hand makes you turn away, cut it off!
It is better for you to enter life without a hand than to keep both
hands and go off to hell, to the fire that never goes out. [44There
'their worms never die, and the fire is never put out.'] 45And if
your foot makes you turn away, cut it off! It is better for you to
enter life without a foot than to keep both feet and be thrown into
hell. [46There 'their worms never die, and the fire is never put
out.'] 47And if your eye makes you turn away, take it out! It is
better for you to enter the Kingdom of God with only one eye,
than to keep both eyes and be thrown into hell. 48There 'their
worms never die, and the fire is never put out.'
49"For everyone will be salted with fire. 50Salt is good. But
if it loses its saltness, how can you make it salty again? Have salt
in yourselves, and be at peace with one another."

(Vs. 48: Isa. 66:24.)

The catchword "in the name of . . ." may have been the reason why vs. 41 was joined to vs. 37 (and 38-40) in a collection of proverbs which was used for purposes of instruction and which was available to Mark. It may be that the original reading was: "Anyone who gives to one of these little ones . . ." It still reads that way in Matthew 10:42 (Greek). Then it is easy to understand how vs. 42 has been attached to the catchword "little." Vss. 43-48 have been added to the catchword "turn away" in vs. 42; vs. 49 to "fire" in vs. 48; and vs. 50 to "salt" in vs. 49. Such catchwords served as aids to memory for those who learned these proverbs by heart. In the same way the first words of each stanza in the German hymn *"Befiehl du deine Wege . . ."* (English translation: "Commit Whatever Grieves Thee") reproduce a Scripture passage (Ps. 37:5) and aid in remembering the stanzas in proper sequence. The suggestion that vss. 37 and 41 were associated before Mark is supported by the fact that they occur together also in Matthew 10:40, 42. It is likely that Mark inserted vss. 38-40 on account of the catchword "in your name." As a result, the saying referred directly to the disciples, and Mark replaced the words "one of these little ones" in vs. 41 with "you." The phrase "belong to Christ" is conceivable only in the church, because Jesus never applied that title directly to himself. In several manuscripts the words of vs. 48 follow vss. 43 and 45 also (vss. 44, 46), which shows how easily such collections of proverbs grow in transmission. Only the proverbs about the eye and the hand are included in Matthew 5:29 f. This may be because the eye and the hand are often instruments of temptation in the case of adultery, with which that passage is dealing. Nevertheless, one may wonder whether at first there was only one proverb which has been expanded through the inclusion of other parts of the body.

[41] Originally the first proverb may have charged Christian missionaries to be hospitable. When connected to vs. 40 it implies for Mark that not even the most insignificant service will be forgotten, nor is the one who renders such service to be numbered with those who are being warned in vss. 42-48. "Reward" is discussed candidly in other places in the New Testament also, but in a rather strange manner; cf. Matthew 20:1-16. In this passage from Mark, reward is promised in return for a single cup of water; however, in 1 Corinthians 13:3 the reward is denied under certain circumstances, even to one who gives everything, including his own life. Reward, therefore, is always based only on the kindness of God, who takes our actions so seriously that he does not forget the slightest deed which has really been done for him ("because you belong to Christ"). Whoever wishes to raise a claim to reward, shows by that very act that he did not really do what he did for God, but for himself. **[42]** The "little ones" are Jesus' disciples. This expression properly designates those who are "spiritually poor" (Matt. 5:3; cf. the men of lowly, i.e., humble, spirit in Qumran). This expression had become unintelligible, so Mark explained it with the phrase "who believe." Matthew has applied the saying to children because he did not understand it correctly (Matt. 18:6 is put next to 18:5). In Luke 17:1 f. (cf. Matt. 18:7) this proverb is preserved in greater detail. There it refers clearly to the tempters of the end-time who want to pervert these "little ones"—the defenseless disciples—before the final redemption. Even Mark's version places the disciples with all their insignificance and vulnerability under God's special care. It is the unimportant, the unattractive, the downtrodden, the indifferent, the odd, and the wearisome for whom the church was urged to show special concern. One will think also of those who with a certain simplicity are not able to comprehend all the theological issues, but not of those "little ones" who consider themselves to be the only true believers and try to dominate everyone else. The "millstone" is a stone which is shaped like a bell and rotates on a cone-shaped stone pivot. In large mills the millstone had a hole in the top in which to put the grain, and was driven by a donkey. The metaphor is grotesque and for that reason terribly impressive, particularly since drowning was to the Jews an especially detestable form of death. **[43-47]** The following verses express a warning which is equally terrible. It does not refer to one's influence upon others, but is a warning against corrupting oneself. This, of course, has nothing to do with self-mutilation, which was practiced by many religions in that time. The severing of parts of the body is not an end in itself and does not promote the perfecting of the spirit with any idea that the flesh is evil in itself. This is a radical way of stating that it is more important to be obedient to God in all circumstances than it is to retain all the parts of the body intact. Nevertheless, the parts of one's body should not be despised; they are to be valued as man's greatest treasure. It is clear, then, that one is not required to observe these statements literally (cf. Matt. 19:11 f.). They are affirming that God is even more important than the most important parts of our bodies. One must guard particularly against attributing any merit to such an action. The passage is not describing an especially difficult self-mutilation which is, therefore, more meritorious. The objective is to free oneself from anything which might hinder fellowship with God. In each case this will be something different. The notion that an individual part of the body may commit sin is in keeping with Jewish thought (cf. Prov. 6:17 f.; 23:33; 27:20). *Geenna,* which is translated "hell," corresponds to the Hebrew *ge-ben-hinnom,* which is the name of a valley south of Jerusalem (Joshua 15:8; 18:16). Because offerings were presented to idols in that valley, the prophets threatened it with the judgment of God (Jer. 7:32; 19:6). From this fact the idea arose later that the last judgment would be held in this valley, and ultimately it became the designation of the place where the damned would be punished. **[48]** The most severe warning is expressed by means of an Old Testament quotation. When interpreted correctly, this does not teach everlasting torment in hell. In refutation of that idea one could refer to Romans 11:32 or 1 Timothy 2:4. It is just as impossible to state that some will be punished in hell someday as it is to state the opposite—that eventually all will be saved. Both anticipate something which is God's prerogative. If the former statement can only be interpreted as God's ultimate warning to me when I am facing temptation, then the latter must be understood as God's ultimate promise to me in the same circumstances. As soon as I transform these words into dogmatic statements about a future situation, I am no longer listening with an attitude of submission in which I am willing to be called to faith. My desire then is to take into my own hands what belongs to God, and in so doing I tie God's hands so that in the future he has no freedom of action.

[49] Vs. 49 is found in different forms in the various manuscripts. The most reasonable interpretation of this verse is that the fire of God (the affliction of persecution, or of the end-time, or of the Holy Spirit?) preserves from decay like salt (with which meat is cured). **[50]** Vs. 50 is even more difficult to explain. It is clear that salt is something good, but it must retain its pungency. "Have salt" is likely older than the wording "You are like salt," which is recorded in Matthew 5:13. Does this have reference to being ready to be sacrificed? This seems to be a reasonable explanation since salt is used in the preparation of sacrifices. Or is it the message of the disciples which is likened to salt? Does it perhaps stand for common sense (Col. 4:6), love for neighbor (according to a rabbinic saying), wisdom in the end-time, fellowship at table (which in the Orient is symbolized by salt), or is it simply a symbol of peace? All of these interpretations have been suggested. This interpretation is the most plausible: Have the spirit of being willing to suffer and of resisting the world, but have peace among yourselves.

Mark has added to the second announcement of Jesus' Passion another section which portrays the ignorance of the disciples in stark terms. While Jesus knowingly moves toward his suffering, the disciples are quarreling about greatness. In the light of this Jesus reiterates the call to discipleship in a collection of proverbs, all of which are assembled around the concept of "little ones." They exhort one to receive the defenseless child, to be tolerant with outsiders, and to supply the simplest necessities of life. They warn against temptation and self-deception. Perhaps the last two verses demand that one be ready to be sacrificed, like the demand made in 8:34 ff. after the first announcement of Jesus' Passion. What was true there applies here also: Only as a disciple follows Jesus can he travel this road; such discipleship is not possible unless Jesus has set a man free; and only in this kind of discipleship is a person able to truly understand Jesus' career.

Discipleship in Marriage 10:1-12;
cf. Matt. 19:1-12

1Then Jesus left that place, went to the region of Judea, and
crossed the Jordan river. Again crowds came flocking to him and
he taught them, as he always did.

2Some Pharisees came to him and tried to trap him. "Tell
us," they asked, "does our Law allow a man to divorce his wife?"
3Jesus answered with a question: "What commandment did Moses
give you?" 4Their answer was, "Moses gave permission for a man
to write a divorce notice and send his wife away." 5Jesus said to
them: "Moses wrote this commandment for you because you are
so hard to teach. 6But in the beginning, at the time of creation,

it was said, 'God made them male and female. [7]And for this reason a man will leave his father and mother and unite with his wife, [8]and the two will become one.' So they are no longer two, but one. [9]Man must not separate, then, what God has joined together."

[10]When they went back into the house, the disciples asked Jesus about this matter. [11]He said to them: "The man who divorces his wife and marries another woman commits adultery against his wife; [12]in the same way, the woman who divorces her husband and marries another man commits adultery."

(Vss. 4 f.: Deut. 24:1; vss. 6 f.: Gen. 1:27; vss. 7 f.: Gen. 2:24.)

This entire passage is representative of the kind of controversy in which the church frequently was engaged, as, e.g., in its quarrel with Judaism. Therefore it is difficult to say whether or not a nucleus can be traced to Jesus, and if there is such a nucleus, how much it included. First Corinthians 7:10 f. presupposes a "word of the Lord" in answer to this same question. Certainly vs. 1 exhibits Markan style (cf. 7:24). And we may be confident that vss. 10-12, which are given a typical Markan setting in vs. 10, are a later addition. Other sayings have been added in Matthew 19:10-12. Vs. 12 is absolutely inconceivable within Jewish relationships; consequently, it must have been added by the Hellenistic church. Vss. 11 f. appear also in Matthew 5:32, but in a little different form. The idea that the woman who remarries commits adultery, while the man does not, is thoroughly Jewish (see comment on vs. 11). In this respect Matthew 5:32 has preserved the original form. Moreover, the declaration in Mark 10:11, where the man is not considered guilty unless he remarries, was certainly stated in this way before Mark, so he has merely added it to this discussion of divorce. Matthew has rearranged vss. 1-9 and changed some of the details, because he no longer understood the train of thought. Possibly the entire section, Mark 10:1-31, already shows characteristics of the composition of a catechism—something like family rules of conduct which provide guidance for various groups (cf. 1 Tim. 2:8—3:13; 5:1—6:2; Titus 1:5-9; 2:2-10; Eph. 5:22—6:9; 1 Peter 2:13—3:7; 5:1-5). This passage describes discipleship in marriage, discipleship as it relates to children, and discipleship as it relates to possessions.

[1] The journey southward to the place where Jesus' Passion would occur follows immediately after the announcement of that Passion. Possibly Mark has a vague conception of the geography, because Jesus ordinarily would have traveled through Transjordan first and then to Judea; or Mark may have assumed that Jesus has spent some time in Judea previously and that now he is returning, although nothing is reported from such a visit (cf. 10:46-52). Perhaps he has mentioned Judea first merely to emphasize a particular theological point—to show that Jesus goes to his suffering deliberately. This fact is given special prominence by the assembling of the crowds, which is something Mark emphasizes frequently; and by the communication of revelation through Jesus' "teaching" (cf. 1:22). Nevertheless, these details reveal how greatly men are in need of God's revelation and that as yet they do not understand it. **[2]** The hypocrisy in the Pharisees' question is exposed at once. Their only interest was to "trap" Jesus. Actually no Pharisee would have asked such a radical question, because among the Jews divorce was regulated by Deuteronomy 24:1-4 (which was designed originally to protect the wife and guarantee her a certain amount of freedom). Dispute centered on the question of what could be considered grounds for divorce. If a man's wife burned his food, or if he found another woman who was more beautiful, would that be sufficient grounds for divorce, or would adultery on the part of the wife be the only just cause? Of course the answer to this question would determine whether or not it was possible to change wives frequently. Such a practice would actually be a kind of sequential polygamy. No very clear answer is given to the question whether, in spite of her bill of divorce, a woman still actually belongs to her first husband and therefore is not free to remarry. Consequently, strict exegetes, such as were found in the Qumran community, insisted that if a man married two women during his lifetime he would be guilty of "whoredom." They contended that "the basis in creation" is: "a male and a female He created them" and, furthermore, that those who went into the ark entered two by two (Damascus Document 4:20 ff.). The Christian church universally enforced this more strict practice. **[2-5]** In these verses it is noteworthy that Jesus refers twice to the "commandment" while the opponents refer twice to the matter of "permission" (vs. 2 "allow"). This means that Jesus was concerned about God's will; the others were concerned about their own rights. When a person begins to ask this kind of question, he is seeking the greatest possible advantage for himself within the limits of what is permissible. In so doing he will have destroyed the marriage before it has begun. Vs. 5 has been viewed most often as a concession, but this would make the construction meaningless: The counter-question of Jesus in vs. 3 elicits the statement in vs. 4 which contradicts him. This puts Jesus in a position where he has to criticize the biblical quotation, which is exactly what his opponents wanted him to do. Actually, the arrangement found in Matthew would be much more logical. It does not say "on account of your stubbornness," but "to your . . ." (i.e., "directed at it") or "against your . . ." Viewed this way, vs. 5 is not a concession made by Moses in resignation, but a judgment upon the people. It is an evidence of their stubbornness and a continual accusation. **[6]** In view of this Jesus holds firmly to Scripture. He contends that there has never been any other way (this is the meaning of the brief formula "in the beginning") than that *one* woman was created for *one* man. The existence of two sexes was ordained by God. This view of marriage is not just some ideal, nor is it something to be overcome in the interest of platonic love. This view is something given by nature that must be gratefully accepted without sentimentality or contempt. **[7]** "For this reason . . ."—the fact that Genesis 2:24 refers back to the creation of the woman out of Adam's rib is now applied to what has been said in vs. 6. The forsaking of the house of one's father was far more meaningful at that time, since a man would forsake the solidarity and protection of his own clan. To the present day this forsaking is the proper prerequisite for marriage. **[8]** That the two sexes become one ("the two" first appears in the LXX, which presupposes monogamy; the Hebrew text merely has "they") is clearly regarded in the Bible as God's will and not as a consequence of sin. **[9]** Marriage is based upon the plain fact of creation in all its simplicity: God created two sexes.

[10] The private instruction in the "house" (cf. 2:1) is a typical Markan addition. The whole matter has been explained, but man cannot understand God's revelation. Although the principle should have been adequate for them, it is still necessary to spell out the ethical implications. **[11]** In the process, Mark's interpretation attributes greater guilt to remarriage after divorce than to the divorce. The first statement is contrary to the customary Jewish regulation: "For it is (only) the man who is permitted by us to do this [dissolve a marriage], and not even a divorced woman may marry again on her own initiative unless her former husband consents" (Josephus, *Antiquities* XV. 259). **[12]** The second statement is possible only in Graeco-Roman relationships, where a woman is free to divorce her husband and remarry. Consequently, the first statement must have been expanded in a new situation and revised to fit the new relationships. In no other way could it continue to be vital and have relevance for men in succeeding generations. In this connection both aspects of this process are important: The saying speaks in each succeeding age in terms which can be understood, and yet is not essentially different in substance from the ancient saying.

Ephesians 5:23 ff. bases monogamy upon God's love as it has taken concrete form in Christ. It is the proper basis upon which marriage exists. This idea is implied in Jesus' answer though it is not stated explicitly, because he interprets the way in which God created man as an expression of God's loving concern for man. At first glance Jesus' position seems to correspond to the more severe tendency in Judaism; but the persistence with which Jesus changes the question of what is permissible into the question of what God wills shows a fundamental victory over legalism. No longer can one ask: What is forbidden by the law, or, where can I find an area unfettered by any legal requirements? Jesus reminds one of the gift of the Creator and calls him to live on that basis. This is far more demanding, because God's gift can be received only if one lives in the way God has planned. This not only involves the avoidance of what is forbidden, but it also invades the area of things "permitted." The goal of creation is achieved in the freedom which Jesus gives, by which men are delivered from every regulation that is purely legalistic.

As a teacher, has Jesus merely repeated something which has always been true? Obviously Mark has more than this in mind. It is not an accident that he has assembled in this section most of the instruction dealing with discipleship, and on the basis of 8:31 this must be regarded as a discipleship of suffering. Until the destiny of the suffering Son of Man was proclaimed, it was not clear that the light of the grace and gift of God has always had its basis in creation. Creation must be understood as God's first step toward man, which now has reached its ultimate fulfillment in the coming of the Son of Man. A legalistic requirement forbidding divorce does not help in any event, but a freedom in which man can avoid the confession of his guilt is even less beneficial. Divorce *can* be a sign of repentance by which two people face up to their failure. It *can* be a confession that they have not succeeded in living according to God's will, i.e., on the basis of his gift. Divorce *can,* therefore, set one free to experience anew the mercy of God. On the other hand, the preservation of the outward appearance of a marriage which has actually been destroyed *can* blur that consciousness of guilt. But divorce is only a last resort after a person has made every effort to be reconciled to the other, and must finally, for the sake of the other person or for the sake of the children, face up to his own failure and suffer the practical consequences. What this means in practice is that the marriage of a divorced person cannot be forbidden in a rigid legalism; nor can divorce proceedings be started indiscriminately, or without considering the principles which have been declared here. Jesus' statement on the subject is very clear, and in the marriage relationship there are times when his straightforward approach to this subject is most helpful.

Discipleship in Childlike Faith 10:13-16;
cf. Matt. 19:13-15; Luke 18:15-17

13Some people brought children to Jesus for him to touch them, but the disciples scolded those people. 14When Jesus noticed it, he was angry and said to his disciples: "Let the children come to me! Do not stop them, because the Kingdom of God belongs to such as these. [15]Remember this! Whoever does not receive the Kingdom of God like a child will never enter it." [16]Then he took the children in his arms, placed his hands on each of them, and blessed them.

It seems that vs. 15 may have been circulated as a separate saying because Matthew includes it in a different passage (18:3), and John 3:5 (translated into even more typical Johannine style in 3:3) has probably been derived from it. Possibly Mark considered this verse to be the real focal point and gathered the other material around it merely to serve as illustrations. He is spelling out what it means to be a disciple of Jesus. This may be a genuine saying of Jesus, since tension between the future and the contemporary aspects of the Kingdom of God is characteristic of his teaching (cf. below). Moreover, so far as we know, children have never played any special role in the church.

[13] We are not told who it is that brings the children. (The Greek word indicates a newborn babe in John 16:21, and a twelve-year-old child in Mark 5:39-42. The Gospel of Thomas [22] is thinking of a nursing infant.) This shows how little interest Mark has in historical detail. We can understand the concern of the disciples for the purity of faith: Is not the idea that the simple touch can mediate miraculous divine power even without faith indicative of belief in magic? **[14]** Nevertheless, Jesus becomes angry with them in the way that he became angry with illness and unbelief (1:41, 43; 3:5). It would appear that his reply defends the children, who are passive, and not the adults who are bringing the children. He is not speaking of their sinlessness or purity and there is no truth in the idea that "child" is a symbol for the ascetic, as it is interpreted in the Gospel of Thomas (22). This much is clear: the children play no active role and cannot defend themselves against the overzealous disciples. But this is the reason they are blessed—just because they have nothing to show for themselves. They cannot count on any achievements of their own—

their hands are empty like those of a beggar. [15] Jesus enlarges the promise to include everyone. With an authority such as only God can claim, he promises the Kingdom to those whose faith resembles the empty hand of a beggar. Such faith is possible because they have no achievements of their own nor any conceptions of God which can intrude between them and God (cf. Matt. 11:25; 21:15 f.). For this reason Jesus speaks of "receiving" and "entering" the Kingdom of God, but not of building it or of forcing it to come. Jesus can speak in this way because he knows that in himself the future Kingdom is already encountering man and taking possession of him; consequently, what will not be fulfilled visibly until sometime in the future is given at this very moment to childlike faith. As in 2:5-7, Jesus exercises an authority here which properly belongs to God alone. He promises fellowship with God; he promises to give the future Kingdom of God immediately to those who have nothing to show for themselves. [16] Jesus' outward actions simply re-emphasize how sincerely he means that promise.

This brief episode is frequently used in support of infant baptism. However, that is not what is being discussed. In this passage the Kingdom is promised to the little ones much as it is in Matthew 5:3. John 3:5 shows that the church had applied this saying of Jesus to baptism even before John wrote his Gospel. Perhaps the question in Acts 8:36, "What is to keep me from being baptized?" is evidence that some such question was regularly included in the liturgy of baptism. This custom may have been inspired by Mark 10:14. Nevertheless, no direct evidence can be derived from this for the practice of infant baptism. It says indirectly that God's Kingdom is promised to us without any conditions and without our meriting it. In fact, the Kingdom is promised to man without his desiring it. Infant baptism is an appropriate symbol insofar as it actually gives expression to this truth. The real question is whether the indiscriminate baptism of children, as is practiced at the present time, has become symbolic of something else—of the fact that the church itself views baptism as something so insignificant and harmless that baptism and its blessing are no longer taken seriously. This leads to the second question, whether baptism is losing the characteristic of testimony. Although this may not be its primary or exclusive significance, baptism is intended to be a testimony to others. In principle, infant baptism is in conformity with the New Testament message when viewed as a symbol of God's gracious promise which obviates the necessity of any human effort. It is clear according to Acts 16:31-33 (cf. 1 Cor. 1:16) that often a whole "family," including all the servants, were baptized at the same time. Whether children were included in this or not, it was not restricted to persons who, like the jailer, had come to believe from conviction and could give testimony of their faith (observe that "believe," which is singular, leads to the salvation of the whole family). One may seriously question whether infant baptism can still be performed in a meaningful way under the present conditions. This symbolic character has largely been lost—even perverted.

Discipleship in Freedom from Possessions 10:17-31;
cf. Matt. 19:16-30; Luke 18:18-30

17As Jesus was starting again on his way, a man ran up, knelt
before him, and asked him: "Good Teacher, what must I do to
receive eternal life?" 18"Why do you call me good?" Jesus
asked him. "No one is good except God alone. 19You know the
commandments: 'Do not murder; do not commit adultery; do not
steal; do not lie; do not cheat; honor your father and mother.'"
20"Teacher," the man said, "ever since I was young I have obeyed
all these commandments." 21With love Jesus looked straight at
him and said: "You need only one thing. Go and sell all you
have and give the money to the poor, and you will have riches
in heaven; then come and follow me." 22When the man heard
this, gloom spread over his face and he went away sad, because he
was very rich.

23Jesus looked around at his disciples and said to them,
"How hard it will be for rich people to enter the Kingdom of
God!" 24The disciples were shocked at these words, but Jesus
went on to say: "My children, how hard it is to enter the Kingdom

God! 25It is much harder for a rich man to enter the Kingdom of God than for a camel to go through the eye of a needle." 26At this the disciples were completely amazed, and asked one another, "Who, then, can be saved?" 27Jesus looked straight at them and answered: "This is impossible for men, but not for God; everything is possible for God."

28Then Peter spoke up: "Look, we have left everything and followed you." 29"Yes," Jesus said to them, "and I tell you this: anyone who leaves home or brothers or sisters or mother or father or children or fields for me, and for the gospel, 30will receive much more in this present age. He will receive a hundred times more houses, brothers, sisters, mothers, children, and fields—and persecutions as well; and in the age to come he will receive eternal life. 31But many who now are first will be last, and many who now are last will be first."

(Vs. 19: Exod. 20:12-16; Deut. 5:16-20.)

The story itself (vss. 17-22) is a unit. It corresponds to sections such as Luke 9:57-62. It is not likely that vss. 28-30 were always included. Possibly they can be traced to some particular experiences of the church (persecutions!). Matthew 19:28 adds another saying which Luke 22:28-30 relates in connection with the Last Supper. Probably vs. 31, which appears in various places in the Gospels (Matt. 20:16; Luke 13:30), has been added here by Mark.

Vss. 23-27 may have developed gradually. By means of one of Mark's favorite expressions, vs. 23 makes the transition from an individual case to a universal teaching (cf. 3:5, 34, and 5:32). Moreover, the shock of the disciples in vs. 24 corresponds to 1:27 and 10:32, but it is more significant that this shock is essentially consistent with Mark's plan to emphasize the disciples' lack of understanding in this part of his Gospel. The insertion of this material makes it necessary for the substance of the statement in vs. 23b to be repeated in 24b in order to return to the saying of Jesus. Furthermore, vs. 26 and the introduction in vs. 27 may have come from Mark. Apparently vss. 23b, 25, and 27 are ancient sayings of Jesus which deal with the dangers of riches.

The church may have added them to this story, since up to this point the story has not been dealing with riches but with discipleship. In any case, these sayings were added before Mark.

[17] The story simply mentions "a man," but purposely does not specify who he was; consequently, every reader can identify with him. A person would not kneel before a mere rabbi (cf. 1:40; 5:22). For centuries the question "What must I do to enter and to share in life?" had been asked by those who came to the temple in Israel, and the priests reminded them of the commandments, as Jesus does here (Pss. 15; 24:3-6). Students of the rabbis asked similar questions. But this story deals with a man who wants to accomplish something more than the ordinary man does. It was common in Israel to speak of "inheriting" (translated: "receive") what God had promised, because it was known that the future inheritance depended upon God's gracious promise alone. Therefore any personal merit was just as inconsequential as it is in the matter of inheritance. Only when in the course of history the unity of Israel—particularly in religious matters—was destroyed did the question arise: "Who then belongs to the Israel to whom God's promise applies?" This particular individual is inquiring for the same reason. But the person who enters into dialogue with Jesus must be very serious as he asks this question. It is not simply a well-adjusted, happy life which is at stake. The question is concerned with "eternal life," i.e., final existence in the presence of God on the other side of death. This is what makes the dialogue so profound.

[18] The address "Good Teacher" is not customary for either Jew or Greek. It is not the complimentary nature of this form of address which is emphasized in Jesus' reply but the fact that he would not accept this name. This is what has made Jesus' answer a problem for the exegetes. One interpretation is that Jesus merely intended to say it is not fitting to exchange compliments when discussing a matter which concerns God and no other. If we inquire what this reply meant to Jesus, we will find this explanation appropriate. In this story, as in the preceding one, Jesus acts in the place of God. With Jesus' call to discipleship eternal life comes to this man, and thus God himself comes to him. When the man says yes or no to Jesus, he is saying yes or no to God (see 8:38). In this story God encounters the man in Jesus and nowhere else; nevertheless, this same Jesus always turns man's attention away from himself to the "only one who is good," to use Philo's expression (*On the Changing of Names* 7), before whom not even the angels are pure (Job 4:18; 15:15; 25:3 f.). But how has the church interpreted Jesus' renunciation of this title, since the church considers the sinlessness of Jesus an important matter? (John 8:46; 2 Cor. 5:21; Heb. 7:26; 1 Peter 2:22).

In its concept of Jesus' sinlessness the church did not include the Greek idea that Jesus was divine in his substance, which would never change. Consequently, the church did not regard his sinlessness as an unchanging attribute but as something which became manifest in the midst of temptation (Heb. 4:15). It is in this respect that Jesus is like "sinners." What is the ultimate meaning of this for the present-day church which speaks of "God the Father" and "God the Son"? Our passage is saying that these terms do not describe a condition of eternal equality which would allow one to use Father and Son interchangeably. This is the means by which the church is attempting to set forth the mystery that it really encounters God in the Son. The church encounters God in the Son because the Son is seeking nothing for himself. He desires that no facet of his life might call attention to himself, but that all may point to One who is greater. This truth is not treated adequately in the classical doctrine of the Trinity. Accordingly, a proper interpretation of the doctrine of the Trinity will not view it merely as a definition of God but rather as the description of an event. God wills to encounter the world in his Son (cf. 15:39), and this has been his will from the very beginning (John 1:1-3).

[19] It is surprising that when questioned by a man who is intent upon some special achievement in order to receive eternal life, Jesus, in contrast to the rabbis, simply reminds him of the commandments without giving any further explanation of them. He quotes from memory the more practical ones from the second half of the Ten Commandments in a carefree manner and in random order. This shows the absence of all legalistic pedantry.

Jesus' position is very close to the teaching of Micah 6:8. He reminds the simple person in the church, who is fascinated by the great achievement of some particular saint, of all the people who are trying to be obedient to God. That is where "life" may be found.

[20] The assertion of the inquirer that he has kept all the commandments could not be an expression of pride, since Jesus loved him. It is an indication of obedience and a day-by-day life with God—and these are good qualities. **[21]** How Jesus seeks the man by fixing his gaze on him is reported here in much the same way as in 1:16, 19, and 2:14 (see comment). In this passage Jesus' interest in him is emphasized very strongly. The only thing which this man needs is to become a follower of Jesus. It is clear that this is not a prerequisite which must be fulfilled in a legalistic manner. It is often thought that every disciple of the earthly Jesus traveled with him, but Jesus has already established a pattern of not requiring this from everyone (5:19). For Mark the word "following" describes the situation of the disciple in a far more comprehensive way. Unless one is "following" Jesus he cannot come to a true understanding of him. Mark is simply giving a universal application to what Jesus says to the individual who stands before him in this specific instance—the one who has kept all the commandments but now, in the presence of Jesus, must prove the intrinsic worth of that obedience by being willing to become a follower of Jesus. This must not be regarded as a demand for some additional achievement. It is an invitation to understand the meaning of the lesson given here: obedience to God must be demonstrated by acknowledging that God meets us in Jesus. In any case, the giving up of one's possessions is not a prerequisite for discipleship. It is the consequence of discipleship, as it was in 1:18, 20, and 2:14; it is the concrete manner in which discipleship is carried out. For this reason Jesus prescribes no rules which might apply to everyone. For one person it is a fishing boat or a tax collector's desk which must be abandoned. For another person it is his parents, or it may be a prophet (John 1:35-37, 46) or some religious preconception which must be forsaken. There is simply no other way whereby it is possible to be close to Jesus.

And so the call to discipleship is always a matter of total commitment. It involves a divine call which gives while it makes demands. The man is asked if he will receive the future life here and now in a completeness from which nothing is withheld. Moreover, God's offer, which would grant him everything he is seeking, makes his refusal especially conspicuous. **[22]** The gloom on his face as he goes away does not indicate any rebellion against Jesus, but a certain sense of dismay which, however, was not able to bring him to the point of being willing to receive. Obviously, the story has been retold many times. It is also found in the Gospel of the Nazarenes. In that account there are two rich men, one of whom scratches his head thoughtfully as Jesus explicitly challenges his right to say that he has fulfilled the law and the prophets while he is not prepared for discipleship. This shows how such stories have grown in the process of being told and retold.

[23] Mark wants to stress that what follows applies to every disciple, and wants to declare that at the present time Jesus is soliciting the assent of the reader also. **[24]** The alarm of the disciples shows how fear will seize the man who is truly confronted by God. Whenever God becomes a reality, his greatness becomes so overpowering that it terrifies man. Therefore, the reaction of the disciples here is very similar to that in vs. 22. Jesus' concern for the tempted and fearful is manifested by the form of address—"children"—which, except for this passage, is found only in John. This is not the full significance of his reply, however, for it has a universal application and concerns the disciples also. The difficulty is not due to some specific requirement which is extremely demanding or to an inordinate attachment to riches —it is due to the fact that God does not become so real to the man that, by comparison, trifles are recognized as trifles. The metaphor of the camel is grotesque, and for that reason is all the more impressive. **[25]** Later rabbis speak of maxims concerning an elephant who goes through the eye of a needle. The metaphor must not be weakened by changing the word "camel" to "rope" (through altering a Greek letter) or by referring to a note in a commentary from the ninth century A.D.(!) which asserts that a small gate to the city of Jerusalem was called the Needle's Eye. Even in contemporary preaching on this passage there are edifying reflections about bowing in humility, as the poor camel was forced to do if the large city gate was closed. **[26]** The disciples understood Jesus correctly. The application of this saying of Jesus is not limited to the particular case of this rich man but is relevant for everyone, and what applies to everyone in general can be seen in the rich man in a concrete way. However, the disciples still do not fully understand. Although they have a correct doctrine of man, they continue to see things from a human point of view when they ought to look not at man but at the mighty work of God. **[27]** This is why Jesus searchingly looks at them once more. This enhances the significance of the final statement. Jesus points to the miracle of divine grace just as the Old Testament does (Zech. 8:6 LXX; Gen. 18:14; Job 10:13 LXX; 42:2). While this statement is being proclaimed, salvation occurs—the hearer is arrested by God, i.e., he is chosen. As was true in 1:16-20 and 2:14, discipleship comes only as the act of God; it is entirely a gift of grace. One can only receive it obediently and continue to hold it fast, while resisting any sloth or cowardice.

[28] Vs. 28 probably was inserted for transition to the promise in vs. 29. In verse 28 Peter first mentions the forsaking of all things, then discipleship, although when viewed in the proper sequence the forsaking really is the result of discipleship. Moreover, 1 Corinthians 9:5 shows that at a later time Peter took his wife with him on his missionary journeys (the wife is omitted from the list in vs. 29!). **[29]** The expression "for the sake of the Kingdom of God" (Luke 18:29) is probably nearer to the original wording (see 8:35). **[30]** This promise is very remarkable. For one thing it encompasses every aspect of earthly life (cf. 8:35). Jesus' demand, therefore, is actually an invitation to find the gift of life in the giving of self. Discipleship to Jesus does not lead to poverty and deprivation, but to wholeness—to the experience of real life. This promise is fulfilled wherever there is genuine, joyous abandonment motivated by the gift of God. One concrete way in which it will be fulfilled is in the fellowship which the disciple will find in the church. Nevertheless, the other side of discipleship is affirmed realistically and without any illusions: Discipleship is accompanied by "persecutions as well." This present fulfillment is, as a matter of fact, different from the complete fulfillment "in the age to come," because only then will life be free from temptation. Thus both truths are upheld: Life is experienced in real fullness in the here and now, and one is not merely reminded of empty promises about a hereafter. Nevertheless, everything which happens in the present is only a token of another far richer and more complete fulfillment which will be free from temptation. **[31]** With the final statement Mark accentuates the strangeness of this divine law.

Mark is not making poverty a special virtue. What he says is much more profound. The point of all this discussion is found in vss. 25-27, which say virtually the same thing as Romans 3:23 f. The statement that all are sinners must not be interpreted purely in terms of moral principles. Vs. 20 is still true and, in addition, vs. 19 is appropriate. However, let the true life actually be offered to man here and now in his own particular situation as life comes to him in Jesus, and at that very moment it becomes apparent that no one really wants it—that is, unless the miracle in vs. 27 should happen. This process can never be reversed. Man would like to do something outstanding, or make some great sacrifice, in order that God might become predominant in his thinking. Experience does not support this, however. Sex, for example, becomes more of an obsession when repressed than it may become in marriage. Only when God has become pre-eminent—and this is the miracle which is intended in vs. 27—will the other things become insignificant. This, of course, does not mean that once the miracle of God has begun it will not be necessary for man to practice making God pre-eminent even in the face of difficulties. It is a general principle that the gift of discipleship is absolutely miraculous. No amount of exertion, not even self-denial or asceticism, can make one a disciple. Discipleship is purely a gift of God. This is what makes the section so very important in the composition of the Gospel of Mark and this is why it is necessary for vss. 32-34 to follow.

Jesus' Third Teaching Concerning the Suffering of the Son of Man 10:32-34;
cf. Matt. 20:17-19; Luke 18:31-34

32They were now on the road going up to Jerusalem. Jesus was going ahead of the disciples, who were filled with alarm; the people who followed behind were afraid. Once again Jesus took the twelve disciples aside and spoke of the things that were going to happen to him. 33"Look," Jesus told them, "we are going up to Jerusalem where the Son of Man will be handed over to the chief priests and the teachers of the Law. They will condemn him to death and then hand him over to the Gentiles. 34These will make fun of him, spit on him, whip him, and kill him. And after three days he will be raised to life."

This section which immediately precedes the beginning of the Passion story has been edited extensively by Mark. He begins and ends (vs. 52) with the phrase "on the road." This is the road to Jerusalem—the place where the Passion will take place. Here, as there, the catchword "followed" occurs. So Mark may consider it to be very significant that Jesus "was going ahead"—a thought which is resumed in 14:28 (16:7). In this passage the prophecy of the Passion is replete with details, which could not have been included before Easter. The mention of his being "handed over to the Gentiles" and the great emphasis upon the manner in which they will treat him may indicate that this segment was formulated in a Jewish-Christian church (in Palestine?) and, therefore, is not Mark's creation. Mark may be responsible for the introduction in which reference is made to their "going up" and the editorial comment with which vs. 32 is concluded.

[32] The fact that Jesus is going to his Passion deliberately is what sets him apart from all others. Those who followed are distinguished from the rest of the people in an unusual way.* It is

* The word "disciple" is not found in the Greek text. It has only the ambiguous pronoun "them."

hardly possible that this designation refers to any persons other than those who said in 10:28, "We have . . . followed you." If this be true, then it is the anonymous "them" who were "filled with alarm," i.e., all those who went along. The expression "were afraid" refers, then, to the disciples in the narrower sense of the term. Both groups suspect something of the special significance of this road. For the disciples who have heard what Jesus said previously this suspicion takes the form of fear. Both reactions show to what a great extent this procession bears the characteristics of an act of divine revelation. As they proceed to Jesus' Passion the incomprehensibility of the divine action becomes even more dreadfully clear than it was in 1:27. **[33]** Therefore, the saying of Jesus returns to the subject of his "going up" and emphasizes its significance. This announcement of the Passion is more detailed than the previous ones and is like a brief summary of the Passion story such as may have been used in a liturgy or a catechism. **[34]** Isaiah 50:6 (cf. 14:65) also speaks of being whipped and spit upon. It is surprising that the reference to the crucifixion which was added to the story later by Matthew (20:19) is not found here. Possibly that reference is part of a later stage of the confession as it was formulated by Paul (cf. Mark 16:6; Acts 2:36; 4:10).

It is important to Mark that emphasis be given to the great significance which this event has for the future, since it would not be possible otherwise to understand anything about Jesus. Hence he places these elements in succession once again: the description of the blindness of the disciples (vss. 35-41), the call to discipleship (vss. 42-45), and the reference to the divine miracle apart from which discipleship would be an impossibility (vss. 46-52).

The Ignorance of the Disciples and Discipleship 10:35-45;
cf. Matt. 20:20-28; Luke 22:24-27

[35]Then James and John, the sons of Zebedee, came to Jesus. "Teacher," they said, "there is something we want you to do for us." [36]"What do you want me to do for you?" Jesus asked them.

[37]They answered: "When you sit on your throne in the glorious Kingdom, we want you to let us sit with you, one at your right and one at your left." [38]Jesus said to them: "You don't know what you are asking for. Can you drink the cup that I must drink? Can you be baptized in the way I must be baptized?" [39]"We can," they answered. Jesus said to them: "You will indeed drink the cup I must drink and be baptized in the way I must be baptized. [40]But I do not have the right to choose who will sit at my right and my left. It is God who will give these places to those for whom he has prepared them."

[41]When the other ten disciples heard about this they became angry with James and John. [42]So Jesus called them all together to him and said: "You know that the men who are considered rulers of the people have power over them, and the leaders rule over them. [43]This, however, is not the way it is among you. If one of you wants to be great, he must be the servant of the rest; [44]and if one of you wants to be first, he must be the slave of all. [45]For even the Son of Man did not come to be served; he came to serve and to give his life to redeem many people."

The arrangement of this material can be traced to Mark, since the announcement of Jesus' Passion is followed by the misunderstanding of the disciples and the call to discipleship as it was in 8:32 ff. and 9:33 ff. The saying concerning the drinking of the cup is found also in John 18:11 (cf. Mark 14:36) and the one about baptism occurs in Luke 12:50. So far as we know, the sons of Zebedee did not share a common experience of martyrdom. (Acts 12:2 may be dated A.D. 44; Gal. 2:9 must be later, the same time as Acts 15:1 ff., since Gal. 2:1 should be dated 14 years [+3?] after the conversion of Paul according to Gal. 1:18.) This must be an authentic saying of Jesus, since it is not likely that the church would have worded it in this way. The present wording ("Can you . . .?") does not suggest that the saying merely implied that the sons of Zebedee would experience baptism and the Lord's Supper someday. Furthermore, vss. 38 f. actually run counter to vs. 40. Are they a later addition? Matthew is offended by this very uncomplimentary description of the two disciples;

therefore, he has their mother make the request, but he neglected to correct vss. 22, 23, and 24. Luke omits the story completely. Does this brief narrative (excluding the prophecy in vs. 39) reflect strained relations between the sons of Zebedee and others in the leadership of the early church (Matt. 16:18)? The expression "Jesus called them all together" found in vs. 41 is one of Mark's favorites (cf. 3:23; 7:14; 8:34) and shows that he has formulated that verse as a transition with which to add the sayings in vss. 42-45. These sayings are found in similar form in Luke 22:24-27 in the account of the Lord's Supper (with the exception that vs. 45 is lacking). This indicates that vs. 45 is an explanation which has been added by the church. The church also added the name "Son of Man" (cf. 8:27-33), which has not been added in Luke. Although it is not possible to point to any allusions to Isaiah 53 in the wording of this passage, probably it is based upon the church's understanding of that chapter.

It is surprising that there is no evidence that Isaiah 53 had any appreciable influence upon the theology of the church until relatively late. The first actual quotation from that chapter which is applied to Jesus' Passion is found in Acts 8:32 f. (and there the emphasis is upon the sequence of humiliation and exaltation rather than on the atoning nature of Jesus' death; cf. 1 Peter 2:24 f., where Jesus' suffering is interpreted as an example). The title "servant of God" is found only in Matthew 12:18 (where it is used with reference to Jesus' healings); Acts 3:13, 26 (reminiscent of Isa. 53); and Acts 4:27, 30 (where comparison is made to God's servant David in vs. 25 and not to Isa. 53). On the other hand, a quotation in Romans 4:25 shows that, in a rather restricted line of the development, Isaiah 53 was applied to Jesus relatively early in the church. All of this favors the view that vs. 45 did not originate with Jesus but with the Jewish-Christian church. Therefore, it is necessary to consider the possibility that the Greek-speaking Jewish church was the first to discover this relationship to the Old Testament. Luke 22:27 makes Jesus' service the pattern for the conduct of the disciples. The fact that the saying about "serving" (in Greek this word primarily indicates waiting on tables) and "servant" is so firmly embedded here (vs. 43; 9:35; Matt. 23:11) indicates that from a historical point of view the setting for these statements has been preserved best in Luke 22:26 f., where the situation is a meal (cf. 9:33-37).

[35-37] The request of the sons of Zebedee is intended to show once more the completely incomprehensible manner in which God's way runs counter to all human thinking. The glory of Jesus is what is portrayed in Matthew 25:31 (cf. Mark 8:38). **[38]** The cup of suffering is an Old Testament metaphor: Isaiah 51:17, 22; Lamentations 4:21; Psalm 75:8; Martyrdom of Isaiah (a Jewish writing from the second century A.D.) 5:13: "For me only God hath mingled the cup [of martyrdom]."

There has been a great deal of debate over the meaning of the saying about baptism. Irenaeus (end of the second century) was the first to speak of a baptism in blood. In Greek the word "baptize" means "to drown"—in the passive "to go under." There is in the Old Testament the figure of the supplicant whom the waters submerged and who feels that he is at the bottom of the sea (Pss. 42:7; 69:1 f.; Isa. 43:2); but different words are used for this idea in the Greek Old Testament. There is one passage which reads, "Unrighteousness baptizes [submerges] me" (Isa. 21:4 LXX). It may be that Jesus himself was using an Old Testament expression such as this, or perhaps he was merely making a general reference to the death of the two brothers. Luke 12:50 may be the oldest form in which this saying can be recovered with any certainty. The Jewish apocalyptists were expecting that the death and "regeneration" of all men would occur at the end of the world. The word "regeneration" must be distinguished from the word "be born again" which is used elsewhere in the New Testament. "Regeneration" (TEV: New Age) occurs only in Matthew 19:28, where it is clearly apocalyptic and in Titus 3:5, where it indicates baptism. In Paul's writings the concept of being "with Christ" is apocalyptic and describes life in the Kingdom of God (1 Thess. 4:14, 17; 5:10; 2 Cor. 4:14; 13:4; Phil. 1:23). It also designates what baptism gives to man before that time (Rom. 6:3-8). Since John's baptism clearly possessed apocalyptic characteristics, baptism may have been interpreted as an anticipation of eschatological sorrow and "regeneration" even before Jesus. It seems natural, then, to think that Jesus would have used an appropriate expression from the Old Testament. Indeed, it is possible to imagine a "universal baptism" by which Jesus in some sense assumes the eschatological sorrow as a part of his own destiny and thus brings about the "regeneration" of the world (cf. vs. 45). Whether or not such ideas are really implied in the figure, whether this was always the case or simply developed in transmission, whether it should be considered purely as an Old Testament simile—these are questions which can no longer be answered.

[39] In any case, the idea that this suffering would be for the benefit of everyone is not stated in the text as yet (in contrast to vs. 45). All that is affirmed in the text is that these two disciples will share in the suffering. When the church repeated this saying, the words "cup" (the Gospel of the Naassenes connects this saying directly to the saying about the cup at the Last Supper) and "baptism" reminded them of the Lord's Supper and the ritual of baptism, and particularly of the fact that by means of these it would have a share in the destiny of Jesus (Rom. 6:3-8). Probably this is what led to the inclusion of vss. 42-45. The church must have understood the case to be similar to that of the Israelite in the Old Testament who shares in the promises of God and in the land which his forefathers inherited. Through circumcision and the covenant meal he is "incorporated" into the nation, and as a result he travels the same road his forefathers did. The "incorporation" into the destiny of Jesus which bestows a share in his blessing makes one subject to his sovereign demand. Then, as a rule, this "incorporation" is expressed in a life which is similar to the life of Jesus (2 Cor. 4:7-15; 5:18—6:10). The same thing is indicated here by the fact that vs. 38 is in the present tense while vs. 39 is in the future tense: Jesus' pathway in the here and now and the disciples' pathway which will join his in the future, lie on two different planes. All "following after" is, in principle, a sharing in the pathway which he has traveled before. It is the road of vs. 32a and vs. 52b. It is Jesus' own pathway to the cross, and it encompasses every experience of the church. Traveling on Jesus' pathway is something real; therefore, the fact that one is traveling this way will be manifested again and again in many similarities between the life of the disciple and the life of Jesus.

[40] The concluding remark in vs. 40 is grammatically difficult even in Greek. Probably this is due to the fact that, out of reverence, the use of God's name was avoided.* The fact that Jesus has left open the question for whom these places of honor have been prepared (by God) makes it very clear that to Jesus, discipleship does not allow one to claim any special reward. In a very pointed manner Jesus rejects the idea that suffering is meritorious. The fact that one suffers in some specific way as a part of sharing in the pathway of Jesus does not qualify him to receive a reward, neither does it allow him to make any special demand. It is certain, however, that God will never forget it (9:41).

[41] In the following conversation with all the disciples Jesus unfolds the ethical (vss. 42-44) and doctrinal (vs. 45) significance of the principle by which his pathway is organized. **[42]** For this reason Mark emphasizes "calling them all together" (3:23; cf. 3:20-35, et al.). **[43]** In comparison with 9:35 (*q.v.*) the statement of this principle is much more detailed here. Perhaps the contrast to the organization of the world was not formulated until after the organization of the church had been established. Nevertheless, it is clear that the latter cannot simply be patterned after political organization so that the synod becomes the legislature and spiritual decisions become a matter of popular voting according to party platforms. **[45]** The expression "for many" (RSV) is typically Jewish and actually means "for the sake of all" (not "instead of"). "Many" merely designates the vast multitude in contrast to the individual, without intending to indicate that some might not be included (of course, that remains a possibility). The only other place in Mark where the death of Jesus is designated explicitly as a "ransom" or an atonement is 14:24. The idea that all innocent suffering was borne on account of one's own sin as

* The English translation supplies the word "God," which is not found in the Greek.

well as on account of the sins of others was widespread in Judaism. This concept could not express the uniqueness of the sufferings of Jesus, and this may be the reason why in the New Testament it is not applied very often to his sufferings. His was to be an "eschatological" suffering, which as the end of Israel's mission fulfills all previous suffering. Moreover, his suffering would mean that a new age was dawning and the Kingdom of God was coming near. The church followed Jesus' custom (2:27 f.; 3:4; 7:29; Matt. 8:10-12; et al.) and applied this statement to all nations, restricting it no longer to Israelites (at least after the time of Acts 11:20 and the time of Paul). This is a new idea which is contrary to all Jewish patterns. Even in this context vs. 45 is not only a doctrinally correct explanation of Jesus' pathway but also a justification of the previous statements (cf. vs. 39). Jesus' suffering is explained, but not in a way which makes it possible to take note of it or preach it in a purely intellectual manner. The explanation makes it possible to believe only if one pursues the life of a disciple in the kind of discipleship described in vss. 42-44. Consequently it also forms a transition to vs. 52 (which see). **[43]** This is why vs. 43 begins with the words, "This, however, is not the way it is among you." The absence of any hierarchy in the church such as is described in vs. 42 is one result of Jesus' Passion which cannot be abolished. Not even all the mistakes of a church can undo it.

Discipleship as a Divine Miracle 10:46-52;
cf. Matt. 20:29-34; Luke 18:35-43

46They came to Jericho. As Jesus was leaving with his disciples
and a large crowd, a blind man named Bartimaeus, the son of
Timaeus, was sitting and begging by the road. 47When he heard
that it was Jesus of Nazareth, he began to shout, "Jesus! Son of
David! Have mercy on me!" 48Many scolded him and told him
to be quiet. But he shouted even more loudly, "Son of David, have
mercy on me!" 49Jesus stopped and said, "Call him." So they called
the blind man. "Cheer up!" they said. "Get up, he is calling you."
50He threw off his cloak, jumped up and came to Jesus. 51"What do

you want me to do for you?" Jesus asked him. "Teacher," the blind man answered, "I want to see again." [52]"Go," Jesus told him, "your faith has made you well." At once he was able to see, and followed Jesus on the road.

This story has been put here by Mark, who transformed it into a picture of discipleship by the addition of the last few words. It emphasizes the importance of the Passion story, which follows immediately, in the same way that 8:22-26 emphasizes the importance of Jesus' first clear teaching about the suffering of the Son of Man (8:27-32). The words "with his disciples and a large crowd" (vs. 46) are a later addition which Mark uses as another reference to discipleship. The setting of the story in Jericho has always been a part of the tradition. "Leaving" comes, then, from the tradition, and "to Jericho" comes from Mark. The idea that Jesus made a journey from Galilee through Transjordan to Jerusalem by way of Jericho may have arisen from the way Mark arranged the story, although his reasons for this arrangement are purely theological (a late manuscript has this correction in 10:1: "to Judea through Transjordan"). Luke 17:14 (there were official priests only in Jerusalem); John 2:23; 5:1; 7:10; 10:40; 11:54 may be evidence that Jesus was in Jerusalem or its environs more than once; however, it is not possible to be certain about this.

[46] "Bar" is Aramaic for "son"; consequently, both names have the same meaning. This may indicate that the story was told first in Aramaic, and then was taken over by a Greek-speaking church which added the translation of the foreign-sounding name. **[47]** This is the only place in Mark where "Son of David" occurs. On the basis of 2 Samuel 7:12 ff. the Messiah was expected to be a descendant of David (cf. Ps. 89:3 f., 19-37; Pss. of Sol. 17:5, 23-49; in Qumran, 4Q Flor. 1:10 ff.). **[48-50]** The comment that "many scolded him" gives far greater prominence to the persistence of the blind man's faith and to Jesus' determination to give his attention to this helpless and handicapped man. This is what Jesus' present pathway to Jerusalem means, and only those who are like the blind man will share in the miracle of enlightenment. The story clearly states that Jesus turned to the blind man; moreover, it affirms positively that the blind man came to Jesus. These two actions are indicative of the correct interpretation of the Passion narrative. **[51]** The order of events in the healing has been constructed deliberately. The form of address "Master" (RSV) is more meaningful here, and perhaps more reverent, than the usual address (*rabbuni* is used here instead of *rabbi*). The word that is used in the request and in the description of the healing occurs in the promise to the blind in Isaiah 42:18. **[52]** Jesus' reply re-emphasizes the fact that the objective of this story is to present an illustration of genuine faith (cf. 5:34). In this connection the word translated "make well" also means "save" (as in 5:34).

Once more, immediately before the Passion narrative, Mark demonstrates to his readers what faith is and what it means to be a disciple of Jesus. These elements follow one another: persistent pleading, continual shouting when opposed, cheering up, coming to Jesus, being questioned by him, having him open one's eyes, and following him on the road. When a man's eyes have been opened by a divine miracle, he can see what is happening in Jesus and can "follow Jesus on the road." This is the only way a man can understand what now will be made known—the pathway of the Son of Man in suffering.

VI

THE PASSION
AND THE RESURRECTION
OF THE SON OF MAN
11:1—16:8

A. The Last Days in Jerusalem
11:1—13:37

Entering the Temple 11:1-11;
cf. Matt. 21:1-11; Luke 19:29-38, 45

[1]As they came near Jerusalem, at the towns of Bethphage and
Bethany they came to the Mount of Olives. Jesus sent two of his
disciples on ahead [2]with these instructions: "Go to the village
there ahead of you. As soon as you get there you will find a colt
tied up that has never been ridden. Untie it and bring it here.
[3]And if someone asks you, 'Why are you doing that?' tell him,
'The Master needs it and will send it back here at once.' " [4]So they
went and found a colt out in the street, tied to the door of a house.
As they were untying it, [5]some of the bystanders asked them,
"What are you doing, untying that colt?" [6]They answered just as
Jesus had told them, so the men let them go. [7]They brought the
colt to Jesus, threw their cloaks over the animal, and Jesus got on.
[8]Many people spread their cloaks on the road, while others cut
branches in the fields and spread them on the road. [9]The people
who were in front and those who followed behind began to shout,
"Praise God! God bless him who comes in the name of the Lord!
[10]God bless the coming kingdom of our father David! Praise be to
God!"

[11]Jesus entered Jerusalem, went into the Temple, and looked
around at everything. But since it was already late in the day, he
went out to Bethany with the twelve disciples.

(Vs. 9: Ps. 118:25 f.)

This story is remarkable. The preparation for the triumphal entry and the great enthusiasm of the people come to naught. Shouts of joy ring out—but only outside the city. There is no announcement that the Messiah has come. Zechariah 9:9 is neither quoted nor clearly alluded to, although the expression "young colt" in the Greek Bible also means "a fresh, new colt" and, therefore, led to the composition of vs. 2b even before Mark. Finally all the excitement ends without anything being accomplished, since Jesus looks at the temple as a tourist might and then leaves. Apart from the enthusiasm of the people the triumphal entry must have seemed very insignificant. It is obvious that the church was tempted to describe it with greater splendor than it actually possessed. Only a few embellishments if any have been added in vs. 8. It is possible that in contrast to the general expectation of a Davidic Messiah who would drive out the Romans by force, Jesus consciously desired to present the completely different character of the peaceful king of Zechariah 9:9, but was misunderstood. In any case, he did not take advantage of this outbreak of enthusiasm on the part of the people in order to reach his goal. It is unlikely that the whole story has been fabricated at some later time on the basis of Zechariah 9:9, because if that were the case, much clearer reference to that prophecy would have been made.

[1] The geographical references are peculiar because Bethphage is closer to Jerusalem than Bethany, which is about one and one-half miles away. Did Jesus go to Bethany by way of Bethphage, and wait until the next day or later before proceeding to Jerusalem? It is clear that Mark, writing at a later date, is not acquainted with these places. According to Zechariah 14:4, God was expected to appear on the Mount of Olives at the time of the end; according to Josephus (*Antiquities* XX:169; from the year A.D. 93/94), it was the Messiah who was to appear there (cf. Ezek. 11:23; 2 Sam. 15:30). **[2]** The text does not specify whether this is the colt of a horse or of a donkey. Nevertheless, the latter is more common in Palestine, although the Greek word when used alone usually meant the colt of a horse. Even without taking into account that there is no other passage which portrays

Jesus riding an animal, the statement that the colt had never been ridden before gets the point across emphatically (cf. Zech. 9:9). **[3]** Jesus' instructions in vs. 3 strengthen that emphasis. This is the only place in Mark's Gospel where Jesus is called "Master" (*kurios,* cf. 12:36 f. and the form of address in 7:28). Perhaps there was a time when this word meant "our Master"; however, at the time Mark wrote it could only be a declaration of the fact that Jesus is the absolute "Master" over everyone. **[4]** The church fathers deduced from Genesis 49:11 that the colt was tied to a vine (Justin, *Apology* 32:6, from the middle of the second century; Clement, *Paid.* I, 5:15, from about A.D. 200). This is a typical example of the way Old Testament passages led to the inclusion of additional details in the story of Jesus. **[5-7]** The significance of Jesus' ride is accentuated by the fact that things happened exactly as he had anticipated. The ride signifies that God directs everything and moves men according to his will. **[8]** The spreading of the cloaks (2 Kings 9:13; Acts of Pilate 1:3, from the 4/5 century?) is a rather strange way of paying homage, especially since Jesus is riding and the road is long. The "branches" can hardly be palm branches (in spite of John 12:13) since palm trees are not common in Jerusalem. They may indicate that the triumphal entry took place in the fall, since it was customary to cut branches at the Feast of Tabernacles. **[9]** The Hallel, found in vs. 9, was used regularly as a part of the celebration at that feast. Obviously Jesus is riding in the middle of the crowd, part of which went before him and part followed after. "Hosannah" (translated here: "Praise God") literally means "please help" and was familiar to every Israelite, since it comes at the end of the Hallel (Ps. 118:25), which included Psalms 113-118 and was read after the morning prayer at every major feast. Apparently, "Hosannah" had a strong eschatological connotation at the time of Jesus and was a call for God's final intervention. **[10]** Nevertheless, Mark uses it to indicate no more than a shout of praise (vs. 10b; cf. Ps. 148:1; Didache 10:6: "Hosannah to the God of David"—or should this be interpreted as "from heaven"?). The first cheer (Ps. 118:25 f.) might be for any pilgrim, but the second reveals an anticipation of the promised Kingdom of the Messiah (cf. 10:48)—perhaps it forms a contrast to the cry of Bartimaeus, who had understood that the "Son of David" and his kingdom had already come. Furthermore, David is never called "our father" in Judaism; it is David's relationship to his son which is important (Luke 1:32). We may surmise, then, that this statement was created as a parallel to the first cheer by the church, for whom Jesus was the Son of David (cf. 12:35). **[11]** The jubilation seems to have died down before Jesus entered Jerusalem, as there is no record of any intervention by the Jewish or Roman authorities. The statement that he entered Jerusalem appears to be another of those geographical details which are found occasionally at the end of a section. Not until vss. 15-18 will it become apparent that this visit to the temple was not accidental.

Here, at the beginning of the Passion narrative, Mark portrays Jesus as the Lord who has everything at his command, including even the donkey of a farmer whom he did not know. The people have correctly perceived Jesus' authority in these events. Yes, unless this dimension is recognized, the depth of Jesus' Passion cannot be comprehended. And yet, the people did not fully understand what was happening here, before their eyes. This will be made clear in what follows.

The End of the Temple of Israel and God's Turning Toward the Gentiles 11:12-26;

cf. Matt. 21:12-22; Luke 19:45-48

[12]The next day, as they were coming back from Bethany,
Jesus was hungry. [13]He saw in the distance a fig tree covered with
leaves, so he went to it to see if he could find any figs on it; but
when he came to it he found only leaves, because it was not the
right time for figs. [14]Jesus said to the fig tree: "No one shall ever
eat figs from you again!" And his disciples heard him.

[15]When they arrived in Jerusalem, Jesus went to the Temple and
began to drive out all those who bought and sold in the Temple.
He overturned the tables of the money-changers and the stools of
those who sold pigeons, [16]and would not let anyone carry anything

through the Temple courts. 17He then taught the people, "It is
written in the Scriptures that God said, 'My house will be called a
house of prayer for all peoples.' But you have turned it into a
hideout for thieves!"

18The chief priests and the teachers of the Law heard of this,
so they began looking for some way to kill Jesus. They were afraid
of him, because the whole crowd was amazed at his teaching.

19When evening came, Jesus and his disciples left the city.

20Early next morning, as they walked along the road, they saw
the fig tree. It was dead all the way down to its roots. 21Peter
remembered what had happened and said to Jesus, "Look,
Teacher, the fig tree you cursed has died!" 22Jesus answered them:
"Remember this! If you have faith in God, 23you can say to this
hill, 'Get up and throw yourself in the sea.' If you do not doubt
in your heart, but believe that what you say will happen, it will be
done for you. 24For this reason I tell you: When you pray and ask
for something, believe that you have received it, and everything
will be given you. 25And when you stand praying, forgive whatever you have against anyone, so that your Father in heaven will
forgive your sins. [26If you do not forgive others, neither will your
Father in heaven forgive your sins.]"

(Vs. 17: Isa. 56:7; Jer. 7:11.)

The outcome of vss. 12-14 is found in vss. 20 f. Since Mark has a preference for this style of composition (cf. 5:21-43), it is likely that he has purposely arranged the story about the cursing of the fig tree as a framework around the cleansing of the temple. Therefore, we must pay attention to the message he wants to convey in this manner. The story which forms the framework is rather strange. Why does Jesus look for figs and curse the tree when he does not find any, although it is not the right season for figs? This is the only miracle which Jesus performs in Jerusalem; moreover, it is the only one of his miracles which involves cursing. Obviously, the entire story must be interpreted symbolically whether or not it is historical. Moreover, it is clear that it refers to unfruitful Israel (or to the scribes or priests. Cf. Jer. 8:13; Joel 1:7; Ezek. 17:24; Micah 7:1; Hosea 9:10, 16 f.). The story may have developed from a saying of Jesus, such as Luke 13:6-9, and perhaps it was told in order to emphasize the seriousness of his warning, even as the Old Testament prophets emphasized the seriousness of their admonitions by means of symbolical acts. If we ask whether or not the story really happened in this way, it is obvious that we have not reached a proper understanding of it. We will understand the story correctly only if we ask what Mark wants to tell us about Jesus in it. However, the story of the cleansing of the temple must be based upon some historical act of Jesus. It would have been almost impossible for Jesus to have cleared the vast temple court—especially to have done so without causing the intervention of the Jewish temple police or of the Roman military stationed nearby. It is recorded that a single merchant once offered 3,000 sheep for sale in the court of the temple.

It is more likely that Jesus, in a symbolic way, cleared only a limited area of the temple court, and that the manner in which the story was handed down in the tradition created the impression of an operation which was much more extensive. The story was revised later to make it appear that Jesus had been involved only in a reformation of the management of the temple (cf. vs. 16) in order to make the story inoffensive in a time when the church still lived within the bounds of Judaism. Certainly Jesus was using the symbolic act of driving out a few money-changers and merchants to emphasize some particular word of warning, but that warning has been omitted in the process of development. This warning is found in Mark 14:58, where it appears as slanderous testimony against Jesus (see comment). The possibility that Zechariah 14:21a (cf. vs. 4a) had an effect upon the further development is not ruled out. Even before Mark, this Old Testament passage was used to clarify the meaning of Jesus' intervention. Mark has placed it within a framework that refers to Jesus' teaching, because he regards this quotation as the theme of the entire section. It constitutes the center around which everything else in the section has been arranged. Perhaps he even referred the pronoun "my" to Jesus (instead of to God). The traditions vary considerably as to the time when the cleansing of the temple occurred. According to Matthew 21:12 it followed immediately after the triumphal entry and came before the cursing of the fig tree. This is probably because Matthew wants to make it a climax to the story of the triumphal entry. According to John 2:13 ff. it occurred at the beginning of Jesus' ministry. This is probably because John wants to point out the fundamental cleavage between Jesus and official Judaism from the very first. The chronology of the Synoptics is probably correct, because 11:28 presupposes some demonstration of the authority of Jesus such as apparently took place in the cleansing of the temple. Vss. 22-25 are found in various places in the other Gospels. This shows that they are independent sayings on the subject of prayer which are incorporated in the story wherever it seems appropriate. They present the cursing of the fig tree as an example of the power of prayer, and are important to Mark (and possibly to the first narrator also) as a sign of divine judgment. It follows, then, that the church must have added these sayings here before Mark. Jesus' curse was interpreted differently by the first narrator, by the church, and by Mark, in the way that a living proclamation is adapted again and again to meet the needs of the contemporary situation.

[12] That Jesus was "hungry" must be an explanation that was added later, since the disappointment of a hungry person is not sufficient provocation for a curse like this. Such a curse can be understood only as a sign of judgment upon Israel. **[13]** The leaves are mentioned in order to make the miracle of the withering more vivid. The reference to the fact that it was not the season for figs makes it absurd for Jesus to look for any. One may surmise that this remark was not a part of the story at first, but was added later when the story was included in the events of the days before the Passover. For this reason some scholars place the triumphal entry in the fall, in which case Jesus would have spent half a year in Jerusalem. Of course, such sweeping conclusions are not justified by one single story which has been handed down without any connection to the Passion narrative. Nevertheless, there are other reasons to suspect that Jesus' stay in Jerusalem continued somewhat longer (see comment on 11:8), e.g., 14:49 presupposes a minimum of more than five days. **[14]** The significance of the curse is not made clear until later. **[15]** Immediately following this, Jesus' judgment upon the temple is recorded. This is Mark's indication that Jesus is thinking of Israel when he utters the curse—that Israel which does not open its temple to him, thus keeping it closed to all nations. There is no other reason for disturbing the money-changers and merchants. They were situated in the Court of the Gentiles, which was not sacred although it was not totally secular. It corresponded to the square before a church visited by pilgrims and was not to be used as a shortcut by those who passed by. These business dealings were necessary since the worshipers had to purchase animals for sacrifice and exchange foreign money for ancient Hebrew or Tyrian currency to pay the temple tax. According to Mark, Jesus' symbolic action is not part of a reform, and he has interpreted Jesus' action correctly. He regards Jesus' action as a sign indicating the disappearance of the old temple (and the construction of an entirely new one), an event which had been expected on the basis of Ezekiel 40–48 and Ethiopian Enoch 90:28-29 (2/1 century B.C.) (cf. the cleansing of Jerusalem by the Messiah and the entry of the heathen in Psalms of Solomon 17:32 f., 2nd century B.C.). **[16]** Vs. 16 is strange, because in it Jesus appears to be no more than a reformer who defends Jewish laws of holiness. Such regulations are actually found in the writings of Josephus (*Contra Apion* II. 106) and the rabbis. **[17]** By mentioning that Jesus taught (cf. 1:21-28), Mark emphasizes the fundamental meaning of what is being said here. The Greek tense expresses an action which is repeated. At first we heard of Jesus' teaching in parables and next of his clear teaching about the suffering of the Son of Man; now we hear of something new: "for all peoples" (or: Gentiles). According to this, Mark understands the cleansing of the temple to indicate the abolition in principle of an institution which was restricted entirely to Jews. As a place of prayer the temple should reflect the attitude that man has nothing to achieve or offer to God; consequently, it should be open to all men. In this way the whole principle of legalism is fully overcome, the completion of what was begun in 2:23—3:6. **[18]** The reaction of the authorities, which is almost identical to that which is described in 3:6, underlines the importance of this truth. Mark emphasizes this a third time when he refers to the amazement of the crowd at the "teaching" of Jesus. The law gave Israel a certain exclusiveness which now has been abolished. God can be approached in prayer—through Israel—by all people. This is made plain at the beginning of Jesus' pathway of suffering. Even his disciples do not comprehend it, and a Gentile will be the first to understand (15:39). Mark's position is much the same as Paul's, who regarded the cross as the end of the law and the beginning of a life based upon grace and offered to all nations. **[19]** Jesus' leaving the city may symbolize the same separation. **[20, 21]** Peter's remark calls attention to the fulfillment of Jesus' curse, which emphasizes even more clearly Jesus' break with the leaders of Israel. Mark understands this as a sign of the judgment of God which puts an end to that separatism in the temple. **[22]** Mark has Jesus answer "them" and not Peter alone, because he wants to emphasize the fact that what follows has a general application. **[23]** This saying has been preserved in its original form in Matthew 17:20. Moreover, the wording of 1 Corinthians 13:2 is probably reminiscent of this saying of Jesus. Luke 17:6 records the same saying but has replaced "hill" with "mulberry tree." Perhaps this happened because the saying was associated with the cursing of the fig tree before Mark and the two were confused in the process of oral transmission so that "hill" was replaced by "tree." As a result the statement reached Luke in this form. There are rabbinical parallels which speak of uprooting a tree by the power of prayer. In comparison with these, what is new in the original form of Jesus' saying is that such a promise is granted to a faith which is as tiny as a mustard seed. The decisive feature is not a larger amount or special quality of faith or theological insight. Jesus' saying takes no account of any measurable difference in the quantity of faith. It refers simply to the existence of a faith to which everything has been promised just because it expects everything from God and nothing from itself. Of course, a person with this kind of faith always prays that the will of God will be done, not his own. In Mark's version "faith" is defined as "not doubting." This is certainly true, especially since the Greek word (and the German) contrasts "duplicity" with the absolute simplicity of faith. Doubt describes man in his indecision and in his wavering between God and every other source of help. Mark's version is more susceptible to misunderstanding since the comparison of faith to a mustard seed has been omitted. One might infer that faith is regarded as an outstanding achievement. The statement about faith as tiny as a mustard seed appears in various contexts. In Matthew 17:20 it follows the healing of the epileptic whom the disciples failed to help. It is introduced in Luke 17:6 by the disciples' request for greater faith. Before Mark, the church connected it to the cursing of the fig tree. As stated above, Mark uses the cursing of the fig tree as a framework around the cleansing of the temple. Therefore it is more likely that for him vss. 23-25 illustrate the expression "house of prayer." In this respect Mark's position is very similar to 1 Corinthians 13:2, which clearly declares that faith manifested in love, rather than extraordinary miracles accomplished by faith, is decisive. The continuation in vss. 27-33 will show that there is no possibility of proving Jesus' authority and that the way to him is obstructed if one asks for such proof. **[24]** The wording "have received" shows that the passage is speaking of the kind of faith which knows God gives even before man asks. **[25]** The rule about forgiving has simply been added to the theme "praying." It is similar to Matthew 6:14 (cf. Matt. 5:23 f.) and signifies that a right relationship to God always includes a right relationship to one's fellowmen. **[26]** Vs. 26 is found in only a few manuscripts. Here copyists have added Matthew 6:15 and at the same time have assimilated it to Mark 11:25. Although sayings of this kind were handed down correctly in substance, this particular instance shows how long the process continued by which they were changed in form when they were placed in a new context.

The development is interesting. The cursing of the fig tree was originally interpreted as a prophetic sign of the judgment of God upon stubborn Israel (similar to Luke 13:6-9). When this was no longer an immediate concern in the Gentile-Christian church, they found its general relevance in the demonstration of the power of prayer, and added vss. 22-24. Finally, Mark used it as a framework for the cleansing of the temple, thereby strongly emphasizing the great and crucial transition from a temple which was open only to Israel to one open to all nations. This, in essence, is what Jesus' Passion means to Mark.

The Question Concerning Jesus' Authority 11:27-33;
cf. Matt. 21:23-27; Luke 20:1-8

27So they came back to Jerusalem. As Jesus was walking in the
Temple, the chief priests, the teachers of the Law, and the elders
came to him 28and asked him: "What right do you have to do these
things? Who gave you the right to do them?" 29Jesus answered
them: "I will ask you just one question, and if you give me an
answer I will tell you what right I have to do these things. 30Tell
me, where did John's right to baptize come from: from God or
from man?" 31They started to argue among themselves: "What
shall we say? If we answer, 'From God,' he will say, 'Why, then,
did you not believe John?' 32But if we say, 'From man . . .' "
(They were afraid of the people, because everyone was convinced that John had been a prophet.) 33So their answer to Jesus
was, "We don't know." And Jesus said to them, "Neither will I tell you, then, by what right I do these things."

At this point one last controversy begins which is similar to those at the beginning of Jesus' ministry (2:1—3:6). The present form may be attributed in large part to the church's arguments with Judaism, which have had an influence even on the formation of details. Even if they had considered the consequences of answering as indicated in vss. 31 f., the leaders named in vs. 27 would not have admitted that they did not know the answer. It is likely that the church in its controversies with Judaism referred in this way to John's baptism, which was recognized to some extent by everyone. Of course, this does not deny that Jesus himself engaged in similar controversies with the leading Jewish authorities in Jerusalem. The reference in vs. 28 to "these things" merely indicates that the question might have been joined directly to vss. 15-17 in the tradition (cf. John 2:18). In the present arrangement this episode occurs on a later day, and it is not clear how the affairs of the temple are able to proceed peacefully in spite of vs. 15. This is one more confirmation of the supposition that Mark is the one who adapted the story of the cursing of the fig tree as a framework for the cleansing of the temple. Vs. 27 makes the necessary transition back to the setting in the temple. Mark must have applied "these things" in a more general sense to all of Jesus' activity (cf. 1:22, 27). The construction is very instructive insofar as his proclamation is concerned. In the cleansing of the temple, Jesus' action is carried out as a judgment upon the temple although that judgment is visible only in token fashion. The temple is replaced by a "house of prayer for all peoples" and the withered fig tree is replaced by the power of God which is given in response to faith and prayer. But this power will be experienced only by faith—not by those who are uninvolved or who ask for external proof. 12:1-12 will show in a definitive way that those who do not perceive the judgment of God pass sentence upon Jesus and in so doing bring judgment upon themselves. Accordingly, 12:12 places this section in brackets by repeating what was said in 11:18.

[27] Once again all the parties who compose the Sanhedrin appear (cf. 8:31). **[28, 29]** The subject of debate is the authority of Jesus, which was also central in 1:27 (see comment). **[30]** "From God" is an interpretation of the Greek phrase "from heaven." The Jews, out of reverence, would not mention God's name and used "from heaven" as a paraphrase for "from God." Whether or not Jesus ever asked it, the question about John's baptism shows that there were situations in which it was not possible to evade a "yes" or "no" or to consider the question in an impersonal way. **[29, 30]** Accordingly, Jesus twice demands an answer, and the way his question is formulated in the Greek text clearly indicates that he expects an unequivocal answer. **[31, 32]** It would have been logical to have them reason this way: "He will say, 'That is the source of my authority also.' " However, having Jesus reproach them for their unbelief gave greater emphasis to the point which the narrator wanted to make here. What their indecision really exposes is their disbelief. The question was asked so that they might receive the kind of faith which no longer requires any proof. This may not be an accurate description of the thinking of the enemies of Jesus, yet it is very appropriate for the subject around which the conversation revolves. **[33]** They cannot deny the work of God. They do not wish to be irreligious, so they insist that they do not know. Their attitude is simply one of wanting to reserve judgment. Therefore, God is not able to give himself to them even though he confronts them directly in Jesus.

The Parable Concerning Jesus' Passion 12:1-12;
cf. Matt. 21:33-46; Luke 20:9-19

1Then Jesus spoke to them in parables: "There was a man who
planted a vineyard, put a fence around it, dug a hole for the
winepress, and built a watch tower. Then he rented the vineyard
to tenants and left home on a trip. 2When the time came for
gathering the grapes, he sent a slave to the tenants to receive
from them his share of the harvest. 3The tenants grabbed the
slave, beat him and sent him back without a thing. 4Then the
owner sent another slave; the tenants beat him over the head
and treated him shamefully. 5The owner sent another slave, and
they killed him; and they treated many others the same way,
beating some and killing others. 6The only one left to send was
the man's own dear son. Last of all, then, he sent his son to the
tenants. 'I am sure they will respect my son,' he said. 7But those
tenants said to one another, 'This is the owner's son. Come on, let
us kill him, and the vineyard will be ours!' 8So they took the son
and killed him, and threw his body out of the vineyard.

9"What, then, will the owner of the vineyard do?" asked
Jesus. "He will come and kill those men and turn over the vineyard to other tenants. 10Surely you have read this scripture?

'The stone which the builders rejected as worthless
Turned out to be the most important stone.
11This was done by the Lord,
How wonderful it is!' "

[12]The Jewish leaders tried to arrest Jesus, because they knew that he had told this parable against them. They were afraid of the crowd, however, so they left him and went away.

(Vs. 1: Isa. 5:1 f.; vss. 10 f.: Ps. 118:22 f.)

The short introduction in vs. 1 and the conclusion in vs. 12 have been written by Mark. Both reveal his hand in style and in content. The quotation in vss. 10 f. is not pertinent to the point of vs. 9 since the rejection of the stone is only an incidental feature, while the decisive thing is its being placed as the cornerstone. This is an example of the witness of the church which found a reference to the Easter event in this Old Testament saying. This passage and others which liken Christ to a stone were frequently cited in the church and combined in various ways (Acts 4:11; Rom. 9:33; 1 Peter 2:6-8; cf. Eph. 2:20; Barnabas 6:2-4; Justin, *Dial.* 36:1). It is not clear whether the parable originated with Jesus or if it can be traced to the church, which used it to describe what actually happened in Jesus' Passion. The latter view is favored not only by the clear designation of Jesus as "Son" (cf. 15:39), but also by the nature of the parable. It is the only parable in the Synoptics which strongly resembles an allegory (cf. 4:1-9). The whole becomes meaningful when the tenants are seen as representative of Israel, the servants representative of the prophets, the son representative of Jesus, etc. In most instances such an interpretation of individual details is characteristic of the church (cf. 4:13-20). Furthermore, in vs. 1, Isaiah 5:1 f. is quoted from the Septuagint, which would have been done only in the Greek-speaking church. In this way the vineyard was interpreted allegorically to mean Israel. The "many" servants must refer to the many prophets of Israel, because insofar as the story itself is concerned it would have been absurd to send more servants. Finally, the "dear son" is a direct reference to Jesus as the Son of God (1:11). Moreover, vs. 9 presupposes the mission to the Gentiles and vss. 10 f. are quoted word for word from the Septuagint. Undoubtedly this is an allegory which was formulated by the church and further developed by Matthew and Luke. It is likely that it is based upon a real parable. A much simpler version is found in the Gospel of Thomas (65) in which two servants are beaten and the son killed. The parable concludes with the exhortation, "Whoever has ears let him hear." Could this be the original form of a parable of Jesus? It is possible that servants would have been treated in this way, since large areas of land were held by foreigners and the Jews were inclined to revolt against them. Even the sending of the son is conceivable, at least as a development from the preceding events. And yet it is unlikely that such things really happened—especially the killing of the son—so it would be more reasonable to consider this to be a parable in which the church uses the figure of the son to refer to the person and the destiny of the Son of God. This first attempt at forming an allegory led to further embellishments.

[1] With the basic assertion that Jesus spoke once more "in parables" (although only one parable follows; cf. 3:23), Mark emphasizes the significance of what follows. No private instruction of the disciples is included here—that instruction took place in 8:31. **[12]** In contrast to what has happened previously, here the leaders of Israel understand what Jesus intends to say (vs. 12). It is, however, an understanding which leads to judgment—not to salvation. This is another indication that Mark does not regard parables as pedagogical aids to illustrate what otherwise would be difficult to comprehend. For Mark a parable is a way of speaking about God, to which a mere intellectual response is not possible. The only person who can understand a parable is one who is willing to accept or to reject its message. It must produce either faith or disbelief. **[1]** The vineyard is described exactly as it is in Isaiah 5:1 f. The tower, on the top of which there was a lookout, is the farm building in which the workers lived during the harvest. It is apparent, however, that the main concern here is not the conduct of the vineyard (Israel) as it was in Isaiah, but the conduct of the tenants. **[2]** The owner is pictured as a foreigner. It was customary for the rent to be a share of the harvest. **[3, 4]** Perhaps the conduct of the tenants should be regarded as a rebellion. Vss. 5 and 8 indicate that the emphasis should be put upon that element which cannot be explained and which staggers the imagination. Obviously, the metaphor has been shaped by the things which it is supposed to represent—the persecution of the prophets and the slaying of Jesus. **[5, 6]** Verse 5 makes the point of the passage very conspicuous: Although the action of Israel is difficult to comprehend, the action of the owner is far more incomprehensible—that is, the gracious action of God. **[7]** Moreover, it is obvious that the reasoning of the tenants is illogical, because the owner is still living. This only serves to portray their frightful maliciousness. **[8]** The feature about throwing his body out of the vineyard probably serves the same purpose and is not likely to be a reference to Hebrews 13:12. **[9-11]** The "other tenants" to whom the vineyard ultimately will be given are of course the Gentiles. This is why Mark added this parable right after 11:15-17 (and after the question about Jesus' authority in 11:27-33, which was connected to 11:15-17 in the tradition. Compare the introduction to 11:27-33). Israel's rejection of the gospel is the reason why the gospel passed from Israel to the other nations. Matthew 8:11 f.; 12:41 f.; and 23:29 ff., 37, speak of Israel's disbelief in a similar way, but no reference is made to the crucifixion of Jesus in connection with it (cf. Acts 3:13 ff.; 7:31 ff.; 13:27 f.). Thus the parable describes God's history, his way with regard to Israel and then away from Israel to the Gentile world. Obviously, this creates a problem. The passages in Matthew are clearly regarded as messages to Israel. They are not meant to exalt Gentile Christendom, but to call Israel to repentance. Mark's solution to the problem emphasizes, on the one hand, the contrast between the way the Jews treated Jesus and his treatment by their leaders (vs. 12); on the other hand, Mark uses the example of the disciples to show how deeply all men are entangled in unbelief and how they are threatened by it (cf. 8:14-21). A Gentile Christian church (accordingly, the vast majority of churches today) needs to be told that its unbelief and its haughtiness with respect to Israel will have even more disastrous consequences (Rom. 11:17-24). So the parable ends with a warning which must not be ignored: God is not bound to Israel (nor to a Christian church which has become disobedient). The church has added the Old Testament verses which triumphantly witness to the Easter victory over the adversary. **[12]**

The conclusion is typical of Mark. For one thing, he distinguished between the teachers of Israel, who wanted to kill Jesus, and the common people, who admired him even though they did not understand the mystery of his suffering. For another thing, Jesus' attack upon the misinterpretation of the privileged position of Israel in comparison with the Gentiles is followed by the decision to kill him, as it was in 11:18 and before that in 3:6 (see comment).

Taken by itself the parable explains that Jesus' Passion is a result of Israel's disbelief just as was the fate of the prophets. Viewed in this way the parable is a call to repentance. The church's conviction that in the Easter event God would triumph over man's rejection has been made one of the primary emphases in this passage by the addition of vss. 10 f. Finally, with his editorial remarks at the beginning and the end of the parable Mark emphasizes the fact that Jesus' message can be understood only by one who permits himself to be so gripped by it that he himself becomes involved. Mark considers this involvement as resulting in a "yes" or "no" to Jesus. Which it is depends upon whether a man thinks he has a special place in God's favor and can make special demands upon God; or whether he, like the Gentiles, waits for the grace of God with empty hands (cf. 7:24-30).

The Pharisees' Question 12:13-17;
cf. Matt. 22:15-22; Luke 20:20-26

[13]Some Pharisees and some members of Herod's party were sent to Jesus to trap him with questions. [14]They came to him and said: "Teacher, we know that you are an honest man. You don't worry about what people think, because you pay no attention to what a man seems to be, but you teach the truth about God's will for man. Tell us, is it against our Law to pay taxes to the Roman Emperor? Should we pay them, or not?" [15]But Jesus saw through their trick and answered: "Why are you trying to trap me? Bring a silver coin, and let me see it." [16]They brought him

one and he asked, "Whose face and name are these?" "The
Emperor's," they answered. 17So Jesus said, "Well, then, pay to
the Emperor what belongs to him, and pay to God what belongs
to God." And they were filled with wonder at him.

The information given about the situation and the person who questions Jesus is very vague. Apparently the wording and, to some extent, the substance also, have been preserved from debates between Jewish groups and the church. Whenever the church encountered a problem it endeavored to ask, "What answer would Jesus have given?" This passage may contain some sayings which have come from Jesus. It is possible, for example, that vs. 17a is his response to those who were hoping for an earthly "Kingdom of God" with an ethnic-political character. If this is true, then Jesus' answer, which had been handed down as an independent saying, was developed subsequently into a debate with the Pharisees, as was done in the following section. A collection of such controversies may have been assembled before Mark wrote his Gospel, and he included them here in order to illustrate the growing hostility toward Jesus.

[13] Herod's supporters were also mentioned with the Pharisees in 3:6. The insincerity in the conversation is pointed out immediately. The discussion is being misused in an effort to defeat Jesus and get the upper hand. **[14]** Therefore, even the compliments are provocative and intended to trip him up. He is thus addressed as a teacher who teaches "God's will for man," i.e., a teacher of ethics. The conversation centers around the Roman poll tax, which was introduced in A.D. 6 and which the nationalistic party of the Zealots refused to pay (cf. 3:18). **[15]** Jesus characterizes the question as hypocrisy because they merely want to "trap" him (cf. 8:11; 10:2); accordingly, it is not a question at all—it is a snare: Jesus must alienate either the Romans or the majority of the people. 12:28-34 (cf. 10:17-22) shows that Mark does not see things merely in terms of black and white; he does not consider everyone a hypocrite who is not a member of the band of Jesus' disciples. This passage (vss. 13-17) presents the kind of question which disguises an attitude that has already rejected Jesus. Therefore, the story is a warning against the kind of discussion in which a person does not seek to learn but already has a closed mind toward Jesus. **[16]** The inscription on a denarius reads, "Tiberius, Caesar, son of the divine Augustus [in Syria: "the majestic son of God"; Augustus means "majestic"], the high priest." **[17]** Jesus' answer is based upon the principle that the property which belongs to another person should be returned without asking whether or not it had been acquired justly. By this statement early Christianity clearly set itself and Jesus apart from an apocalyptic view according to which the world was something completely unimportant and would disappear, and from the attitude of the Zealots who believed the world was something which one must fight because it belonged to the evil one (cf. Rom. 13:1-7; 1 Tim. 2:2; Titus 3:1; 1 Peter 2:13 f.; contrast Rev. 13). The last two statements are crucial and have a significance which is not limited to this questioning. Jesus' reply rejects in principle any ready-made formula which can be applied in each new situation that arises in order to ascertain immediately how one should act. Everything belongs to God—even the person who asks the question.

Thus there is no fixed boundary between a civil sphere ruled by Caesar and a religious one ruled by God. The second statement takes precedence over the first. Who is to determine what really belongs to Caesar and where loyalty to Caesar reaches its limit? This is something only God can do. Despite Jesus' answer, the question cannot simply be dismissed once and for all. As each new problem arises it is necessary to seek for the will of God. Ultimately, neither the Pharisees' truce with the Romans nor the rebellion of the Zealots, neither political conservatism nor revolution, is justified in every situation. With this practical decision Jesus does not relieve man of the responsibility to choose. Instead, he confronts him with God before whom man must decide in each concrete situation whether to say "yes" or "no" and must be held responsible for his decision. It is both possible and necessary to give instructions such as are found in Romans 13:1-7, but they can only be appropriated and applied in the making of a responsible decision.

The Sadducees' Question 12:18-27;
cf. Matt. 22:23-33; Luke 20:27-40

[18]Some Sadducees came to Jesus. (They are the ones who
say that people will not be raised from death.) [19]"Teacher," they
said, "Moses wrote this law for us: 'If a man dies and leaves a
wife, but no children, that man's brother must marry the widow
so they can have children for the dead man.' [20]Once there were
seven brothers; the oldest got married, and died without having
children. [21]Then the next one married the widow, and he died
without having children. The same thing happened to the third
brother, [22]and then to the rest: all seven brothers married the
woman and died without having children. Last of all, the woman
died. [23]Now, when all the dead are raised to life on the day of
resurrection, whose wife will she be? All seven of them had
married her!"

[24]Jesus answered them: "How wrong you are! And do you
know why? It is because you don't know the Scriptures or God's
power. [25]For when the dead are raised to life they will be like the
angels in heaven, and men and women will not marry. [26]Now,
about the dead being raised: haven't you ever read in the book of
Moses the passage about the burning bush? For there it is
written that God said to Moses, 'I am the God of Abraham, the
God of Isaac, and the God of Jacob.' [27]That means that he is the
God of the living, not of the dead. You are completely wrong!"

(Vs. 19: Deut. 25:5 f.; vs. 26: Exod. 3:2-6.)

The exposition will show that two entirely different questions are being grappled with and answered in this passage: the question asked by the Pharisees as to what the resurrection will be like (vs. 25), and the question asked by the Sadducees in regard to whether or not there really is a resurrection (vss. 26 f.). Early Christianity had to defend its faith on both fronts—against a dogmatic confidence which considered itself to be the master of divine mysteries, and against a skepticism which would no longer reckon with God's power to create something new. Questions like those presented in vss. 19-23 were actually discussed by the Pharisees, whose decision was that the woman would belong to the first husband. However, the answer given in vs. 25 agrees perfectly with the beliefs current in Jewish apocalyptic circles (see below). Accordingly, this passage may have dealt originally with the kind of discussion that was carried on between Pharisees and apocalyptically-inclined Jews. The church stood clearly on the side of the latter group and adopted this answer for that reason. Vss. 26 f. may be an argument against those who did not believe in the resurrection, which was handed down separately and may have come from Jewish sources. Jesus may have adopted one or the other of these sayings. It is more likely, however, that they arose in the polemic of the church. Discussions like this, where one Scripture passage is pitted against another, were carried on among the Jews as well as between Jewish and Christian teachers (cf. 2:23-28 and 10:1-12).

[18] The Sadducees were the priestly party, i.e., the Jewish aristocracy. The only authority which they recognized was the "Law," i.e., the five books of Moses. Therefore, they did not consider the doctrine of the resurrection to be scriptural, since it does not appear until Isaiah 26:19 and Daniel 12:2 (Job 19:25 f.; Ps. 73:23 f.?). This fact is confirmed by Acts 23:8 and the Jewish author Josephus (*Antiq.* XVIII. 16; *Wars* II. 165). In actual fact these rather late passages are the only places where the Old Testament mentions an existence after death which deserves to be called "life" (cf. Pss. 88:5; 115:17; Isa. 38:18). The Old Testament faith which rejects any thought of reward in the hereafter has almost no parallel in the history of religion. Nevertheless, the later development is anchored in the numerous and varied experiences of God who has proven to be mightier than all other powers. But the Sadducees are justified in their doubting if one refers only to the Hebrew Scriptures and neglects the few late passages which were not generally accepted as being canonical. It is not likely, however, that the Sadducees had any influence among the followers of Jesus. And so it is easy to understand what the resurrection of Jesus meant to the church by way of corroboration and reformulation. Acts 24:15 and 26:6-8 show how the church defended its faith against attacks by the Jews. From the belief in a general resurrection, which was held by the Pharisees and the people as a whole, the church concluded that the resurrection of Jesus was not incredible. The church also concluded that the resurrection of Jesus provided an example to prove the truth of the general resurrection (Acts 4:2). In 1 Corinthians 15:12 ff. (see comment), Paul argues in an entirely different way which, theologically, is more sound. He affirms that faith in the resurrected One (the experience of the living Christ) knows that those who belong to him will continue to belong to him even on the other side of death and will therefore be raised with Jesus (2 Cor. 4:14). John 11:24-26 asserts even more emphatically that to accept the truth of the resurrection in general is of no value until a person recognizes that the certainty of the resurrection is found in Jesus, who encounters him right now.

[19-23] Levirate marriage (Deut. 25:5 ff.) serves to preserve the male's posterity. It is hardly possible that the Sadducees would have used this regulation as an argument against the resurrection. As mentioned above, this type of discussion was carried on among the Pharisees and obviously presupposes the reality of the resurrection (vs. 23a!). **[25]** Actually the first answer is not directed to the Sadducees' question as to whether or not there is a resurrection. It refers to the question that really interested the Pharisees—they wanted to know what the resurrection would be like. The ideas that angels neither eat nor drink (Tobit 12:19) nor marry (Ethiopian Enoch 15:7) and that the dead become angels after the resurrection (Ethiopian Enoch 51:4; cf. 104:4; Syriac Baruch 51:9 f.) were found in Jewish writings. This part of Jesus' answer is no different from what many of his Jewish contemporaries might have said. **[24]** The introductory sentence, however, is more penetrating: "God's power" is the ability to create something new which the human mind is not able to comprehend. Here the fact is taken seriously that God is God; he is God in that he cannot be limited or confined by human thought. In this passage both truths are maintained: Life on the other side of the resurrection is not kept secret—clear statements are made concerning it, and yet the statements are made in a way that preserves the mystery as something which surpasses human categories and concepts. This answer resembles the one given in 12:13-17 inasmuch as a clear message is granted to faith. Faith can never speculate on this message or use it to solve every possible theoretical problem without regard for the fact that it is faith. Thus an answer is given to the question about the manner of the resurrection—a question which was actually raised by the Pharisees in their discussions of every conceivable situation involving Levirate marriage.

[26] The second answer is very different; it approaches the question of the Sadducees in regard to whether or not there is a resurrection and acknowledges this as a separate problem. The awkward way in which the sentence begins is another indication that a transition has been made. Moreover, the form of the reply is different from the one in vss. 24 f. Here Scripture is set against Scripture. Gamaliel, the Pharisee, used Deuteronomy 11:9 to argue more forcibly against the Sadducees' denial of the resurrection. Since God had promised to give the land of Canaan to Abraham, Isaac, and Jacob and the land was not given to Israel until centuries later, God must have raised the patriarchs back to life. Perhaps it is because the meaning of this formula is not immediately obvious that the one really decisive declaration is implied more clearly: When God becomes the God of a particular person, he gives him a promise which nothing and no one other than God himself can abrogate. This means that not even death can annul it. It is absurd to assert that God pledges himself to a dead person unless this implies that the person is raised to life. **[27]** Truly, God is never the God of the dead; he is always the God of the living, and of those who will be raised to life. This last assurance of the reality of the resurrection is found in the awareness that God has made a promise to man which death cannot abolish, since God is greater than death (Rom. 4:5, 17, 24 f.). Therefore, Jesus' reply concludes in the same way that it began—with a reference to the fact that the questioners are basically in error.

Jesus does not refer to an indisputable miracle which would guarantee the reality of the miracle of the general resurrection. He points to God's power which goes beyond the limits of our imagination and to God's present promise which exceeds our power of comprehension and will therefore be stronger than death. What he expects from man is that he will turn away from himself and his own potentialities, cast himself completely upon God, and believe that God will create something new which will exceed every human imagination. Whenever a man begins to magnify God, he is freed from his error.

In this discussion of the resurrection it is assumed that the reader is a believer. Consequently, resurrection is viewed as a saving experience in which only believers will share. It is not regarded as resurrection to condemnation in the last judgment. Whoever ponders the question as to whether or not there is any resurrection is in reality engaging in a kind of speculation which shows no regard for God's promise to faith; therefore, whether his conclusion affirms or denies the resurrection, it is a counterfeit of the testimony of faith. Paul, too, speaks consistently of the resurrection in a positive sense (as in 1 Cor. 15:21-23, in spite of Rom. 2:3-11). The same thing is true in John 11:24-27 (contrary to the tradition in John 5:28 f.; compare, however, the genuine Johannine statement in 5:25 f.). Even in Revelation 20:12 f. the word "resurrection" is not used to present the leading of the unbelievers into judgment (in spite of 20:6). The experience of Easter made such a tremendous impression upon the early church that for a long time afterward they used the word "resurrection" exclusively for a saving event in which those persons who by faith have been united with Christ and his resurrection will share.

A Teacher of the Law Asks the Real Question 12:28-34;
cf. Matt. 22:34-40; Luke 10:25-28

28A teacher of the Law was there who heard the discussion. He saw that Jesus had given the Sadducees a good answer, so he came to him with a question: "Which commandment is the most important of all?" [29]"This is the most important one," said Jesus. " 'Hear, Israel! The Lord our God is the only Lord. [30]You must love the Lord your God with all your heart, and with all your soul, and with all your mind, and with all your strength.' [31]The second most important commandment is this: 'You must love your neighbor as yourself.' There is no other commandment more important than these two." [32]The teacher of the Law said to Jesus: "Well done, Teacher! It is true, as you say, that only the Lord is God, and that there is no other god but he. [33]And so man must love God with all his heart, and with all his mind, and with all his strength; and he must love his neighbor as himself. It is much better to obey these two commandments than to bring animals to be burned on the altar and offer other sacrifices to God." [34]Jesus noticed how wise his answer was, and so he told him: "You are not far from the Kingdom of God." After this nobody dared to ask Jesus any more questions.

(Vss. 29 f.: Deut. 6:4 f.; vs. 31: Lev. 19:18; vs. 33: 1 Sam. 15:22.)

The introduction in vs. 28a is cumbersome. Apparently Mark or the church before him used a few incidental remarks to link the original beginning of this passage to the preceding one. Luke has included this conversation in an entirely different context (Luke 10:25-28). However, vs. 34 contradicts Mark's usual opinion of the teachers of the law (2:6 f.; 3:22; 7:1 ff.; 12:38 ff.; et al.). It is necessary to consider the possibility that the story itself arose in the church (see comments on 12:13-17). Nevertheless, the unique character of vs. 34 together with the scarcity of parallels to vss. 28-31 favors its being the record of an incident in the life of Jesus. Vs. 30 does not agree exactly with the passage which was repeated daily by the Jews (Deut. 6:5); therefore, at least its present Greek form has come from a church which no longer recited this confession.

[28] The rabbis also distinguished between commandments of greater and lesser importance. They searched in particular for the commandment which outweighed all others. **[29, 30]** Each morning and evening every Israelite man had to recite Deuteronomy 6:4-9; 11:13-21; and Numbers 15:37-41 as his confession of faith. Jesus quoted the first statements from this confession as his answer to the question asked by this teacher of the law. Accordingly, he has nothing to say which is different from that which Israel has known all along through the law. **[31]** But the ancient command takes on new meaning when a "second" commandment is placed alongside it. Of course, it is not completely clear in what way this commandment is "second." Matthew 22:39 indicates in so many words that these commandments are of equal importance, and Luke 10:27 connects them without any break between. The same thing is implied by the concluding statement in Mark (vs. 31b). This means that it is impossible to keep the first commandment unless one lives according to the second. When Mark introduces it expressly as a second commandment, he does so in order to indicate the proper sequence. Though love for God is something concrete and can be experienced only as one exercises love for his neighbor, still everything depends upon the recognition that the latter becomes possible only on the basis of the former. **[29, 30]** Love for God is the first thing that will be revealed to men by love for one's neighbor. But what does it mean to love God? In contrast to Matthew and Luke, but in conformity with the Jewish confession, Mark begins by declaring that God is one before he proceeds to summon man to love God. This is how he expresses the truth perceived in 1 John 4:10 and Romans 5:5, 8—that God himself and his love which chooses and saves are the source of that stream which flows on as man's love to God and to his fellowmen.

[31] The addition of the second commandment was not entirely new, but it was not customary. Rabbi Akiba, who died as a martyr in A.D. 135 with the beginning of the Jewish confession on his lips, stated at one time: "To love your neighbor as yourself . . . , this is a great general principle of the law." However, he did not connect it with the first commandment. On the other hand, Philo of Alexandria, the Hellenistic Jew who was a contemporary of Jesus, spoke of two basic doctrines, "One of duty to God as shewn by piety and holiness, one of duty to men as shewn by humanity and justice" (*Special Laws* II, 63). He explicitly applied the term "neighbor" to all men, although originally in the Old Testament it designated only Jewish fellow citizens or, later, resident aliens also. It is difficult to determine how widespread this general interpretation of the word may have been in Palestinian Judaism (cf. Luke 10:29 ff.). The two commandments were placed side by side in the Testaments of the Twelve Patriarchs (Issachar 5:2; 7:6; cf. Dan 5:3; Zebulun 5:1 f.; Benjamin 3:3). This document shows many similarities to the teachings of the Qumran community, and just how extensively it has been influenced and interpolated by Christians is not known. Therefore the question as to whether or not Jesus stated it this way is not important—what is important is that the demeanor of Jesus gives a seriousness and a power to the answer which it does not have in Philo or in the Testaments of the Twelve Patriarchs. In accordance with the Old Testament and all Jewish statements, Jesus understands love as volition and thinks of all the everyday ways in which it is expressed. But Jesus' action gives these statements their power which unsettles all legalism. This has been illustrated in 2:1—3:6. He called the tax collectors into fellowship with God. He excluded any kind of legalism which lost sight of God's will while seeking simply to observe all sorts of specific commandments. And thus Jesus' action led inevitably to his execution on the cross. This is the only way that the truth of Romans 13:8-10 could become known. If these two commandments are interpreted in such a radical manner by the life and death of Jesus that they actually incorporate all the other commandments, then it is not possible for man to use the law as a means of making himself secure before God or of raising any claim against him. Then man is placed before God in such a way that he never arrives at the goal; if anyone were to achieve his goal in loving, he would cease loving. And yet this does not cause him to fall into despair as one who never reaches his objective. No, the opposite is true: He has the confidence of one who knows that God loves him, and he so lives in this confidence that love flows on and on.

[32] There is no other instance in the Gospels where a teacher of the law is found agreeing with Jesus. **[33]** The repetition of what Jesus said and the assertion that this is "much better" than numerous sacrifices indicate a correct understanding: These two commandments are not simply given a place with the other commandments, not even a place of greater importance. No, all of the other commandments derive their significance from these two. In agreement with many prophetic utterances (1 Sam. 15:22; Hos. 6:6; Isa. 1:11; Prov. 21:3; and the rabbis) the teacher of the law has in mind primarily the disparaging of ritual requirements. Nevertheless, he does not merely want to set an ethic of inwardness against external ritual—this would not have transcended the ethics of the Pharisees, because they also relegated ritual to a subordinate position. As a matter of fact he was comparing love which comes from the whole heart and can no longer be measured quantitatively with the legalism which allows one to ascertain how many commandments he has kept and how many he has violated. **[34]** Furthermore, Jesus' answer is without parallel. It is an invitation to take the final step which leads from "not far from" to "into the Kingdom of God." This is the part of the story which is really new. Although the Kingdom of God will not dawn until sometime in the future, it is something which is already present so that it is possible for one to be near it and even enter into it. In Jesus himself, in his actions, and in his words the Kingdom of God has come to man, and Jesus determines who is close to him. According to Mark, Jesus makes this statement in Jerusalem, of all places, where he will be executed in a few days. Consequently, one can no longer be disposed to employ certain legal prescriptions as a means of determining for himself how near to the Kingdom of God, or how far from it, he or anyone else might be. That "nobody dared to ask Jesus any more questions" must be interpreted in the same way as 1:22. This shows what happens when the Kingdom of God comes near. Salvation and judgment are accomplished when one meets Jesus. This makes it impossible to carry on a disinterested discussion. With this Mark concludes the controversies.

Jesus' Decisive Question 12:35-40;
cf. Matt. 22:41-46; 23:1-36; Luke 20:41-47

35As Jesus was teaching in the Temple he asked the question: "How can the teachers of the Law say that the Messiah will be the descendant of David? [36]The Holy Spirit inspired David to say:

'The Lord said to my Lord:
Sit here at my right side,
Until I put your enemies under your feet.'

[37]David himself called him 'Lord': how, then, can the Messiah be David's descendant?"

The large crowd heard Jesus gladly. [38]As he taught them he said: "Watch out for the teachers of the Law, who like to walk around in their long robes and be greeted with respect in the market place; [39]who choose the reserved seats in the synagogues and the best places at feasts. [40]They take advantage of widows and rob them of their homes, then make a show of saying long prayers! Their punishment will be all the worse!"

(Vs. 36: Ps. 110:1.)

There are many indications that all of the material up to 12:44 was already combined with the preceding controversies before Mark. The most significant of these indications are the catchwords which link the controversies together (see comment on 9:41-50)—"teacher of the Law" connects vss. 28 and 32 to vss. 35 and 38; "widow" connects vs. 40 to vs. 42. Yet Mark's editing is particularly evident in this passage. The observation in vs. 35a that Jesus was "teaching in the Temple" (he had been there ever since 11:27), the renewed reference to his "teaching" in vs. 38, and the comment which clearly distinguishes the attitude of the people from the attitude of the leaders show that Mark sees an important break here. Actually the public activity of Jesus is concluded in this section. Mark 14:43 f., 13:1 ff. in particular, and the farewell suppers in 14:3-9 and 17-25, all occur within the narrower circle of the band of disciples. Perhaps the quotation in vs. 36 began to be applied to Jesus in the Greek-speaking church. The Aramaic-speaking church addressed Jesus as *marana,* "our Lord" (1 Cor. 16:22). It is unlikely that the Hebrew word in Psalm 110:1 *adoni,* "my lord," would have been applied to Jesus, since it connoted a position of higher honor. This word is used in the customary way in Psalm 110:5 where it refers to God, and this is how it was interpreted in Jesus' time. On the other hand, there was only one word for "Lord" (*kurios*) in the Greek-speaking church. This word is used in Psalm 110:1 (LXX) and was frequently applied to Jesus. This Psalm was never quoted in the Qumran community even though the hope of a Davidic king and a special salvation-time during his reign was vital among them. This is generally true of the ancient Jewish writings. Consequently, it is clear that the suggestion that this Psalm was given a Messianic interpretation in Judaism but that this was suppressed later on account of the polemic with the Christians cannot be accepted. The saying in vss. 38b and 39 occurs in Luke 11:43 as a warning to the Pharisees and is addressed to them directly: "How terrible for you . . . You . . ." This makes the saying more meaningful and is likely its original form. As Mark uses it in this passage the saying no longer presents a specific warning by Jesus to a particular group. It expresses the decision of the church which must finally separate itself from the leaders of the Jewish people, though not from the people themselves. Vs. 40 has been added in a way that is rather awkward grammatically (literally: "Watch out for the teachers of the Law who like to . . .; who devour the houses . . .; these shall receive . . ."). Apparently vs. 40 circulated as a separate saying and was formulated correctly in the nominative. It was not added to vss. 38 f. until sometime later, although the connection to vs. 42 by a common catchword shows that this must have occurred before Mark. Moreover, the nature of this warning is very different from the one in vss. 38 f. Accordingly, Mark has taken up two common warnings with minor changes ("Watch out for" as in 8:15, which is found nowhere else in the New Testament) in order to place the decisive separation of the fellowship of Jesus from the teachers of the law at the end of the public ministry of Jesus. In this way he points out the break which occurs here.

[35] The controversies are concluded with vs. 34b. At this point Jesus begins his message of revelation once more. The death sentence in 11:18 and the tense situation in 11:27—12:12 are not forgotten, but they remain in the background. Here again Jesus is presented as the teacher who reveals God to the world before he goes on his way to death. Jesus' question might lead us to suppose that he is disputing the Davidic descent of the Messiah. Certainly that would be the easiest interpretation of the statement. The Davidic descent of the Messiah, however, is not denied in the Christian writings prior to the Epistle of Barnabas (12:10 f.), and there it occurred as the result of an anti-Jewish attitude. Otherwise Jesus is regarded universally as David's descendant. The Davidic descent of the Messiah was always a tremendous burden for early Christianity, since in Judaism it was understood with a nationalistic flavor. The origin of this concept can be explained only if Jesus' family actually did trace its lineage back to David and if the church knew this fact but neither denied it nor covered it up. **[37]** This is why vs. 37 should not be translated "how" (although this is possible), but "to what extent" or "in what way." What does this mean?

[36] The introduction to the quotation is unique within the Synoptics; the only other places where similar introductions are found are Hebrews 3:7 and 10:15 (cf. Heb. 9:8; Acts 1:16; 4:25; 28:25). It conforms to the rabbinical formula, i.e., a kind of theology which restricts the activity of the Holy Spirit to salvation history in the distant past so that in the present the Holy Spirit can only be found "packaged and preserved" in the Scriptures. The uncommon formula used in this passage emphasizes the special significance of the quotation which follows. In the Old Testament it was stated that the Psalm was written by David. "My Lord" refers to the king. In the Old Testament the king may be addressed by the name which rightly belongs to God alone, because he sits "upon the throne of the kingdom of the Lord over Israel" (1 Chron. 28:5; cf. 29:23; 2 Chron. 9:8). Psalm 110 has played an especially important role in the New Testament. The statement that the exalted One is seated at the right hand of God is very common. Moreover, the words of the Psalm are used in Acts 2:34 f.; 1 Corinthians 15:25; and Hebrews 1:13 to declare that his enemies will be subject to him. The fourth verse, which speaks of the honor which he would receive as a priest after the order of Melchizedek, is included only in Hebrews 5:6 (cf. 7:21). The extremely interesting statement about the testimony which God bore to him before creation (vs. 3, LXX only) is not referred to anywhere in the New Testament. The New Testament consistently sees the fulfillment of this Psalm in the victory of Easter. The statement that Jesus is sitting at the right hand of God describes his position between the exaltation and the final fulfillment in the Second Coming ("until I . . ."; cf. 1 Cor. 15:25-28). **[37]** Therefore "son" and "Lord" stand in a certain tension. The Davidic descent of Jesus is not questioned anywhere in the New Testament; consequently, the question arises: In what way should this descent be viewed? Its primary meaning for the church was simply that all of the Old Testament hopes and promises were fulfilled in Jesus. Of course, the church had to clarify for itself and for others the concrete implications of Davidic descent. In Romans 1:3 f. Paul quotes an early confession of the church which explicitly affirms that Jesus was the son of David. But it immediately makes clear that this is not the most decisive thing that could be said. It only expresses what is obvious and can be summed up in human terms. What was really most important came to pass on Easter when Jesus was installed in his function as Son of God and, therefore, as the royal sovereign, God's representative. Emphasis is given to the fact that all the Old Testament passages about the coming descendant of David and his everlasting kingdom would actually be fulfilled. In contrast to the Jewish expectation, however, Jesus was not enthroned at Easter in an earthly, political kingship, but in the heavenly, and therefore everlasting, Kingdom of God. The way had been prepared for such an interpretation by Judaism, inasmuch as the anticipated kingdom of the son of David was conceived of in earthly, national terms but was given more and more miraculous and divine features as the idea developed (see Pss. of Sol. 17, first century B.C.). Romans 1:3 f. represents a Christology in two stages. Paul perceived that it would not do to resolve this in terms of a temporal succession, i.e., one stage after the other. Accordingly he placed the title of honor "Son of God" (cf. Mark 15:39) in Romans 1:3 before the quotation and in this way affirmed that Christ has always been the Son of God and that his divine Sonship was manifested in the humility of his earthly life and death (Gal. 4:4 f.; cf. Gal. 3:13). Thus the church discovered Jesus' secret step by step. It is not important to know when or where each specific statement was made. What is important is whether or not these statements adequately describe the reality of Jesus. We may be confident, therefore, that what is crucial has really been perceived in Mark 12:36 f. and that the formulation of this conviction reached its full clarity and force with Paul, who affirmed both truths: In the person of the Son of God, God is for us from eternity past and in eternity future, and within history God's "being-for-us" lives in the man Jesus. Mark is absolutely correct in his perception that this is where the line is drawn which separates the teachers of the law from the fellowship of Jesus. **[37b-40]** This separation is given added emphasis when Mark includes the note indicating the approval of the crowd and then presents Jesus' teaching of a general truth which, according to Mark's understanding, proclaims the final cleavage between the Christian church and the teachers of the law. Of course, in themselves the statements which are quoted here do not say this. Vs. 40 can be found in a similar and even more sarcastic form in Judaism, but there it refers only to exceptionally bad cases. Vss. 38 f. are clearly more to the point. Moreover, Matthew 23:8-11 has declared that a system based upon a new principle must take effect in the fellowship of Jesus. The new principle will not permit the devout person to cherish any desire for special honor. Accordingly, this does not describe some detested individual who was an exceptional case, but is obviously the description of a regular custom which was closely associated with an attitude of holding human religious achievements in high esteem. However, these verses do not penetrate as deeply as does Jesus' parable in Luke 18:10-14. The Pharisee in that parable was consistent, obedient, and flawless (as Paul was, according to Phil. 3:6); he is not the inconsistent one who does not obey his own teaching.

The Widow's Offering 12:41-44

41As Jesus sat near the Temple treasury he watched the people
as they dropped in their money. Many rich men dropped in much
money; 42then a poor widow came along and dropped in two

little copper coins, worth about a penny. [43]He called his disciples together and said to them: "I tell you that this poor widow put more in the offering box than all the others. [44]For the others put in what they had to spare of their riches; but she, poor as she is, put in all she had—she gave all she had to live on."

This story may have been added here before Mark (see comment on 12:35-40). It offers him a welcome opportunity to use one of his characteristic editorial expressions in vs. 43a to pass from Jesus' public ministry in the temple to the smaller circle of the band of disciples. At the same time this story, by presenting an example of true Jewish piety, reinforces the cleavage Mark saw between the Jewish people, who are devoted to Jesus, and their leaders (see 12:37b). There are Indian, Greek, and Jewish parallels; for example, God is supposed to have spoken (in a dream) to a rabbi who had refused to receive a handful of meal as a gift from a widow, saying, "Do not look down on her, it is as if she has offered herself." Actually the story would be easier to understand as a simple report or a divine instruction, because Jesus was not able to see what the individuals put in nor was it possible for him to know that this was all that the widow had. What has happened is that a common theme has been clothed in the form of a conversation between Jesus and his disciples. Another possibility is that a story has developed from one of Jesus' illustrations.

[41] Perhaps the "Temple treasury" was one of the thirteen trumpet-shaped containers which were placed in the court of the temple. **[42]** According to Roman standards the gift was hardly worth a penny. It is significant that she gave two *lepta,* because she could have divided them and kept one for herself. **[43]** With vs. 43a Mark makes it clear that the church is being addressed here. **[44]** The final statement, "all she had to live on," re-emphasizes the greatness of the offering.

Thus this brief story exalts that quiet, matter-of-course, and total giving which does not make a big fuss about the deed. Letting go of himself and every security the person commits himself completely to God's mercy. Accordingly, it makes a good conclusion for Jesus' public ministry.

The Parousia of the Son of Man 13:1-27;
cf. Matt. 24:1-31; Luke 21:5-28

1As Jesus was leaving the Temple, one of his disciples said, "Look, Teacher! What wonderful stones and buildings!" 2Jesus answered: "You see these great buildings? Not a single stone here will be left in its place; every one of them will be thrown down."

3Jesus was sitting on the Mount of Olives, across from the Temple, when Peter, James, John, and Andrew came to him in private. 4"Tell us when this will be," they said; "and tell us what is the sign that will show that it is the time for all these things to happen."

5Jesus began to teach them: "Watch out, and don't let anyone fool you. 6Many men will come in my name, saying, 'I am he!' and fool many people. 7And don't be troubled when you hear the noise of battles close by and news of battles far away. Such things must happen, but they do not mean that the end has come. 8One country will fight another country, one kingdom will attack another kingdom. There will be earthquakes everywhere, and there will be famines. These things are like the first pains of childbirth.

9"You yourselves must watch out. For men will arrest you and take you to court. You will be beaten in the synagogues; you will stand before rulers and kings for my sake, to tell them the Good News. 10The gospel must first be preached to all peoples. 11And when they arrest you and take you to court, do not worry ahead of time about what you are going to say; when the time comes, say whatever is given to you then. For the words you speak will not be yours; they will come from the Holy Spirit. 12Men will hand over their own brothers to be put to death, and fathers will do the same to their children; children will turn against their parents and have them put to death. 13Everyone will hate you because of me. But the person who holds out to the end will be saved."

[14]"You will see 'The Awful Horror' standing in the place where he should not be." (Note to the reader: understand what this means!) "Then those who are in Judea must run away to the hills. [15]The man who is on the roof of his house must not lose time by going down into the house to get anything to take with him. [16]The man who is in the field must not go back to the house for his cloak. [17]How terrible it will be in those days for women who are pregnant, and for mothers who have little babies! [18]Pray to God that these things will not happen in wintertime! [19]For the trouble of those days will be far worse than any the world has ever known, from the very beginning when God created the world until the present time. Nor will there ever again be anything like it. [20]But the Lord has reduced the number of those days; if he had not, nobody would survive. For the sake of his chosen people, however, he has reduced those days.

[21]"Then, if anyone says to you, 'Look, here is the Messiah!' or, 'Look, there he is!'—do not believe him. [22]For false Messiahs and false prophets will appear. They will perform signs and wonders for the purpose of deceiving God's chosen people, if possible. [23]Be on your guard! I have told you everything ahead of time."

[24]"In the days after that time of trouble the sun will grow dark, the moon will no longer shine, [25]the stars will fall from heaven, and the powers in space will be driven from their course. [26]Then the Son of Man will appear, coming in the clouds with great power and glory. [27]He will send out the angels to the four corners of the earth and gather God's chosen people from one end of the world to the other."

(Vs. 7: Dan. 2:28; vs. 8: Isa. 19:2; 2 Chron. 15:6; vs. 12: Micah 7:6; vs. 14: Dan. 9:27; 11:31; 12:11; vs. 19: Dan. 12:1; vs. 22: Deut. 13:1 ff.; vs. 24 f.: Isa. 13:10; 34:4; vs. 26: Dan. 7:13; vs. 27: Zech. 2:6; Deut. 30:4.)

This chapter is easily divided into introduction (vss. 1 f. and 3 f.), signs (vss. 5-13), events in Judea (vss. 14-20), warnings (vss. 21-23), parousia of the Son of Man (vss. 24-27), and concluding parables (vss. 28-37). The Greek word *parousia* means "presence," or "to become present," "to come." Strictly speaking it does not designate the "return," but simply the appearance of Jesus. In the mother tongue of Jesus and the early church there is no word for "return" or "come again" (cf. Matt. 24:3). In the introduction, vs. 1a is the Markan transition from the preceding subject matter to the new theme of eschatology, the doctrine of last things. In the Christian Scriptures this doctrine traditionally comes at the end of a section or book (Matt. 25; John 14-17; Heb. 6:1 f.; at the end of the five great discourses in Matthew; Didache 16; and apparently at the end of Q), and here it concludes Jesus' ministry before the beginning of his Passion. Deuteronomy 29-30 is the first example of the literary technique where a discourse is included shortly before the death of a great man (found also in Greek authors). It has been suggested that originally the Gospel of Mark ended with chapter 13. This seems very unlikely. References to the importance of Jesus' parousia and the signs which will precede it are so extremely rare in the rest of Mark that chapter 13 can hardly be regarded as the high point of his book. Furthermore, there are no indications in any manuscript that the Passion story is a later addition. Ever since 8:31, perhaps even since 3:6, everything has been moving toward Jesus' Passion. The saying about the destruction of the temple in vs. 2 has been handed down in a different version in 14:58 and 15:29. It must be an authentic saying of Jesus since it caused the church obvious embarrassment. It is difficult to restore the original reading. In its present formulation the passive voice ("will be thrown down") might be original; all of the other versions, however, testify that Jesus in some way or other spoke of a rebuilding (by the church?). Mark makes a new beginning in vs. 3. This verse has to connect the announcement of the destruction of the temple with the great eschatological discourse in which that announcement has no part whatever. Therefore the words "all these things" in vs. 4 do not refer to what is said in vs. 2, but to the things described in vss. 5-27 (see vss. 4 f.). It is certain that eschatological instruction was carried on in the inner circle of the church, but this particular formulation is typical of Mark. It is no longer known whether Mark is responsible for the inclusion of Andrew with the three who are usually singled out as Jesus' intimate friends.

[14-20] It is necessary, first of all, to separate the passage concerning the events in Judea (vss. 14-20) from the discourse proper, as it forms a distinct segment of the tradition. In contrast to vss. 8, 9 f., for example, and more particularly to vss. 24-27, it is only the inhabitants of a rather restricted war zone (Palestine) who are addressed in this passage and called to flee from the cities into the Judean mountains and from the houses into the open fields. This would still be true even if "Judea" were to be traced to Daniel (see 1:6; 2:25). Nothing is mentioned concerning a destruction of Jerusalem or of the temple. The prophecy of a Jewish or a Christian prophet may have been taken over here, possibly from about A.D. 40 when Caligula ordered the erection of his statue in the temple in Jerusalem (which would have constituted the highest kind of blasphemy for Judaism). Sometime in the sixties would be a more likely date, when the Roman war could be seen on the horizon and the country was already involved in all kinds of disorders. In this case the way everything is viewed is colored not only by Daniel, but also by the madness of Caligula. The reference to "the reader" can hardly be attributed to Mark, who is not particularly interested in "The Awful Horror." It indicates that this prophecy was already committed to writing, that is, unless this is a marginal note which a copyist incorporated into the text, or simply an allusion to the passage in Daniel.

[21-23] The warnings in vss. 21-23 are a digression which brings everything to bear upon the situation of the readers. These verses are connected to vs. 20 and to vs. 27 by the catchword "chosen people." The fact that vss. 5 f. contain a very similar warning shows that vss. 21-23 were firmly established in the tradition when Mark received it and that he inserted them here.

[5-13, 24-27] This leaves vss. 5-13 and 24-27, which present an authentic description of the events of the end-time. The warning in vss. 5 f. has the same meaning as vss. 21-23 and should be viewed as a special adaptation to the situation of the church. Isaiah 13:2-10 (and 2 Esdras 5:4 f., from the end of the 1st century A.D.) associates war with changes in the sun and moon. Amos 8:8 f. (cf. Joel 2:10; the Assumption of Moses 10:4, which is from the beginning of the 1st century A.D.; and Ethiopian

Enoch 102:2, which is earlier) links an earthquake with that phenomenon. It is clear that these Old Testament passages were still being quoted in the writings of the first century A.D. It is possible that on the basis of Isaiah 13 and Amos 8 the Christian church expected war, earthquake, and cosmic signs in the sun and moon as indications of the coming of the end-time just as their Jewish contemporaries did. These are the same phenomena which are mentioned in vss. 7 f., 24b, and 25. In the Old Testament the three horrors of war are portrayed as being the sword, famine, and pestilence (in nearly every possible sequence: Jer. 14:12; 21:7; 38:2; Ezek. 5:12; cf. Ezek. 14:21; 1 Kings 8:37), and this is fully in agreement with Luke 21:10 f. (parallel to Mark 13:8). It may be accidental that "pestilence" is not found in Mark, since "famine" and "pestilence" sound nearly alike in Greek. This is why "pestilence" occasionally dropped out in translation into Greek, e.g., Jeremiah 38:2. Finally, there was a general expectation that a time of turbulence would come before the end when even the members of the same family would fight against one another: Isaiah 3:5; Jeremiah 9:4; Ezekiel 38:21; and Micah 7:6. (This had been applied to the destiny of the church in Matthew 10:34-36.) This expectation is responsible for the statement in vs. 12.

And so by carefully reading its Bible the church discovered seven signs of the approach of the end: war (vs. 7), imperialism (vs. 8a; we may wonder to what extent this should be regarded as the outbreak of the wars which had been rumored [vs. 7]), earthquake (vs. 8b), famine (vs. 8c), pestilence (Luke 21:11), internecine rebellion, which was interpreted by the Christian church as persecution for the sake of faith (vs. 12), and the fading of sun and moon accompanied by the falling of the stars as prophesied in Isaiah 34:4 (vss. 24 f.). This series exhibits a remarkable degree of correspondence to the one found in Revelation 6. The earthquake, however, is included with the cosmic signs so that it is the shaking of the heavenly powers. This makes it possible to leave the "seventh seal" available, because in Revelation 8:1 f. it has to inaugurate another series of seven (apart from this even the order is the same). The interpretation of the first rider is not certain. The fourth rider is called "Death." Hell, the sword, famine, death, and wild beasts follow after him. The word "death," however, is frequently used for "pestilence." In this way a more or less fixed scheme for the events of the end-time was developed gradually in the Christian church from reading the Bible and particularly from reading the prophets. Moreover, as a result of the things which had been experienced by the church, the insurrection which had been expected traditionally and even the rebellion within families came to be interpreted generally as representing persecution for Jesus' sake (Matt. 10:28-36; Mark 13:9-13; Rev. 6:9-11).

The material found in Mark 13:9-13 occurs in Matthew 10:17-21 in an entirely different context. There it is found within an exhortation to confess the faith fearlessly. Matthew 10:21 agrees word for word with Mark 13:12. Matthew 10:19 f. (Mark 13:11) clearly resembles Luke 12:11 f., and this shows that the statement was found in Q also. Matthew 10:17 f. (Mark 13:9 f.) is worded somewhat differently from its parallel in Mark. Therefore, we need to ask whether the content of Mark 13:9-11 (without vs. 12, which is the only part formulated in the third person rather than the normal apocalyptic style in the second person) formerly was handed down by itself as an exhortation to testify boldly. It is possible that the apocalyptic statement in Mark 13:12 (Micah 7:6; and Ethiopian Enoch 99:5; 100:1 f.; Jubilees 23:16, 19; 2 Esdras 6:24; Syriac Baruch 70:6 as an aftereffect) was traditionally interpreted by the church as referring to religious persecution. In the earlier stages it may have been associated with the hostility among the nations (vs. 8). Vs. 12 had attracted verses 9 and 11 before Mark. These then attracted vs. 13 to serve as a conclusion. Mark may have contributed vs. 10 which intrudes between vss. 9 and 11 which are linked together by the catchword "arrest." We will have to consider the possibility that the saying in Matthew 10:18 (". . . to tell the Good News to them and to the Gentiles") is what stimulated the expanding of this passage to read: ". . . to tell them the Good News. The gospel must first be preached to all peoples" (Mark 13:9 f.). However, a reliable reconstruction of this passage has not been attained.

Finally, vss. 26 f. add, in the language of the Old Testament, the expectation of the coming of the Son of Man (cf. 8:31), which was important to the Christian church as the goal to which all of the signs were directed. This would have been possible only in the Greek-speaking church, since this particular reading of Zechariah is found only in the Greek translation, while the Hebrew text, which was used by the early church, speaks of the scattering of Israel to the four winds—a concept which is the exact reverse. It is clear that this section has not come from Jesus, since here Old Testament statements simply follow one another in a way that is not attributed to Jesus anywhere else. It may have arisen in the church which read the Old Testament in Greek. This does not reflect in any way upon the truth or importance of the section; but it does raise the question whether or not the truth about Jesus is expressed correctly and adequately in this way. We will have to answer this in the exposition.

Thus the description of the events of the end-time in Mark 13 has arisen, in the main, from the church's reading of the Bible and has developed gradually. It is an extension of the sayings of Jesus concerning the end of the temple and is consistent with Jesus' general attitude. Although the world and its riches are affirmed by him in a positive way, he considers them as something merely penultimate when compared with God. The description has been augmented by the addition of the prophecy of a Jewish or Christian prophet. Vs. 14 seems to indicate that this prophecy had already been prepared in written form. The addition of the exhortations has important theological significance since they portray the church in its present situation as standing right before the end, and then address the church there (vss. 5 f., 9-13, 21-23). The formulation of the question in vs. 4 and Jesus' preliminary answer in vs. 5 may be traced to Mark with reasonable certainty, along with vs. 10. By greatly emphasizing the exhortation to the church, Mark deliberately wards off a strongly apocalyptic expectation of an immediate end and summons the church to be watchful in the interim. This raises the question whether it was Mark who also inserted the parenthetical remarks "they do not mean that the end has come" (vs. 7), "you yourselves must watch out" (vs. 9), and "be on your guard" (vs. 23). In any case they are well suited to vss. 33-37. This view of the future has been attributed to Jesus not merely because it was obvious to the church that the glorified Jesus was the one who gave it such insight into the Old Testament and first enabled the church to express these things, but primarily because it was not possible to speak about Jesus in an appropriate way without being mindful of the fact that he is Lord of the future even to the final consummation. Moreover, it is necessary to observe that in this passage Jesus has no vital role in the period between Easter and the end of the world (in contrast to those passages where the exalted Lord is the center of faith), except that his preaching is remembered and his coming is anticipated.

[1] That Jesus "was leaving the Temple" may represent for Mark the definitive schism. **[2]** The destruction of the temple was foreseen by the prophets also (Micah 3:12; Jer. 7:14; 26:6) and by Jewish seers both before and after Jesus (Ethiopian Enoch 90: 28; Jochanan ben Zakkai *ca.* A.D. 1-80, B. Joma IV, 1 = 39b; Josephus, *Wars* VI. 300 ff.). This is an example of genuine prophecy. It is not prophecy *post eventu,* nor has the passage undergone later emendation, because in A.D. 70 the temple was not torn down—it was burned. If the temple was "torn down," it was only after it had been burned. It is not important that the events of the future be foretold here with perfect accuracy. What is really important is stressed by the question in vs. 1b, which was framed (by Mark?) as an introduction to the prophecy: Every false security of man which builds upon his own excellent achievements—here they are even pious achievements—will be attacked and destroyed by the Good News. **[3]** The Mount of Olives, which is higher than the mountain upon which the temple stood, is the appropriate scene for the prophetic discourse which follows (cf. Zech. 14:4). It is strange that Andrew, who nowhere else is included with the three intimate friends, is mentioned here and named last instead of with Peter, especially since he is Peter's brother. **[4]** Jesus is questioned about "the time for all these things to happen" (*suntelesthai,* "to be consummated"). Therefore it is a question not only about the destruction of the temple, which was an event that would happen within history, but also about the end of the world, since that is frequently designated as the consummation. To be more precise one should say: The question is asked about the "sign" (the singular stands in contrast to the kind of curiosity which is interested in a series of different signs); in other words, about something in the present situation of the inquirer which will serve as an indication of things which have not happened yet.

[5] This new introduction marks the beginning of something far more important than anything that was stated in vs. 2. The answer to the question in vs. 4 is not given any priority. In vs. 32 that question is simply dismissed as being inappropriate. **[6]** A warning must be uttered concerning an immediate danger which the church is facing at the present time. This is a danger which threatens the reader also, not something which endangers only future generations. Apparently there were men at that time who claimed to be the Christ. The expression "in my name" means: "with an appeal to me and to my words." This shows that these men worked within the fellowship of Jesus (this is more apparent in vs. 22). It is clear that they claimed to be either Christ himself who had reappeared, or a reincarnation of Christ. This is evidence that there was a time of extreme fanaticism in early Christendom (2 Thess. 2:1-12). Since Acts 20:29 f. and 1 John 2:18 witness to the presence of such persons within the Christian church, these were not simply instances where some Jews claimed to be the Messiah. These were persons such as Simon the Magician, who Justin (*Apology,* I, 26:1-3) reports was addressed as God in prayer. Furthermore, Irenaeus (*Heresies,* I, 23:1) asserts that Simon appeared among the Jews as "the Son," among the Samaritans as "the Father," and among the Gentiles as "the Holy Spirit." All of this leads one to suspect that the beginnings of Gnosticism were inspired by the fanatical attitude of early Christianity. All religious boundaries were quickly crossed, and much that was Jewish or heathen was assimilated wherever the church lacked a healthy rooting in the gospel. Certainly the expectation that "many" such persons would yet appear was not fulfilled in the time of Mark and indicates that he did not expect the end to come in the immediate future. According to the parallel passage in Luke (21:8), the enemies of Christ are the ones who assert that the end is near. This is typical of Luke's attitude. **[7]** The period of war before the end (in 2 Esdras 13:30-32 before the appearance of the "Servant of God") is subject to the divine "necessity" of which the Jewish apocalyptics spoke frequently. The wording of this verse came from the Greek version of Daniel 2:28. This does not provide an explanation of the calamity of war, but faith has made it subject to God's sovereignty. The wars are clearly distinguished from the end of the world. This may have been done to counteract a pessimistic mood in early Christianity which interpreted the distress of the war in the sixties as a sign that the end of the world would dawn immediately. It may have been done to counteract the Jewish nationalistic hopes as well. **[8]** Vs. 8 substantiates the last brief statement in vs. 7. In Mark's source the spreading of the conflict to world-wide proportions was distinguished as a new development, in contrast to limited local war. But even this is only the "first pains of childbirth" and is not to be identified with the end. According to Mark, in a special way the times of distress point to the life to come and to the future glory of God. It is not possible to infer from this whether there will be a period of relief after the "birthpains" (this word had already come to be a technical term in Jewish apocalyptic thought from the metaphor of an eschatological rebirth), or whether, figuratively speaking, it is dealing with the final birth pains that come just before the baby is born. In the suffering of all creation, Paul heard the approach of God (Rom. 8:18-25). In a way that is less likely to be misunderstood than the passage from Mark, Paul stated that no suffering will be understood properly until God comes and that the understanding of suffering will always be something which must be asserted by faith. Consequently, man will never so comprehend God that he can explain everything or be able to arrange the events of the end-time on a timetable.

[9] "You yourselves must watch out" is a typical Markan expression. Since it has no accompanying subordinate clause, it calls the attention of the readers to the significance which the passage has for them and repudiates any reading which is motivated merely by curiosity. The first half of the statement originated in a time when the church still considered itself a part of the Jewish commonwealth and subject to Jewish jurisdiction and to the discipline of the synagogue. It is only the second half of the statement which makes it adaptable to the new relationships. The interpretation of *marturion* (the Greek word translated: "to tell them the Good News") is crucial. The formula "to bear testimony before them" (RSV) originally indicated the "witness" borne in court which incriminates another person. Since this passage is in juxtaposition to vss. 10 and 11, Mark must be thinking of the witness of Jesus' disciples which calls men to faith. **[11]** Then vs. 11 states that in bearing this witness it is not essential for the suffering martyr to be brave—he may be weak and full of fear. It is important, however, that his behavior have the character of witnessing. This enables the disciple to completely forget himself and his own abilities or weaknesses so that he can give his attention to the one who is persecuting him, because he is his brother and he must make Christ real to him. **[10]** The worldwide proclamation is of primary importance to Mark (cf. 4:32; 11:17; 15:39). Therefore under no circumstances can this proclamation be omitted from a survey of the future. It must be included here where the discussion is about witnessing in order to make it impossible to entertain the mistaken notion that witnessing is necessary only in the (Jewish) courts. This sentence is based upon an understanding which is expressed primarily in the post-Pauline statements of Romans 16:25 f. and Colossians 1:23, where the catchwords "Good News," "preach," and "all nations" (Romans 16:26; Col. 1:27; Col. 1:23 has "everybody") are also placed in combination. Paul indicates in Romans 1:5, 8-17; 11:11 ff.; 15: 16, 19, the importance which he attributes to the dissemination of the Good News into the world of the Gentiles and how he sees this as the fulfillment of Old Testament prophecy (Ps. 98:2 f. in Rom. 1:16; Isa. 66:20 in Rom. 15:16). Ephesians 3:2-9 also underscores the importance of the mission to the Gentiles, and in 1 Timothy 3:16 this mission appears as a central article of faith in a brief hymn. In this passage the spread of preaching beyond the borders of Israel into the Gentile world becomes an actual saving-event and Christ's victorious procession through the Gentile world becomes parallel to his victorious procession through the heavenly spheres in his exaltation at Easter. This understanding is in a certain tension with the Jewish-Christian scheme of the events of the end-time which Mark has utilized in this chapter and which does not take the mission to the Gentiles into account. The word "first," which puts off the coming of the end, refers, strictly speaking, to the sufferings of persecution (even in the synagogue); however, it is clear that Mark has understood it as applying to all the events of the end-time.

[11] The Old Testament and Jewish understanding of the Holy Spirit is implicit in the promise in vs. 11: The Spirit is given to inspire especially marvelous utterances and is given only to special men—the martyrs—in times of special need—in court proceedings (cf. 1:12). The book of Acts and the letters of Paul in particular emphasize that the Holy Spirit is given to every member of the church and that he initiates those actions, and attitudes also, which do not appear miraculous in any way (1 Cor. 12:1-3; observe that among the gifts of the Spirit are found: power to help and to lead others, generosity, and kindness, 1 Cor. 12:28 and Rom. 12:8). The parallel verse Luke 21:15 (cf. Luke 12:12) speaks of the exalted Jesus instead of the Spirit. The change may be attributed to Luke, who equates the two in other passages also. This procedure shows how very conscious the church was that no one other than Jesus Christ himself addressed it in the Holy Spirit (see Introduction 3, last paragraph). **[12]** When there is a conflict with one's responsibility to his family, obedience and the ready confession of Christ become especially difficult. It is stated here just as clearly as in 10:29 f. that these persons must not be permitted to prevent one from saying "yes" to Jesus. **[13]** In the following verse this is illustrated from the experience of the church. In the apocalyptic scheme (e.g., vs. 8) the word "everyone" referred to the nations of the whole world, as in Matthew 24:9. In Mark, however, "everyone" refers to the members of the persecuted person's family and his fellow citizens. Accordingly, we have here a clear example of how a description that had reference to the whole world, and for that reason was not very binding, was reformulated so that it addressed the church directly and gave light to the church in its present situation. The word "end" placed alongside vs. 7 and in contrast to "first" (beginning) in vs. 8 must really be the end of the world. Since the aphorism was probably handed down as a separate saying, it may have had reference to the end of a witness's life, as in Revelation 2:10 (in contrast to 2 Esdras 6:25). Probably this is the way Mark understood it, since it does not seem that he thought (all of) his readers would survive until the end of the world. So the entire passage about the signs leads up to these exhortations which concern the present situation of the reader. Consequently, the narrative has not degenerated into a mere compilation of strange signs. On the contrary, it derives the importance and justification which it now has from the consummation which is still future.

[14] Vs. 14 marks the beginning of something quite extraordinary (see above). Vs. 13 might have led us to expect that the discussion would continue to be about the end, but it has turned to other symbolic events. In Daniel 9:27, "The Awful Horror" designates the pagan altar which was erected at that time upon the altar of burnt offering in the temple courtyard. The discussion which follows clearly indicates that here in Mark 13:14 the term refers to a person. Perhaps the seer expected a sacrilege similar to what Caligula planned when he ordered his statue to be set up in the temple. Is it possible that he used this expression to signify the appearance of the Antichrist in the temple? The suddenness of the event might favor this interpretation (2 Thess. 2:3 f.). Undoubtedly the phrase "where he should not be" refers to the temple, since the entire passage presupposes a Jewish situation. It is evident in vs. 18 that the prophecy was formulated before the anticipated tribulation began. Flight into the mountains would not be reasonable except in the event of a very limited war such as the one which occurred at the beginning of the Maccabean revolt in the second century B.C. (1 Macc. 2:28; Josephus, *Wars* I. 36). Perhaps this passage is important to Mark because it shows that the troubles of the war in Judea in the sixties did not indicate the end of the world, but were simply "signs." It has been suggested that in this passage Mark is calling the church to leave Jerusalem and go to Galilee in order to witness the imminent parousia of the Son of Man (cf. 16:1-8). This is very unlikely. To the best of our knowledge the church escaped to Transjordan, not to Galilee. It is impossible to imagine that the church would have fled to Galilee, since that is where the war between the Jews and the Romans began. This passage, however, does not speak of an exodus to Galilee, but of a state of emergency in the uncertain future which would necessitate a panicky flight to the mountains (in Judea) and out into the open fields. The erroneous information about Palestinian geography shows how improbable it is that Mark lived in this vicinity. Therefore his interest cannot have been confined to the Jerusalem church and its exodus. Above all, the overall construction of the Gospel contradicts the idea that this passage was drawn up as a document dealing with flight in the last days before the end of the world and that it was intended to appeal to men to conduct themselves properly in the last hour. **[15]** Obviously, it is impossible to get off the "roof" without going down. The meaning of this injunction is that he should go down by way of the outside stairway and not enter the house. **[16]** Perhaps the rather formal statement, which translated literally is "let him not turn himself toward the rear," has been phrased with Genesis 19:26 in mind. If so, it is an indication of the knowledge of the Bible upon which this chapter is based. **[17]** Except for Jesus' influence, it is likely that the defiling of the temple would have become the center of interest in this passage rather than the bitter distress of the weakest persons—the mothers. **[18]** It is not the swollen rivers which make winter an especially dangerous time for flight, but the lack of provisions in the fields. **[19]** This very limited local emergency, which differs from the world-wide perspective of vss. 8, 10, and 24-27, is looked upon here as the crucial and unparalleled tribulation of the end-time. Moreover, the conclusion of vs. 19, if taken literally, presupposes an additional lapse of time before the end. **[20]** "Nobody" represents an expression in the Greek text which literally is: "no flesh." This is translation-Greek and would be understood only by one who was acquainted with the Old Testament where "flesh" designates humanity in its weakness and finiteness. It is possible to speak of reducing the days (cf. Syriac Baruch 20:1 f.; 83:1, from the end of the first century A.D.; and the Epistle of Barnabas 4:3), because the Jewish apocalyptists conceived of a divine timetable which was rigidly and precisely defined.

What has happened here? In a particular time of emergency in Judea—which from the standpoint of world history represented an obscure event similar to the suppression of the revolt of an Arab sheik—a prophet arose and in accordance with apocalyptic notions interpreted this distress as the coming of God. Mark takes up this prophecy without referring concretely to any historical event. Surely in this context the prophecy has reference to some event which is yet to happen. This emphasizes the fact that behind those agonizing experiences which are full of apocalyptic horror God stands as the God who is accomplishing his objective. Thus the sketch is a call to put faith in him and in his future despite every appearance to the contrary. This call is made explicit in the following verses.

[21] Once more the description of the end-time leads to an appeal to the church which is living in the present. Luke 17:23 records a similar statement in a different context. The appearance of "false Messiahs" in addition to "false prophets" is something new when compared with the Old Testament anticipations. In addition, false teachers were expected to come in the last times according to 1 Timothy 4:1 (cf. 2 Tim. 3:1), and antichrists were expected according to 1 John 2:18 f. As early as Deuteronomy 13:1-3 miracles were not considered to be unambiguous proofs of God's presence. **[23]** It is emphasized here as in vs. 5 that one must "be on guard." Even before Mark there was a time of extreme fanaticism when it was not enough to call for preparation, as is done in vs. 9. It was necessary to warn against so-called saviors of every description. Mark appropriated this warning because he recognized the need to invoke the authority of Jesus in warning against a fanatical faith in Christ (cf. 1 John 4:2 f.) which is not inseparably connected with the suffering Son of Man (cf. 13:9 with 14:53—15:15; 13:22 f. with 14:33-46, 50, 66-

72; 13:26 with 14:62; 13:32 f. with 14:35, 37; and 13:35 with 14:17, 43, 72; 15:1). This is where Mark's real battle can be seen. It is not without good reason that he discerned the first clear revelation of God in 8:31.

[24] The transitional phrase "In the days" refers, strictly speaking, to the time of vs. 17. It is a formula which is characteristic of Mark (except for Luke 9:36 and the deliberate emendation in Luke 5:35 it is found only in passages which are dependent upon Mark). In 1:9 and 8:1* it links two very different passages without implying that they occurred at the same time (as is made clear in the TEV). In this passage, therefore, a statement is inserted that it will come to pass (in a short time which cannot be defined more precisely) "after that time of trouble." However, what happens affects the whole universe. Nothing is stated about any relationship between what is reported here and "The Awful Horror" who obviously still stands "where he should not be." It simply takes place later than the events in Judea. **[25, 26]** The collapse of the entire universe is not important in itself. It is only the framework for that one thing which is important—the coming of the Son of Man—which is portrayed in conformity with the picture in Daniel 7:13 (see the excursus to 8:27-33). **[27]** Deuteronomy 30:4 f. and Isaiah 60:4 ff. have spoken already of the gathering of Israel from all nations which was expected to happen in the end-time. Compare the flowing together of all nations in Micah 4:1 ff. and elsewhere. This concept is taken up in the New Testament, and its fulfillment is seen partly in the future home-gathering into the Kingdom of God (Mark 13:27; Didache 9:4) and partly in the mission to the Gentiles, who are brought into the unity of the church (John 11:52; Rom. 15:16). The description of their range reads literally: "from the end of the earth to the end of the heaven." It is a rather illogical blending of the two figures "from one end of heaven to the other" (Deut. 30:4 LXX, which speaks of the regathering of the scattered Israelites) and "from the one end of the earth to the other" (Deut. 13:7). The meaning is not altered, however. The gathering is restricted to the chosen

---

* The phrase literally is: "in those days," although in 1:9 and 8:1 it is translated: "not long afterward."

people; consequently, there is no expectation of a universal resurrection or judgment of all people both good and evil (cf. 12:25-27). There is no anticipation of the horror of the end, which comes upon all the inhabitants of the earth (cf., e.g., Rev. 6:15-17), nor of the Antichrist (however, cf. vss. 14 and 22). In contrast to the Jewish apocalypses, this passage contains no description of the punishment or annihilation of the enemies (in contrast to 2 Thess. 1:6-10). The description is especially crude in the contemporary Jewish document, the Assumption of Moses 10:10, where the redeemed are permitted to look from heaven and watch the punishment of their enemies. Great importance is placed upon the fulfillment of the Old Testament promises, which are quoted almost word for word. Therefore what is important is the ultimate fellowship of God's chosen people with their Lord (cf. 1 Thess. 4:17).

At the end of each individual passage we might have looked for the abiding significance of the statements in view of the changing interests which have had an effect upon the development of the tradition. As we review the whole discourse we will need to indicate again how it differs from a typical apocalypse. (a) Mark 13 does not provide anything which resembles a travel guide for the events of the end-time whereby the reader could determine exactly how far he had come on the journey. It is not the report of some past history which is only made to appear prophetic (which the author writes under the pseudonym of some famous personage in history). No contemporary events nor any events in the foreseeable future are presented in such a way that they would be helpful in determining what point had been reached in the program of future events, even though this may have been the original intention of vss. 14-20. Since the dating of events is kept general, it is more likely that this passage is a collection of various bits of tradition combined by the editor without any special emphasis other than that of marking out an exact succession of events. Thus this passage simply preserves the Old Testament point of view, where God's hand is seen even in war, famine, and pestilence. He is seen as the one who leads his people through any experience of suffering to his benevolent goal. (b) This goal is not the annihilation of his enemies or their condemnation to everlasting punishment. It is the power and glory of the Son of Man, which involves the homecoming of the dispersed to ultimate fellowship with their God. So in the last analysis this passage is dealing with the fulfillment of the prayer: "May your name be kept holy, May your kingdom come, May your will be done," which also includes "Keep us safe . . ." (c) Above all, it is evident how the style of this account, which concerns future events, was interrupted again and again by appeals made directly to the church in reference to its present situation. Moreover, Mark 13 reminds one of the Old Testament prophets whose only reason for speaking about future things was to make the matter of Israel's repentance urgent and unavoidable in the time of the prophet. We may be able to explain the gradual rise of all sorts of details, but this account can hardly be considered a presentation of the course of eschatological events that are accurately described and must be accepted as true. The statements of this chapter are, however, central and important: (a) All suffering in the present time is subject to God's sovereignty. This suffering is part of a history over which God is Lord and which he will bring to its fulfillment. Thus keen anticipation and glad hope characterize the attitude of the church toward history despite all its suffering. (b) This goal is the power and glory of God and the return of his chosen people into full fellowship with him. With this two things are asserted: In the end what really matters is God, his triumph and his honor; and God, who will meet us in this triumph, will at that time have the appearance of the Son of Man. When he is all in all, and all opposition to him has ceased, he will not be an abstract God "in and by himself." On the contrary, he will be the God who turns his attention toward us, as the God whom he revealed himself to be in the Son of Man, Jesus of Nazareth. (c) This is why the events of the present are no minor matters, but are signs of the final coming of God. Therefore these events represent the world and the age in which the church is subjected to trials. The church is able to endure only through the strength which it is supplied in the Son of Man, and in the present time it is able to experience the power and glory of

God afresh. This is the way a person must believe today. Then everything from the "trivial" experience of the fugitive who does not have sufficient time to go to his room to get his coat (vs. 16) to the "greatness" of the world mission (vs. 10) will be seen in the light of the coming of God. This is what gives everything its meaning and its goal.

Parables about the Proper Way to Wait 13:28-37;
cf. Matt. 24:32-36; Luke 21:29-33

28"Let the fig tree teach you a lesson. When its branches become green and tender, and it starts putting out leaves, you know
that summer is near. 29In the same way, when you see these things
happening, you will know that the time is near, ready to begin.
30Remember this! All these things will happen before the people
now living have all died. 31Heaven and earth will pass away; my
words will never pass away."

32"No one knows, however, when that day or hour will come—
neither the angels in heaven, nor the Son; only the Father knows.
33Be on watch, be alert, for you do not know when the time will be.
34It will be like a man who goes away from home on a trip and
leaves his servants in charge, each one with his own work to do;
and he tells the doorkeeper to keep watch. 35Watch, then, because you do not know when the master of the house is coming—
it might be in the evening, or at midnight, or before dawn, or at
sunrise. 36If he comes suddenly, he must not find you asleep!
37What I say to you, then, I say to all: Watch!"

The last section of this discourse is made up of a number of separate parts. Vss. 28 f. are a parable which is an exhortation to pay careful attention to the signs of the one who is coming, similar to Luke 12:54-56. Both passages may go back to Jesus, since he frequently expressed the same thought in two figures. That this parable was not found originally in this context is indicated by the fact that "these things" in vs. 29 cannot refer to vss. 24-27 and is different from "all these things" in vs. 30. At one time this phrase may have referred to Jesus' activity (see vs. 29). Consequently, vs. 30 is also a separate saying and can be compared with 9:1. Probably it was added here in the tradition because the catchword "these things will happen" appears in both verses, 29 and 30. The catchword "die—pass away" is the only reason why vs. 31 has been added here. This verse is related to Matthew 5:18 (cf. Luke 16:17). The statement is meaningful only if Jesus' words—or the law (Matt. 5:18)—are declared to be the standard by which everything will be decided even after heaven and earth have passed away, i.e., in the last judgment. This is the kind of context in which the saying belonged originally. Although this version is old, the one in Matthew 5:18 is older, so that the transition from the law to Jesus' word presents the second stage. Vs. 32 is difficult to evaluate. It, too, is based upon a separate saying, because this is the only place where "the Father" and "the Son" are mentioned—also because it is in tension with vss. 29 f. This may be a genuine saying of Jesus. The designation as "the Son" indicates a position of honor in comparison with all other men. The title also distinguishes him from God, and thus does not in any way present a definitive formula which can simply be accepted as true (see below on vs. 32). The limitation of Jesus' knowledge which is enunciated here caused the church great difficulty later. Since it seems that Jesus spoke of himself as "the Son" nowhere else (see 15:39), we will have to consider the possibility that this saying arose in an early period because the church possessed no saying of Jesus about when these things would happen. At that time many were asking why the end had not come as yet. Others were making rather precise announcements concerning the imminent end of the world (cf. 2 Thess. 2:2; Luke 21:8).

It is clear that two different figures are combined in the last parable. Vs. 35 refers only to the master's return home during the night. In the conditions of that time such a thing would be almost inconceivable if the master had gone on a trip to a foreign country, but it could happen if he had gone to a banquet. Under those circumstances the doorkeeper, who is mentioned in a rather strange addition at the end of vs. 34, has his role as the one who watches throughout the night and opens the door for the master when he comes home. This is how the parable is recorded in Luke 12:36. The watching is the real point here, since one must be ready at all times to open the door for the master when he comes. In the parallel verses Matthew inserted a second metaphor, that of a thief in the night (the same metaphor pictures the sudden coming of the "day" of judgment in 1 Thess. 5:2, but it signifies the coming of the Son of Man in Luke 12:39) in order to illustrate this intense vigilance during the night-watch. On the other hand, a completely different metaphor is combined with it in Mark 13:34. The wording of Matthew 25:14 f. and Luke 19:12 f., which is largely in agreement with Mark 13:34, shows that this metaphor belonged in another context originally—the context of the "man" who traveled to another country and gave his servants certain tasks to do in the interim (which was a much longer time than in the case of the "master" who went to a banquet). As Matthew 25:19-30 and Luke 19:15-26 indicate, the salient point here is the faithfulness with which the servants carry out their tasks during the long period of the man's absence. When the simple metaphor of the sudden coming of the master in the night was no longer adequate—since it was impossible to wait for years and decades for the single apocalyptic moment of the appearance of the Son of Man—the second metaphor had to become dominant as the center of interest for the church. Mark has combined both metaphors even though the summons to watch for the unknown hour when the master would return is all that is relevant in this passage. This is why the charge to the doorkeeper is added in a way that is awkward grammatically and why the summons "watch" is repeated by Mark in vs. 37 and is directed to "all." In contrast to his source, Mark certainly regarded the faithfulness of the church in the time before the end as the real "watching," not the adherence to a belief that the end would come soon.

[28] Once again it is clear that every description of the events of the end-time is tantamount to an exhortation to the church. The answer to the question in vs. 4 about when these things will happen will be given only in the form of the summons to be ready. **[29]** The position of these verses is rather unfortunate since "these things" cannot refer to events in the near future, but only to those things which will happen before the end. Yet Mark prefers not to specify what is actually meant by "these things." Since the coming of Jesus, every event had in principle taken on the character of a sign and pointed to the coming of the Son of Man. This is what made the events meaningful. Furthermore, the passage does not state what it is or who it is that is about to begin (Greek: "is near the door"). According to what has preceded it must be the parousia of Jesus. In the parallel saying in Luke 12:54-56 Jesus and his activity are the "sign" which ought to make men take notice. This is no longer clear in Mark 13, where many kinds of events are enumerated between Jesus' death and the end. We must not overlook the fact that even the events recorded in this passage are given the character of signs only by Jesus and by the good news about him. This is seen most clearly in the explanation of 13:12 by vss. 9-13. Ever since God in Jesus turned his attention to the world, the church has seen God moving toward his objective in the progress of world history. This does not mean that the church is able to explain or understand the progress of history, but that again and again it is able to catch a glimpse of signs and to recognize a connection here and there in which the promised future is already manifest. In this respect there is no basic difference between Luke 12:54-56 where the activity of the earthly Jesus is interpreted as the sign which should be heeded, and Mark 13 where that sign is the activity of Jesus throughout the entire history of the world. The nearness of summer is more noticeable in Palestine than it is in our country, because it sets in very quickly there, immediately after the end of the rainy season. **[30]** Certainly "all these things" (vs. 30) must include the parousia of the Son of Man. The use of *genea* (translated here: "people") in Luke 16:8 shows that this word can designate the whole human race—not merely a generation as it usually does (cf. 8:38). If, however, it were understood with that meaning here, the statement would be rather inane. The possibility that the human race might die out before the end of the world is not entertained in any contemporary document either within or outside the Bible. The statement must be understood to mean that "all these things" would happen before all of the generation which was living at the time of Jesus had died. Consequently it is similar to 9:1. This is another passage designed to impress the reader with the truth that the Son of Man is determined to encounter him. He must not suppose that it will be a long time before this encounter will happen, and that future generations are the only ones who need to prepare for it. **[31]** The phrase "my words" is not Mark's formulation. He would have said "my teaching" (see 1:22). Nevertheless, he does not apply this saying, which has been handed down to him, exclusively to chapter 13. He applies it to what in other places he calls Jesus' "teaching," i.e., the revelation of God which has been given in Jesus, which includes above all the suffering of the Son of Man. It is the one thing which has stability in the midst of all the change of the rapidly occurring events of the end-time. It is the firm ground upon which the church can dare to live and to meet courageously all the terrors which are coming before the end.

[32] The fact that one is prepared to listen now instead of wishing to transfer this message to future generations does not entitle him to a knowledge of God's plans such as is striven for continually in apocalyptic calculations. This is a method by which man would like to control God and have a better chance to postpone meeting him until that particular time which man has determined by his calculations. Thus Mark emphasizes that Jesus is not understood correctly unless he is understood as the "Son." It is surprising that Jesus is classified together with the angels. This is customary in eschatological assertions about the Son of Man (Mark 8:38; 13:27; Matt. 25:31; Luke 12:8; cf. John 1:51) so that in passages of this type a kind of trinity of Father, Son, and holy angels is developed (see 8:38). When this passage speaks of the "Son" instead of the "Son of Man," the emphasis falls upon his subordination to God instead of his majesty and honor. "Son of God" (see 15:39) is an expression of majesty, in contrast to "son of a human father." But whenever "the Son" is used absolutely, it calls to mind the contrast to "the Father" and at the same time it describes a subordinate position in relation to the Father. In the same way, 1 Corinthians 15:28 uses this expression in an eschatological context to warn against the misunderstanding of

Christ the Lord of the end-time as a second God alongside the Father. The strong emphasis upon the exaltation of Jesus as the Son of God who reigns in heaven (Rom. 1:4) must have compelled the church, which had its roots in the Old Testament, to stress that Jesus was not a second God, but that in him the one God turned his attention to the world. This reservation is made clear here also. Jesus is the one who in a unique way stands on the side of the "angels" and yet is distinct from them. He it is who always turns the attention from himself to God and makes God a present reality.

[33] Mark's concern becomes especially clear in vs. 33. The formula "be on watch" is certainly typical of him. Probably he is the one who made the transition to what follows by adding the statement that the Son does not know the day or the hour (vs. 32). The "time," which cannot be calculated, is always immediately at hand. It summons us to wakefulness—to that attitude toward life which characterizes the man who always stands accountable before the coming Lord and permits nothing to hinder him from being ready for the Lord at all times. And so this "time" which is future becomes the factor which fully determines the present and gives it its tension, its hope, its objective, and its meaning. **[34]** This is what is emphasized by the figure of the tasks which were assigned by the master to be carried out in the present—before the time of his return. **[35]** The figure of the watching and the reference to the uncertain hour of his return give urgency to this responsibility: No moment is unimportant, because any one could be the moment of the Lord's final return. **[36]** For this reason the church cannot sleep the time away as if it were unfulfilled time, i.e., time not fulfilled by the future coming of the Lord, and as if it would not matter how this time was used by the church. **[37]** By his last comment Mark re-emphasizes that, in contrast to sayings which are truly apocalyptic, this one applies to everyone and not simply to the four intimate friends (vs. 3). In so doing he is giving another indication that in this passage his real interest is centered in the exhortation.

It was already traditional for the discourse about the events of the end-time to come at the close of Jesus' public ministry (cf.

introduction to vss. 1-27). Nevertheless, this arrangement has special significance for Mark, because with this discourse Jesus once more summoned "everyone" to that "watching" which characterizes the life of the church between the time of the suffering of the Son of Man and his return which will bring everything to fulfillment. The only other reference to his return (8:38—9:1) serves equally to emphasize the urgency of the call to discipleship. Mark uses the return of the Son of Man as an opportunity to refer specifically to the need for endurance in persecution and in confrontation with false teachers. In this connection Mark is particularly concerned about the world-wide proclamation. At the present time the church lives in the midst of persecution and temptation and yet confidently proclaims the Good News to the whole Gentile world. This kind of living and proclaiming makes it imperative—and glorious—to know about the coming of the Lord.

B. THE DAYS OF JESUS' PASSION AND RESURRECTION 14:1—16:8

The Passion Narrative. It is likely that the oldest account of the Passion still preserved begins with 14:1 f. From the beginning this account possesses a character completely different from what has been treated up to this point (see sections 2 and 3 of the Introduction). In this narrative the sequence of the most important passages is the same as it is in John. The degree of accordance with John was very limited before this point (see comment on 6:32-44). Luke probably was acquainted with another source which must have followed the same sequence in the essential matters (see Luke 22:47-53, 54-71; 23:13-25). There is a whole series of individual passages which, on the whole, are meaningful only in context; consequently, they never could have been handed down as separate units (see Judas' bargain to betray Jesus, the identifying of the betrayer at the Last Supper, the arrest in Gethsemane, and the trials before the Jewish and Roman authorities). Therefore, the Passion story must have been told from the very first in a specific order. This applies even to brief excerpts such as we have discovered in 8:31; 9:31; 10:33 f. and particularly to a confession of faith as in 1 Corinthians 15:3-5. However, it certainly does not apply to every portion (cf. 14:3-9, 12-17, 22-25). Moreover, new passages were added after Mark, e.g., Matthew 27:3-10, 62-66; and Luke 23:6-16, 27-31. It will be necessary for us to seek to establish what was included in the oldest account. Rudolf Bultmann accepts only a very brief sketch which contained Jesus' arrest, his sentencing in Jewish and Roman courts, his being led away to be crucified, his crucifixion, and his death. However, there probably was an ancient Passion story which basically contained those passages which also appear in the same order in John. In addition to 14:1 f. this story would have contained the betrayal by Judas; the Last Supper, with the identification of the betrayer; the arrest and the hearing; the trial before Pilate; and the crucifixion. Of course, the account was not in its present form (see the specific introductions). Martin Dibelius suggested the possibility that Peter's denial (14:66-72) along with the account of how it had been predicted (14:29-31) and parts of the scene in Gethsemane had always been included.

On what occasions was such a Passion story narrated? First Corinthians 11:23 ff. indicates that at the celebration of the Lord's Supper reference was made not only to Jesus' death but also to certain details of his Passion ("on the night"). The first kernel of such a presentation may actually have been formed in the liturgy of the Lord's Supper, and that liturgy would have been more elaborate on Easter Sunday. A number of scholars have suggested that the nucleus of the Passion story arose in public worship commemorating the Passion, with set hours for prayer, or in a lectionary which was read during Holy Week. Others suggest that the Passion story originated in preaching. The various parts of the story must be differentiated. A portion such as 14:22-25, which contained the institution of this ritual that continued to be observed, certainly was recited regularly in the liturgy of the Lord's Supper (see the introduction to 14:22-25). Other passages are simple accounts which may have had a significant place in the church's program of instruction. Possibly this was true of the oldest version of the account of the crucifixion. Others were developed more for edification in view of their significance for the church. The scene in Gethsemane may be an example of such a passage. This development occurred most likely in homiletical discourses addressed to the church. The interweaving of Peter's denial (particularly if this should belong to the earliest stage) with Jesus' testimony before the high council certainly had a parenetic purpose; consequently it was intended as an exhortation to the church (or to the catechumens) to be faithful in confessing their faith. Explicit references to Scripture such as the one in 15:24 reveal a later stage involving theological reflection, while the almost instinctive manner of speaking in Old Testament phraseology implies that it originated in a church which lived with its Bible and found the Christ-events predicted in it. Still later the matter of apologetics became more and more important in the discussions with non-Christians. This is especially true of Matthew who, e.g., defends the crucifixion of Jesus as a saving-event which was part of God's will (cf. Matt. 27:62-66). Therefore it is necessary to predicate a number of different situations to account for the rise of the individual portions which have accrued in the development of the tradition. Most likely the first brief summary of the Passion was formed in the liturgy of the church.

The inclusion of chapters 11-13 in the Passion narrative was Mark's most important contribution. He may have fashioned all of the material in these chapters as a kind of introduction to the Passion by locating the events in Jerusalem (where according to Mark, Jesus had never been before!) and by suggesting a special Passion Week (this is about the only place in Mark where we find any chronology). In reality he extended the Passion story all the way back to 8:31, or perhaps 3:6, or even 1:14. The Gospel of Mark cannot be adequately described as a "Passion story with an extensive introduction," since it contains the "Book of the Secret Epiphany" as well as Jesus' struggle to reveal God to man. Nevertheless, such a designation does indicate something of critical importance to our understanding of Mark.

The Conspiracy to Kill Jesus 14:1-2;
cf. Matt. 26:1-5; Luke 22:1-2

[1]It was now two days before the Feast of Passover and Unleavened Bread. The chief priests and teachers of the Law were looking for a way to arrest Jesus secretly and put him to death. [2]"We must not do it during the feast," they said, "or the people might riot."

[1] This chronology was not always included in the account of the Passion. In John the conspiracy and the anointing are put before Jesus' triumphal entry. The Passover begins at sunset (cf. 14:12-16) on the evening of the first full moon after the spring equinox. According to Jewish reckoning this is the fifteenth of Nisan. The "Feast of Unleavened Bread" (Jewish "Matzoth") includes the whole week from the Passover to the twenty-first of Nisan. The combination of "the Feast of the Passover and Unleavened Bread" is customary, although the latter actually includes the former. Possibly this dating is intended to stress the fact that each step has been foreordained by God and has turned out according to his plan: There are two days until the Passover; its night and day are divided into three periods of three hours each, and then there are two more days until the resurrection. Even at this time (after 3:6; 11:18) all that is considered is how to destroy Jesus. In these considerations the expression "put him to death," and certainly the planning of a strategy by which to seize Jesus, may indicate that these plans had matured even down to the details. **[2]** Here again we see that distinction between the common people and their leaders (cf. 12:12) which is important to Mark. One might translate: "not in the gathering at the feast." It is more likely, however, that Mark wants to assert that the very thing which men desire to prevent must be brought to pass by God: It is "during the feast" that he will be executed (at least according to Mark; see 14:12-16).

The Anointing of Jesus in Preparation for His Death 14:3-9;
cf. Matt. 26:6-13; Luke 7:36-50; John 12:1-8

[3]Jesus was in the house of Simon the leper, in Bethany; while he was eating, a woman came in with an alabaster jar full of a very expensive perfume, made of pure nard. She broke the jar and poured the perfume on Jesus' head. [4]Some of the people there became angry, and said to each other, "What was the use of wasting the perfume? [5]It could have been sold for more than three hundred dollars, and the money given to the poor!" And they criticized her harshly. [6]But Jesus said: "Leave her alone! Why are you bothering her? She has done a fine and beautiful thing for me. [7]You will always have poor people with you, and any time you want to you can help them. But I shall not be with you always. [8]She did what she could: she poured perfume on my body to prepare it for burial ahead of time. [9]Now, remember this! Wherever the gospel is preached, all over the world, what she has done will be told in memory of her."

Luke omitted the story from this place, because he had recorded a different version of it in 7:36-50. In that version also the man with whom Jesus is staying is named "Simon," although he is a Pharisee. John must have known both versions. Part of John 12:3b agrees with Luke 7:38b, while the rest of his account follows the Markan version rather closely. The drying of Jesus' feet with the woman's hair is logical in Luke, where they have been covered with her tears, but the drying of his feet is not logical in John, where they have been anointed. This can only be understood as a reminiscence of the Lukan account which has not been preserved accurately. It is almost certain that these two versions were not only told independently but were also woven together before they were written down by Mark and Luke, and that they came to John in this combined form. The Markan version is probably the older of the two. The story of the anointing may have been used in the church as an illustration of the parable in Luke 7:40-43 or may have been compared with some other incident where a harlot (for whom the anointing oil is very appropriate) bathed Jesus' feet with her tears and dried them with her hair. The location in Bethany (in John 12:1 also) and in the house of Simon (in Luke 7:40 also) was already a part of this story in the tradition. The observation that Simon was a leper must have come from a time when either he or his story was still known, since the possibility that he had been healed by Jesus is not referred to in the story. On the other hand, the difficult construction in vs. 3a (*ontos autou . . . katakeimenou autou . . .*) is an indication that the oldest tradition may have started with the second Greek participle, i.e., with the words, "while they were eating." Then the more specific statement of location was added later (by Mark from oral tradition, or possibly because the words "home of Simon" were already included in the second participial clause?). Certainly in the development of the tradition something was added at the conclusion. Probably in the oldest layer, which might easily correspond with what happened in the life of Jesus, vs. 7a,c was the real point of the story: Jesus' time is distinguished from all other time. It is the time of the "bridegroom" (2:19), in which the religious duties of fasting (2:19) and giving to charity (14:5; occasionally the two occur together in Jewish writings, frequently alongside repentance and prayer, cf. Matthew 6:1-18) can no longer be given primary importance, because the presence of Jesus calls for a kind of conduct which surpasses the standards of everyday life. The story may have been linked to the imminent death of Jesus even before any additions were made. It was then necessary to avoid the misconception that expressions of love had become unnecessary because of his approaching death. This was accomplished by the insertion of vs. 7b. Sayings of Jesus which were eschatologically oriented, and which by emphasizing the uniqueness of what happened in Jesus distinguished his time from all other times, were usually expanded, reinterpreted, or reformulated. This was done because ethical problems, which remain more or less unchanged through the years, became more important for the church (cf. 4:13-20). In vs. 8a there seems to be a new explanation of the woman's act which corresponds to 12:44b: She gave all that she had. Vs. 8b may be a later accretion. Her perception that at that moment Jesus was more important than any financial or charitable considerations is no longer the only thing that makes her deed distinctive—it is the fact that the anointing became a prophetic allusion to Jesus' Passion. What was implicit in vs. 7 has become explicit here. Finally, with vs. 9 Mark emphasized that the kernel of the proclamation of the Good News is found in the reference to the Passion as it has been anticipated in the action of this woman (according to vs. 8). This passage presupposes knowledge of the world-wide proclamation of the Good News. This is something which was not thought of in the church before Acts 8:1 and 11:19 f. This statement is surprising, because the woman's name is not mentioned in the story even though the assertion is made that in all future generations this incident will be told "in memory of her." Her name is not given until John 12:3. Then in the fourth century the Syrian church-father Ephraem identified this Mary with Mary Magdalene (Mark 15:40, et al.) and with the sinful woman in Luke 7:37. This is the basis for the portrayal of Mary Magdalene as one who repented of her sin and later became the first witness of the resurrection. The statement in vs. 9 must have been added later when the world-mission had become an established fact and the name of the woman was no longer known. Then the interest in the story which persisted must have been of an entirely different nature. The only one who could have made this addition is Mark, since the Passion of Jesus had become so extremely important to him.

It is obvious that this story breaks the continuity between 14:1 f. and 14:10 f. It has been placed at the beginning of the Passion story on account of vs. 8. Mark set it between the conspiracy to kill Jesus and the betrayal (see comment on 5:21-43). John put it before the triumphal entry. In this way Mark has presented a very impressive contrast between the conspiracy of the authorities and the love of this woman who was one of the common people. Hers was a love which showed profound insight. At the same time the concluding verse (vs. 9) calls attention to the great significance of this insight into the importance of Jesus' Passion.

[3] According to 11:1 and 11 f. Jesus had been spending the nights in Bethany. The woman's action is unorthodox by the standards of that time, because she breaks into the company of men and suddenly anoints Jesus during the meal—not before it. **[4]** Mark does not specify who asked the indignant question. Who it was is stated differently and has become more specific in Matthew 26:8 and John 12:4 (cf. Luke 7:39). **[5]** The value mentioned probably represents a year's wages for a laborer. It is understandable that the people mentioned in vs. 4 would begin to calculate the value of the ointment, and ordinarily this would have been proper. Even their anger is understandable. **[6]** And yet it is wrong here even as it was in 10:13. The lack of understanding of these persons who have become angry is so much more noticeable in this situation where they have reason and sober reflection on their side, because when Jesus is present every regular custom is broken. Jesus sees the "beautiful thing" which she has done. **[7]** Once again it is affirmed in words reminiscent of Deuteronomy 15:11 that normally the objections of vss. 4 f. would have been altogether proper. However, through Jesus—here it is not through his action or speech, but simply through his personal presence and the shadow of his death which was already standing over him —an exceptional situation has been created in which those correct statements are incorrect. **[8]** The first phrase of vs. 8 emphasizes another element—the magnitude of the sacrifice. Most important, in 8b the anointing is interpreted as a symbolic and prophetic action which prepared Jesus for his path of suffering. Perhaps this even implies that the usual anointing of the body would not take place on account of the resurrection (16:1). **[9]** For Mark this woman is the first person who knew of the central importance of Jesus' Passion which was alluded to in vs. 8. Here belief in the gospel (1:15) is expressed in a remarkable way. So in Mark's account she stands at the beginning of the Passion, and her ministration emphasizes that the pathway of Jesus leading to death (perhaps he even has the resurrection explicitly in mind) is the heart of the message.

Judas' Betrayal 14:10-11;
cf. Matt. 26:14-16; Luke 22:3-6

[10]Then Judas Iscariot, one of the twelve disciples, went off to the chief priests in order to hand Jesus over to them. [11]They were

greatly pleased to hear what he had to say, and promised to give him money. So Judas started looking for a good chance to betray Jesus.

Originally this brief record came immediately after vss. 1 f. It may have been the beginning of an ancient account of the Passion (cf. vss. 3-9). That Judas was "one of the twelve disciples" (in Greek he is called here "the one . . .") is firmly embedded in the tradition (14:10, 20, 43; John 6:71). It is extremely unlikely that this idea arose later in order to make the suffering of Jesus that much more grievous (cf. 6:7-13). On the contrary, it was more common later on to make excuses for the disciples. From an historian's point of view it is no longer very clear what it was precisely that Judas betrayed. John 18:2 asserts that it was the place where Jesus often went at night. However, if Jesus regularly stayed at a certain place, it would have been relatively easy to discover its location without Judas' help. If Jesus stayed there only for that one night, Judas would scarcely have known in advance where it was. It is rather fantastic to assume that Jesus might have founded anything like an underground movement against the Romans with carefully selected hide-outs. Some have supposed that Judas betrayed the fact that Jesus considered himself to be the Messiah. However, this hypothesis is hardly conceivable either, since it is obvious that the hostility against Jesus had been aroused much earlier by his attitude toward the law and the temple (3:6; 11:18; 14:58). Moreover, Judas did not appear as a witness at the trial; on the contrary, everything depended on the testimony of the accused (14:61 f.). It is possible that Judas was attracted by the objectives of the Zealots (cf. 3:18 f.). Even if it is likely that his surname means "man" (Hebrew: *ish*) from Kerioth (in southern Judea), it is still conceivable that Judas, being very disappointed by Jesus' inactivity, made contact with old friends among the opponents of Jesus in order to force him into action at last and thus to set events in motion. It is a possibility that during or after the meal he indicated to someone that Jesus would not go home this night until after dark. Nevertheless, these ideas are no more than conjectures which at best are merely probabilities.

[10] The text emphasizes the bitterness of the fate of Jesus, who is betrayed by one for whom he had taken special pains and who should have had insight and understanding (see comment on 4:34; 8:26). Judas' act is consistently called a "handing-over." It is mentioned without any reference to Judas in 9:31; 10:33; 14:41; Luke 9:44; 18:32; et al. This suggests the interplay of human action and divine predestination. Judas merely fulfills the prediction in 9:31 that the Son of Man would be handed over to men. In 8:31 the statement is made that these things "must" come to pass. A wild horse can be mastered by an experienced rider and thus render great service to him. In the process his wildness is not removed nor is it "excused." Nevertheless, it is a fact that the horse now serves the rider with that very same wildness; yes, it is specifically with that wildness that it serves him. So here also it becomes clear that Judas' guilt must not be measured according to moral standards alone. **[11]** This is even more applicable to the next verse, because according to Mark the reward was not promised until after the decisive conversation had been held. Matthew 26:15 first makes Judas' greed the motive for the betrayal (cf. John 12:6). It also specifies the amount of the reward, which, obviously, has been taken from Zechariah 11:12 f. (Matt. 27:9). However, Mark leaves open the possibility that he may not have been motivated by any abysmal moral depravity but by an idealistic nationalism which in itself was something extolled by many. This illustrates the inadequacy of purely moral standards in measuring a person's guilt in the sight of God, when men either wish to pass Jesus by or do so in going their own way.

The Preparation for the Last Supper 14:12-16;
cf. Matt. 26:17-19; Luke 22:7-13

[12]On the first day of the Feast of Unleavened Bread, the day the lambs for the Passover meal were killed, Jesus' disciples asked him: "Where do you want us to go and get your Passover supper ready?" [13]Then Jesus sent two of them out with these instructions: "Go into the city, and a man carrying a jar of water will meet you. [14]Follow him to the house he enters, and say to the

owner of the house: 'The Teacher says, Where is my room where my disciples and I shall eat the Passover supper?' [15]Then he will show you a large upstairs room, fixed up and furnished, where you will get things ready for us." [16]The disciples left, went to the city, and found everything just as Jesus had told them; and they prepared the Passover supper.

This section stands out clearly from the rest of the context. The "disciples" are mentioned four times in the Greek text (the only other place where they are mentioned in the Passion story is in 14:32), while in vs. 17 as in vss. 10, 20, and 43 they are designated as "the twelve." The way it works out is that Jesus sends two disciples ahead, while vs. 17 declares that he came "with the twelve disciples." Furthermore, the statement "on the first day of the Feast of Unleavened Bread" (cf. 14:1) would be correct for Greeks and Romans, for whom the day began in the morning, but the day began at sunset for the Jews. This applied also in the case of the Passover and the Week of Unleavened Bread, so that one would have to say "on the day before the Feast of Unleavened Bread." It may be nothing more than an inaccurate statement, since this calculation is found occasionally in Jewish writings. Finally, whole clauses in vss. 13a and 16 (cf. vs. 14 also) are the same as those in 11:1 f., 4, 6 (cf. vs. 3 also). Since the entire incident is omitted from John it is impossible to avoid the conclusion that this is a later accretion, which has been formed after the pattern of 11:1 ff. as an introduction to vss. 17 ff. or on the basis of the description of some other feast. This is important, since it is the only passage in Mark where the Last Supper is designated as the Passover (found also in Luke 22:15). According to this, Jesus would have died on the Feast of the Passover, or the fifteenth of Nisan. It may be that the composition goes back to the church, which was disposed to view the Lord's Supper as replacing the Passover meal. John 18:28 and 19:14 state with equal clarity that Jesus died on the fourteenth of Nisan, the day before the Passover, which is the time when the Passover lamb was slaughtered. This may be explained by the fact that John regarded Jesus as the Passover lamb (John 1:29, 36; 19:36; cf. 1 Cor. 5:7). It is clear that Jesus died on Friday (see comment on 15:42), but since we do not know what year it was, we do not know whether Friday was the day of the Passover or the day before.

Luke 22:15 favors the fifteenth of Nisan as does the singing of the hymn (Mark 14:26), since this was a custom at the Passover. The same might be said concerning the late hour of the meal, which is recorded only in 1 Corinthians 11:23 (?) and John 13:30 (where it is interpreted symbolically). However, the late hour as well as the use of wine and the reclining at the table might all be true of a formal dinner which the host wanted to be something out of the ordinary. Finally, the fact that the supper took place in Jerusalem is appropriate for the Passover. To be sure, 14:12-16 is the only passage in Mark that mentions this, but it is assumed in John 18:1. The subsequent stay on the Mount of Olives, which was a part of the larger area of the city, was nothing extraordinary. It is recorded, however, only in John 18:1; Luke 21:37 and 22:39. The following considerations favor the fourteenth of Nisan: There is no reference to the Passover either in Mark 14:17-21 or in 14:22-25. With the exception of Luke 22:15, none of the accounts of the Last Supper contain any reference to the lamb which was the central feature of the Passover. The words of explanation are not assimilated to the form which was customary at the Passover, nor do they appear at the same point in the course of the meal. In contrast to the Passover, no women are present. And finally, the blessing of the cup is pronounced by Jesus and not by some other person at the table. The main objection is that although the convening of the court and the execution of Jesus could have happened on the day of the Passover feast, it is difficult to imagine that it really did. Moreover, details such as the statement that Simon was coming from a field and that weapons were carried (14:47; Luke 22:38) preclude its being a feast day. Finally, we would expect the Lord's Supper to have been celebrated annually in the church rather than daily or weekly if the original one had been a Passover meal. Thus the dating in John is a little more probable. Moreover, according to a (later) Jewish tradition, Jesus was crucified on the Day of Preparation before the Passover. Of course, if the Last Supper was held on the eve of the Passover, it would still be a Passover meal even as a meal on Christmas Eve is a Christmas dinner according to our customs.

The Passover. For the Passover meal a one-year-old lamb or kid that was free from any blemish was slaughtered in the temple in the afternoon. The dinner party had to assemble inside the city of Jerusalem and, as a rule, had to include at least ten persons, since no more than one lamb could be prepared for each group, and because it was imperative that the entire lamb be eaten that night. The eating of the meal did not begin until after sunset. It began with the first cup, which was mixed while a blessing was being said. Green herbs and, very often, a paste of mashed fruits were served with unleavened bread. This was followed by the second cup, at which time an explanation was given of the way in which this meal differed from an ordinary one. This may have taken the following form, which was recorded at a later date: "Look, this is the bread of affliction (cf. Deut. 16:3) which our forefathers ate when they departed from Egypt." In any case, "the men in each generation are obligated to look upon themselves as if they had come out of Egypt." Then a part of the Hallel (Pss. 113—118) was recited, followed by a prayer of thanksgiving. After this the meal was served. It began with the breaking of bread. The father of the house pronounced the blessing, then broke the bread and gave a piece to each person. The third cup followed with the table grace. This was the "cup of blessing" (1 Cor. 10:16), after which there was a fourth cup and the conclusion of the Hallel. At customary formal dinners an appetizer was served for which each pronounced his own blessing. In contrast to the usual meal, the guests reclined at the table for the main dish, and wine was served. The formal dinners began in the same way as the Passover meal, with a cup of wine and the breaking of bread. After the meal the leftover pieces were gathered, grace was said, and the "cup of blessing" was drunk. When compared with both of these festal occasions, the blessing in connection with the breaking of the bread at the Lord's Supper corresponds to the blessing of the meal at the breaking of the bread. This was not the point where the Passover was explained;

that came before the main dish. The saying in connection with the cup corresponds to the blessing of the "cup of blessing" at the end of the meal (as 1 Cor. 11:25 and Luke 22:20 report explicitly). Accordingly these sayings simply take the place of the table grace before and after the meal. Thus in the course of the Lord's Supper there is nothing which would indicate whether it was the Passover meal or a formal dinner on the preceding evening.

[12] The fact that, as a matter of course, the question was worded with "you" and not "we" clearly indicates that Jesus was the central figure in the band of disciples. **[13]** The miraculous foreknowledge of Jesus is described similarly to the way it was in 11:2 f. Of course, a water carrier was a common sight, although a jar may have been more unusual than the customary leather bag. **[14]** Naturally the miracle consists in the precise prediction of what follows. "The Teacher" could mean "our teacher." In this case it would have been the usual request of a pilgrim for permission to use a room. This request was always complied with on the eve of the Passover if at all possible. But the way in which Jesus' saying is worded shows that something more is meant. He is "the Master" who has all mankind at his service. With the exception of where it is used as a noun of address the only other place in Mark where this title occurs is in 5:35, where an onlooker speaks of him as "the Teacher." Here it is congruous with "disciple," which is a characteristic expression in this passage. **[15]** The house must have been extraordinary since an upper room suitable for a large gathering was available and already furnished with carpets and sofas. **[16]** There is a brief statement that everything was fulfilled as Jesus had predicted.

Thus this passage serves two objectives: It puts the Lord's Supper into the place of the Jewish Passover and at the same time emphasizes that what happened on this day did not come upon Jesus as a catastrophe but was predicted by him, and that he chose to endure it.

Jesus Identifies His Betrayer 14:17-21;
cf. Matt. 26:20-25; Luke 22:14, 21-23

17When it was evening, Jesus came with the twelve disciples.
18While they were at the table eating, Jesus said: "I tell you this: one of you will betray me—one who is eating with me." 19The
disciples were upset and began to ask him, one after the other, "Surely you don't mean me, do you?" 20Jesus answered: "It will be one of you twelve, one who dips his bread in the dish with me.
21The Son of Man will die as the Scriptures say he will; but how terrible for that man who will betray the Son of Man! It would have been better for that man if he had never been born!"

(Vs. 18: Ps. 41:9.)

Vs. 18 is reminiscent of Psalm 41:9 ("who ate of my bread, has lifted his heel against me." [RSV] Quoted in John 13:18). The correspondence in wording is hardly literal; however, it had become a proverbial expression (1QH 5:23 f.: "All that ate of my bread lifted their heels against me; . . . mouthed distortions about me"). It is conceivable that the entire scene might be merely a symbolical presentation of the proposition that one of those closest to Jesus "who ate of his bread" delivered him over. Anyway, John also records that the betrayer was singled out at the Last Supper, and the tradition found in Luke 22:21 reports the same thing. It may be assumed, therefore, that the statements correspond to the historical event. On the other hand, Jesus' knowledge, his readiness to submit to the will of God (vs. 21a), and above all the conduct of the disciples, which is incomprehensible from a psychological point of view but typical of the Markan characterizations (vs. 19b, cf. vs. 29!), further the proclamation. Strictly speaking, they are theological statements—not historical statements.

[17] This statement can refer to late afternoon as well as the actual evening. **[18]** It is assumed—in spite of vs. 22—that the meal had already begun. Accordingly it is clear that the breaking of bread at the beginning of the meal and the saying of Jesus which accompanied it were never a part of this passage. The exposure of Judas is the only point of interest (as is true in John 13:21-30). The use of the word "betray" without any additional details is striking (cf. vs. 10 f.). **[19]** The fact that all of the disciples ask the same question (cf. 14:31 also) can hardly be interpreted as nothing more than a warning to the reader to examine himself in the same way (cf. Heb. 6:6). It is a part of Mark's desire to emphasize again and again that even the disciples remain undiscerning to the very end (cf. 8:17-21). **[20]** Jesus would not have said "one of the twelve" (the Greek lacks "you"). He must have said "one of you" as is found in vs. 18. This shows how well established the formula already was (cf. vs. 10). The dipping is not necessarily the dipping of bitter herbs during the Passover meal. As in John 13:26 it can be interpreted as any kind of reaching for food or the dipping into a sauce. This feature is simply another indication of the close fellowship which existed between Jesus and his betrayer. **[21]** The Greek word used here, *hupago* "to go away," is not customarily used for "to die." Perhaps it indicates that Jesus was going the way God had ordained. 9:12 has already declared that the Passion of the "Son of Man" was attested in the Scriptures, and "Son of Man" appears frequently in connection with "be handed over," or "be betrayed" (see 9:31). Therefore, this saying re-emphasizes the fact that everything will happen in accordance with the will of God, but that this does not remove the guilt of the one who "betrayed" Jesus (cf. vss. 10 f.).

The Promises at the Last Supper 14:22-25;
cf. Matt. 26:26-29; Luke 22:15-20; 1 Cor. 11:23-25

22While they were eating, Jesus took the bread, gave a prayer
of thanks, broke it, and gave it to his disciples. "Take it," he
said, "this is my body." 23Then he took the cup, gave thanks to
God, and handed it to them; and they all drank from it. 24Jesus
said: "This is my blood which is poured out for many, my blood
which seals God's covenant. 25I tell you, I will never again drink

this wine until the day I drink the new wine in the Kingdom of God."

(Vs. 24: Exod. 24:8; Jer. 31:31 ff.; Zech. 9:11.)

The Words of Institution of the Lord's Supper. The repetition of the phrase "while they were eating . . ." (cf. vs. 18) shows that vss. 22-25 were at one time handed down independently, without any connection to vss. 17-21. Since the breaking of bread signified the beginning of the meal, it is not possible that the meal had begun earlier. The style is terse, listing only the words and actions that have liturgical importance, in a manner which is almost ceremonious; consequently, apart from the brief observation that all of them drank from the cup, only the words and actions of Jesus are reported. This style probably indicates that this passage was recited regularly at the celebration of the Lord's Supper. In fact, 1 Corinthians 11:23-25 shows that from the beginning Paul taught in the church at Corinth a similar brief summary of Jesus' last supper. Therefore, these verses were handed down by themselves and could be earlier or later than verses 17-21.

A comparison with 1 Corinthians 11:23-25 shows that that passage is based upon a different account of the Last Supper. Matthew 26:26-29 follows Mark's account except for some small alterations and additions. That Luke 22:19 f. is a combination of the Pauline and Markan versions is very clear in vs. 20 (literally: ". . . in my blood which is poured out for you"), while vss. 15-18 represent a third tradition which is essentially parallel to Mark 14:25. A comparison of the Pauline and Markan renderings shows that the latter has preserved a few Semiticisms, principally the expression "for many" (cf. 10:45). As a whole, however, it is likely to be the later version. On the other hand, the statement preserved in the Pauline account that Jesus did not take the cup until "after the supper" is very old (cf. vss. 12-16). Originally the explanatory statements made in connection with the bread and the cup were separated from one another by the time spent in eating the meal. In 1 Corinthians the wording of these statements is not parallel: "This is my body, which is given for you . . . This cup is God's new covenant, sealed with my blood." It is much easier to assume that two sayings, which originally were not parallel in wording, gradually have been assimilated to one another, than to assume the opposite. This is especially true since in the process of development the account of the eating of the meal was omitted. The juxtaposition of vss. 17-21 and vs. 22 may indicate that it was true also in the Markan church that an entire meal was eaten before bread and wine were served. The wording of the two sayings is parallel in Mark. If this was always true, then the words used must have been "flesh" and "blood," because "body" is never found in combination with "blood." This is not a problem in the Pauline version because "covenant" corresponds to the term "body" in the first saying. Finally, to Jews the drinking of blood is so offensive that it is inconceivable that the saying would have been uttered in Jewish circles without an explanation of the necessity for such a shocking action (cf. Gen. 9:4; Lev. 17: 10 ff.) unless it was always considered nothing more than a metaphor. These ideas are not included in the Pauline version. Even if this should happen to be the older of the two versions, it has not been handed down unaltered. "My body for you" cannot be said in Aramaic (without any verb). Probably in the time when Greek was spoken the phrase "for you" was added from the saying which Mark records in connection with the cup. On the other hand, the phrase "which seals God's covenant" has been taken from the formulation handed down by Paul. Furthermore, the (repeated) command to observe the Lord's Supper is not found in Mark although it is included by Paul. This may be a later addition which explicitly requires the observance of the Lord's Supper. Thus even in the oldest form which can be recovered, the statements which explain the significance of the bread and the cup have been shaped significantly by the idea of the new covenant between God and his people (cf. Exod. 24:8-10, where "the blood of the covenant" is connected with eating and drinking in the presence of God and in eschatological glory). The (new) covenant was very important in the Qumran community, where a fellowship meal with the blessing of bread and wine was held daily (1QS 6:2-5; 1QSa 2:17-22; cf. Joseph and Asenath 15:5; 16; 19:5; the dating of this document is uncertain).

We may suspect that Luke 22:15-18, 25-30 contained a third account of the Last Supper which at one time was independent, before the explanatory sayings were introduced from the Pauline and Markan traditions. The reference to Jesus' serving would have been combined in this passage with the prospect of his future glory without any special word of explanation, as is true also in John 13 and 14–16. Anticipations of a glorious banquet in the end-time are found in Isaiah 25:6; 65:13; Ethiopian Enoch 62: 14; Syriac Baruch 29:8; and Pirkē Aboth 3:20. We might easily assume that the oldest account of the Lord's Supper is found in Luke. Here, however, the meal is clearly presented as the eating of the Passover lamb (cf. introduction to vss. 12-16). This passage may be based upon a version which can be traced to a Jewish-Christian Passover celebration. Mark's version, which appears to be the latest when compared with the Pauline and Lukan accounts, has likely been formulated according to the pattern of the Jewish sacrificial dinner which allowed the participants to share in the blessing of the offering (cf. 1 Cor. 10:16-18).

When we review the various accounts of Jesus' last supper, three essential elements appear in all, but with differing emphases: (1) The meal anticipates the future fulfillment of the Kingdom of God in which the eschatological meal was expected to be a manifestation of complete fellowship between God and man. This is emphasized most strongly in Luke 22:15-18, 25-30, but is found also in Mark 14:25; and there is at least a reminiscence of this feature in 1 Corinthians 11:26 ("until the Lord comes"). Moreover, 1 Corinthians 16:22 f. may be an indication that the eschatological summons "Our Lord, come!" was a part of the liturgy of the Lord's Supper (cf. Didache 10:6; Rev. 22:20 f.). (2) The Supper represents the present covenant relationship between God and his people. This is central in 1 Corinthians 11:23-25, but even in Luke 22:15 and Mark 14:22a, 23b it is the basis of the table fellowship which is emphasized in those passages. In Mark it is mentioned explicitly by the addition of "covenant" in vs. 24. (3) Each time it is celebrated the Supper recalls Jesus' death which took place once for all and is the basis of this fellowship. This is most strongly emphasized in Mark 14:24, but is contained also in Luke 22:20b (spoken on the night before the Crucifixion!) and in 1 Corinthians 11:24. It is specifically expressed in 1 Corinthians 11:24 by the addition of the words "for you." With this background we can proceed to the exposition of the Markan tradition.

[22] Jesus' action is fully in accord with the way the meal was ordinarily begun (see the introduction to vss. 12-16). Moreover, this action is described the same way in 6:41 and 8:6. It is a ritual which binds together those who have gathered for fellowship at the table. For this reason, when Jews served a formal dinner they made a clear distinction between the appetizer and the meal itself. Each guest said his own grace with the appetizer so that those who came later could join the fellowship. Fellowship was instituted at the meal proper when thanksgiving was offered on behalf of everyone at the breaking of the bread. We cannot determine whether the Aramaic word in the first statement was *bisra* "flesh" or *guph* "body." If it was the second word, which corresponds exactly to the Greek expression, it signifies "body, self, I" (cf. John 6:32, 35, 48, 51a), which makes it necessary to consider the possibility that the first word would also signify Jesus' whole person. In general, words like "flesh" or "body" describe the whole man in both Hebrew and Aramaic and, of course, each word considers him from a specific point of view. Thus the bread which Jesus breaks and distributes is to be understood as the sign and guarantee of the presence of Jesus, his "personality," his "person." This is the case in Mark also. But now "body," placed so closely parallel to "blood," designates with even greater emphasis that it was the person of Jesus which was given for everyone in death. Accordingly, the idea of the "body" which was sacrificed for the table fellowship becomes predominant. **[23]** Jesus' action in connection with the cup corresponds fully with the normal conclusion of the meal. The observation that "they all drank from it" is probably aimed against any tendencies toward asceticism or frugality which would eliminate the wine from the celebration of the Lord's Supper. There is a series of records of such celebrations in early church history. It is significant that the disciples drank before Jesus uttered the saying; consequently there is no implication here that Jesus' saying altered the wine in any substantial or material way. His saying does bestow upon the cup its special character, but this is due to the promise it contains. It is similar to the way the imprint and signature of the bank on the paper of a bank note or bond gives it its value. The imprint is the promise that the bank will be liable for the value of this paper, although its substance has not been changed in any way. Therefore, this saying which contains the promise that Jesus will be surety for that which is pledged to man in the Lord's Supper can be uttered after the drinking just as well as before. **[24]** The second statement clearly emphasizes the idea of sacrifice. The blood poured out at the making of a covenant was originally only an expression of an obligation to complete fidelity. It may have meant something like this: "May I suffer the same fate as this animal if I break the obligations of this covenant!" (cf. Gen. 15:10; 1 Sam. 11:7). Nevertheless, what is expressed in Mark is that God's covenant with his church is established solely upon the foundation of Jesus' death, which he suffered for its sake (cf. 10:45). Of course the fact that Jesus died on the cross only a few hours after this meal has had an effect upon the words spoken here from the very beginning and, therefore, before Mark. Thus it becomes clear to those who have gathered at the Lord's Supper that God is to be found standing by Jesus' pathway to humility. In this way they are brought into a new fellowship with God and become subject to the new lordship of Christ. Luke may be essentially correct when he connects the regulation found in Mark 10:42-45 directly with the Last Supper. **[25]** The Lord's Supper would not be the Lord's Supper without the anticipation of the final end. To be "present" at this table fellowship is to be "present" in the future. Fellowship in the present time is genuine fellowship simply because it occurs in the presence of Christ. For this reason it is impossible to conceive of such fellowship apart from its accomplishment in Christ's future, when being "with Christ" will have become a reality (cf. 1 Thess. 4:17 and many other places). This is the basis of the joyous character of the Lord's Supper (Acts 2:46). Obviously excessive joy was more of a danger to the early church than were fear and solemnity (cf. 1 Cor. 11:23 ff. also). Such joy is possible only when the settled conviction persists that what happens now in a symbolic manner in the midst of temptation will be fulfilled as a gift in the future Kingdom of God. With this kind of anticipation the church celebrated the Supper as the table fellowship which God had given them in the present time but which was looking forward to greater fulfillment in the future. By the insertion of this passage (which belongs here chronologically) Mark has emphasized once more the significance of Jesus' Passion.

The question concerning the significance of the word "is," which was debated so vigorously in the time of the Reformation, is not relevant, because Jesus and the early church did not have our concept of a "substance." They were concerned about the function of something or the service which it performed. In Aramaic the sentence must have been formulated without the word "is": "This—my body." The question as to what a thing might be, of what it consisted, which seems so obvious to the Greek mind and especially to the modern mind as a consequence of the development of natural science, was far removed from their thinking. Therefore, the phrase means that Jesus himself will be active in the present and will confront the church whenever it partakes of the bread and the cup (see comment on vs. 23).

The Blindness of the Disciples and Jesus' Promise 14:26-31;
cf. Matt. 26:30-35; Luke 22:39 (31-34)

[26]Then they sang a hymn and went out to the Mount of Olives.
[27]Jesus said to them: "All of you will run away and leave
me, for the scripture says, 'God will kill the shepherd and the
sheep will all be scattered.' [28]But after I am raised to life I will
go to Galilee ahead of you." [29]Peter answered, "I will never leave
you, even though all the rest do!" [30]"Remember this!" Jesus said to
Peter. "Before the rooster crows two times tonight, you will say
three times that you do not know me." [31]Peter answered even

more strongly: "I will never say I do not know you, even if I have to die with you!" And all the disciples said the same thing.

(Vs. 27: Zech. 13:7.)

It is evident that the continuity is interrupted by vs. 28. This announcement is not found in the summary of this passage in a certain papyrus fragment; however, in the papyrus the passage is abbreviated in other ways also. In view of Matthew 26:32 it cannot be doubted that the statement is an authentic part of Mark's Gospel, but it is possible that it was handed down at first as a saying of the resurrected One (16:7) and that Mark inserted it here. Vs. 29 then continues vs. 27 ("will leave" occurs in both verses). This is in essential agreement with Luke 22:31-34 and John 13:36-38. It is clear that the quotation from Zechariah 13:7 (vs. 27b) circulated independently in the church, because it influenced John 16:32 also. Vss. 27b and 28 presuppose a description of the Passion in which the main emphasis was upon the failure of the disciples and the fact that Jesus again goes on ahead of them (cf. 16:7). This makes it more imperative for us to pay careful attention to what Mark wanted to say by the inclusion of vs. 28. The second observation which can be made is that the warning to all the disciples (vs. 27) is not found in Luke, nor is the remark in vs. 31 that all of the disciples had concurred with Peter's statement. This may be connected with the fact that the flight of the disciples (Mark 14:50) is not reported by Luke. His account, however, presupposes that they were still staying in Jerusalem on Easter morning. It is hardly possible that this idea originated with Luke. It is more likely that it comes from the tradition which he follows in reporting Peter's denial (Luke 22:31-34). A parallel to the announcement of the scattering of the disciples is found in John 16:32. Moreover, the prediction of Peter's denial occurs in a slightly altered form in John 13:36-38. Accordingly, the two sayings, the one addressed to all the disciples and the one addressed to Peter, were not handed down together. Luke refers only to one, and the sayings are found in widely separated passages in John. We may suspect that in the first place the church, which generally emphasized the foreknowledge of

Jesus, found the flight of the disciples predicted and described in the Scriptures. Then the church expressed this as a saying of Jesus, while it included in Jesus' counseling with Peter (more pronounced in Luke 22:31 f.; John 13:36—14:7; 21:15-17) what the exalted One would say to him (and ultimately to every believer) concerning this denial.

[26] It was customary to sing a hymn of praise at the end of the Passover meal. Most likely this custom was continued by the Christian church at the Lord's Supper (cf. 1 Cor. 14:26; Col. 3:16; Eph. 5:19); consequently, this comment may reflect the fact that the narrator rather naturally was portraying Jesus' last supper in conformity with the manner in which the Lord's Supper was celebrated in his own church. With reference to the Mount of Olives, compare 13:3. **[27]** By presenting Jesus' prediction and this reference to the Scripture the church made the flight of the disciples less offensive. To be sure, this did not make them any less guilty. On the contrary, it is extremely important to Mark to give prominence to the significance and inevitability of Jesus' Passion by presenting the blindness of the disciples as a repeated illustration of the fundamental gulf between God and man. But it is still clear that Jesus is fully sovereign even in the matter of the disciples' defection. **[28]** Vs. 28 makes the same point with greater emphasis. The fact that this statement has been taken from the Easter story and interrupts the context rather abruptly is what gives it special significance. For Mark this significance lies in the fact that by this statement Jesus confirms his promise in the face of any human failure. Discipleship does not break down with the defection of the disciples nor with the death of Jesus, in which they bear their share of blame. No, it is at this point that discipleship really begins. The Old Testament picture presents only the smitten shepherd and the scattered flock. But Jesus promises that the scattered flock will be gathered together again in true discipleship. Not until then will true unity be possible. Therefore, Jesus is declaring that the pathway leads through the failure of the disciples and the suffering of the "shepherd" to the resurrection and the church of Jesus. The phrase "ahead of you" can be interpreted spatially: to go at the head of a procession as leader (as in 10:32), or temporally: to go first, with others following later (as in 6:45). Certainly Mark understands it in the latter sense (cf. 16:7 and the introduction to 16:1-8). **[30]** The expression "tonight" (NEB: "today, this very night") is the Jewish way of thinking, because for them the day begins with sunset. **[29]** From a historical point of view it is not easy to connect the prediction of Peter's denial with that of the flight of the disciples in vs. 27, even though Mark employs vs. 29 to do this. However, the manner in which the disciples fled is qualified in 14:50 by the inference that they did not leave Jerusalem and flee to their homes until after the fate of Jesus was sealed. Mark employs the transitional verse to make Peter's blindness even more conspicuous. He who feels secure and considers himself to be different from all others will fall the farthest (cf. Luke 10:15; 14:11; 18:14; James 4:10; 1 Peter 5:6). The fact that this episode has been preserved in three different traditions indicates what a strong impression it made. **[30]** It is strange that the rooster crows twice (found only in Mark). Perhaps the first time was to serve as a warning. **[31]** Readiness to make the supreme sacrifice is not enough—even if a person is sincerely willing to suffer martyrdom. Man is repeatedly deceived into overrating or underrating himself when he judges himself and the strength of his faith before he actually experiences the situation. The only thing which saves him is Jesus' promise (vs. 28). That promise is able to demonstrate its power in ways which are completely unexpected (cf. the conclusion of John 13:36; 21:18 f.). In the situation where everyone fails, including the one closest to Jesus, Jesus proves himself greater than any failure.

Mark has already emphasized in 8:31, 34 ff.; 9:31, 35 ff.; 10:33 f., 39, 52 that Jesus' suffering and the discipleship of his followers go hand in hand. Now in 14:22-31 he shows that this has become possible only as a gift of grace by virtue of the fact that Jesus has gone on before.

Jesus Faces His Bitter Struggle Alone 14:32-42;
cf. Matt. 26:36-46; Luke 22:40-46

[32]They came to a place called Gethsemane, and Jesus said to
his disciples, "Sit here while I pray." [33]Then he took Peter, James,
and John with him. Distress and anguish came over him, [34]and
he said to them: "The sorrow in my heart is so great that it almost crushes me. Stay here and watch." [35]He went a little farther
on, threw himself on the ground and prayed that, if possible, he
might not have to go through the hour of suffering. [36]"Father!"
he prayed, "my Father! All things are possible for you. Take
this cup away from me. But not what I want, but what you
want."

[37]Then he returned and found the three disciples asleep, and
said to Peter, "Simon, are you asleep? Weren't you able to stay
awake for one hour?" [38]And he said to them, "Keep watch, and
pray, so you will not fall into temptation. The spirit is willing, but
the flesh is weak."

[39]He went away once more and prayed, saying the same words.
[40]Then he came back to the disciples and found them asleep;
they could not keep their eyes open. And they did not know what
to say to him.

[41]When he came back the third time, he said to them: "Are
you still sleeping and resting? Enough! The hour has come! Look,
the Son of Man is now handed over to the power of sinful men.
[42]Rise, let us go. Look, here is the man who is betraying me!"

(Vs. 34: Pss. 42:5, 11; 43:5; Jonah 4:9.)

This entire description presents a series of riddles. It is strange how the story begins a second time with the selection of the three intimate friends, who also are left behind instead of being taken with Jesus when he prays. Luke, who seems to be acquainted with a different version of the tradition, knows nothing about this detail. Vs. 36 repeats in direct discourse the prayer which has been reported in indirect discourse in vs. 35. This raises the question as to who could have known the content of Jesus' prayer since the disciples were not with him, and, furthermore, were asleep. Jesus returns three times although he goes away only twice. Moreover, we are not told whether he comes to the three disciples or to the nine. Vss. 43-50 assume that both groups are together again. The events related at the beginning of the story are repeated in a rather general way in vss. 39 f.; this time the word to the disciples is omitted, but it is reported when Jesus returns the third time. If the brief statement "When he came back the third time" were removed, the account would be much more logical and the second episode would form an exact parallel to the first. It is possible that the original story reported that Jesus prayed twice, but then a third time was added since it was customary to report that in distress a person prayed three times (2 Cor. 12:8; Dan. 6:10, 13; there are also examples in extrabiblical Greek writings). When we observe that in addition to the double beginning there are duplicate summaries of the first prayer in vss. 35 f. and that the second prayer is simply a repetition of the first, we may suspect that two accounts (vss. 32, 36-38 and 33-35, 40 f. without 41a) have been combined into one. Moreover, Luke only records that Jesus prayed once. This account corresponds to vss. 32, 36-38 and does not contain the saying about the Son of Man. However, it is easier to assume that a shorter account has been expanded. There is no reason to question the historicity of Jesus' struggle in prayer in Gethsemane. The essence of it has been handed down also in John 12:27 (cf. 18:11b) and Hebrews 4:15; 5:7 f. Moreover, it does not fit the picture of the Servant of God and is even less appropriate for the glorious miracle-worker and divine Lord. However, it is clear that the account has grown. Sayings which were important to the church and had been circulated separately have been added (vs. 41b, which is very similar to 9:31a except that the rather puzzling expression "men" has been explained by the word "sinful"; and vs. 38b which is quoted out of context by Polycarp in Phil. 7:2). In addition, the exhortation to the church has been emphasized (vs. 38a, which echoes the Lord's Prayer and is directly quoted by Polycarp in Phil. 7:2). Old Testament phrases have been appropriated (vs. 34), whereby the exact words of Jesus' prayer are presented and not simply a summary in indirect discourse (as in vs. 35). Consequently, in the present account the "coming" of the hour which has theological importance stands adjacent to the "arrival" of Judas which should be regarded as rather trivial; and the "handing over" to sinners which has theological importance stands adjacent to the "betrayal" to the Jewish authorities which must be considered to be rather unimportant. Moreover, parallel to such passages as Genesis 22:5 and Exodus 24:14 special emphasis may have been given to the fact that Jesus was alone. The three intimate friends (vs. 33), whom Luke does not mention, may have been added later (parallel to 9:2, where it also says "took . . . with him") because this was the way many were telling the story. Or was it added because Mark wanted to emphasize that those closest to Jesus failed him? (cf. 13:3).

[32] Gethsemane means "oilpress." The name must be a part of the tradition, especially since Mark had already indicated where they were in vs. 26. **[33]** Nothing equal to the description of Jesus' distress and anguish is found in any Jewish or Christian accounts of martyrdom, nor is there anything like it in the announcements of the Passion (the only exception is Luke 12:50). Jesus is portrayed here as one whose suffering is real, and we would completely misunderstand this passage were we to consider Jesus as a Stoic standing aloof from all human suffering and ultimately not affected by it. This might be a more impressive picture than the biblical one; but then Jesus would be one of a few exceptional persons or perhaps a superman, but he would not be brother to the man who is plunged into deepest distress (cf. Ignatius, *Ephesians* 7:2; *Polycarp* 3:2, where in himself Jesus is free from suffering but suffers on our behalf). It is surprising how much complaining there is in the Old and New Testaments. But this is due to the fact that these men kept their hearts open to suffering instead of securely shielding themselves from it. This biblical attitude is deeply rooted in the fact that God himself consented to take this path which leads into suffering—not around it. Therefore he consented to endure genuine inner grief in Gethsemane. **[34]** ". . . so great that it almost crushes me" (cf. Jonah 4:9; the rest is from Pss. 42:5, 11; 43:5) might be translated: "So that I would rather be dead." The summons to "watch" is chosen to form a contrast to the sleeping of the disciples which is presented later. **[35]** We will gain a proper understanding of this passage where Jesus separated himself from the disciples only if we assume that it symbolizes preparing oneself for God's action through prayer, or preparing to defend oneself against the coming of the tempter. But it was only in the early church that it gained this significance (and at first in accordance with 13:34-37). The "hour" is the one determined by God. The word received its special connotation in apocalyptic literature where it indicated the hour of the consummation, the final judgment (Dan. 11:40, 45 LXX). What this passage says is that in the midst of history that hour will strike which goes beyond all history. **[36]** Victory over fear is found in the midst of fear because Jesus knows what lies before him and regards it as a charge given by God, which God alone could remove. This address in prayer, "Abba" (in the Greek text), is unique. It may have been a part of the language Jesus used in prayer, which was later taken over by the church in his name and used widely (Rom. 8:15; Gal. 4:6). As far as we know, no Jew before or after Jesus ever called upon God using this form of the name "father." In the Old Testament even the customary word for "father" is not often used with reference to God. This may be due to the myths of the neighboring nations which regarded God as the procreator of the world and humanity. In Judaism God was regarded as father of the individual only in post-biblical times; even so, "my Father" is seldom used in addressing God directly in the prayers of Palestinian Judaism or of the rabbis. Nor is the designation "father" used for God very often in any other way. This applies equally to the early church. God is rarely called "father" in Mark, in Q, or in the material which is peculiar to Luke. It is only in Matthew (about 37 times) and John (about 100 times) that this occurs frequently. We should add one more observation. It is recorded that Jesus said "your Father" and "my Father," but nowhere did Jesus include himself with the disciples by the expression "our Father." Without even taking into account the fact that the older form in Luke omits the "our," Matthew 6:9 was not prayed by Jesus with the disciples—Jesus is simply instructing his disciples to pray in this way. All of this clearly indicates that Jesus knew he had a special relationship to "his Father" which was different from that of all other men. Only through Jesus did God become "your Father" (John 20:17). The "cup" is the cup of suffering which had been given him by God (see 10:38). "I" and "you," Son and Father, are set in contrast to each other but are united in the submission of obedience. Theirs is not a physical unity which exists from their very nature and is taken for granted since it could not be otherwise. It is the unity of love which is always renewed and reestablished time and again while enduring temptation. The severity of the suffering is accentuated in that there is no mention of any divine reply to Jesus' prayer (different from Luke 22:43-44, found in many manuscripts; cf. John 12:27 ff.).

[37] Simon Peter represents the entire group of disciples. It may be that he is singled out on account of vss. 29, 31. Often one Gospel writer attributed to Peter alone things which another ascribed to all the disciples (Mark 11:21 compared with Matt. 21:20; Matt. 15:15 with Mark 7:17; cf. Mark 13:3 with Matt. 24:3; also Matt. 18:21 with Luke 17:4, and Luke 12:41 f. with Matt. 24: 45). **[38]** They are given another summons to "keep watch." This time, however, a special reason is given. The Gospel writer repeats the statement here, because he is warning his readers at the same time. The contrast between "flesh" and "spirit" is striking. This contrast had been familiar to Judaism since Isaiah 31:3, but the contrast there is not within a person. "Spirit" always designates God and his world; "flesh" designates man together with his intellectual or spiritual potentialities and his world. Therefore, God himself, his word, his grace, his election, is the most common antithesis to "flesh" (Isa. 40:6-8, et al.). On the other hand, the Greek who had been influenced by Platonism made a sharp distinction between "soul," which originates in heaven and returns there, and the earthly "body" which imprisons the soul, but he did not use the terms "spirit" and "flesh" for these concepts. Accordingly, this passage combines something from both Jewish and Greek thought. But the wording of this passage comes from Psalm 51:12, specifically from the Hebrew text which speaks of a "willing spirit" which God gives to man and which actually is nothing other than God's own "Holy Spirit" (Ps. 51:11). The idea presented here is that God's Spirit dwells continuously in the devout person to whom it has been given (and not only in a prophet or a king). This idea is not found anywhere else in the Old Testament, except where "spirit" is used simply to designate "vitality." Mark 14:38 is an example of how in the Judaism of Jesus' time it was possible to consider as a present reality something which the Old Testament usually expected to occur in the end-time. The "spirit" always is clearly regarded as none other than the Spirit of God, and yet as the spirit God has given to man unconditionally and for all time, so that in a certain sense it is proper to speak of "his," i.e., the man's, spirit. Of course, the Spirit is only entrusted to man and always belongs to God. God is always the subject of the acts of the Spirit. Therefore it is not the strength of the human spirit which is contrasted to human weakness, but the power of God, and that power is bestowed upon man continually.

[39] The deep agony of Jesus' suffering is made more prominent by the repetition of his prayer. **[40]** The loneliness of the Son of Man is accentuated by the fact that while he struggles in prayer he is surrounded by men who do not understand him, but fall asleep. **[41]** The translation of vs. 41a is not certain. The first clause could be translated as a question: "Are you still sleeping and taking your rest?" It is the next word which is the most ambiguous. There are no other passages which can be cited to substantiate the translation "enough"—it is nothing more than a conjecture. Perhaps the literal meaning is: "it is delayed" (because there was something else which had to be done first). Or "Is it (still) a long way off?" (No, the hour has come . . ., etc.). Or "He (Judas) is going to get (me now)." Or with a slightly different reading, "It is the end" (of the sleeping, or of me?). That the word "hour" refers back to vs. 35 is an important consideration. Jesus will have to go through the hour of suffering. In this way emphasis is placed upon the fact that in this temporal "hour" (vs. 37) God's hour (similar to vs. 35) is fulfilled; in the "handing over" of Jesus to the authorities, the "handing over" which had been determined by God is accomplished. **[42]** The action of Judas, which has many parallels in world history, serves as a clue to something far greater than apostasy or the well-intentioned error of a disappointed follower: In this action he who was not a "sinner" was handed over to "sinners" (cf. 9:31). A certain tension exists between vss. 41b, 42 and vss. 34 f. Vss. 41b and 42 emphasize (as John does consistently; cf. John 12:28) that Jesus' sovereignty is that of one who has been victorious in temptation. And so Jesus' willingness to obey is more impressive because he walks this path consciously and deliberately.

In this passage the reality, i.e., the "humanity," of Jesus' suffering is accentuated once more, and the action of God is manifest in that suffering. This is how God demonstrates that he is God—he can consent unconditionally to such a path; consequently, he is able to do what man cannot. Mark looks upon this passage as an illustration summarizing the truth he has been endeavoring to emphasize throughout this entire book. He presents Jesus as the suffering Son of Man who stands in complete contrast to men who sleep and are not able to understand him and who are, for that reason, the greatest cause of his suffering. This is the radical way in which Jesus objectifies the fact that God is for man and with man.

Jesus' Arrest 14:43-52;
cf. Matt. 26:47-56; Luke 22:47-53

43He was still talking when Judas, one of the twelve disciples,
arrived. A crowd carrying swords and clubs was with him, sent
by the chief priests, the teachers of the Law, and the elders. 44The
traitor had given the crowd a signal: "The man I kiss is the one
you want. Arrest him and take him away under guard."
45As soon as Judas arrived he went up to Jesus and said,
"Teacher!" and kissed him. 46So they arrested Jesus and held him
tight. 47But one of those standing by drew his sword and struck at

the High Priest's slave, cutting off his ear. [48]Then Jesus spoke up and said to them: "Did you have to come with swords and clubs to capture me, as though I were an outlaw? [49]Day after day I was with you teaching in the Temple, and you did not arrest me. But the Scriptures must come true." [50]Then all the disciples left him and ran away.

[51]A certain young man, dressed only in a linen cloth, was following Jesus. They tried to arrest him, [52]but he ran away naked, leaving the linen cloth behind.

"Immediately," *euthus* (which does not appear in this verse in TEV), is one of Mark's favorite expressions and occurs frequently in his Gospel. The same is true of the Greek construction of the subordinate clause "while he was still talking." This suggests that Mark was the one who combined this passage and the preceding one, and that the oldest account of the Passion did not include the story of Gethsemane. Several observations reinforce the impression that this account had been formulated before Mark: Judas is introduced again as "one of the twelve" although this had been stated in vss. 10, 18, and 20. The unusual formulation "When he came, at once came to him, he said . . ." (this is a literal translation of vs. 45) might be a wooden translation from Aramaic. The statement that people stood by with swords (in addition to the twelve?) might be an indication that the event occurred some place other than in Gethsemane. Vs. 49a seems to be consistent with Mark's manner of writing, while vs. 49b does not conform to his style. It would seem more reasonable for vs. 50 to precede vss. 48 f., since it is not likely that the disciples would have lingered as long as is indicated by its present position. Has it been placed alongside vs. 49b because it is the fulfillment of vs. 27? It is difficult to evaluate the historical details. Vss. 51 f. contain a brief memorandum that is rather strange. It has frequently been assumed that the young man was Mark himself, and he has been identified with the person named in Acts 12:12, 25; 15:37, 39. In that case he would have been present at the gatherings of the early church in Jerusalem, which probably were held in the upper room of his parents' home (Mark 14:15!). With reference to this matter, see part 6 of the Introduction. But this passage is not the account of an eyewitness. Up to vs. 46 the report is written from the standpoint of a police officer. This may be an ancient record about a young man who, although he was not one of the twelve, was arrested with Jesus and at some later time joined the church. Certainly the incident has not been fabricated on the basis of Amos 2:16. With reference to the historical problems, see the excursus on 14:53-72.

[43] Mark placed this story immediately after vss. 41 f. in order to emphasize that God is at work here and that Jesus submits to this experience in conscious obedience. The reference to the fact that Judas was one of the twelve accentuates the grievousness of Jesus' fate. Even those closest to him have not understood him. Moreover, it is not some misguided outsiders, but the official Jewish leaders who carry out the arrest (the three influential parties are mentioned also in 8:31; 11:27; 14:53; 15:1; see comment on 8:31). **[44]** The matter of Judas giving the sign with a kiss is strange. Jesus had taught publicly in the temple court. Is it possible that they had no one to send along who would recognize Jesus? Would it not have been adequate for Judas to point his finger at Jesus? It is absurd to suggest that this was an attempt to conceal the intention of the mob or the fact of Judas' collaboration, since there could be no doubt about these things when Judas moved in with armed police and soldiers. Obviously this visible action is used figuratively to present Judas' inner attitude in the same way that painters represent Judas' inner attitude at the Last Supper by his outward appearance. **[45]** By this kiss Judas is portrayed as one who lived very close to Jesus but did not dare to express either his doubts about what Jesus was doing or his opposition. Without ever discussing his problem with Jesus or giving any indication of broken fellowship he "handed [him] over to . . . sinful men" (vs. 41). In this verse, the Greek word for "kiss" is more vigorous than the one used in vs. 44 (however, it would probably be an overstatement to translate as "smothered him with kisses"). The statement is made even more impressive by the implication of a firm embrace. **[46]** By way of contrast the arrest is reported with moderation and brevity. There is no suggestion that Jesus attempted to defend himself in any way or that he made the slightest objection. **[47]** The addition of the incident about the blow with the sword does not change this fact. It seems more reasonable to understand this move as symbolic of Jesus' deliberate defenselessness since it was so ridiculously ineffective. This is probably a historical incident, as it has been reported without any theological motive. The text does not specify that this action was taken by one of the twelve. On the contrary, the report of the incident seems to suggest that it was someone from a larger circle of onlookers who wanted to defend Jesus. Thus Jesus was defended only by a clumsy onlooker who sympathized with him. **[48]** The word "outlaw" is rather common. It is difficult to see, in the use of this word, any allusion to the possibility that the Romans looked upon him as an insurgent like the "bandits" in 15:27.

[49] Perhaps "in the daytime" would be a better translation of vs. 49 than "day after day"; however, there is scarcely any significant difference. It is hardly possible that Jesus uttered this reproach in this particular situation. It would be meaningful only if addressed to those who ordered the arrest, but not if directed to the police and the soldiers who had no share in the decision as to when and how it should be carried out. This saying may have been included here to re-emphasize the contrast: Since 8:31 Jesus has been ready to take the pathway which leads to his suffering; in 14:41 f. he clearly expressed this readiness. How absurd, then, is the secrecy which has been observed since 14:1, including all the security measures of a night arrest by armed personnel! Consequently, whether or not this saying is true in the deepest sense—i.e., whether it becomes to us the communication of the Good News—does not depend upon whether Jesus really spoke in this way or at this time. It depends upon whether or not we believe the witness which is given in it. This witness declares that all human devices are ridiculous, because behind these events something entirely different is happening: The Son of Man is being handed over in accordance with God's saving will. It is interesting that in this connection the reference made to the Scripture is very general, as it is also in 14:21 and 1 Corinthians 15:3 f. Therefore it is enough simply to assert that here God's will which has been established throughout ages is being done. It is not necessary to quote any striking passages with the apologetic intent of convincing the doubter. This explains the fact that Judas is not rebuked and why even the subordinate officers are reproached only for the manner of their action—not for the action itself. Only one thing is important: In the midst of human guilt the plan which was foreordained by God has been accomplished, thus fulfilling the revelation which brings to pass the salvation of the world. In the light of this fact all other considerations become secondary. **[50]** The flight of the disciples is reported without any apology for their action. The isolation of the Son of Man is absolute. **[51, 52]** Even the brief incident concerning the young man simply intensifies the atmosphere, which seems to say, "Save yourself if you can." Against this background, the quiet dignity with which Jesus calmly goes on his way stands out clearly.

The entire account is given in a concise and straightforward manner without any edifying embellishments. The purpose of the passage is to indicate how Jesus takes the path which was foreordained for him, lonely and separated from his enemies and also from the sympathetic onlookers and his disciples. As a matter of fact, in his Passion the "Son of Man" is separated from all the "men" to whom he is "handed over" (9:31).

Jesus' Testimony and Peter's Denial 14:53-72;
cf. Matt. 26:57-75; Luke 22:54-71

53Then they took Jesus to the High Priest's house, where all
the chief priests, the elders, and the teachers of the Law were
gathering. 54Peter followed far behind and went into the courtyard
of the High Priest's house. There he sat down with the guards,
keeping himself warm by the fire. 55The chief priests and the
whole Council tried to find some evidence against Jesus, in
order to put him to death, but they could not find any. 56Many
witnesses told lies against Jesus, but their stories did not agree.

57Then some men stood up and told this lie against Jesus:
58"We heard him say, 'I will tear down this Temple which men

made, and after three days I will build one that is not made by men.' " [59]Not even they, however, could make their stories agree.

[60]The High Priest stood up in front of them all and questioned Jesus: "Have you no answer to the accusation they bring against you?" [61]But Jesus kept quiet and would not say a word. Again the High Priest questioned him: "Are you the Messiah, the Son of the Blessed God?" [62]"I am," answered Jesus, "and you will all see the Son of Man seated at the right side of the Almighty, and coming with the clouds of heaven!" [63]The High Priest tore his robes and said, "We don't need any more witnesses! [64]You heard his wicked words. What is your decision?" They all voted against him: he was guilty and should be put to death.

[65]Some of them began to spit on Jesus, and they blindfolded him and hit him. "Guess who hit you!" they said. And the guards took him and slapped him.

[66]Peter was still down in the courtyard when one of the High Priest's servant girls came by. [67]When she saw Peter warming himself, she looked straight at him and said, "You, too, were with Jesus of Nazareth." [68]But he denied it. "I don't know . . . I don't understand what you are talking about," he answered, and went out into the passageway. Just then a rooster crowed. [69]The servant girl saw him there and began to repeat to the bystanders, "He is one of them!" [70]But Peter denied it again. A little while later the bystanders accused Peter again: "You can't deny that you are one of them, because you, too, are from Galilee." [71]Then Peter made a vow: "May God punish me if I am not telling the truth! I do not know the man you are talking about!" [72]Just then a rooster crowed a second time, and Peter remembered how Jesus had said to him, "Before the rooster crows two times you will say three times that you do not know me." And he broke down and cried.

(Vs. 62: Dan. 7:13; Ps. 110:1.)

Peter's denial forms a framework around Jesus' testimony. His unfaithfulness is contrasted to the faithfulness of Jesus, who remains true until death. Surely at one time the story of Peter's denial was told by itself as a continuous unit. It is told in that way in Luke 22:54-62, which comes from another tradition. Mark takes delight in telling one story within another as he does here (cf. 5:21-43). We could conclude, therefore, that Mark was the one who combined these two stories. **[53, 54]** It is more likely, however, that vss. 53 f. were formulated almost entirely by Mark as an introduction to both incidents. That Peter's following was "far behind" (as in 15:40) and was not, therefore, what it ought to be (vs. 54), is fully consistent with Mark's theology. The rest of the process could be inferred from vss. 67 and 68; it is more likely, however, that parts of the original introduction were moved forward by Mark and replaced by a new introduction in vs. 66 (in a form which is one of Mark's favorite constructions). Then vs. 53b could also be traced to Mark (see comment on vs. 53). This line of reasoning is not conclusive since the same bracketing is found in John, although John's story of the trial and the denial are somewhat different in other respects. And yet it should be observed that John 18:18b which immediately precedes the passage about Jesus' trial is resumed in vs. 25a and continues the story of Peter's denial. In the interim Jesus had been taken from the house of Annas to the palace of Caiaphas; therefore Peter must also have gone to the palace, although this is not stated. Consequently, it appears that the story of Peter's denial might have been added later, in a rather mechanical way, as a framework around the trial of Jesus. There is a possibility that this was done during the final compilation of the Gospel (by the author of 21:24?).

The Historical Problems Concerning the Trial of Jesus are very complicated, hotly debated, and difficult to solve. It is not clear who gave the command for Jesus' arrest. Usually the military terminology in John 18:3, 12 is applied exclusively to the Roman army; consequently, it can hardly be understood as an inexact reference to the Jewish temple police. Since John ordinarily tries as much as possible to suppress the collaboration of the Romans (as is generally true in the New Testament), their collaboration in this instance could be historical (see comment on vs. 48). Moreover, it is difficult to believe that a death sentence would have been reached so swiftly through the Roman procurator if some kind of an agreement had not previously been made between the two parties. In A.D. 26-36 Pilate resided in Caesarea on the Mediterranean Sea but came to Jerusalem frequently and stayed in Herod's palace in the western part of the city. From the way in which he is portrayed in all the sources, Pilate was not a man who would have given in so easily to pressure from the Jews. According to Philo of Alexandria, a contemporary of Jesus, Pilate was "naturally inflexible, a blend of self-will and relentlessness" (*Embassy to Gaius,* 301). Unquestionably it was the Romans who condemned and executed Jesus, since crucifixion was practiced only by them—not by the Jews. Nevertheless, the involvement of the Jews cannot be questioned. According to all the accounts Jesus was taken into custody first of all by the Jewish authorities and probably was interrogated by them also. Just as anyone who was greeted by the people as a prophet or messiah was considered dangerous by Rome, so anyone who attacked the proper observance of the law and temple ritual was considered dangerous by the Jewish authorities. This is evidenced by the fact that, even without taking into consideration the Passion story, there are many references to opposition by Jewish officials and religious parties to Jesus' inflammatory teaching of freedom from the law. Moreover, Jesus' followers were persecuted almost immediately after his death (Gal. 1:18; 2:1). So it is certain that Jews and Gentiles, religious and secular authorities, co-operated, and that from a purely historical standpoint it is impossible to place the blame solely upon any particular group. This is fortunate, since there is but one answer for those who are really interested in Mark's message—the answer of Hebrews 6:6. Whoever is conscious of his own negligence in obedience, of his own failure to love, of the lethargy of his own heart in the midst of the demands of everyday life, cannot escape from his responsibility before God for Jesus' death by fixing the blame upon some other person.

A series of difficult problems arises in connection with the conduct of the trial itself. In the first place it is strange that according to 15:1 the chief priests convene the court early in the morning (if this is a proper reading of the text), as if the court had not functioned already during the night and had not sentenced the accused to death. It has been suggested that it would have been necessary for the court to assemble a second time in order to make the sentence valid. All that is stipulated by the regulations of court procedure which were laid down later by the Pharisees is that a death sentence may not be passed until the second day, and that such a sentence may not be passed during the night. In this case the sentence was passed at night and at the first session. Moreover, the second session took place on the same day as the first (the day began with sunset). Therefore this rule was grossly violated, if it was actually in force at that time. In case a "Sadducean" law was in force, there are a number of clues which would lead us to surmise that agreement of the testimony of the witnesses (vss. 56, 59), the rending of the garments (vs. 63), and the offering of a pain-killing drink (15:23) were both required and observed. However, the regulations of the Sadducees would not have permitted a trial to be held on the day of the Passover (see 14:12-16), nor would they have required a second session of the court. According to Luke 22:54, 63-71 Jesus is merely held in custody in the palace of the high priest and tormented by his guards (not by the court as in Mark 14:65) throughout the night. Only one session of the court is called, and that occurs in the morning (Luke 22:66=Mark 15:1). The proceedings at this hearing (Luke 22:67-71) are identical with those which had taken place during the night according to Mark 14:60-64. It is no longer possible to be sure about these matters, especially since the text of 15:1 is doubtful and may refer simply to the conclusion of the night session. Nevertheless, it is at least possible that Luke was acquainted with another tradition which seemed more plausible from a historical standpoint. It is difficult to imagine that the court was convened during the night without preparation, and even more difficult to believe that it was reconvened in the morning. It so happens that the name of the Roman procurator is known and is handed down consistently in all layers of the tradition. The name of the high priest, however, is not given at all in Mark and it is reported incorrectly by Luke in 3:2 and in Acts 4:6 (5:17?). Only in Matthew 26:3, 57 is his name recorded correctly. According to John 18:13, 24, Jesus was led first to Annas and then to Caiaphas, who actually was high priest. This might imply that the oldest tradition presented Pilate not only as the one who carried out the death sentence, but also as the one who pronounced it. The question of whether the Jewish authorities at that time had the right to pronounce and carry out a death sentence is vigorously debated. Even if the Jews did have the authority to administer the death penalty, it would be clear that the Romans were the ones who actually took the initiative, since Jesus' countrymen would have executed him by stoning. Our sources seem to indicate that John 18:31b is correct and that the Jews had no other recourse than to turn to the Roman procurator. This raises the question whether the Jews merely decided to hand him over to Pilate, an action which was likely to result in a death sentence, without any necessity for the Jews to actually deliver the sentence themselves. It is amazing that Luke makes no mention of any death sentence, although he usually accentuates the guilt of the Jews and excuses the Romans (see comment on Mark 15:16-20).

Furthermore there are numerous details which are difficult to evaluate. It is not impossible that the church received direct information about the trial from an eyewitness (Mark 15:43), although on the basis of the text it is very doubtful. Jesus' saying about the temple (vs. 58) was apparently the cause of great difficulties for the church. Mark solves these difficulties by designating the statement as false testimony against Jesus. According to Matthew 26:60 f., it seems that the testimony of the witnesses agreed on this point, but Jesus said only that he could do this—not that he would do it. Luke omits the saying altogether; but Acts 6:13 f. records that a similar charge was brought against Stephen at his trial. John 2:19, 21 interprets the prophecy allegorically and finds its fulfillment in the death and resurrection of Jesus. These many efforts to qualify the saying are evidence of the fact that it was firmly embedded in the tradition and could not be repudiated easily. This favors the supposition that in some form or other it is a genuine saying of Jesus. If this is true, the statement must have been made by Jesus on some occasion. Under these circumstances the church would have been acquainted with the saying and had no need to learn it from a report of the trial (cf. 15:29 also). Which of the many forms of the saying is the oldest? The contrast between "which men made" and "not made by men" is typical of Hellenistic thought, where external worship in temple and sacrifice was contrasted with purely spiritual, inner worship (Acts 7:48; 17:24; cf. 2 Cor. 5:1; Eph. 2:11; Heb. 9:11, 24). The fact that this addition is not found in 15:29 or in Matthew 26:61 indicates that it is an explanation which was added later. In prophetic speech "three days" may indicate simply a short time (Hosea 6:2), so this is not necessarily based upon the Easter experience of the church. Nevertheless, it is difficult to imagine that Jesus would have said, "I will destroy this temple." Mark 13:2 may have preserved the original form in that it says only that the temple "will be" destroyed. It is possible, therefore, that this saying really did play a part in the trial. Since vss. 57b and 59 merely repeat vs. 56 and are almost the same in wording, we may surmise that the saying about the temple was part of the tradition and that Mark took it from the tradition he received and presented it here as false testimony. From a historical standpoint the objection might be made that false witnesses could easily have collaborated in their testimony. This raises the question whether or not in an early stage the account might have terminated with vs. 58 and the sentence of death or the decision to hand Jesus over to Pilate. This theory may receive support from the possibility that vss. 60 f., which resemble the statement in 15:4 f., could have been formed parallel to that passage in the process of narration. From a historical point of view it is unlikely that the high priest would have asked whether or not Jesus was the Son of God, since the Jews did not use "Son of God" as a title for the Messiah. And, so far as we know, Judaism did not prosecute anyone for claiming to be the Messiah. Barcochba, who died a martyr's death in A.D. 135 after he had led the whole Jewish community into severe persecution, was publicly declared to be the Messiah, honored as such, and still held in high regard despite that catastrophe. However, these accusations were considered significant by the Romans because they indicated that Jesus was a dangerous person. Therefore it may be true that Jesus' claim to be the

Messiah was either suggested or explicitly presented to the Romans as justification for the death sentence. His claim to be the Messiah could have been inferred from the saying about the temple without any question being asked, since according to a Jewish paraphrase of Isaiah 53:5 (which is somewhat like a commentary), the Messiah was to rebuild the temple which had been profaned by the guilt of the people. It is possible, therefore, that the explicit question in vs. 61 represents another stage in the development of the story.

The literary history of vs. 62 is even more difficult to evaluate. The exaltation and parousia of Jesus are not mentioned together in any other passage. Moreover, the wording which states that they would see him "seated" and "coming" is very strange. Obviously two Old Testament quotations have been combined here. Therefore the application of Psalm 110:1 to the Messiah may have been discovered rather late by the church, which used the Bible in Greek translation (see comment on 12:35-40). Daniel 7:13 is quoted also in Mark 13:26, but translated differently ("in the clouds" instead of "with the clouds of heaven"). It is not likely that this expectation originated with Jesus (cf. 8:27-33). Old Testament statements apparently were put together by the church as in increasing measure it discovered the story of Jesus there (cf. 15:20-26). This process can be traced one step further here. As John 19:37 indicates, the crucifixion of Jesus was understood in the light of Zechariah 12:10. Later the crucifixion was connected with Jesus' return and with Daniel 7:13, as shown in Revelation 1:7. Moreover, this may explain the fact that in Mark 13:26 and 14:62 this statement came to be associated with the expression "they will [or: you will] see," which came originally from Zechariah 12. On the other hand, the statement about seeing the heaven opened and seeing the Son of Man is found in both John 1:51 and Acts 7:55 f.—passages which are different in every other aspect. Surely Acts 7:55 f. refers to the exalted One who is portrayed, in keeping with Psalm 110:1, as abiding "at the right side of God"; however, he is standing, not sitting. This may be due to the fact that originally Daniel 7:13 spoke of the exaltation of the "son of man" (=Israel) and, consequently, of his coming to the throne of God, not his coming from it (this is also the Jewish interpretation in the Midrash on Ps. 2, pars. 9 and 21, par. 5). Whatever the case may be, in Mark 14:62 the idea of the exalted Son of Man has been combined with the idea of the vision of one coming with the clouds, which indicates that this representation is the result of a long preoccupation with the Bible.

The account of the mocking of Jesus in Luke (where the guards are the aggressors) does not mention the spitting and the smiting (although it alludes in a general way to a "flaying" or beating). These are the two expressions which appear in the Greek text of the prophecy concerning the Servant of the Lord in Isaiah 50:6. Since that passage combines spitting and smiting with the scourging of the Servant of the Lord, it could be the source of these details which have become a part of the scene before Pilate in Mark 15:19 (where, however, a different Greek word is used for "beat," while in John 19:3 the same word is used as in Isaiah 50:6 and Mark 14:65). These details then were introduced into the parallel incident in the palace of the high priest. The brief summary in Mark 10:34 refers to mocking, spitting, and scourging by the "Gentiles." As we look back it seems possible, from a historical point of view, that Jesus' saying about the temple constituted the real reason for the action of the Jewish court, while the accusation about his pretension to Messianic dignity formed the official indictment for the ears of Pilate. For the Pharisees, Jesus' attacks on righteousness based upon law must have been far more dangerous than any attack on the temple. Nevertheless, every member of the court could concur in this charge since the temple cult was fundamental for the Sadducees, and the Pharisees viewed the temple ritual as one aspect of obedience to the law. The mocking by the guards also possesses historical probability. These events were then supplemented by other factors which the church found in the Old Testament. Furthermore, Jesus' saying about destroying the temple and rebuilding it was rendered inoffensive in various ways. The first half of the saying was embarrassing so long as the church was still a part of the Jewish community, while the second half could have caused problems after the church separated from Judaism.

The account of Peter's denial in vss. 66-72 probably corresponds to the historical facts. It is told in a very straightforward and credible manner. According to Mark it all began with a single disavowal to an insignificant servant girl, which Peter then was obliged to uphold. Since Peter had such an important place in the church, it is difficult to believe that the church would have invented a story like this about him. This account appears in all four Gospels, which indicates that it must have been formed during Peter's lifetime. But there is no period in the history of the New Testament church where any hostility toward Peter is evident. The Markan expression *(euthus)* "just then" suggests that the dramatic conclusion wherein the rooster crows immediately after the third denial (although chickens were not permitted in Jerusalem) should be attributed to Mark. Of course, he must have based this on Jesus' words recorded in 14:30. It is strange that the words "a second time" are added. This accentuates the literal correspondence with 14:30, even though there does not seem to have been any mention of a first crowing.* We cannot be certain about this matter, however, since a number of good manuscripts do mention a first crowing in vs. 68. This detail may have been inserted by later copyists in order to make intelligible the words "a second time" in vs. 72; it is not likely that they would have crossed it out if it had been recorded by Mark. Nevertheless, the latter alternative is not impossible, since they may have considered it premature to include the crowing in vs. 68.

[53] The three groups which are mentioned in the introductory verse represent those whom Mark considers to be the real enemies of Jesus (cf. 8:31; 14:43). **[54]** Logically, vs. 66 could follow immediately after vs. 54. By placing the one story within the other Mark has made his message to the reader very clear. The visible parallel between Jesus and Peter makes the fundamental difference between them all the more prominent. The first two verses present both Jesus and Peter, as they go to face the hour of temptation and the necessary testing. Although they are some-

* Schweizer is following the older manuscripts which do not contain the words "Just then a rooster crowed" in vs. 68.

what separated physically, they proceed along the same path to the same situation. However, it is obvious immediately that the situation is far more serious for Jesus since it has been evident (since 3:6!) that he is threatened with a sentence of death. If Peter faces any danger at all it is rather nebulous.

[55] Mark begins the trial of Jesus with a remark which is reminiscent of 3:6; 11:18; 12:12; and 14:1: The result of the trial has been decided more or less from the very beginning. **[56, 57, 59]** Thus it is ironical that the legal principle which required that the testimony of at least two witnesses be in agreement is adhered to so scrupulously. The irony of the proceeding is heightened by the obvious fact that there are more than enough false witnesses to satisfy the legal requirements as well as to bring about the decision which already had been reached. In this way Mark sets forth in bold relief the magnitude of the guilt of human action and the severity of the suffering which Jesus experiences as he travels God's pathway for the sake of these very same men. **[58]** Certainly the church regarded itself as the new temple which had been promised, since it was frequently designated as a building (Matt. 16:18) or a temple (1 Cor. 3:17; 2 Cor. 6:16; Eph. 2:22; and perhaps Rev. 3:12). Evidently Mark also interpreted the saying in this way. Whether we should attribute the same view to Jesus (since it seems likely that the promise to build a new temple originated with him) depends upon how we evaluate his other sayings. As early as the first century A.D., Ethiopian Enoch 90:28-36 (cf. Jubilees 1:17, 27 f.) expected the destruction of the old temple and the building of a heavenly temple (in contrast to Rev. 21:22). Accordingly, we may suspect that Jesus was referring to the Kingdom of God when he spoke of the new temple. However, since he emphasized time and again the great significance of God's offer and his demand in the present time (cf. 8:38, et al.) it is more likely that he was thinking of his disciples as a new Israel called by God to obedience. In a way that is similar to Jesus' many sayings about the law (2:1—3:6, 7), the saying about the temple which is included here opposes that complacent security which presumes that possession of the temple and proper observation of the cult are a guarantee of salvation. Salvation can be anticipated only as a gift of grace which comes from God's new order. Since it includes the obedience of discipleship, salvation can be expected only within the fellowship of Jesus' disciples. When interpreted this way, the saying corresponds with Jesus' action in 11:15-19, and especially with the Markan interpretation which regards that action as the opening of the door to the Gentile world. Another typical feature found in this saying is the fact that Jesus does away with complacent and secure temple religion but does not deny that the temple was God's good gift and must continue to exist as a spiritual temple along with the "cult" that must be practiced in it (Rom. 12:1 f.). Similar considerations apply to Jesus' sayings about the law. This was no longer understood in the Gospel of Thomas (71), which continues: ". . . and no one will be able to build it [again]." **[60, 61]** The question of the high priest makes the incomprehensibility of Jesus' silence especially prominent. It is an impressive sign of what occurs in Jesus' Passion: Man has to gain his point and defend himself, therefore he is not able to understand how anyone can behave in a different way. The Son of Man who goes his way at God's command is able to be silent, whereas man is compelled to protest either outwardly or inwardly against any suffering or death, even when he accepts it as unavoidable. The Son of Man enters into the humility of his suffering and death without protest. This is the truth expressed here by Jesus' silence which sealed his death sentence (cf. Isa. 53:7). The chief priest's second question about Jesus' divine Sonship is important to Mark, primarily, as a question which faces the church as it reads this account. The church is asked the question because this is the profession it makes even in the midst of persecution. In modern-day terms this question would be: Is it enough merely to profess faith in God in a general way, without clearly specifying whom we mean when we say "God"? Or are we able to confess God, who is really God, only if we have encountered him in Jesus—if in Jesus' promises and demands we have discerned features which are no longer vague or indistinct, but definite and clear? The latter answer is the one given by Mark and by the sum total of the church's traditions. **[62]** In contrast to Matthew, Mark reports Jesus' answer to this question as a clear "yes." To be sure, it is only here at the depth of Jesus' weakness and failure that his answer could be expressed in this way. Matthew is more reserved in his formulation because the title of Messiah might be misunderstood (cf. 8:29 f.). Both of these Gospel writers interpret this answer by referring to Jesus' position as Lord, and to his future parousia. When the church confessed the divine Sonship of Jesus, it indicated primarily that it recognized Jesus as "Lord" and that it was waiting for the fulfillment wherein Jesus' sovereignty would be manifested and would bring an end to all temptation and establish God's Kingdom over all things. The church at various times and in various places has been divided in its interpretation of the lordship of Jesus. Did it designate him first and foremost as its Lord to whom it owed obedience and from whom it expected guidance and help, or as Lord of the world to whom all earthly and heavenly powers are subject? **[63]** The tearing of the clothing is an expression of horror (2 Kings 18:37; 19:1), and it is probably correct to include it here (see the introduction). **[64]** Since only those cases were regarded as blasphemy where the most holy Name was uttered, the sentencing of Jesus to death for this statement can hardly be thought to be justified. This gives greater prominence to the theological aspect: It was not while in a fit of passion that the world said "no" to God's way as it is found in Jesus. It did so after deliberate court proceedings conducted according to long-established rules.

[65] This is illustrated more dramatically by the reference to the way in which the same court personnel, of all people, made fun of Jesus and tormented him, which surely was contrary to all court regulations. The correct procedure which had been maintained in some measure up to this point is obviously abandoned; and the human triumph, which appears here in the form of the rejection of God's way, or even of the apparent victory over Jesus, gives free rein to the rage of men.

[66] While Jesus was faithful in temptation and sustained his testimony clearly and unmistakably whether by keeping silent or by speaking, Peter was standing in the courtyard below. **[67]** In the Greek text the servant girl's accusation mentions "Nazarene" first and adds Jesus' name afterward. It seems that it was customary to designate Jesus and particularly his disciples (Acts 24:5) simply as "Nazarenes" or "Nazarites" (cf. 1:24). Peter's temptation came in a very unimpressive and incidental way. It was not the appropriate situation for confessing one's faith. The question he was asked did not really concern his faith at all. It was a purely objective question as to whether or not he was the one whom the servant girl thought she had seen with Jesus on some particular occasion. Furthermore, there was no reason for him to vindicate himself publicly. The one who asked was simply a servant girl who probably had no idea what it really meant to be a "Nazarene," so neither a "yes" nor a "no" would have indicated anything about faith. Consequently, if Peter had replied in the affirmative, he would have risked his safety without giving any witness to his faith. **[68]** His rather wordy response, which in the Greek resembles the form of an oath used by the rabbis, conceals his confusion. Moreover, his escape into the passageway is a halfway retreat. **[69-71]** Since it is the same servant girl who makes the assertion a second and a third time, Peter has no choice but to repeat his denial before a larger number of witnesses and to make his statements more emphatic. This was especially necessary since his Galilean dialect apparently was a liability to him—which is something else that had nothing to do with his religious profession. **[72]** With the concluding verse Mark stresses the fact that this was the denial predicted by Jesus (14:30), which now had come to pass. Any situation which calls for the confession of one's faith is appropriate for such a confession, i.e., whenever a disciple of Jesus is confronted by some person, even a single individual such as a servant girl, in such a way that his belonging or not belonging to the "Nazarene" must be made known. It makes no difference whether or not that person has any religious interest. When God expects such a testimony from a disciple then the disciple's refusal to give it is sin. All Peter can do is break down and cry, by which action he proves that he is a disciple of Jesus. This forms a complete contrast to penance by which one wishes to make his own amends (Matt. 27:3-5).

What Mark is trying to say to the reader by the whole structure of his book becomes especially clear in this section. In Jesus,

God is present among men. In Jesus, God wants to make himself available to men. But men close their hearts against God. Even the disciple fails who is very close to Jesus, who knows the joy of sacrifice and is ready to die (14:31). Thus the faithfulness of the Son of Man and the unfaithfulness of men stand in sharp contrast. This clearly discloses the difficulty God encounters when he tries to reveal himself to man. The conclusion of the passage shows that man can meet God only when he does not imagine himself to be invincible, in the cheerful self-confidence of 14:29, but knows that he is placed under the judgment of God.

Jesus Is Handed Over to Pilate 15:1;
cf. Matt. 27:1-2; Luke 23:1

1Early in the morning the chief priests met hurriedly with the elders, the teachers of the Law, and the whole Council, and made their plans. They put Jesus in chains, took him away and handed him over to Pilate.

With reference to the historical problems, see comment on 14:53-72. Unfortunately the wording of the original text can no longer be ascertained. Ancient manuscripts which are equally reliable read "they passed a decision" or "they wrote out a decision." Since this is an exact parallel to 3:6, which is an editorial insertion, we can assume that Mark had in mind a continuation of the same session—not a new one. With his favorite expression *euthus* (rendered "hurriedly" in TEV) he is taking up the thread of the story which had been interrupted by the account of Peter's denial. The addition of "and the whole Council" is superfluous, since this council consisted of the three groups that are named (cf. 14:53, 55). These terms are amassed to emphasize the official nature of the condemnation: The sentence was not passed by a few men whose circumstances were responsible for their error, nor was it a momentary surge of hate which delivered Jesus over to death on the cross. It was the result of a considered decision. In this experience we see evidence of the Pauline thesis that, without exception, everyone is shown to be a sinner in the light of the gospel (Rom. 3:23). Pilate was so well known that it was no longer necessary to specify that he was the Roman procurator. Handing Jesus over to the Romans was the obvious thing to do. Josephus (from the end of the first century A.D.) wrote of a prophet named Jesus, the son of Ananias, who had announced the destruction of the temple and for that reason was handed over by the Jewish authorities to the Romans, who scourged him (*Wars* VI. 300 ff.).

The Condemnation of the King of the Jews 15:2-15;
cf. Matt. 27:11-26; Luke 23:2-5, 17-25

[2]Pilate questioned him: "Are you the king of the Jews?" Jesus
answered: "So you say." [3]The chief priests accused Jesus of many
things, [4]so Pilate questioned him again: "Aren't you going to
answer? See how many things they accuse you of!" [5]Again Jesus
refused to say a word, and Pilate was filled with surprise.

[6]At every Passover Feast Pilate would set free any prisoner
the people asked for. [7]At that time a man named Barabbas was
in prison with the rebels who had committed murder in the riot.
[8]When the crowd gathered and began to ask Pilate to do them the
usual favor, [9]Pilate asked them: "Do you want me to set free for
you the king of the Jews?" [10]He knew very well that the chief
priests had handed Jesus over to him because they were jealous.
[11]But the chief priests stirred up the crowd to ask, instead, for
Pilate to set Barabbas free for them. [12]Pilate spoke again to the
crowd: "What then, do you want me to do with the one you call
the king of the Jews!" [13]They shouted back, "Nail him to the
cross!" [14]"But what crime has he committed?" Pilate asked. They
shouted all the louder, "Nail him to the cross!" [15]Pilate wanted
to please the crowd, so he set Barabbas free for them. Then he
had Jesus whipped and handed him over to be nailed to the cross.

With reference to the historical problems, see comment on 14:53-72. The whole hearing is related in a stylized manner so that those details are omitted which are interesting for historical reasons but not essential for proclamation, e.g., the place where the hearing was held. (The Tower of Antonia, which is in the northwest corner of the temple area, is one possible location. It was the prison where criminals were held pending trial. Matthew 27:27 favors this location, but Mark 15:16 does not. The latter verse suggests Herod's palace.) Also omitted were the content of the accusation (which is presupposed in vs. 2) and the rebellion (which must have taken place, according to vs. 7). It would have been more logical to expect vs. 2 after vs. 5; however, it is clear that the decisive title had to be stated at the very beginning in order to make known what everything depended upon. Jesus' consistent silence, which is added as a development of vs. 2, Pilate's discreet and yet ineffective and unconvincing washing of his hands (Matt. 27:24), the methodical action of the high priest (Mark 14:60-64), and the shout of the fanatical crowd are stylistic elements which are more than just a report of what happened at that time. They are meant to portray what really took place in the depths which are known only by faith. Thus the sole interest of the entire passage is the defenseless silence of Jesus in the face of all the questioning by his interrogators, all the sly accusations of the religious-political leaders, and all the shouting by the mob. This is how the passage proclaims that Jesus suffered deliberately and willingly. It is most unlikely that there was a custom of setting a prisoner free each year. Neither Roman nor Jewish sources report anything of this kind, and there is no reference to a parallel practice anywhere else. Moreover, it is not recorded in Luke, even though he tells of the people's decision in favor of Barabbas. Furthermore, it is not likely that the details of the account are historically correct. The offer in vs. 9 to set him free before he had been sentenced, and even before the question of his guilt had been investigated (vs. 14), is a mockery of Roman jurisprudence. It is both possible and probable that this represented a single case of clemency which was reported here to form a contrast to the condemnation of Jesus and to make the latter appear even more grievous, and, moreover, to remind one immediately of the vicarious nature of Jesus' suffering—the murderer goes free; his punishment is borne by the Son of God. Matthew 27:17, 21 increase the possibility that such an interpretation is correct; in that account Pilate himself takes the initiative and merely gives the people the option of choosing between these two. It would be difficult to believe that Barabbas was no more than a fictitious character. The conviction that he is a historical personage is reinforced by the observation that he was not introduced at the beginning as "Barabbas, the murderer." Mark does not even specify what his actual relationship to the rebellion was. It is clear that some small rebellion against Rome had occurred at that time, but in the absence of any documentation no sober historical investigation would connect it with the movement which was initiated by Jesus.

[2] Pilate's question (see excursus on 14:53-72) is worded the same in all four Gospels and corresponds to the inscription on the cross (15:26). It is a Graeco-Roman formulation of the question which the high priest asked in a Jewish version in 14:61. Naturally, for the Roman procurator this amounted to an accusation of political insurrection. There was no longer any Jewish king, only a "tetrarch" who ruled with others as a vassal of Rome over the land which had been divided into several parts. The people followed the ancient custom and called this person "king" (6:14, et al.). If, however, someone who had not sworn allegiance to Rome had usurped this title, it would have amounted to high treason; and if the people had tolerated such a person, they would have been guilty of insurrection. Of course, it would not have been possible for Pilate to ask the question in this way. Most likely he would have said, "Do you claim to be the king of the Jews?" or something similar. Pilate could not acknowledge the existence of such a person. Jesus' answer is strange. Obviously he had to avoid a clear "yes," because the title in this form was apt to be misunderstood as having a nationalistic connotation. While "Israel" designates the Jewish nation in the sense of God's chosen people and does not always include all who belong racially or politically, "the Jews" is merely a designation of nationality. Jesus could not easily deny that he had a genuine right to this title, since he actually was "King of Israel" according to faith (15:32; John 1:49; 12:13), and as such he truly was king of some who were Jews. Pilate would have to examine the words and deeds of Jesus by questioning the witnesses and the accused. No account of this procedure has been handed down, although Roman trials were public. The church did not consider such details worth preserving.

[3-5] The silence of Jesus, which is unique even when compared with similar trials of Jesus' disciples (13:11; Acts 7:1 ff.; 22:1 ff.; 23:1 ff.; 2 Tim. 4:16 f.; cf. Phil. 1:12 f.), was the only feature which continued to impress the church, because it revealed Jesus' will to suffer. It may have reminded the church of Isaiah 53:7. So these two complement each another—the spoken "yes" in 14:62 (15:2) in response to the question about his Messiahship and the silent and suffering "yes" in response to the divine commission which was a part of that Messiahship (14:60 f. and 15:3-5). **[7]** The one whom they are allowed to choose is always introduced as "the Barabbas" (the son of Abbas), the well-known individual whose release the people requested and for whom Jesus had to die. **[8, 9]** Pilate's question implies that the people had not asked for any specific person. It is irrelevant to ask if the people had actually flocked to Pilate and made a general request for the release of a prisoner without having any particular person in mind. Pilate's question is intentionally phrased so that it accentuates the difficulty of making the choice which now faces them. Jesus is the one whom they are about to reject, and the reader is asked whether he will accept the assertion of the text that it is really "the King of the Jews" who is repudiated when Jesus is rejected. **[10]** Actually vs. 10 is a declaration of Jesus' innocence; it asserts that Pilate himself was convinced of this fact. "Jealousy" is not mentioned by Mark anywhere else (cf. John 12:19). This verse must be a parenthetical explanation which the Gospel writer included to distinguish the general public from the authorities, which is his consistent practice (cf. 11:8, 18; 12:12, 37; 14:1 f., 11; et al.). **[11]** Although the populace was incited by the authorities (vs. 11) to shout the demands recorded in vss. 13 f., it is upon the authorities alone that Mark places the blame. Moreover, in Greek "the chief priests" are the last words of the sentence and stand immediately before vs. 11. In this way the responsibility of these men is doubly emphasized, and the reader becomes aware of this when he senses the harshness of the grammatical construction.

[12] Pilate's next question is also very strange; surely he was able to pardon the accused. Moreover, the Roman procurator as representative of the occupying power was not obliged to ask a subject people what he should do. **[13]** This is another attempt to present the indecision of the judge, on the one hand, and the deliberate incurrence of responsibility by the entire nation, on the other. These two attitudes lead to the rejection of Jesus. Perhaps Mark intended to emphasize the irony of the fact that the people who had acclaimed Jesus as their king are the very ones who bring about his death. The word *palin* "again" (TEV "back") is surprising (just as it is in John 18:40), since neither the shouting of the people nor the demand that Jesus be crucified has been mentioned before this. So far, the specific punishment that was to be inflicted upon Jesus had not been announced. Perhaps this is a device to express the stubborn and repeated rejection of Jesus. Similarly it is important to the story that the specific form of the punishment be explicitly requested by the entire nation. **[14]** Pilate's next question, which is actually another affirmation of Jesus' innocence, is a subtle indication that he has decided to yield to the demand of the crowd. While the prisoner in his silence is the one who is truly free, Pilate is characterized as the one who has no freedom whatever. **[15]** Without any dogmatic statement, the idea of vicarious suffering is suggested by placing side by side Barabbas who was set free and Jesus who was handed over to be crucified. It is surprising that the whipping is mentioned so briefly (literally: "and he delivered Jesus, having whipped [him], in order that he should be crucified"). Other documents inform us that condemned criminals who were not Roman citizens (Acts 22:25) were flogged with a leather whip to which bits of metal were attached. Any description of the gruesome procedure which might arouse either sympathy or hatred is deliberately avoided in the account. Neither emotion is appropriate in view of the seriousness of what is happening here. Either one would place Jesus' Passion on a level with thousands of other executions which frequently were more brutal. Furthermore, in this instance a complete and precise historical description was deliberately avoided.

Therefore the reader is not asked whether he regards the presentation of the facts as historically accurate. There is little likelihood that these are accurately reported, at least when it comes to the details. The real question here is the same one asked by Mark and by the church before him as it proclaimed the Good News: Are men in the same situation as the disciples who fled? As Peter who denies his Lord? Or even as the residents of Jerusalem who, rather than consent to God's way, prefer to request the release of some obscure condemned criminal although they do not know whether or not he deserves sympathy? If they followed God's way they might encounter God's promise and demand in such a way that they would be stripped of their self-confidence. The question has a second part: Is it really true that when Jesus dies, the "Son of the Blessed God" who is also the "King of the Jews" sent from God goes to his death in order that man may become free?

Ridiculing the King of the Jews 15:16-20a;
cf. Matt. 27:27-31a

16The soldiers took Jesus inside the courtyard (that is, of the
Governor's palace) and called together the rest of the company.
17They put a purple robe on Jesus, made a crown out of thorny
branches, and put it on his head. 18Then they began to salute him:
"Long live the King of the Jews!" 19And they beat him over the
head with a stick, spat on him, fell on their knees and bowed
down to him. 20When they had finished making fun of him, they
took off the purple robe and put his own clothes back on him.

The account reads very well without vss. 16-20a. It has been suggested that this incident is a later addition. This suggestion is favored because the incident is not found in Luke and because Luke gives the impression that it was the Jews who crucified Jesus (the Roman soldiers are not mentioned until Luke 23:36). Furthermore, John 19:16 moves immediately from Pilate's pronouncement of the death sentence to the crucifixion (by Roman soldiers, as is clearly stated in John 19:23). However, a similar account of the mockery of Jesus is found in John 19:2 f., immediately following the whipping. The only difference is that the mocking appears a little earlier in John. Perhaps the omission of this incident by Luke should be attributed to his tendency to report as little as possible that is negative about the Romans. Moreover, Luke records a similar incident in which they made fun of Jesus before Herod (Luke 22:63-65). There Luke also suggests the theme of Jesus' silence. This shows how easily such themes were transferred from one incident to another. There are some interesting parallels to this account. When King Agrippa arrived in Egypt the populace ridiculed him by laying hold of an imbecile named Carabas to whom they gave a "crown," a "royal robe," and a "scepter"; they paid homage to him, and addressed him as *"Mare"* (i.e., "lord." Philo, *Flaccus* 36-39). This is the title which the early church used when addressing Jesus. The mockery in the case of Agrippa was a part of anti-Semitic rioting in opposition to one who was recognized by Rome as "King of the Jews." This fact calls attention to the great similarity between the two incidents and the wretched role of those who were mocked. In one instance Jesus had to play the part of one who was exposed to scorn and humiliation, whereas in the other the poor imbecile had to play the part of the king, whom the crowd could not get their hands on. There were other customs which have even greater resemblance. It is reported that the Persians at the end of the first century A.D. placed a condemned criminal upon the throne at the Sacaean festival, where for a short time he was allowed to exercise some type of mock rule. There are records of similar customs among the Romans. The mocking and mistreatment of the emperor Vitellius before he was beheaded is a comparable incident. This indicates how common this kind of treatment was and favors the historicity of this incident, which has been recounted in varying independent traditions (in Mark 15:16-20; John 19:2 f.; and in the brief ancient summary of the Passion in Mark 10:33b, 34a, which must have originated in a purely Jewish church). We may suspect that the matter of the spitting and the beating, which interrupts the story of their saluting (vs. 18) and falling on their knees (end of vs. 19), has been brought in here from the scene in 14:65. Without the spitting and the beating there would be a more consistent picture of their ridiculing him by honoring him as king, i.e., pure mockery without any mistreatment. At the end of the account in John (19:3) a reference to beating is added which uses the same word from Isaiah 50:6 as is found in Mark 14:64. (It should be observed in this connection that John knows of no mocking in the palace of the chief priest to parallel Mark 14:65.)

[16] It is not possible to determine whether this refers to the "palace" (see comment on 14:43-52) or to the inner "courtyard." The Greek word can signify either. The explanation added by the Gospel writer, which is difficult grammatically, favors the first alternative. **[17]** A purple robe (here it may be a red military coat) and a golden crown are, of course, symbols of royal dignity. They represent a type of decoration for special merit. Accordingly, these are the items which were presented to Jonathan Maccabaeus as "the king's Friend" for special bravery (I Macc. 10:20). **[18]** The title "King of the Jews" in vs. 18 is firmly embedded in the tradition (cf. vs. 26). This corresponds to the customary Roman salutation, *"Ave Caesar."* The story is more elaborate in the Gospel of Peter (6-9, from the middle of the second century). In that account Jesus' sitting on the throne and the shout "Judge righteously, O King of Israel!" call to mind his role as judge of the world. The scorn of those who scourged him, expressed in the words "With such honour let us honour the Son of God," intensifies the marked contrast between the unbelief of men and the action of God which is really taking place here. **[19]** Falling upon the knees is an oriental custom for according the most solemn homage. **[20]** The summary of the Passion in Mark 10:33b, 34a also includes the feature of the Gentiles mocking Jesus.

In the context of Mark's Gospel, special emphasis is put upon the fact that Pilate's question in vs. 2 and the reference to the notice of the accusation in vs. 26 are unintentional testimony to Jesus' kingship. John underscores this thought with Pilate's *"Ecce homo"* ("Look! Here is the man!" John 19:5; cf. 19:19-22); the

Gospel of Peter elaborates this theologically in terms of Jesus' being the judge of the world. Furthermore, the theme of his humiliation has been added (Isa. 50:6 and Jesus' saying in 10:34). Thus with increasing deliberateness the entire account becomes a concealed reference to Jesus' royal dignity and to the secret fulfillment of the plan of God which occurs in the midst of overt humiliation that would seem to prove the opposite.

The Crucifixion of Jesus 15:20b-26;
cf. Matt. 27:31b-37; Luke 23:26, 33-35a, 38

20Then they led him out to nail him to the cross.
21On the way they met a man named Simon, who was coming
into the city from the country, and they forced him to carry Jesus'
cross. (This was Simon from Cyrene, the father of Alexander and
Rufus.) 22They brought Jesus to a place called Golgotha, which
means "The Place of the Skull." 23There they tried to give him
wine mixed with a drug called myrrh, but Jesus would not drink
it. 24So they nailed him to the cross and divided his clothes among
themselves, throwing dice to see who would get which piece of
clothing. 25It was nine o'clock in the morning when they nailed
him to the cross. 26The notice of the accusation against him was
written, "The King of the Jews."

(Vs. 24: Ps. 22: 18.)

This passage contains a very simple account of the crucifixion in vss. 20b-24a which, obviously, is very old. The verbs in this account are in the present tense and are simply joined with "and." Vs. 23 alone is in the past tense, but it is quite believable (see below). The quotation in vs. 24b, however, may be a later addition, like vs. 25, which seems to be an appendage. The fact that this is the second time that the crucifixion is mentioned has caused some to suspect that a second account has been interwoven; however, this cannot be proven. Since the "and" *(kai)* may be a dialectical peculiarity in the place of "when" (as in TEV), all that we can be sure of is that some emphasis was put on the chronology (cf. vss. 33 f.) when it was added by Mark or the narrator before him. Vs. 26 may have been a part of the account from the very beginning.

The brief reference to Simon, of Cyrene (which is in North Africa; perhaps Simon was living in Jerusalem), was handed down because his two sons were still well known. Otherwise it is not likely that their names would have been mentioned. Probably the sons had joined the church. (Is the Rufus mentioned in Romans 16:13 the son of Simon?) No theological tendency can be detected. This event does not portray the weakness of Jesus or his collapse under torture. Later the details began to disappear, first the names of the sons (Matt. 27:32; Luke 23:26), and then the fact that Simon was coming from the country (Matt. 27:32). Moreover, the wording was carefully chosen so that the hearer or reader could understand the deeper significance. Mark formulated the passage in the same way as 8:34 although the verb, particularly in the specific Greek tense which was chosen, really means "take up"—not "carry." Luke actually said "carry," but added the words "behind Jesus" to remind one of Luke 9:23 and 14:27. Consequently, a historical detail which has been handed down began to "speak" to the church and became for the hearers a picture of the discipleship to which they were called. The next stage of development appears in John, where the story has been forgotten or deliberately omitted. Probably this was done because all human weakness vanishes at the proclamation of victory and even in the midst of Jesus' Passion. Finally, since the Synoptics state that Simon carried the cross, while according to John, Jesus bore it himself, Basilides (Irenaeus, *Heresies* I, 24:4) concluded that the Son of God exchanged his form with that of Simon so that Simon was crucified in the place of the Son of God without any of his enemies being aware of the fact.

From the very beginning the name Golgotha was included in the tradition, and the translation of the name was supplied in those areas where Greek was spoken (Luke 23:33; in John 19:17 the form is a little different). **[23]** The proffering of the stupefying drink is in keeping with Jewish custom, which follows the directive given in Proverbs 31:6. In conformity with Psalm 69:21, Matthew 27:34 substitutes gall for the myrrh (the fragrant resin of a bush, which was used as incense). A drink of vinegar (TEV: wine) is reported in Mark 15:36 (Matt. 27:48), which also conforms to Psalm 69:21. The first half of the verse in that Psalm reads, "They gave me also gall for my meat" (KJV). Both expressions in the Psalm must be taken figuratively and merely describe the distress of the righteous (the same thing is true in 1QH 4:11, "And given them in their thirst vinegar to drink"). Since the tradition reported that Jesus was offered a drink on two different occasions and the second time the drink contained vinegar, Matthew concluded that the first half of the verse from the Psalm must have been fulfilled by the first drink that was offered. This explains why he inserted the corresponding word from the Psalm. A few manuscripts also supplied "vinegar" in this passage in Mark. This shows how with the passing of time the church found in its Bible more and more passages by which to interpret Jesus' Passion. Indeed, the Old Testament was the only document in which the church was able to read the story of Jesus. The dividing of his clothes is described in Psalm 22:18. Just as was true of Psalm 69:21, this action is presented in two parallel statements in keeping with Old Testament style. And even as Matthew 27:34 derived from the parallel statements in Psalm 69:21 two different drinks for the cup which was offered to Jesus, so John 19:23 f. applied "cast lots" from Psalm 22:18 to the seamless robe and "divided" to the other articles of clothing. Although it seems reasonable, it cannot be demonstrated that the Romans had a practice of dividing the clothing of criminals who were executed. Therefore, we must consider the possibility that the church discovered this feature in its Bible. Psalm 22 became for the church the principal biblical description of Jesus' Passion and had a place in its worship similar to that which the Passion story has with us (cf. vss. 29, 34; Matt. 27:43; John 19:28). At Roman crucifixions it was customary to place a title on the cross to indicate the offense of the criminal. It is conceivable that this was the actual wording of the title if it is construed as casting derision upon Jewish expectations. The fact that Jesus was executed as Messiah and that this was declared by the inscription on the cross may be related to the fact that so soon after his death he was generally designated as the Messiah (Christ).

[20] The condemned person was required to carry the horizontal beam of the cross to the place of execution. **[21]** The fact that another had to do this for Jesus, who apparently was exhausted by the scourging to the point of collapse, became a picture of discipleship for the church in accordance with the saying of Jesus in 8:34. This is important for a proper understanding of the meaning of discipleship. Even here (cf. 1:18, 20) the disciple is not given any credit for his decision; he was compelled by others to do what he did. Moreover, discipleship is expressed very concretely in the literal carrying of a timber and following after Jesus. Discipleship here is not a subjective experience or a frame of mind. Although stories and sayings about discipleship were handed down in order to make it possible for those who lived after Easter to become disciples of Jesus, the realistic aspect of the church's understanding of discipleship caused it to use the word *akoloutheo* exclusively for following the earthly Jesus (with the exception of Revelation 14:4). The phrase "from the field" (TEV: "country") implies that it was not the day of the Passover (cf. 14:12-16). However, it is possible to interpret this phrase to mean that he was coming from a farm—not from the city.

[22] The place where the Church of the Holy Sepulchre was completed in A.D. 335 may be the approximate location of Golgotha since at that time it still lay outside the city wall. The legend that Adam's skull was buried on Golgotha probably arose at a later time (cf. the parallels drawn between Adam and Christ in Romans 5:12 ff.; 1 Corinthians 15:21 f., 45 ff.). The place may have received its name from a hill shaped like the top of a skull. **[23]** The refusal of the stupefying drink shows that Jesus wanted to be conscious during his suffering. **[24]** The cross extended only a little higher than the top of a man's head. The person died from the exhaustion of having been beaten until bloody, and from being exposed naked to insects. It was not unusual for a criminal to live until the second day. He was either tied or nailed to the cross (nailing is presupposed in Luke 24:39a and John 20:25).

None of these details are described here. The story could not be told any more concisely; only the use of the present tense (crucify) in the Greek makes this decisive action more prominent than the others. Once again what was said concerning vs. 15b proves true: Since the physical anguish did not constitute Jesus' real suffering, it is not described. His real suffering was caused by his rejection, which, beginning with 3:6, has been traced in every conceivable variation and in increasing measure, culminating with the fact that none of the disciples have appeared since 14:72. The use of the words of Psalm 22:18 presents the dividing of his clothing as the fulfillment of Old Testament statements, although this is not asserted explicitly. **[25]** It is impossible to reconcile the reference to the hour of the day (9 o'clock in the morning) with John 19:14 (where Jesus was condemned to die at 12 o'clock noon). The time is stated simply to indicate that hour after hour passed in perfect accord with the will of God (cf. vss. 33 f.). He was Lord over every hour of this day. In a similar way the statement in John declared that Jesus died at the hour when the Passover lamb was slaughtered. He who wants to completely reconcile these two statements of time prevents himself from listening humbly to the crucial affirmation which Mark and John wish to make. **[26]** When placed alongside this sober account of a gruesome though relatively common proceeding, the inscription on the cross appears to be sarcastic, and this is what the civil court which passed the sentence wanted it to be. The reader knows, however, that this expresses most profound truth concerning the events which took place here.

If we reflect a moment we will recognize, first of all, that this description is surprisingly sober and concise. It avoids sentimentality and does not seek to arouse sympathy or hatred. At the same time, it preserves historical details such as the names of Simon's sons. Jesus' deliberate determination to suffer was early recognized and emphasized. In various stages this passage expresses the church's discernment of the truth that in Jesus' suffering the path of every righteous sufferer in Israel was fulfilled in an all-encompassing manner (see comment on 8:27-33); consequently, that in this event God brought his plan for Israel to its goal. Therefore

Jesus' Passion is viewed primarily in the light of Psalm 22 (and Psalm 69), while the much closer parallel in Wisdom of Solomon 2 seems to have had its effect first in Matthew 27:43. The chronology gives further expression to the conviction that these things have not been determined by any accident or human intervention —God's will has been the decisive factor. The inscription, to which John has given special significance, declares what actually took place. The main idea is the insight that God triumphs in the humiliation of an execution.

The Mocking of the Crucified 15:27-32;
cf. Matt. 27:38-44

27They also nailed two bandits to crosses with Jesus, one on his
right and the other on his left. 28[In this way the scripture came
true which says: "He was included with the criminals."]

29People passing by shook their heads and threw insults at
Jesus: "Aha! You were going to tear down the Temple and build
it up in three days! 30Now come down from the cross and save
yourself!" 31In the same way the chief priests and the teachers of
the Law made fun of Jesus, saying to each other: "He saved others,
but he cannot save himself! 32Let us see the Messiah, the king of
Israel, come down from the cross now, and we will believe in
him!" And the two who were crucified with Jesus insulted him
also.

(Vs. 29: Ps. 22:7; Lam. 2:15.)

All the Gospel writers state that Jesus was crucified between two criminals, and this is certainly reliable historically. No particular theological tendency is discernible in this detail. In the course of textual transmission, later copyists inserted the comment found in vs. 28 that Isaiah 53:12 was fulfilled in this manner ("he was numbered with the transgressors"), which indicates that they interpreted this incident as a divine fulfillment of Old Testament prophecy. This shows the extent to which this account disturbed the church. This is seen also in Luke, where the story of the two robbers serves to indicate Jesus' loving concern for the spiritual needs of the afflicted and also to depict the difference between human acceptance and rejection of divine love. An even better example is the way the penitent robber both confesses his guilt and rebukes the soldiers, according to the Gospel of Peter (4:13, from the middle of the second century). Finally, in John the two criminals present a contrast to accentuate the uniqueness of Jesus (19:31-34). Accordingly, features which identified Jesus with criminals, such as are found in this passage from Mark, were removed gradually, thus emphasizing the fact that his position was truly unique. Since the two robbers are not mentioned immediately in connection with Jesus' crucifixion (as is appropriately done in John 19:18), it is strange that they are mentioned at all before the reference to their insulting Jesus (vs. 32b). This would be easier to understand if a brief statement about the way the people who passed by were making fun of Jesus (vs. 29a) had originally been connected with the reference to the way Jesus was insulted by those who were crucified with him. The most surprising feature in the intervening verses is that vss. 28b-30 and 31-32a describe two different mockings, each of which mentions "saving himself" and "coming down from the cross" in almost the same words. The first of these contains a reference to 14:58 and the second to 14:61 (or 15:26?). Are these merely two variant accounts of the same event? If so, vss. 31 f. must be the later version, coming from a time when the saying about the temple was no longer understood and Jesus' dignity as the Christ was regarded as a far more important cause of contention. In this later version the chief priests and teachers take the place of the unnamed persons. This tendency can be observed in other passages also (cf. Mark 3:22 and Luke 11:15; Mark 8:11 and Luke 11:16; Mark 3:6 and 3:1-5). Mark may have made this change, since he knew two different versions of the event and had to assume that a different group of people spoke in the second instance. However, there is more to be seen here. The shaking of the head is mentioned in Psalm 22:7—the Psalm in which the church was able to discover the Passion of Jesus more clearly than in any other passage (cf. vs. 24). Moreover, this phrase occurs in Lamentations 2:15, where there is also a reference to the people who were passing by. It is likely, therefore, that at some time a narrator well versed in the Bible introduced the phrase in this place. The same verse, Psalm 22:7, states that all who saw him mocked at him (Luke 23:35 has repeated this literally from the Greek Old Testament) and that they "shoot out the lip" (KJV, in agreement with the Hebrew text; the Greek text reads "murmured with their lips"). Both expressions were adopted by Justin (*Dialogue* 101:3; *Apology,* I, 38:6; from the middle of the second century. Cf. 1 Clement 16:16, from the end of the first century). In Psalm 22:6 these actions are characterized as "scorned by men, and despised by the people." Did the church regard this double statement as a reference to the two mockings? Obviously Psalm 22:8 has been appropriated in Matthew 27:43 (and similarly in Wisdom of Solomon 2:18). It is doubtful that this passage had any influence upon the words "save yourself."

What conclusions may be drawn? It stands to reason that Jesus would be ridiculed since his great expectations appeared to be so tragically shattered. It is conceivable that at first the report of this ridicule was very concise. It may have been something like the beginning of vs. 29, which completely contradicts the Markan tendency to accuse only the authorities and excuse the general public. The Old Testament expression about the shaking of heads may have been added later, as well as the specific words of those who mocked Jesus by referring to his saying about the temple. Then vss. 31, 32a would have been another version of this same story which Mark inserted immediately after the first. This has resulted in the wide separation of vs. 32b from vs. 27, for which it is the proper conclusion.

[27, 28] Perhaps the "bandits" are two of the rebels who were mentioned in vs. 7. No details are given, however, because everything is oriented toward Jesus' Passion and for that reason the picture of his death between two criminals is the only thing which is important. **[29]** That the "people . . . threw insults" (literally: blasphemed) is a very strong accusation and an implicit assumption that in blaspheming Jesus they are really blaspheming God. Consequently, the mockers are doing the very thing which 14:64

presents as the justification for condemning Jesus to death. With reference to the saying about the temple, see comment on 14:58. **[30]** The scoffing of the people assumes that Jesus' primary objective would have been to save his own life; therefore his failure to do so must be proof that he lacked either the power or the opportunity. Previously, in 8:35, Jesus stated that God does not look upon things in this way. **[31]** The chief priests and teachers of the law were introduced later as the principal scoffers—a feature that conforms to Mark's editorial pattern. **[32]** "King of Israel" is what they would have called him, but they had his religious dignity in mind, not his position as a national leader. What appears most crude is the misunderstanding revealed by the demand that he display his power in order that they might believe. This is the very thing which would destroy the possibility of belief, just as a marriage would be destroyed if one of the partners were to employ a private detective to gather visible evidence of the other's faithfulness. In addition, it would be an astonishing miracle indeed if Jesus were to come down from the cross, but this would prove only that he was a superman—not that he was "Messiah and King of Israel." This is how God differs from any man or superman—he does not have to assert himself, nor is it necessary for him to prove that he is right or to crush his enemies. This is the message of Jesus' Passion. It is emphasized more intensely by the final remark which declares that those who were crucified with Jesus insulted him. In this way they renounced that companionship with him which fate had decreed and in so doing they made the loneliness of his Passion complete. He did not even belong to those who suffered with him.

If we stop to examine the gradual formation of a passage like this, we will discover that a large number of witnesses stand before us, all of whom are directing our attention to the same event. It is obvious that what moved the church primarily and most impressively was the loneliness of Jesus, which was the real cause of his intense suffering. This is proof of the amazing difference between God's way and everything which men consider their goal or conceive of as being God's way. Gradually this difference was made more prominent as the church discovered the prototype of this suffering in the Psalms of the innocent sufferer. By appropriating these Psalms the church explicitly stated that God's plan of salvation was being fulfilled in this experience. And, finally, even the figures of the two criminals served to emphasize the uniqueness of Jesus.

The Death of Jesus as the Revelation of God 15:33-39;
cf. Matt. 27:45-54; Luke 23:44-47

33At noon the whole country was covered with darkness, which
lasted for three hours. 34At three o'clock Jesus cried out with a
loud shout, *Eloi, Eloi, lema sabachthani?* which means, "My God,
my God, why did you abandon me?" 35Some of the people who
were there heard him and said, "Listen, he is calling for Elijah!"
36One of them ran up with a sponge, soaked it in wine, and put it
on the end of a stick. Then he held it up to Jesus' lips and said,
"Wait! Let us see if Elijah is coming to bring him down from the
cross!" 37With a loud cry Jesus died.
38The curtain hanging in the Temple was torn in two, from
top to bottom. 39The army officer, who was standing there in front
of the cross, saw how Jesus had cried out and died. "This man was
really the Son of God!" he said.

(Vs. 34: Ps. 22:1; vs. 36: Ps. 69:21.)

The climax of this account is the statement that Jesus died with a loud cry. In Mark's formulation the notion of "giving up the spirit" is obvious (Matt. 27:50; Luke 23:46; John 19:30, although different Greek verbs are used). In vs. 34 another shout by Jesus is added in the words of Psalm 22:1. We may easily suspect that the church derived the content of Jesus' inarticulate cry from the description of the Passion which the church found in the Old Testament (cf. vs. 24) and thus attributed the words to him. This suggestion is particularly appealing since a Jewish version of the story of Esther reports that on the first and second days she prayed "My God," but that she was heard on the third day when in her distress she cried out, "My God, my

God, why did you abandon me?" The outcry could have been worded this way in Aramaic; however, it is difficult to conceive how the misunderstanding recorded in vs. 35 would be possible. No one who knew Aramaic could be so mistaken as to the meaning of the cry; and unless he did misunderstand completely, no one would have misconstrued it as a cry to Elijah for help. Probably the Greek-speaking church translated Jesus' cry found in vs. 34a (34b). Then with vs. 35 it presented the traditional incident where Jesus was offered a drink from a sponge as an act which revealed absurd misunderstanding and ridicule. The offering of vinegar to drink could have been derived from Psalm 69:21 (cf. vs. 23 above). Since, however, the same word designates a cheap, bitter wine, we might easily suppose that the action of a sympathetic soldier who took pity upon the martyr was later interpreted differently. Finally, Jesus' death is placed in a framework of two apocalyptic signs, neither of which is found in John. An eclipse of the sun would not have been possible at Easter time when the moon was full. This phenomenon is referred to in Amos 8:9 where "mourning for an only son" is mentioned in the very next verse: "And on that day," says the Lord God, "I will make the sun go down at noon, and darken the earth in broad daylight" (Amos 8:9). The fact that the same occurrence was reported at the death of Caesar and in connection with other great events indicates how widespread this idea was. The sign of the splitting of the curtain in the temple originated with the church, which regarded Jesus' death as the end of all temple ritual. Consequently it is a theological statement and not a historical one. Probably Mark received it from tradition. Normally he (or someone before him) would have added vs. 39 to vs. 37, because vs. 39 refers to the manner of Jesus' death. Mark may have added vs. 39, since the confession that Jesus was the Son of God was so important to him. It may be taken for granted that the army officer was a Gentile, although this is not stated explicitly.

[33] The darkness mentioned in Amos 8:9, which in Luke 23:44 is regarded as an actual eclipse of the sun, shows the sweeping effect of Jesus' death. Not only the earth was affected, but the entire universe as well. What happened, therefore, is similar to what will accompany the Day of Judgment, according to 13:24. Therefore the death of Jesus is compared to that event: Even the future world catastrophe will not be left to wild chance or to insane human action. It will be subject to the cross of Christ, i.e., subject to the will of God who has offered his grace to the world whenever it experiences judgment of any kind. If we concern ourselves with the question whether or not such darkness was possible, perhaps as the result of a sandstorm, we will miss the real message of the passage, because we will not be listening properly. **[34]** The chronology must be interpreted in a similar manner (see comment on vs. 25). For the third time a period of three hours has passed, and now the hour of fulfillment has come. The cry of Jesus summarizes in an extraordinarily meaningful way both aspects of what is happening here: it is a radical expression of the loneliness of Jesus' suffering. He has to bear not only the experience of being abandoned by men, but also of being forsaken by God. At the same time, however, it is a radical expression of a devotion to God which endures in every adverse experience—a devotion which continues to claim God as "my" God and will not let him go although he can be experienced only as the absent One who has forsaken the petitioner. Because the church wanted to express this, it used the words of the Psalm to represent the inarticulate cry of Jesus (vs. 37). This cry clings to the fact that God is real in all times, even in those times when neither experience nor thought can lay hold of him. It is not a question here of whether or not Jesus uttered this saying, or even the sayings handed down by Luke and John. It makes no difference whether he said any part of it or none of it. This passage presents the search for a faith which knows that God is real even in times when the believer feels forsaken and when the resources of thinking and experience have been exhausted. **[35]** It would have been impossible to portray such a misunderstanding unless at that time (in Hellenistic Judaism?) Elijah was regarded as a helper sent from heaven in cases of distress. According to 2 Kings 2:11, Elijah was translated to heaven. This is the basis of a Jewish legend (admittedly, it is not documented until later) according to which Elijah lives among the departed and comes to the aid of the godly. **[36]** Even the soldier (this person is identified as a soldier in Luke 23:36 f.) wants to see before he believes, as did the chief priests in vs. 32 and the enemies of the righteous sufferer in Wisdom of Solomon 2:18. And so it is likely that Mark understood the offering of vinegar to drink as mockery (this is certainly true in Luke 23:36; cf. vs. 23).

[37] Jesus' death is described with stark simplicity. Nothing is glossed over, nor is there any reference to an unshakable inner peace. Of primary significance is the absence of any imposing gestures or statements such as are usually found in Jewish and Christian stories of martyrdom. Nothing needs to be added to the concise account of the event itself. It acquires its magnificence through all that has been related previously about Jesus. The loud cry is strange, since one who was crucified died of exhaustion. For this reason the suggestion has been made that this cry is an embellishment added by an apocalyptically-minded church which conceived of Jesus as dying with the victor's shout of triumph. Although there are a few parallels (Ethiopian Enoch 62:2; 2 Esdras 13:4, 10: the voice of judgment which slays the sinners and the enemies; Ethiopian Enoch 71:11: the voice of praise to God Most High; 2 Esdras 10:26 f.: the fearful cry of Zion which shook the earth and terrified the seer), this cry remains completely incomprehensible when no additional information is given. In the New Testament, where loud cries are mentioned rather frequently (in the Apocalypse), only the cries of the vanquished demons (Mark 1:26; 5:7; Acts 8:7) are presented as inarticulate and are left unexplained. Therefore it is conceivable, at least, that the account of Jesus' dying with a loud cry was handed down to the church and was historically correct—and that the church later interpreted this cry in the way presented above on the basis of the parallels mentioned and on the basis of vss. 33 and 38 in particular. However, it seems that even for Mark this simply emphasizes the intensity of Jesus' suffering.

[38] Signs indicative of the future destruction of the temple (the bursting open of the gates, the quaking and the noise) were mentioned also in Jewish sources. What is intended here, however, is not an announcement of future events but the description of a consummation which has come already in the death of Jesus. After what was said in 11:17; 13:2; and 15:29 f., vs. 38 must be interpreted as a reference to the end of the temple cult which comes in Jesus' death. More precisely, this is the end of the exclusion from the place of God's presence of all who were not priests, of all who were not Jews (cf. Eph. 2:13 f.). The chief priests continue to appear as the real enemies of Jesus (vs. 31). The following saying of Jesus has been preserved in the Gospel of the Ebionites (surely the negative formulation is not genuine): "I am come to do away with sacrifices." The events which occurred in connection with Jesus' death were made more and more miraculous in the process of transmission (cf. Matt. 27:51-53!). According to the Gospel of the Nazarenes (21) the immense lintel of the temple was split; furthermore, thousands of Jews were said to be converted at that time. The Gospel of Peter (15-27) relates that it became so dark that many thought it was already nighttime and went to bed; that when Jesus' dead body was laid upon the earth, the earth shook mightily; and that the entire nation was so terrified by this and by the reappearance of the sun that they all perceived the wrong which they had committed and lamented the future destruction of Jerusalem. **[39]** Mark, on the other hand, deliberately places the Gentile, as the first person to really understand what happened, alongside these signs which presage the end of all Jewish temple worship. This man's statement could be translated "a son of God" just as readily as "the Son of God." If Mark had wanted to make clear that he meant the only Son of God besides whom there are no others, he could have worded the statement differently in Greek (this does not seem to be the usual significance of the wording used here). There is no doubt, however, that in Matthew 14:33; 27:40, 43; Luke 1:35; and John 10:36, where the same Greek construction is found, "the Son of God" is intended—not "a son of God." It is clear that in Mark's mind this expression is not merely a conjecture on the part of a Gentile that Jesus was some kind of divine person; it is an unqualified confession. This is confirmed by the recognition that the confession of Jesus as the Son of God determines the overall construction of this Gospel.

Son of God. Since the writing of 2 Samuel 7:12-16 Israel had waited for a descendant of David who would ascend David's throne as the "Son" of God and establish the rule of the Davidic dynasty over Israel forever. This hope continued to live in both Palestinian and Hellenistic Judaism until the time of Jesus, and it appears in the documents from Qumran (4Q Flor. 1:7 ff.). What was clear in connection with the title "Christ" (see comment on 8:29) applies here also: Jesus actually called upon God as his Father in a unique way (see 14:36), but he did not use the title "Son of God" to refer to himself. Simply to adopt a title which was already current would only hinder men from truly encountering the unique significance of his life, which could not easily be dismissed with some kind of label. The church was groping its way when it adopted the title, and this fact in itself is evidence of the truthfulness of the confession. Here men who have been mastered by God are seeking to express in human language the knowledge given them. In so doing they must guard continually against misunderstandings which lurk in the forms of speech they employ. In Romans 1:3 f. Paul quotes a creed according to which Jesus was installed as "Son of God" at Easter (see 12:37). In the same way Acts 13:33 applies to Easter the "today" of Psalm 2:7 when the Son of God would be "begotten." This assertion contradicts current Christology but is in complete agreement with the thought of Psalm 2:7, according to which the King of Israel is "begotten," i.e., installed, as Son of God on the day of his enthronement. This indicates that in Old Testament terminology "son" was purely a statement of function and described the authority of the one who reigned on behalf of God over his people. A contemporary of Jesus who was instructed in the Old Testament would be more concerned about a person's action or a thing's function than about its nature. He would not be interested in the question of whether a person was God's Son "in and of himself"; in fact, he would not have been able to understand such a question. He considered a person's actions to be important because they really indicated that this person encountered him as one who demanded obedience, exercised authority over him, protected and guided him. It was in this sense that the church confessed it had experienced Jesus' authority since Easter, i.e., his divine Sonship, and had proclaimed this to the whole world. But if the one who arose on Easter was the same person who lived on earth as Jesus of Nazareth, his baptism must be regarded as the actual beginning of his reign as God's representative (see 1:9-11). Even before this fact was recognized by men, God's Son, in the person of the earthly Jesus, encountered them as the One who sought their obedience and extended to them God's eschatological promises. But the church perceived that what had happened was more than simply another fortuitous event among thousands of others in human history; this was actually God's encounter with the world, in which all is fulfilled. As soon as the church perceived this truth it was necessary for it to affirm that Jesus' office as Son began with his birth (Luke 1:32, 35) or, really, before his birth, because God's plan to encounter the world in the "Son" was no sudden decision. From eternity this purpose had characterized his "being for the world," without which God would not actually be God but would be some kind of false god created by human imagination (cf. Gal. 4:4; John 3:16; et al.). To implement this affirmation familiar contemporary ideas were used, such as the Hellenistic notion that many great men were born without the involvement of a human father, or the idea that the Logos would be sent as the messenger or child of the gods. In Hellenistic Judaism these ideas already had been linked to the Old Testament stories about the miraculous births of the Patriarchs and the sending of angels. Here again the important thing is not the ideational forms in which the faith expressed itself, but the substance which the form was designed to convey: That God himself encounters the world in Jesus Christ; that this does not happen by accident, but is an expression of God's eternal purpose for the world—the purpose which makes him God; and that this did not happen only after Easter but before that time in the earthly Jesus of Nazareth.

But the decisive question which is asked by Mark is this: How does it happen? It was very tempting to see God revealed in all sorts of miracles worked by Jesus. There were movements in the church which regarded Jesus simply as a "divine person" who had more ability than the average mortal (see the Epilogue). In this way Jesus would be placed on a level with a variety of rather doubtful miracle-workers and his divine Sonship would have been limited to the giving of special miraculous assistance in cases of extraordinary need. This process shows how very little is achieved by regarding even such a majestic title to be true, and what consummate wisdom lay in Jesus' rejection of any title which had already been coined and filled with all kinds of ideas. Such titles always create preconceived notions in a person's mind before he meets the living Jesus Christ, who proves to be different from what he was imagined to be. It was to counteract such tendencies that Mark formulated his Gospel. It has been suggested that he tried to represent Jesus' adoption as Son of God (1:11), his presentation before the court (9:7), and his actual enthronement (14:61 f.; 15:39) in accordance with an Old Egyptian enthronement ceremony, so that Jesus became Son of God in the deepest sense at the crucifixion. But it is difficult to believe that such a ceremony or even the form of it was known to Mark. There is no indication that Jesus was any other than the Son of God in the fullest sense from the very beginning. The only element of truth in this suggestion is that Mark considered the Passion to be the decisive revelation of Jesus' divine Sonship. Of course, Jesus is the Son of God, as was perhaps already asserted in 1:1, but this is based upon God's commission which set him upon a very specific pathway (1:9-11). Therefore the faith which ascribes deity to Jesus on the basis of his miracles alone is merely the faith of demons (3:11; 5:7) and consequently should not be proclaimed under any circumstances. God did not reveal Jesus' divine Sonship to Jesus' three intimate friends until Peter's misunderstanding had been corrected. Moreover, he did not do so until the crucial revelation of God, which up to this point was concealed in the parabolic teaching, had been accomplished in the announcement of the suffering of the Son of Man, and the possibility of genuine faith had been promised solely to those who followed in the way of the cross. In making this revelation God did not refer to Jesus' miracles but to his words (9:7). Only when his Passion had begun did Jesus acknowledge the title which was used by the chief priest (not by Jesus himself), and even then in a curiously restrained way. Not until Jesus died with a loud cry was any man able in faith to say by himself, "This man was really the Son of God!" Furthermore, the fact that the first to do so was a Gentile shows how Jesus' death opened the door to the Gentile world.

Little by little other statements were added to a brief account telling of Jesus' death with a loud cry, the mockery of the people, and the sympathy of an individual who wanted to alleviate Jesus' suffering with cheap wine. In these statements the church attempted to express what had really happened. As we might expect, it is at the crucial passages that we meet a vast throng of witnesses who were not content simply to report historical details in the way that a disinterested eyewitness might testify at the trial following a traffic accident. What really happened in those hours can be stated only by one who is so involved personally that he interprets the story as he tells it. Faith alone can decide who is correct—the one who interprets it as the dying of a misguided fanatic who cried in vain to Elijah for deliverance, or the one who regards it as the dying of the Son of God. Mark does not withhold the first interpretation from us, though he indicates clearly that he has decided in favor of the second. A person cannot report this incident without attempting to state what God has done here, whether by interpreting the historical events or even by adding new features. This is similar to the way an artist paints a halo around a person's head (which, of course, could not be seen in everyday life) in order to indicate who the subject really was. Sometimes an artist places Jesus in a modern environment in order to say that he is still living today. The early Christians spoke in this way of such things as darkness and a torn curtain in the temple in order to testify to the unique significance of Jesus.

The Women Who Were Disciples of Jesus 15:40-41;
cf. Matt. 27:55 f.; Luke 23:49

40Some women were there, looking on from a distance. Among
them were Salome, Mary Magdalene, and Mary the mother of the

younger James and of Joses. [41]They had followed Jesus while he was in Galilee and helped him. Many other women were there also, who had come to Jerusalem with him.

[40] Those who spread the tradition of Jesus' death and burial and of the discovery of the empty tomb were women. They were women who came from Galilee—not residents of Jerusalem or Judea. This is in agreement with the historical situation. It indicates that the movement begun by Jesus was largely confined to Galilee during his lifetime, and that the disciples had fled before Jesus' death, probably back to Galilee, their home country. Examined historically, it is likely that the picture of the loneliness of Jesus when he died is accurate, since even the women who were his followers were able to watch only from a distance. With reference to the problem of their names, see introduction to 16:1-8. **[41]** This is the only place in the Gospels where the discipleship of women is mentioned (and in Luke 8:1 ff., but see the "waiting" in 1:31). The passage also suggests that the women did not lose their heads as the disciples did. This is remarkable when seen in the light of the humble role allotted to women in Judaism and the ancient world in general. The emphasis upon following and upon going up to Jerusalem are characteristic of Mark (cf. 10:32!). Perhaps he included vs. 41 to prepare for 16:1 ff. Disciples of Jesus are the first to whom the true meaning of Jesus' resurrection will be revealed: the death of Jesus is not the end for the disciple; instead, it is actually the beginning of a new life.

The Burial of Jesus 15:42-47;
cf. Matt. 27:57-61; Luke 23:50-56

[42]It was getting on toward evening when Joseph of Arimathea arrived. [43]He was a respected member of the Council, who looked for the coming of the Kingdom of God. It was Preparation day (that is, the day before the Sabbath); so Joseph went in bravely to the presence of Pilate and asked him for the body of Jesus. [44]Pilate was surprised to hear that Jesus was already dead. He called the army officer and asked him if Jesus had been dead a long

time. [45]After hearing the officer's report, Pilate told Joseph he could have the body. [46]Joseph bought a linen sheet, took the body down, wrapped it in the sheet and placed it in a grave which had been dug out of rock. Then he rolled a large stone across the entrance to the grave. [47]Mary Magdalene and Mary the mother of Joses were watching, and saw where Jesus was laid.

The fact that the names of the women are repeated here, although they are not the same names as in 15:40 (or 16:1; see comment), shows that formerly this story was told by itself. This lack of correspondence is evidence of the fact that this account actually was based upon the testimony of a few women and was not fabricated later to explain how in 16:1 the women knew where Jesus was buried. The fact that it was not one of the disciples but a sympathizer from a larger circle of friends who cared for Jesus' burial is surely historical and favors the historicity of this entire incident. At the same time it confirms the impression that the disciples had fled. It is not possible to detect any theological motive here. On the contrary, this description contradicts Isaiah 53:9. In John 19:38-42 the burial of Jesus is handed down in essentially the same way. This account, then, is primarily interested in the historical course of events and most likely has reproduced it correctly.

[42] This is where we first learn that Jesus died on Friday. According to the interpolation in 14:12-16 it was the Passover as well, which could have made the purchase of linen cloth an impossibility. Friday is in agreement with John 19:42, but John 18:28 indicates that the Passover was not celebrated until Saturday. Nevertheless, the day of the week must have been handed down correctly, since it explains the hasty and temporary burial of Jesus. In order for Joseph to be able to complete all that was necessary before the beginning of the Sabbath—his visit to Pilate, including all the questions Pilate would necessarily ask, the purchase of supplies, and the burial itself—Jesus' death would have had to occur rather early in the afternoon. Therefore, the hours indicated in Mark 15:25 and 33 f. are to be preferred to those in

John 19:14. **[43]** "Member of the Council" may signify a member of the high council (as in Luke 23:51), or of some local council. Mark's description leads to the conclusion that Joseph was a Jew who belonged to a group which had a keen interest in the coming of God's Kingdom and was sympathetic toward Jesus, but did not actually join him (in contrast to Matthew 27:57). It is likely that groups such as this continued to have close contact with the early Christian church as late as A.D. 70 without breaking off from the Jewish community. This, too, is probably historical. The theology of the disciples was so shaken that they were utterly confused, and there was nothing for them to do but flee. For this reason what had to be done at the moment was done by an interested onlooker; perhaps he remained open to whatever God expected from him at that moment simply because he had no theological preconception of Jesus. However, according to Acts 13:28 f. it was the residents of Jerusalem who buried Jesus. The fact that Joseph went "bravely" to Pilate implies that Pilate was not disposed to be as friendly to Jesus as it may seem in 15:2 ff. According to Roman custom a body was turned over to friends or relatives, while according to Jewish custom a person who was executed had no right to a private grave. **[44]** Official confirmation of death was necessary in order to prevent rescue of a condemned criminal by friends while he was still alive. Consequently, this feature may have been included purposely (by Mark?) to preclude any rumors that Jesus merely appeared to be dead (cf. 1 Cor. 15:3). **[45]** The word *ptoma* is replaced in Matthew 27:59 (Luke 23:52 f.) and John 19:38, 40 by *soma,* which is very similar in sound. This may have been done because it was not a corpse which was presented to the church at the Lord's Supper, but the Lord's "body," which was given for them and which manifested its vitality ever anew. **[46]** Cemeteries were unknown at that time. People were buried on their own land away from their dwellings. The stone was rolled in front of the grave as a protection against animals and, possibly, to keep out grave robbers. As a rule, however, one person would be able to roll the stone away. Josephus also attests the fact that it was important to the Jews to bury the dead before sundown, even in the case of someone who had been crucified (*Wars,* IV. 317). **[47]** Here again the only witnesses are women. The very persons who in general held a rather despised position among Jews and Greeks were in this instance more persevering than the disciples. This feature delineates the new position of women in the fellowship of Jesus.

God's Triumph 16:1-8;
cf. Matt. 28:1-10; Luke 24:1-11

1After the Sabbath day was over, Mary Magdalene, Mary the
mother of James, and Salome bought spices to go and anoint the
body of Jesus. 2Very early on Sunday morning, at sunrise, they
went to the grave. 3On the way they said to one another, "Who
will roll away the stone from the entrance to the grave for us?"
4(It was a very large stone.) Then they looked up and saw that
the stone had already been rolled back. 5So they entered the grave,
where they saw a young man, sitting at the right, who wore a white
robe—and they were filled with alarm. 6"Don't be alarmed," he
said. "You are looking for Jesus of Nazareth, who was nailed to the
cross. But he is not here—he has risen! Look, here is the place
where they laid him. 7Now go and give this message to his disciples,
including Peter: 'He is going to Galilee ahead of you; there you
will see him, just as he told you.' " 8So they went out and ran from
the grave, because fear and terror were upon them. And they
said nothing to anyone, because they were afraid.

This story presents a whole series of riddles. The names of the women agree to some extent with those given in 15:40, but not as well with those in 15:47. In any case it is strange that these names are repeated. Since the Sabbath ended at sundown it is necessary to assume that the women made their purchase in the evening (according to Luke 23:54 ff. this was done on Friday), but did not go back to the grave. Normally the wording in Mark would lead one to believe that they made their purchases before sunrise, but that is hard to imagine. It is clearly taken for granted that Jesus was given a temporary burial without anointing (in contrast to John 19:39 f.; cf. Mark 14:8). Jewish sources testify that the grave of a dead person was visited for three days (cf. John 11:31-39, which must be a special case). It is doubtful, however, that in the climate of the Near East women would have dared to enter a grave after a day and a half. It is especially striking that they had given no consideration to the rolling away of the stone before they set out for the tomb. The angel's words (where "of Nazareth" and "who was nailed to the cross" follow the name of Jesus) sound like a creedal formula of the church (cf. Acts 4:10). But the most remarkable thing is the sudden ending at vs. 8. Verses 9 ff. are not found in the oldest manuscripts.

The Easter Story. The transmission of this story is very difficult to unravel. Its earliest traces are found in 1 Corinthians 15:3-8 (written about A.D. 55; it was quoted word for word by Paul from the tradition of the church—in Jerusalem? in Antioch?). In that passage a number of appearances of Jesus are listed—to Peter and the twelve; to more than five hundred brethren "most of whom are still alive"; to James and all the apostles (which therefore must represent a larger circle that included more than the twelve); and finally to Paul himself. With the exception of a brief statement in Luke 24:34 about an appearance to Peter (which sounds like a set formula and shows by its brevity that this is all Luke knew about it), only the second of these is reported in the Gospels. According to Luke 24:36-49 and a very different account in John 20:19-23, this event took place in Jerusalem on Easter Sunday. Matthew 28:16-20 reports that it happened in Galilee. If we were to postulate that the latter appearance occurred after the ones in Jerusalem, which Matthew neither mentions nor alludes to, it would not have been possible for any of the disciples to entertain doubts when they had had the experience recorded in Luke 24:36-49, and the one recorded in John 20:24-29 in particular. Moreover, the journey to Galilee would have been an act of open disobedience to the command of the resurrected One in Luke 24:49. An appearance in Galilee which apparently was portrayed as the first appearance but which happened in a way altogether different from the one in Matthew 28:16-20 is reported in the supplementary chapter of John (21) and in the Gospel of Peter. The varying accounts can no longer be reconciled if we seek to establish the historical course of events. Undoubtedly, Paul's list is the most reliable historically. He was commissioned shortly after Jesus' death; he worked with the members of the Jerusalem church for a long time, and he knew a great number of the witnesses personally. Nothing can be inferred from this concerning the place or the manner of the appearances except the fact that Paul simply lists his own experience along with the others. This suggests that he is reckoning with appearances of the heavenly Lord, rather than appearances of one who walks on earth; however, he clearly distinguishes these appearances from mere visions (cf. Gal. 1:15 f. and 1 Cor. 9:1 with 2 Cor. 11:16-18 and 12:1-11a). However, Matthew 28:18b presupposes that Jesus had been exalted as the heavenly Lord "to the right hand of God" and it is only the expression "drew near" which suggests an encounter upon earth. Since this is an expression used frequently by Matthew, it is necessary to assume that he added it here. Above all, in contrast to the Lukan and Johannine accounts, the appearance in this passage is interpreted at once as a sending-forth to preach, as was true in the case of Paul (Gal. 1:15 f.)—not as an authentication of the resurrection (see comment on 16:15). Mark 16:7 alludes to the setting in Galilee in the same way as Matthew 28:16-20, and this interpretation appears to be more in keeping with the ancient tradition. At this point the question arises as to why nothing is reported of the appearances in that locality.

The Conclusion of Mark can be explained in various ways. It is very unlikely that vs. 7 contains a genuine but unfulfilled saying of Jesus which anticipated that as the resurrected One he would go to Galilee leading a band of disciples (see comment, 14:28). Nowhere else do we find Jesus having apocalyptic notions such as this. At least Mark did not interpret it that way—the change to the present tense in this passage (the future was used in 14:28) implies that Jesus was already on his way to the meeting place, and it is stated that the disciples will not see him until they are "there." Moreover, there is no basis for the supposition that Mark expected the Day of Judgment to come when the Son of

Man would appear in Galilee and that he therefore ended his Gospel abruptly with vs. 8 because, interpreted in this way, the fulfillment of vs. 7 only awaited the coming of the church (see comment on 13:14). To be sure, the word "see" can refer to the experiencing of the parousia (Mark 13:26; 1 John 3:2; Rev. 1:7; 22:4), but it can also refer to the encounter with the resurrected One (1 Cor. 9:1; John 20:18). In addition to this, the expression "he appeared to . . . ," which occurs so frequently, when translated literally reads: "he was seen by . . ." Mark 14:62, the closest parallel, combines in the same saying the seeing of the One who was exalted at Easter and the seeing of the One who is coming in the future. According to Mark 13:5-7 the parousia seems to be rather distant; however, the resurrection is clearly announced in 8:31; 9:9, 31; and 10:34, so it is necessary to report the fulfillment of these prophecies. Above all, however, churches which were acquainted with accounts of the appearances of the resurrected One would not be able to interpret Mark 16:7 other than as a reference to an encounter with the risen Jesus. Finally, the fact that Peter is mentioned separately indicates that the story of his denial and repentance has not been finished as yet and that we should still expect the resurrected Jesus to encounter him (1 Cor. 15:5; Luke 24:34; John 21:15-19). Therefore, the conjecture that the resurrection (of which the church was already aware) is merely alluded to as a mystery—like the Messianic secret—is not very probable. It is necessary to assume that the conclusion of the Gospel has been lost. Aside from any other argument, it is difficult to imagine that a book would have ended with the statements made in vs. 8, and with the little word "because." The conclusion may have mentioned certain appearances in Galilee—perhaps a first appearance to Peter and another to the twelve (1 Cor. 15:5). It is not impossible that Mark was the source of the information found in Matthew 28:9 f. and 16 ff. It would be more natural to expect Jesus to repeat the angel's command after Mark 16:8 than after Matthew 28:8. Moreover, the description of an appearance from heaven, which is the basis of Matthew 28:16 ff., might have been deliberately dropped later on because it had become offensive. This, however, is only a conjecture and cannot be proven. It is more likely that the conclusion was lost accidentally, since there are many examples of books with papyrus pages where the ending has been lost, and similar examples of incomplete scrolls. It is clear that Mark took for granted that the disciples were in Jerusalem. From a historical point of view, vs. 7 might be an attempt made prior to Mark to link together the traditions of the empty grave and the appearances in Galilee, which had circulated independently, and at the same time to make an excuse for the disciples' flight to Galilee by tracing it to a command by Jesus (see below). Since there is no mention whatever of the disciples at the crucifixion, burial, and tomb of Jesus, it is likely that the disciples actually fled to their homes. Moreover, Luke, who reports that the first appearances occurred in Jerusalem, shows in general a theological preference for that city. Furthermore, the disciples must have been in Galilee (sooner or later) because after this they lived in Jerusalem permanently (consequently, with their families, who had not accompanied them previously).

It is difficult to determine the details of what happened at the discovery of the empty tomb, since the accounts vary considerably. The command of the angel has been changed deliberately in Luke 24:6-8, as the reference to Galilee indicates. Here it is used in a completely different way and sounds a little strange. There is, in addition, another command recorded in John 20:17. Matthew 28:1 seems to postulate a visit on Saturday after sunset. As in John 20:1, this visit is motivated solely by devotion without any intention of anointing Jesus' body or entering the grave, and this solves several difficulties in the Markan account. Thus none of the other accounts include the deliberation about the stone. Matthew 28:2 f., without relating the story of the resurrection itself, tells of the descent of the angel. (Does this indicate that the resurrection of Jesus might have taken place after the guards had fainted?) According to Matthew 28:2-5 the angel was in front of the tomb when he spoke to the women (so that after 28:8 they "go away" and do not "go out" as in the source of Mark 16:8). According to Luke 24:4 there were two angels in the tomb. The details about the announcement of the resurrection vary also. Finally, the carrying of the command to the disciples is only contemplated in Matthew 28:8; according to Luke 24:9 it is carried out.

From the original wealth of traditions about the appearances in 1 Corinthians 15:5-8 only the appearances to the twelve are contained in the Gospels, where they have been handled in a very different manner (wherein Matthew seems to come nearest to the historical course of events). Moreover, the discovery of the empty tomb, which is related by all four Gospel writers, is never mentioned outside of the Gospels. These two traditions have, therefore, been handed down separately. Certainly a Jewish narrator of the appearances of Jesus would assume quite naturally that the grave was empty; nevertheless, no reference is made to any witnesses of that fact. This is why some have suggested that the story arose after the ideas about the resurrection had become more "concrete." But this seems very unlikely. Even if there were many different concepts of resurrection in Judaism, it would have been assumed at once that the tomb was empty—rather than to come to this conclusion later on when the resurrection was thought of in more concrete terms. Naturally, if Jesus met the disciples, he was no longer in the grave (Acts 2:29-32). It is clear that the accounts of the empty tomb and those of the appearances were not combined until later. The empty tomb was discovered in Jerusalem, but the appearances took place in Galilee. Therefore the news of this discovery could not have been passed on to the disciples and verified by them. From the historical point of view this is the background of Mark 16:8. That this verse is an attempt to explain how it happened that so much time passed before there was any report of the discovery of the empty tomb is too modern a suggestion. A critically trained historian would think this way, but not the early Christian church. It is still necessary to inquire what theological truth Mark is attempting to express when he reports the silence of the women. In Judaism a woman did not really have any right to act as a witness. It stands to reason, then, that the women disappear among the many far more important witnesses to the encounter with the resurrected One. Celsus (reported in Origen, *Contra Celsum,* 2:55) ridiculed the women's gossip about an empty tomb.

If we examine the matter historically, we must begin with the fact that the discovery of an empty tomb by women on Sunday morning (it may have been in the evening at the end of the Sabbath) is reported in all four Gospels. This fact was expanded by various additions. Is the discovery trustworthy historically? It is strange how few witnesses are named. Only Luke 24:24 and John 20:3-10 report a verification by the disciples. Matthew 28:9 f. (contrary to Luke 24:23 f.) is the only record that Jesus himself appeared to the women. Above all, the list of witnesses seems to narrow down to one single woman in the original version. Even within the Gospel of Mark the list of names is different in 15:40, 47, and 16:1. When a person's name is followed by another name in the genitive case, the second name normally indicates the person's father. Accordingly, in 15:47 the daughter of Joses is named and in 16:1 the daughter of James, both of whom are called Mary. Since she might easily have had two sons, but not two fathers, 15:40 may be an attempt to combine the two variants. The disagreement between the details in Matthew 28:1 and those in Luke 24:10 is even greater. The only name which is handed down the same in every account is the name of Mary Magdalene. According to John 20:1, she is the only one who went out to the grave on Sunday morning, and she did so simply out of devotion—not in order to anoint Jesus. John 20:2-10 was added later in an attempt to authenticate the discovery of the empty tomb (this is clear from vs. 11, wherein Mary is still standing by the tomb). But this state of affairs is in itself a clear argument for a historical kernel. If the discovery of the empty tomb had been developed later as proof of a "concrete" resurrection, the story in its earliest form would have included the largest possible number of good witnesses. A multitude of witnesses and a demonstration of the reality of the miracle are customary features in miracle stories. The fact that in John 20:1 Mary Magdalene appears as the only witness and that she alone is consistently named in the other accounts is another strong argument in favor of the conclusion that it was understood from the very beginning that she was the one who discovered the empty tomb. However, in addition to this, 15:42-47 (containing the name of Joseph of Arimathea, which is not mentioned anywhere else) is trustworthy and makes it obvious that the location of Jesus' grave was not unknown in Jerusalem. The simplest explanation of the fact that the resurrection of Jesus came to be placed "on the third day" (1 Cor. 15:4) very early and quite generally, so that Sunday was celebrated instead of Saturday (1 Cor. 16:2), is that the resurrection had always been placed on Easter Sunday. It is not likely that this would have resulted from an appearance in Galilee, since the disciples could hardly have arrived there so soon, but it could have resulted from the discovery of the empty tomb. This fact is another argument in favor of the historicity of the empty tomb, but it is no proof of the resurrection. Other possible explanations in addition to the one contemplated in Matthew 27:64 are that the body of Jesus, which had been buried temporarily, was moved to another grave; or that Mary went to the wrong grave.

The primary thing which must be pointed out is that the reality of the resurrection does not depend upon the empty tomb (as 1 Cor. 15:3-8 shows). Paul spoke of a "spiritual body" which is something completely different from the physical body (1 Cor. 15:44); consequently, he was speaking of a form of resurrection life which is impossible for us to conceive. He stressed that, after the resurrection, man remains a person in continuity with his earthly personality and that he does not become a vague aura which has fused with God or with the "All." On the contrary, he is the specific individual whom God had accepted into his fellowship before the man died. Furthermore, Paul asserted that this continuity exists only by a miracle of God who through his creative act calls the deceased to life again and thereby creates him anew. Therefore whether the old body (in the case of those who will have died already) decays in the grave or (in the case of those who are still alive at the time of the parousia) is "absorbed" by God's new creative action (2 Cor. 5:4), obviously made very little difference to him (1 Thess. 4:13-18). There is no record in any of the accounts (with the exception of John 20:8) that the discovery of the empty tomb produced faith. This shows that the certainty of Jesus' resurrection is not based on the empty tomb, but on the fact that it is as one who is alive that Jesus encounters man. Of course, for those whom the living Jesus has encountered, the fact of the empty tomb is a sign that what happened here is unique—that this was an act of God like that act which in the beginning brought out of inert matter the thing which we call "life" but are unable to explain.

[1] It is clear again that the women are the only ones who are present to perform the necessary service of love (cf. 15:47). Of course, they are merely fulfilling a duty out of devotion and are by no means anticipating the divine intervention which has already occurred. **[2]** The time of their arrival is stated twice. Perhaps as the story was told, first one time was given and then the other, but Mark places both times side by side. The way this is worded (literally: on the one day of the week) is not proper Greek. It is a Hebrew idiom, since that is the only way it could be expressed in Hebrew; however, it may have been taken from the Greek Old Testament. Since the wording is the same in John 20:1 (Mark 16:9 alone is different) we may conclude that both are based on a common tradition (as are 1 Cor. 16:2; Acts 20:7). **[3]** The question asked by the women is intended to depict the human approach. **[4]** For man the large stone closes the tomb now and forever, and this makes the miraculous intervention of God which has already occurred so much more impressive. This is also the reason for mentioning the size of the stone again after their question—a type of emphasis often used in popular narration. A Latin translation has included a description of Jesus' resurrection at this point. In the New Testament the fact that the mystery of God's action cannot be seen or described by anyone is always of decisive significance. Neither the miracle of the resurrection nor the incomprehensible discovery of the empty tomb produces faith. Faith is created only when the living One encounters his disciples. Faith in God's miraculous intervention will always be based upon such an encounter. Only those to whom the resurrected One has appeared alive can understand the report of the empty tomb. So then, what is visible at the present moment is not God's intervention itself but only the result of his intervention, and there is no immediate explanation of that result. **[5]**

The angel is described with great reserve as a "young man," similar to the description in II Maccabees 3:26, 33; Josephus, *Antiquities* V. 277 ("a spectre appeared to her from God [*aggelos tou theou*], in the likeness of a comely and tall youth"). The white robe is nothing more than a symbol of the heavenly realm. The one to whom he reports the miracle with such remarkable reserve is interested in God who encounters the individual in the miracle rather than in the more or less miraculous nature of that encounter. At times, however, the encounter must come in a miraculous way in order to gain the person's attention. Thus the man's answer and the alarm of the women (cf. vs. 8 also) are the only things which clearly indicate that this is God's messenger and not simply some young man. **[6]** In almost every passage of the Bible where the living God encounters man it is necessary for God's first words to dismiss the person's fears. Man cannot help being afraid when he realizes that he is in the presence of the overwhelming majesty of God. The phrase "You are looking for . . ." is surprising. Emphasis must be given to the fact that man's action, though full of devotion, is meaningless in the light of God's action. With the words "he has risen" God's action is moved into the center of focus. The miracle which the angel proclaims is that God intervenes in history when, from the human point of view, everything is lost. In the resurrection Jesus experienced what men generally did not expect to happen until sometime in the distant future. "He is not here" would be chosen as an epitaph which was original but was clearly true to the New Testament in meaning. **[7]** The significance of what has happened will not be indicated until the encounter with the resurrected One in Galilee. The mention of Peter reminds the reader of his denial. Therefore those who fled when Jesus was arrested and the one who later explicitly denied him are called again by Jesus, who once more goes before the disciples (cf. 10:32) and commands them to follow. This is another experience of the bestowal of grace. In order that they may be received into his service once and for all they are given another opportunity to see the One who did not forsake them when they forsook him. **[8]** As has been true throughout the whole Gospel, man's response is one of total blindness. No joy is visible—only fear. In comparison with God's unprecedented action man has nothing to show except a complete lack of understanding. This is true even of those who are filled with devotion, who love Jesus and show a measure of courage. The resurrected One must open the eyes of the blind once more (note the way 8:22-26 comes before 8:27-31). The conclusion to the Gospel of Mark, which has been lost, told about this miracle of opening blind eyes which is the first expression of the miracle of Easter morning.

The most amazing part of this passage is vs. 8. Far from exploiting the fact of the empty tomb as proof of the resurrection, Mark simply reports the words of the angel, which on the whole merely state what has happened. In addition to this, he asserts that even the words of the angel produce nothing but fear and terror; they do not evoke any faith or understanding. In the entire tradition, even in the accounts of Jesus' appearances to his disciples, we can sense that the truth of Jesus' resurrection had to prevail against men who were very critical and who did not anticipate that such a thing would ever occur. Mark, however, moves beyond this inasmuch as he does not report the inception of any faith whatever. So man's continued inability to understand is contrasted with Jesus' promise to go before them and accomplish what human hearts cannot do; despite every failure he would call the disciples again to discipleship and would encounter them in a way that would enable them to see him.

THE FIRST ATTEMPT TO SUPPLY A CONCLUSION 16:9-20

9After Jesus rose from death, early on the first day of the week,
he appeared first to Mary Magdalene, from whom he had driven
out seven demons. 10She went and told it to his companions. They
were mourning and crying; 11and when they heard her say that
Jesus was alive and that she had seen him, they did not believe
her.

12After this, Jesus appeared in a different manner to two of
them while they were on their way to the country. 13They returned
and told it to the others, but they would not believe it.

14Last of all, Jesus appeared to the eleven disciples as they
were eating. He scolded them, because they did not have faith
and because they were too stubborn to believe those who had
seen him alive. 15He said to them: "Go to the whole world and
preach the gospel to all mankind. 16Whoever believes and is baptized will be saved; whoever does not believe will be condemned.
17Believers will be given these signs of power: they will drive
out demons in my name; they will speak in strange tongues; 18if
they pick up snakes or drink any poison, they will not be harmed;
they will place their hands on the sick, and they will get well."

19After the Lord Jesus had talked with them, he was taken
up to heaven and sat at the right side of God. 20The disciples went
and preached everywhere, and the Lord worked with them and
proved that their preaching was true by giving them the signs of
power.

(Vs. 19: 2 Kings 2:11; Ps. 110:1.)

Unquestionably this passage is a later addition, which has been supplied because the sudden ending in vs. 8 required such a conclusion (see comment on vss. 1-8). It is not found in the oldest manuscripts. A few church fathers were acquainted with this ending; others, however, attest that it was missing. The designation of Jesus as "the Lord" is not typical of Mark (cf. 11:3). Above all, this is an example of a harmony of all the Easter accounts (see vs. 15) which has probably been created for purposes of instruction (originally without any connection to Mark 16:8; the transition to vs. 9 is not smooth). According to a very uncertain tradition this conclusion was originated by the Presbyter Aristion (A.D. 100).

[9] The text had already become so much a part of public worship that it was no longer necessary to say who actually appeared (the name "Jesus" is not found in the Greek text)—vs. 8 dealt only with the women. We cannot be sure whether or not something else originally preceded this conclusion. First of all, the story in John 20:11-18 is briefly summarized. It is clear that this could not have come from Mark since Mary Magdalene had already been mentioned in 16:1. The fact that she apparently is alone once again (at the grave?) needed explanation after 16:1-8. But most important is the fact that the resurrection of Jesus was reported in vs. 6, and these details about Mary, which correspond to Luke 8:2, should have been included in 15:40. It is significant, however, that this supplement still recognizes that an Easter account is incomplete if it does not include the encounter of the living One with his witnesses. **[10]** The report to the disciples (according to vs. 13 it appears to refer to a larger circle which may have included women; Luke 24:33; Acts 1:14) is in agreement with the Johannine account except that more emphasis is put upon their mourning and crying. **[11]** In addition to what is stated in John, their unbelief is mentioned specifically and was especially important to the narrator. **[12]** Then the Emmaus story is added (Luke 24:13-35). The "different," or changed, manner indicates an appearance different from the way the earthly Jesus looked—but not different from the way Jesus appeared to Mary—because Luke records that those who walked with Jesus did not recognize him at first. Those features which are not mentioned here are, therefore, taken for granted. **[13]** The stubborn unbelief of the disciples, which contradicts Luke 24:34, is emphasized again. The fact that the narrator tolerates this contradiction shows how important he considers this point to be. **[14]** When Jesus appears to the disciples this time, only the eleven are assumed as present. This is probably how Luke 24:36-43 was understood. That the appearance occurred at a meal is mentioned also in that passage in Luke and in Acts 10:41. The unbelief, or even stubbornness, of the disciples is stressed again. This narrator understood what it was that Mark wanted to impress upon his readers again and again, especially in 8:17-21: Witnessing, proclamation, grace, and salvation exist only as the result of God's action in the face of all human resistance.

This was too much for one of the copyists; therefore, he added an apology for the disciples: "And they replied saying, This age of lawlessness and unbelief is under Satan, who by means of evil spirits does not permit the true power of God to be apprehended; therefore reveal thy righteousness now. They were speaking to Christ, and Christ said to them in reply: The limit of the years of the authority of Satan has been fulfilled, but other terrible things draw near, even for the sinners on whose behalf I was delivered up to death, that they might turn to the truth and sin no more, in order that they may inherit the spiritual and incorruptible glory of righteousness which is in heaven." This addition, which was supplied much later, is interesting because it shows how for a long time after the resurrection the church was greatly vexed by the problem of sin, temptation, and suffering. What is the relationship of God's Easter victory to the full revelation of the "glory" and "righteousness" of God which still lies in the future? Naturally, the answer given above was not satisfying. It declared that the power of Satan was truly broken, but that "other" terrible things would still come. This has obscured the answer in vss. 11-14, which had the right approach when it asserted that the reason for the paradox lay in the reality of unbelief. As a believer man already lives in the light of God's Easter victory. As one who is always tempted by unbelief he lives at the same time "in this age." Only the fulfillment at the parousia will transform him from a believer to one who sees with his own eyes—one who lives without temptation in the complete fellowship of the child of God.

[15] This is why the author of vss. 9-20 did not try to make any excuses and why the missionary commission follows immediately upon the denunciation of unbelief. Mark had always understood it in this same way: The conquest of unbelief and temptation—that is, the event of the grace of God—comes in such a way that man is accepted into service and thereby enabled to believe. The statement is related to Matthew 28:16-20, but is not a copy of it. It represents a different version in which the emphasis is on the universality of the Gentile mission. This had been expressed in various terms: Mark 13:10, like Matthew 28:19, speaks of "all peoples"; Mark 14:9; 16:15a; and Romans 1:8 of "the whole world"; Mark 16:15b and Colossians 1:23 speak of "all mankind," which is probably the oldest wording. In any event, this is an example of an early Christian way of speaking which was prevalent in a certain stratum of the church. In this stratum, attention was no longer focused as much on the "mystery" of the crucified One (as with Paul in 1 Cor. 2:7 f.); more and more the center of attention was the "mystery" of the One who marches in triumph through the Gentile world by the church's proclamation (1 Tim. 3:16 and the passages cited in the comment on Mark 4:10-12). This is theologically significant inasmuch as unbelief is not conquered simply by the miracle of the resurrection. It is conquered only by the obedience granted to the witness by the living Christ, through which the resurrected One reveals himself "to all mankind" as the living One (see introduction to the Easter account in 16:1-8). **[16]** Baptism is referred to here as it is in Matthew 28:16-20. Here, however, it is more clearly understood as an expression of faith or at least an allusion to it. In the negative statement, unbelief alone is declared to be the reason for condemnation—not the failure to be baptized. The Greek form in each instance indicates the point in time when a man has, in principle, either come to believe or decided in favor of unbelief. And yet it is necessary to place a question mark here. According to Matthew 11:20-24 the cities which had seen Jesus' works and still did not repent were warned of judgment. Such a call to repentance warns a person against blindness in the face of God's mighty act and urges him to repent. This warning has been dangerously abridged, however, when a mere dogmatic condemnation of "unbelief" takes the place of the invitation to see the work of God and heed the call to repentance. The interpretation of unbelief as simply "not considering a thing to be true" is presented in vs. 14, though it must be admitted that something more than this is intended here.

[17] The emphasis upon charismatic gifts, which are still clearly promised and given to all believers (cf. Luke 10:17-19), is interesting. It is indicative of a church which was still rather flexible and not yet strongly institutionalized. **[18]** In this connection particular emphasis is put upon the spectacular. All of the miraculous deeds listed here are found in the book of Acts (2:1 ff.; 3:1 ff.; 9:32 ff.; 14:8 ff.; 16:16 ff.; 19:13 ff.; 28:3 ff.), with the exception of drinking poison without harm; such an incident, however, is reported by Papias. Between A.D. 130 and 140 he gathered a variety of amazing anecdotes ranging from a story about the daughters of Philip (Acts 21:9) who were said to have raised a dead person to life to one about Justus Barsabbas (Acts 1:23) who did not die although he drank poison (Eusebius, *Church Fathers* III 39:9). **[19]** As stated in Luke 24:51, Jesus is taken up to heaven on Easter Sunday immediately after his conversation with the disciples. This is described in Old Testament phraseology taken from the story of Elijah (2 Kings 2:11) and from Psalm 110, a Psalm repeatedly quoted by the church. The theological significance of this incident is that it designates Easter as the beginning of the lordship of Christ, which found expression in the course of the world-wide proclamation. So the resurrection becomes the enthronement of the king who from this point on marches through the world. It is obviously impossible to find room here for any Galilean appearances (as in Matt. 28:16). **[20]** However, the description of the missionary activity of the disciples forms the real conclusion of the Gospel. What Luke does in Acts may be seen in embryo here. In this connection the idea that Christ confirmed their proclamation by means of all kinds of miraculous signs is relatively primitive in comparison with the declaration that he marches through the world.

In addition to the fact that this addendum gives us a glimpse of a development of the church wherein miracles and charismatic gifts were generally held in high esteem, it is valuable because it affirms that the real objective of Jesus' resurrection is found in the proclamation of the gospel in the world. The agents of the proclamation are the disciples whom the resurrected One receives back into his service, and whose unbelief he alone can overcome. His power, dominion, and victory are manifested in the proclamation.

THE SECOND ATTEMPT TO SUPPLY A CONCLUSION 16:9-10

[9]The women went to Peter and his friends and gave them a brief account of all they had been told. [10]After this, Jesus himself sent out through his disciples, from the east to the west, the sacred and ever-living message of eternal salvation.

This second conclusion is very brief. It also reports the fulfilling of the angel's command and stresses particularly the beginning of world-wide proclamation in language totally unlike that of Mark. Apparently the church regarded that proclamation as the real fulfillment of Easter. Peter is given special prominence here as the leader of the band of disciples (cf. 16:7). Expressions like "ever-living" and "eternal" are indicative of Hellenistic thinking. Consequently, what was said above about the centrality of the proclamation applies to this conclusion also.

Epilogue

MARK'S THEOLOGICAL ACHIEVEMENT

When Mark wrote his Gospel the message of Jesus Christ had already reached most of the countries around the Mediterranean Sea. It was no longer possible to halt its progress through the world. This progress was promoted particularly by Paul, but also by numerous other persons whose names are not known (such as those who founded the influential church in Rome). The triumphal march of the exalted One through the Gentile world was interpreted everywhere as the actual revelation of the divine mystery which had been hidden from eternity. This is indicated by the epistles to the Colossians and the Ephesians (which were probably written by disciples of Paul), by the hymn in 1 Timothy 3:16, and by the doxology which has been added at the end of the Epistle to the Romans. But the question as to what the life and death of Jesus really meant had by no means been explained as yet.

There are three explanations which stand out in particular. (1) Jewish-Christian churches were primarily interested in those sayings of Jesus which provided ethical instruction and information of an apocalyptic nature concerning the anticipated end-time. Thus the collection of sayings of Jesus which we call the "sayings-source" (cf. Introduction, section 1) was already substantially in existence when Mark wrote. But a person could collect sayings of Jesus and even memorize them and pass them on to others without knowing the person who had uttered them. This was true in the case of many rabbinical sayings. If Jesus were no more than a particularly outstanding teacher, or even a teacher who was greater than all others, he would be important only for his teaching. At best he would have permanent interest only as an example of one whose life was a confirmation of his teaching.

(2) In the churches which were influenced by Paul, the cross and resurrection of Jesus formed the heart of the creed. This is what we find in early Christian creeds such as 1 Corinthians 15:3-5. In these churches little attention was paid to the traditions about the earthly life of Jesus; consequently, most of these traditions were lost. These churches were interested only in the significance of that life. A fanatical piety arose in Corinth even in Paul's time which based everything on the resurrection and imagined that the believers had already entered the new life where sin could no longer disturb the divine, everlasting element in man which had been granted through the sacrament. They believed that the spiritual gifts, tongues, and miracles gave evidence of this new divine life. In the period which followed, the resurrection seems to have been interpreted more and more as the exaltation of Jesus as Lord of the world, to whom all powers and authorities had already been made subject. Here everything seemed to have been fulfilled; the whole world together with nature seemed to have been mysteriously changed by his glory which permeated all things. The fact that the church alone knew that this redemption had been accomplished seemed to be the only thing that distinguished it from the rest of the world. Paul had taught that the Son of God existed eternally and that he was with God before the incarnation, but now the life of Jesus merely signified the in-breaking of heavenly life and power on earth. So it was necessary to ask whether in the final analysis such knowledge was really linked to Jesus. Jesus of Nazareth had disappeared long ago in the shadow of the heavenly Christ and it was not really clear why the name of some Greek or Roman god or son of a god could not have been chosen as the symbol for the in-breaking of divine grace, the divine dominion of the world, and the unity of the divine with the innermost being of the awakened man. Gnosticism came to this very conclusion in the second century A.D. Of course, it was to counteract such fanaticism that Paul placed the crucified One at the heart of his preaching and proclaimed him as the one who provided freedom from sin and law by means of the righteousness of God. In this way he started man upon the path of the

obedience of faith where, as one who had died with Christ, man was approaching resurrection with Christ, and had to express this obedience in all his conduct. Apparently, when Mark wrote, Paul had already suffered martyrdom and his disciples were calling the church back to its assigned task. This task was the world-wide proclamation through which the exalted One desired to permeate the world—not as a mysterious supernatural power, but as master of those disciples who witnessed for him, walked the streets of the Roman Empire, and frequently lay bound in its prisons. Even if this is how the church was called back to its senses, whether it was sufficient ultimately to conceive of the cross merely as a symbol of justification and the obedience which flows from it is still an unanswered question. The resurrection, then, would be only a symbol of the everlasting life which God had promised. This was an obvious inference because, beginning with Paul's emphasis, many seem to have essentially reduced the whole life of Jesus to the cross and the resurrection.

(3) We may assume that a third answer was given in the Hellenistic churches (perhaps in Syria?) which had not been influenced to any great extent by Paul. In this region there were any number of so-called "divine persons," miracle-workers, who traveled throughout the cities of Greece, Asia Minor, and Syria. They aroused the enthusiasm of the throng by various means—partly through magic tricks and partly through the miraculous deeds produced by the influence of their personalities and their reputations. They were looked upon as some sort of incarnation of divine powers, and amazing things were reported about them. Apparently many churches understood Jesus to be like these persons. Their interest in Jesus centered around the healings he actually performed, which had been exaggerated and described as signs of a "divine being." This stage in the understanding of Jesus is very apparent in the tradition of miracle stories which lies behind the Gospel of Mark, but it is seen even more clearly in the apocryphal gospels and the stories of the apostles from a later period. Here the earthly life of Jesus is truly central, but it becomes more and more otherworldly and his ascension to heaven becomes the consequence which follows more or less naturally from his divinity. His death could only be interpreted as an in-

comprehensible and tragic end—a misfortune caused by the foolishness of men.

Mark was the first to write a Gospel, and in so doing he created an entirely new literary form. This new creation was a major theological achievement. Collections existed of the sayings of Hellenistic peripatetic philosophers and Jewish rabbis which were interspersed with some biographical data or anecdotes. The "sayings-source" was a similar collection of the sayings of Jesus. But Mark turned things the other way around. For him the life of Jesus is most important and only occasionally is that story interrupted by interpretive sayings. Miracle stories of divine persons had been collected and a similar collection of stories about Jesus may have been in existence even before Mark wrote, but we have no way of knowing its proportions. Apparently this collection presented difficulties for Mark most of the time and could not serve as a model for him. The fact that Mark's narration of the Passion story includes many details and the fact that his entire Gospel is interspersed with references to the Passion show that he did not intend it to be merely a collection of amazing events. The decisive details of Jesus' ministry had already been compiled in hymns and creeds. His death was usually mentioned, but not always; his birth was referred to occasionally and his baptism rather seldom. Otherwise the only things mentioned in these hymns and creeds were events outside the earthly life of Jesus, such as his descent from heaven and his exaltation to the right hand of God. It would have been meaningless for Mark to expand these items in his Gospel. A certain theological insight was nascent in these brief creedal statements and hymns: It is necessary to emphasize by faith that it was really God himself who encountered man in all of Jesus' ministry, including his death; however, faith knows that the presence of God is never a simple inference such as primitive reverence for a "divine being" would like to consider it to be. In a time when Jesus and his ignominious death (it was such an unforgettable offense to Paul that before he was called he persecuted the church) were in danger of being forgotten, Mark's theological insight created the completely new literary form which we call a "Gospel" (see Introduction, section 6).

[1:1-13] Two things are apparent in the construction of this book. In the introduction (1:1-13) Mark describes the dimensions in which all that follows must be interpreted. "Horizontally" it must be understood as the eschatological fulfillment of Old Testament prophecy. "Vertically" it must be seen as the in-breaking of God's heavenly realm upon earth. **[1:14—8:26]** In three acts, each of which begins with a summary of Jesus' activity and the call of the disciples or the sending of them, and ends with the rejection of Jesus (1:14—3:6; 3:7—6:6a; 6:6b—8:26), the evangelist describes the following: On the one hand, he presents the revelation of God: (1) in the mighty deeds and the controversies of Jesus; (2) in the parables and the miracles which were already associated with those parables in the tradition; (3) in his battle against legalism, in the turning of his attention to the Gentiles, in the miraculous feedings. On the other hand, he portrays the blindness of the people: (1) of the Pharisees; (2) of the common people, including Jesus' fellow citizens; (3) finally, of the disciples themselves. Here it is already apparent that everything begins with Jesus' authoritative call which enlists men as his disciples. Moreover, it is clear that from the beginning the battle must be waged against a wrong interpretation of the miracles that would venerate Jesus as a miracle man. This is why the demons and the persons who were healed were commanded to be silent. This is why Jesus taught in parables. This is why Jesus' teaching is usually stressed, as well as the attendant progressive hardening of the hearts of men—even within the circle of the disciples. The story of the healing of the blind man leads to the conclusion that it is not possible for men to discover the real meaning of the events in the life of the historical Jesus; only a miracle of the living God can open the eyes of the blind to see that meaning.

[8:27—10:52] Thus the incident in Caesarea Philippi characterizes the heart of the Gospel (8:27—9:1). Even in his confession of Christ, Peter has not progressed as far as the demons, who, more correctly, called Jesus the Son of God (5:6 ff.). Then for the first time Jesus speaks openly and without parables about the Passion and resurrection of the Son of Man. The Word had to become flesh in the body of the Crucified; otherwise he could not reach the hearts of men. However, the abiding difference between God and man becomes more manifest now than ever before: not even the disciples are able to understand the announcement of the Passion. Beyond the narrow circle of the disciples Jesus must summon all men to follow him on the way to the cross. This is the only place where God's action can be understood. Consequently, discipleship, which was emphasized at the beginning of the story of Jesus, appears again at the beginning of Jesus' path from Caesarea Philippi to Jerusalem. This path is the subject of 8:27—10:52, where the word "follow" continues to be used with special significance. Three times the announcement of the Passion of the Son of Man is followed by the misunderstanding of the disciples and Jesus' call to discipleship. Once again the section ends with the miracle by which God himself opens blind eyes, and as a result a man "followed" Jesus on the road. That that road leads to Jerusalem was already stated in 10:32.

[11:1—16:8] With 11:1 the days in Jerusalem begin. These are the days in which the suffering of the Son of Man is fulfilled. The controversies manifested the growing rejection of Jesus, and the discussion about the parousia emphasized the serious nature of discipleship in the interim; Mark is now giving special prominence to those passages which show the gospel breaking away from Jewish legalism and ceremonial piety and breaking through to the Gentiles (11:17 f.; 12:9; 13:10; 14:9; 15:38 f.). The suffering of Jesus is described with great reserve and in this connection special emphasis is given to human failure, which is found even within the most intimate circle of the disciples. It is no longer the historical Jesus who, going before them to Galilee and commanding them to follow, leads the disciples to true understanding; it is the resurrected Jesus, whom the angel proclaimed as being no longer among the dead.

Thus the Gospel of Mark is the account of the unprecedented and incomprehensible incarnate love of God. In the person of Jesus this love seeks and finds man despite many kinds of opposition. Because any direct revelation would lead only to a miracle-faith such as even the demons possess, God has to take the way of death in obscurity, in disgrace and humility. This is clear in the staggering simplicity of Jesus' cry, "My God, my God, why did you abandon me?" and in the statement that Jesus died with a loud cry. Discipleship is the only form in which faith can exist.

A half-committed onlooker who buries Jesus; a Gentile officer who cannot always keep his hands clean, who is even delegated to execute one who is innocent; and a few frightened women who do not trust the word of an angel—these are the signs which show that this miracle really happened and that God's revelation will reach its goal. These—but especially the disciples before whom Jesus goes to Galilee even after their far more serious failure—point to the miracle of the future church. The resurrected One will call that church into being and will send it out into the world.

INDEX
OF NAMES AND SUBJECTS
Compiled originally in German by Gotthold Holzberg

The names and subjects which occur in the Scripture passages can be looked up in the many available reference works, concordances, et al.; therefore, only those words which receive special consideration in the exegesis of a passage are included in this index. The numbers refer to the explanations of the respective Scripture passages. The special excursuses which have been appended to the exposition of individual passages are represented by capital E.

INDEX
TO THE EXCURSUSES